D0437339

HILLSBORO PUBLIC LIBRARIES
Hillsboro, OR
Member of Washington County
COOPERATIVE LIBRARY SERVICES

A MAN'S LIFE

DISPATCHES FROM DANGEROUS PLACES

MARK JENKINS

HILLSBORO PUBLISHING LIBRARIES
An imprint of Rodale Inc.
Hillsboro, OR

Member of Washington County
COOPERATIVE LIBRARY SERVICES

© 2007 by Mark Jenkins

All rights reserved. No part of this publication may be reproduced or transmitted in any form or by any means, electronic or mechanical, including photocopying, recording, or any other information storage and retrieval system, without the written permission of the publisher.

Modern Times is a trademark of Rodale Inc.

Rodale books may be purchased for business or promotional use or for special sales. For information, please write to:
Special Markets Department, Rodale Inc., 733 Third Avenue, New York, NY 10017

Printed in the United States of America
Rodale Inc. makes every effort to use acid-free ∞, recycled paper ☻.

All stories in this collection were first published in *Outside* magazine.

Cover and interior photographs by Mark Jenkins

Interior design by Tara Long
Cover design by Joanna Williams

Library of Congress Cataloging-in-Publication Data

Jenkins, Mark, date
    A man's life : dispatches from dangerous places / Mark Jenkins.
       p.   cm.
    ISBN-13 978–1–59486–707–1 hardcover
    ISBN-10 1–59486–707–0 hardcover 37717237   7/08
    1. Jenkins, Mark, date—Travel.   2. Travelers—United States—Biography.
    3. Voyages and travels—Anecdotes.   I. Title.
    G226.J46A3   2007
    910.4092—dc22
    [B]   2007030652

Distributed to the trade by Holtzbrinck Publishers

2   4   6   8   10   9   7   5   3   hardcover

To Sue, my rock.

And to Addi and Teal,
whose lightheartedness toward my
absences gave me strength.

The fact is, I think I am a verb instead of a personal pronoun.
A verb is anything that signifies to be; to do; or to suffer.
I signify all three.

—*Ulysses S. Grant*

CONTENTS

FROM THE SADDLE

INTO THE WAR ZONE

CONVICTION

LESSONS

LAST RITES

ACKNOWLEDGMENTS

This collection would not have been possible without two people: Katie Arnold and Hal Espen, both former editors at *Outside* magazine. Hal's sense of the nature and balance of a story, combined with Katie's equipoise in tempering sentences and paragraphs, guided my work. Katie and Hal, you saved me from myself.

Leaving Home

GOOD-BYE, AGAIN

I'm going away again, the fourth foreign trip in as many months. My passport, thick as a thin wallet, has another new tattoo, my arm another needle hole, my tattered vaccination record another stamp. I bought a new journal, and the empty pages beckon like a sculptor's block of clay.

I've read the handwritten reports and obscure books and corresponded with one of the few people on Earth who's been to the region of China's western Sichuan province where I'm going, seventy-one-year-old Japanese explorer Tomatsu Nakamura. I've printed out the Landsat photos and managed to obtain the uncannily accurate Soviet topographic maps that have guided me on so many trips before.

Before he died on an expedition in the Arctic, my best friend, red-headed Mike Moe, told me that "half the joy of a journey is planning it; the other half is coming home and bragging about it." So many nights Mike and I had spread maps across his living room floor and dreamed big about some distant place; three months later, we'd be giving a slide show about our adventure in that same living room, roasting each other to the hooting of close friends. Later, when everyone was gone, we'd stretch out on the rug and plan our next trip.

I have been going away and coming back since I was sixteen. I blew off my last semester of high school so Mike and I could escape to Europe and Africa and Russia. We traveled till our money ran out, then kept going, scrounging meals in university cafeterias from Seville to Stockholm. Six months later we made it back to Wyoming to start college.

During my junior year, when I met Sue, the woman who would become my wife, the first thing she and I did was take off to the Grand Canyon for ten days. Two months later I left for three months to bicycle across the United States. When I returned, we moved in together—Sue was the first woman I'd met who was secure enough to accept my wanderlust rather than seeing it as a threat to our relationship. Several months later I left for a month to ski across Yellowstone, and Sue left to bicycle through Europe for six weeks.

Here, then gone. Back, gone again. I chose this recursive path, and it has been my life and livelihood for more than two decades. I can't get enough of the world: the stench of sweat on a Tanzanian bus, the sword of wind on an Andean pass, a little girl in the Sahel carrying her baby sister on her back and a bucket of brown river water on her stiff-necked head.

My gusto for journeying and writing about it has remained inextinguishable—and yet something else, something corded to travel like ligament to bone, has changed over the years: my connection to home.

In my twenties I hardly gave a thought to home. I was wild and self-centered and left without a look back. I remember standing around a campfire in the Tetons, snowflakes hooking together in midair and parachuting to the ground. One of our clan had just learned that his girlfriend was pregnant.

"I'm not going to let it change me or my life," he declared. "I'm still going climbing and kayaking and skiing!"

"Here, here!" We all toasted his commitment to the heroic, self-absorbed dirtbag life.

In 1991, when Sue was pregnant with our first daughter, Addi, I was kayaking down the Niger River, running a gauntlet of hippos and crocs. I'd left in the middle of the second trimester. When I'd expressed my misgivings, Sue had dismissed the issue. "Pregnancy isn't an injury, Mark," she'd said. "I'll just be fine."

And she was. She was focused on her passions—teaching Spanish at the university, volunteering in the community, working on our old house. I was back for the birth, but a part of me still wanted to believe that home was wherever I happened to lay my head.

I was stripped of this sophistry forever when Addi was twenty months old. I was leaving for Burma with three friends to attempt an unclimbed 19,296-foot peak called Hkakabo Razi. It was a dangerous undertaking with an uncertain outcome. I didn't have to go—I wanted to.

Innocent of my imminent departure, Addi, a weeble-wobble toddler, helped me pack. She drummed the black camp pot with ice screws, waddled up and down the hallway dragging my climbing slings and carabiners, flung her chubby, diapered body into my −40°F down sleeping bag, pealing with delight. For her, it was just another game. But I was scraped raw by my duplicity. I didn't have the heart to tell her what was really happening: I was leaving.

At the airport, watching planes take off, Addi suddenly figured it out. "Daddy . . . ," she hesitated, and her lip began to quiver.

The look of shock and hurt and betrayal in her huge brown eyes crushed me more than any avalanche ever could.

• • •

By the time I got home two months later, Addi was potty trained and speaking in full sentences. The mountain that I failed to climb is still there, ice coated and indifferent. It will always be there, but the moment when Addi put together her first sentence was gone, and I'd missed it. Like any anguished father, I brought back a stuffed panda bear that was bigger than she was, and she's been sleeping with it ever since.

When Sue and I decided to have children, we already knew that the adventurous life wasn't enough for either of us; on the other hand, we weren't about to give it up. When feasible, we figured, we'd bring our kids along. Addi was six months old when Sue and I bicycled across Europe with her. We took her, at thirteen months, to Costa Rica. When she was three and her new little sister, Teal, was six months, we went deep into the hinterlands of Mexico, staying in two-dollar-a-night village huts and eating the fiery cantina food. To this day, the girls love Latin culture.

We traveled as a family to Nepal, Russia, Australia, Spain, and Thailand—whenever schedules and finances jibed. It was our way of taking home with us, and we weren't the only ones. Eric Jackson, the world freestyle kayaking champion, and his wife, Kristine, who manages the family kayak business, did something even more extreme.

In 1997 the couple and their two kids, seven-year-old Emily and four-year-old Dane, were living in suburban Washington, DC. Eric, now forty-one, was running a kayak school on the Potomac but training in Colorado and traveling to compete all over the country. "I just couldn't take it anymore," Eric—E.J.—tells me by phone. "I wasn't seeing my kids or my wife, but my kayaking never suffered. I'm extremely selfish about my kayaking."

"Kristine suggested we move into an RV," he says. "It saved our marriage."

She placed a classified ad in the *Washington Post*, and in one weekend they sold everything they owned. "People came into our house and walked out with our TV, silverware, clothes, the sheets on our bed," E.J.

recalls. When it was all gone, the Jackson family drove off in an RV with their kayaks and $7,000 in cash, traveling across North America from one put-in to the next and kayaking at least thirty new rivers a year.

"One of the things that fascinates me most about American culture is the readiness to move," observes Jonathan Raban, sixty-three, winner of a National Book Critics Circle Award for his 1996 *Bad Land: An American Romance* and a British expat who has lived in the States since 1990. "Americans have this inborn readiness to turn themselves into exiles. They have become accustomed to living the temporary life."

For the Jacksons, the strategy worked. "It was a real breakthrough," says E.J. "Every morning the kids were right there, Kristine was right there, we were all together, twenty-four/seven."

Kristine homeschooled the kids, and E.J. competed and taught kayaking clinics to make ends meet. ("I went to the pawnshop plenty of times," he says.) They lived in an RV for five years before settling along the Caney Fork River in central Tennessee and starting Jackson Kayak, now the fourth-largest manufacturer of whitewater kayaks in the country.

"This place has everything we need," E.J. says. "A high-volume river with year-round whitewater, warm weather, and a rural environment."

Even with its gorgeous mountains and huge sky and our extended family nearby, Wyoming doesn't have everything we need. That's why Sue and I and the girls head off on a trip or two a year. The rest of the time, when I leave, I leave alone.

But I'm not gone for months anymore. I'm no longer bicycling across entire continents or climbing 8,000-meter peaks. I've already learned most of what these expeditions can teach; besides, they take too much time. I've become a master at moving fast. Mount Cook in one day rather than four, McKinley in nine days rather than twenty-four, ditto Aconcagua. I immerse myself in the sticky liquid of another culture, do all I possibly can, scribble a book of notes and shoot a box of film, then hightail it back home.

I was there when both Addi and Teal learned to walk. I taught them both how to ride bikes, build a snow cave and use a map and compass, poop in the woods and wipe with snow, climb rocks and canoe rivers. Small skills. They taught me how to see the colors and ants, how to swing with my head thrown back, how to listen and believe.

The truth is, if your kids don't change your life, you—and they—are completely missing out. If you choose to bring them into the world, children are the biggest adventure there is. You only hope you can find the strength and courage and grit and love to live up to the opportunity.

• • •

As I prepare to leave again, I'm culpably conscious of what I will miss: Halloween, eleven-year-old Teal's final soccer game of the year, thirteen-year-old Addi's first dance, Sue's mountain race. All the ordinary, miraculous breakfasts and dinners, when we share each other's minor triumphs and tribulations.

I've been off on assignment on Sue's birthday or our anniversary countless times; usually I remember to have flowers delivered in my absence, an act that I realize is corny and pathetic and somehow still meaningful. I've missed piano recitals and school plays, swim meets and weddings and funerals. Writing about crawling into a wet sleeping bag in Uganda meant I was not home to tuck my kids in and tell them a story and then slip into bed with my wife. Perhaps I now bring home something better than a stuffed panda for my girls—an understanding that the world is full of choices, and that it will someday be up to them to find their own way. They're already becoming writers and athletes themselves.

My daughters, like their mother, miss me, but they don't pine away while I'm gone. Sue says that they bond even tighter, knowing they must take care of one another. That's what I want to be doing.

This is my conundrum, the incurable disease of mountain guides, foreign correspondents, and all kinds of adventurers: We yearn to go, but we don't want to leave.

"I'm not sure I deal with it particularly well," admits Barry Bearak, fifty-six, a *New York Times* reporter who won a Pulitzer Prize in 2001 for his coverage of life in war-torn Afghanistan. "I signed up to be the coach of my older boy's Little League team and missed every game. I felt awful."

Bearak's wife, Celia Dugger, forty-seven, is also a writer, reporting on global poverty issues for the *Times*. They live in Pelham, New York, with their two sons, Max, fifteen, and Sam, ten, but have been known to travel for three or four months over the course of a year.

"Sometimes it is just really, really hard," Bearak tells me over the phone. "I phone home every day. On Thanksgiving in 2001, I was in Afghanistan in the middle of a battle, bullets flying all around, and I called home."

Had he wished he were with his family at that moment?

"No. I felt like I was in the right place for the story. I love my work. The work is important. It's why we all got into journalism: to try to make a difference."

Dugger picks up the phone. "I feel extraordinarily privileged to do what I do," she says, "to travel all over the world and write about something meaningful. But there is a sense of grieving when I leave, and after three to four weeks, I miss the boys so much I just have to come home."

And how is it for Sam and Max?

"I think they've gained from this kind of life," says Dugger. "They have an enormous curiosity about the wider world. But, yes, it's tough. In some sense it's irresolvable. You're always trying to not let it get to the point where you're paying too high a price for this drive you feel to be out in the world."

•   •   •

For me, one of the iconic images of the Katrina disaster was an old, graceful New Orleans house being washed from its foundation, dragged into the tempest of brown water, and gradually torn apart—the roof collapsing, walls shearing off, the structure warping, then sinking.

To be rendered homeless—whether by hurricane, poverty, or choice—is to be deprived of not simply physical shelter but emotional refuge. Home is where we return to, where we stop to rest and think, where we piece together the new pictures in our minds and try to make sense of our planet. Without home, we are unmoored.

And it's a literary lie that you can never go home again. Somehow, like a boomerang, most of us do. It may take a lot of trying and time before we get there. It may be a different home, it may be a home we build or rebuild, but it is home nonetheless: a physical place, a family or friends or both, pets, a community.

Which is not to say that the homecoming will be smooth. Reentry is inevitably bumpy. If you come in at the wrong angle, you can burn up. Contrary to the Hollywood happy ending, homecomings are usually jagged affairs. There's a period of cultural limbo before you regain your sense of place. Meanwhile, your family is struggling to reintegrate you into their lives. Whenever I come home, jet-lagged and weary, Sue and I cautiously circle each other for a couple of days before harmony returns.

Then the whole process starts all over again.

For better or worse, the warmth of the womb of home will eventually start to smother me. I will grow restless and irritable. I will crave, physically and emotionally, another big hit of travel. Sue's used to it. "Time for another trip," she'll say. No sooner said than done.

"I have this terrible sense of regret every time I leave Wyoming," says old friend and fellow Wyomingite Gretel Ehrlich. "It's like some sort of betrayal, as if I'm saying, 'Things aren't good enough here,' although it's not about that at all. I have this great hunger to see and experience how people and animals and plants survive, even thrive, in other difficult places."

Gretel, author of the 1985 classic *The Solace of Open Spaces* and, recently, *The Future of Ice*, lives half the year in a cabin in northwestern Wyoming.

"I believe home requires developing an intimacy with a place," she says. "Intimacy takes time. Every morning I go for an old-fashioned Thoreauvian walk. I like to note how the antelope divide themselves into bands, watch the ravens doing tricks in the sky."

Gretel pauses. "Home isn't my toaster and my toilet; it's the whole community of animals and birds and people and dogs. Home is like a great big tree. It provides shelter, but there are no walls. It doesn't separate you or isolate you from the world. Rather, it's a platform from which to launch."

• • •

I'm leaving in three days and the momentum is building now. That feverish thrill of the prospect of exploring new territory. That curiosity to see what's on the other side of the mountain, the continent, the ocean. The guilt of leaving Sue, Addi, and Teal for the hundredth time, and the fear of what would happen if I didn't come back.

I'm trying to be with them as much as I can. Friday night, a family movie and a bowl of homemade caramel corn. Saturday, Addi's state volleyball tournament; Sunday, Teal's soccer game. Last night Teal read to me from an adventure mystery I read at her age, *The Haunted Treasure of the Espectros*. Addi read me her latest story, "The Perfect Girl," written from a boy's perspective.

When they get home from school, I just want to lie on the couch and listen to them practice piano, but I can't. I'm on deadline. Sometimes even when I'm home, I'm not.

The day before I leave, Teal knocks on my study door and wants me to come out and play. Pained, I tell her no.

"That's okay," she says.

She comes close and peers over my shoulder at the computer screen.

"You know, when you're gone, before bed I come in here and sit in your chair just to be close to you," she says.

I'm gutted.

Without my home, a place to leave from and return to, travel would be impossible for me. In the balancing scale of life, home is the antipodal counterweight to travel. It is the hand that holds the kite string—and, should the string snap, the kite will twist and fold and drop from the sky like a buckshot bird.

Ascents

GUERILLAS IN THE MIST

We all have a place we dream about. We have visited it without ever having set foot there. It's someplace far away, someplace exotic. Although we've never seen it, we know what it looks like, for we half-created it, using a book we read when we were ten, something we overheard at a party at a villa in Italy, and the one unforgettable image from a slide show in Bozeman. This is enough. Like a child in the backyard with a refrigerator box, a bread knife, and crayons, we've fashioned the dream of a place to which we've never been but long to go.

We carry it with us in the backs of our minds. It's our private dream. The way a tomboy keeps a smooth stone in her pocket, we don't share it with just anybody. It's not a place anyone else would necessarily want to go.

As we grow up, this enchanted outpost can disappear inside us, if we let it. But most of us are able to hold onto our magical place, filling in the blank spaces with facts and images we pick up along the way. Then one day something happens. The trigger may be obvious or unconscious—no matter. The time has come to find this place in the flesh.

• • •

I don't remember when I first heard of the Mountains of the Moon. Perhaps it was as far back as elementary school, when we learned that the Nile is the longest river in the world—4,132 miles—and that Ptolemy, second-century Greek polymath, had named as its source the Lunae Montes, or Mountains of the Moon, the mythic snowcapped peaks that rise from the jungles of central Africa. The source actually remained unconfirmed until 1858, when British explorer John Hanning Speke discovered Lake Victoria and declared it the river's origin. But it wasn't until 1888 that Henry Morton Stanley became the first European to see the highest source of the ancient river: the snow mantling the equatorial peaks of the Rwenzori (the modern name for the Mountains of the Moon), on the border between Uganda and the Democratic Republic of the Congo. It was pointed out to him by an African boy who thought the peaks were covered with salt.

My next serendipitous encounter must have been in H. W. Tilman's *Snow on the Equator* (1937), for when you are too young to strike out on your own, the next best thing is to read of men who did. Tilman, a taciturn bachelor with a stiff upper lip, was nevertheless a wordsmith who wrote his autobiography as a series of thirteen adventure books. He lived the life a restless adolescent dreams of: climbing in East Africa, reconnoitering in Iran and Tibet, sailing around Greenland. In the early 1930s, Tilman and his mountaineering partner Eric Shipton ventured into the Rwenzori. His descriptions—"the nightmare landscape," with its constant cold drizzle, tree-size flowers, leg-swallowing mud, jungle "made grotesque by waving beards of lichen hanging from every branch," and elusive peaks hidden in roiling mist—gripped me like lust.

Then, in 1987, descending off Mount Kenya, I had an offhand conversation with a Kiwi who had just been to the fabled Rwenzori: "Times in there we was walkin' on roots suspended ten feet 'bove the ground like they was the backs of snakes," he said. "You can't imagine it."

But I could.

The trigger came in 2003, on the London Tube: I stumbled upon a story in the *Guardian* about University College geographer Richard Taylor, who, during a recent scientific expedition into Rwenzori Mountains National Park, had discovered that, due to global warming, the glaciers were rapidly melting.

I had to go now, before my dreamland disappeared.

• • •

I got in touch with Richard Taylor, who put me in contact with Nelson Kisaka, thirty-one, the Kampala-based president of the Mountain Club of Uganda (MCU). Nelson said that the mountain club, much like the country itself, had been through difficult times but was in the process of rebuilding. By e-mail, he invited me to mount a climbing expedition with the club into the peaks of the Rwenzori.

The MCU was founded in the geography department of Kampala's Makerere University in 1946. Early members—the vast majority of them Europeans living in Uganda—conducted numerous mountaineering and scientific expeditions to the Rwenzori. Between 1948 and 1962, the year Uganda gained independence from Britain, the MCU built a circuit of six huts, published several guidebooks, and began introducing rock and ice climbing to a fledgling nation.

But when Idi Amin came to power in 1971, all semblance of civil life vanished from Uganda. Preternaturally homicidal, Amin overthrew prime minister Milton Obote and then spent the next eight years executing some 300,000 civilians before being ousted by Ugandan exiles and the army of Tanzania in 1979. Milton Obote returned to power in 1980 and ruled for another five bloody years, until former defense minister Yoweri Museveni's rebel army captured the capital of Kampala in January 1986 and installed Museveni as president. A benevolent yet autocratic leader, Museveni has instituted national elections (he was reelected in 1996 and 2001) and rebuilt Uganda's economy on privatization, foreign investment, and coffee exports.

Though better developed and more politically stable than many African nations, Uganda today shares some problems with its neighbors. Since 1982, AIDS has killed a million Ugandans, and Museveni's government faces several rebel insurgencies in the north, as well as sporadic fighting along the western border with the Congo. In the mid-nineties, guerrillas fighting in the Congo began using the Rwenzori as a redoubt, prompting the Ugandan government to close Rwenzori Mountains National Park in July 1997. The Western world heard almost nothing of this conflict until March 1999, when Congolese insurgents slaughtered eight Western tourists and a Ugandan warden in Bwindi National Park, Uganda's popular gorilla sanctuary, a hundred miles south of the Rwenzori. Ugandan military forces were sent to the western frontier, and, trail by trail, the rebels were killed or driven out of the parks. Rwenzori Mountains National Park reopened in July 2001.

With peace come tourists and their desperately needed dollars. In the past four years, the country's tourism industry has tripled, with more than 100,000 travelers visiting the nation's ten game parks in 2003. As for outdoor sports, they too are luxury activities that germinate only in relatively stable conditions. When citizens are simply trying to survive—to eat, to find shelter, to protect their children, to avoid being shot or tortured or raped—they do not climb, hike, or ski.

Nelson said that after a long hiatus, the Mountain Club of Uganda was getting back on its feet, but it had no climbing gear; and of the 300 affiliated members, only eighteen were currently active—and just a handful of those were experienced at altitude. (Most of the 300 members are Ugandans, but more than half of the active climbers are expats.)

Because our expedition would be the club's first major ascent since the early days, Nelson asked if I might teach basic mountaineering skills.

For this I would need a partner, and I had just the man in mind: Steve Roach, forty-four, a former mission programmer for NASA, computer science professor at the University of Texas at El Paso, colorful orator of Robert Service ballads, and solid mountaineer. Steve is unflappable, wry, and up for anything—he once drove a school bus loaded with used computers down to Guatemala to give them to an impoverished school. Before I even explained what the trip was all about, Steve said, "I'm going."

The two of us arrived in Kampala with bulging duffel bags of equipment—donations of clothing, gear, and ropes from fellow climbers, as well as new tents from Mountain Hardwear—for the Mountain Club of Uganda.

• • •

Our eighteen porters are huddled around the fire, squatting like frogs, as we pass by at dawn. It is our fifth day out of Kampala, our third day on the approach inside Rwenzori Mountains National Park. We cross the Bujuku River and pull ourselves up through a stunted, moss-webbed forest to gain the lower Bigo Bog, a narrow defile between two walls of dark, wet granite. Beneath the floating hummocks lies a lake of mud.

The goal is to leap from one meter-high, frost-glazed stump of sedge to the next. The porters, acrobats in disguise, have already caught up. They pass us and commence running over the Bigo Bog, bounding lightly from one tussock to the next as if their fifty-pound loads are no more than knapsacks.

The rest of us follow, with frequent muddy falls. In addition to the porters and our Ugandan trekking guide, Joel Nzwenge, thirty-four, an armed national park ranger, our team consists of Steve, me, Nelson Kisaka, and six other members of the Mountain Club of Uganda. The demographics of our group resemble those of the present-day MCU: Of the seven members, only Nelson and twenty-six-year-old electrical engineer Eric Mugerwa are Ugandan. The rest are expats: Kenyan Ngoki Muhoho, forty, owns her own management consulting business; Greg Smith, twenty-four, a British economist for Uganda's Ministry of Finance and 5.12-grade gritstone climber; Mike Barnett, fifty-nine, an Australian project engineer in Kampala and passionate lepidopterist; and two

Yanks—Glenda Siegrist, forty-two, a nurse at the US Embassy in Kampala and the life of our party, and her husband, Loren Hostetter, forty-three, an agricultural development consultant for the US Agency for International Development and the spirit behind the resurgent MCU. Greg and Loren alone have mountaineering experience; the rest are enthusiastic novices.

It has been raining for days. Two nights ago, at the Nyabitaba hut, it was pouring so violently that the tin roof was shrieking. But when I asked Joel how the weather would affect the alpine moorlands, he said flatly, "It is not raining." He wasn't joking. To the Bakonjo—the people who live in the foothills of the Rwenzori and farm cassava, bananas, beans, and coffee—it is raining only when the air is so full of water you literally can't breathe and must stay indoors.

Above the lower Bigo Bog lies the upper Bigo Bog, at 12,000 feet, which legend has it is capable of gulping down a smallish, uncoordinated climber in a matter of seconds. But when Rwenzori Mountains National Park was declared a World Heritage Site by the United Nations in 1994, a boardwalk was built across this swamp. Dilapidated now but still largely above water, it allows us to chug across the quagmire like engines on a narrow-gauge railroad, entering a landscape I have imagined since childhood.

A forest of hypertrophic plants surrounds us—giant groundsel and giant lobelia and giant heather. The groundsels, twenty-five feet tall, with their enormous, artichoke-like balls atop their furred branches, resemble Joshua trees. The lobelias, purplish spires of hair, stand like solemn, bearded trolls; heathers hover to either side like plants that have morphed into enormous mammals. It is like *Little Shop of Horrors*. At any moment I expect a giant groundsel to reach out and grab me, or a three-foot rosette to spread its labial leaves and speak.

It is this surreal terrain, as much as the summits themselves, that drew me to the Rwenzori. I'm in no hurry to pass through this Seussian ecozone. I revel in each hour, stopping to touch the exotic plants like one would a giant rabbit. Still, it takes us only two more days to reach our alpine high camp, the Elena hut, at 14,900 feet.

The night before our dawn attempt on Margherita, the highest summit of 16,763-foot Mount Stanley, we're all zipped up in our bags on the blackened hut floor. Due to altitude sickness, Eric, Ngoki, and Nelson will stay in the hut while the rest of us make the final push.

"We should split into two roped teams," whispers Steve. "You, Loren, and Greg. Me, Glenda, and Mike. How far did you recon today?"

"To the Stanley Plateau, I think," I say.

"Couldn't see the peaks?" chuckles Steve. The fog, sleet, drizzle, and flurries of snow have been incessant, and we haven't even laid eyes on the summits yet. It is the summer dry season, but the Rwenzori gets eight feet of precipitation a year.

The next morning we set off into an ocean of fog, as usual. Following cairns up recently deglaciated granite slabs, we reach the steep nose of the Elena Glacier, where our two teams separate.

"See you on top," I yell to Steve, a blue ghost in the pearly opacity.

"I doubt it."

Loren, Greg, and I make short work of the Stanley Plateau—a flat, diminishing ice cap—then cut northeast across a rock ridge to gain the Margherita Glacier. Although it is heavily crevassed, meltwater has filled in the cracks. A generation ago we would have been able to climb ice all the way to the top. Today the peak is a shattered helmet of dripping rock.

We summit before noon, eat lunch in swirling clouds, then descend to the base of the rock to find Steve's team arriving. With some swift belaying, Steve, Glenda, and Mike top out.

We're all grinning from ear to ear as we crampon back down the glaciers together. Back at the hut, Mike Barnett, the pentagenarian Aussie, gives me the most vigorous, heartfelt handshake and confides that he's been dreaming of climbing in the Rwenzori since he did Kilimanjaro in 1970.

Dreams are contagious, and dreamers inevitably find each other.

• • •

Once you've spent the time, money, and emotional energy to get yourself to that place you've fantasized about for decades, there's no sense in not having a good look around. So when the MCU climbers descend the next day, Steve and I stay on at the Elena hut. We have a detour in mind.

During the Mountain Club of Uganda's peak years, its most dedicated member was H. A. Osmaston, who with David Pasteur wrote *Guide to the Ruwenzori: The Mountains of the Moon* in 1972. I'd obtained a photocopy, read it carefully, and made e-mail contact with Osmaston, now eighty-four and living in Cumbria, in northern England. In my note I suggested that there appeared to be ample room for a new route on the west face of Mount Stanley.

He responded: "I think all you say is correct. The rock should be clean of moss as it is so steep. But it is entirely in the Congo. A bulletproof jacket would be an important addition to your kit. I don't advise it."

According to Osmaston, the last documented ascent of the west face of Margherita was in 1956. No one knew whether Congolese guerrillas were still using the western slope of the range as a hideout, but after talking to our porters—many of whom live in the high villages of the Rwenzori—I reasoned that if they were, they probably wouldn't bother climbing to 16,000 feet.

"I say we go have a look."

"I say we might get ourselves killed," replies Steve, which doesn't mean he doesn't want to go.

From Osmaston's guide, it appeared that no one had made a complete traverse of the Stanley Plateau. There was once a cabin, the Moraine hut, down on the Congo side, but Osmaston didn't know if it still existed. We decide to aim for this mythical hut, get a peek at the west face if we're lucky, and go from there.

An alpine start is requisite, but it's snowing hard the next morning. We scootch back down in our bags. Steve prepares a leisurely breakfast while I read about the Duke of Abruzzi.

The duke, an indefatigable Italian hero and probably the most meticulous mountain explorer of the early twentieth century, led a professional mountaineering team into the Rwenzoris in 1906. In forty days, the team made thirty first ascents, including the multiple summits of the Rwenzori's two highest mountains, Stanley and Speke.

By nine o'clock it is snowing only lightly.

"If we're gonna go," says Steve, heaving on his pack, "let's go."

We retrace our steps up the Stanley Plateau, then veer left toward the pass. By chance, a hole opens in the clouds, and we spot what we think is a tiny hut before the gap closes. We cross the invisible border and descend the western Stanley Glacier until it disappears, forcing us to rappel down rock ravines. We're in the Congo now.

As the mist momentarily clears, we again spy the hut on the ridgeline—and *two people* standing beside it! We're speechless. This is the last thing we wanted. I stare through the wisps of white with all my might, trying to determine whether they are armed.

"Are they moving?" Steve's voice is a bit higher than normal.

"No. They're not moving."

The mist rolls in and the guerrillas disappear. We move forward like cats, silent, shoulders tensed, creeping low to the ground through the boulders. The mist blows off again.

"They haven't moved," I whisper.

Steve bursts out laughing so loud I jump. "Nope. They sure haven't. Might be because one's a cairn and the other one's a giant groundsel."

We reach the Moraine hut fifteen minutes later. It is empty but still in solid condition. We eat lunch inside with the door open, hoping for a momentary glimpse of the west face of Mount Stanley. Alas, the peak, 2,500 feet above, is engulfed by dark-bellied clouds. The glaciers, the icefalls, the three summits—we can see none of it. So what's new?

Steve strikes out up the face first and I follow, both of us scrambling along steep, verglased granite. Gaining what we presume is the Alexandra Glacier, we rope up and simul-climb for the next three hours, occasionally sinking an ice screw. The ice is not steep, 50 to 60 degrees, but we can never see more than a hundred feet above us, so we don't know where we're going, other than straight up. But it sounds more daring than it is. When you're climbing properly, you're in the moment, working only with the world that's right at the ends of your hands and feet—like a potter or a sculptor or a gymnast.

The last two pitches are a gothic castle of ice—turrets, moats, curtained walls, tenuous drawbridges. Everything above us and everything below us is lost in nubilated white gauze, as if this castle is suspended in the sky. We climb the castle walls straight to the summit.

Standing beside the summit signpost, we have no view whatsoever. No hazy sea of green down in the Congo. No surrounding ridges or arêtes. No falling valleys. But that's fine. We can imagine it without even trying.

• • •

When you finally go to a place you have fictionalized for years, you know that the illusion you've so carefully constructed will vanish forever, as all dreams do when you wake up. Which would be heartbreaking if, before you got home, you didn't discover that you had somehow slipped your secret smooth stone into another person's pocket.

We have a grand pizza party at an upscale Italian restaurant in Kampala following the expedition. The whole team is there along with aspiring members of the MCU, young Ugandans yearning to explore the mountains. They listen to our stories of the Rwenzori, then start planning their own expedition.

The Mountain Club of Uganda is back.

LIVE TO FIGHT
ANOTHER DAY

Perhaps I am alive only because we turned back.

This realization startles me so much that I turn the key and the windshield wipers halt in midslap. I'm sitting behind a line of cars waiting for a road crew to clear away a mud slide blocking the coast highway. I sit listening to the pounding rain, a downpour so copious the car feels submerged, as if I am inside a one-man submarine.

Perhaps I'm alive merely because I was denied the opportunity to make the wrong decision.

· · ·

It has been pouring nonstop since I arrived in New Zealand. I'd been forewarned.

"We have a rather wet weather pattern at the moment," e-mailed Allan Uren, a sardonic Kiwi ice climber with whom I had hoped to do an enchainment of the three highest peaks in New Zealand—Mount Tasman, Mount Dampier, and Aoraki/Mount Cook. "Over 250 mm of rain in the last week. This may sound quite grim, and it is, but things can change quickly."

But they didn't. When I arrived in Fox Glacier, the tourist hamlet on the West Coast of New Zealand's South Island where Allan lives, the gutters were running like rivers. I half expected to see trout jumping. The West Coast is a rainforest to rival the Olympic Peninsula—sphagnum practically hangs in the air. Fox Glacier, like Talkeetna or Grindelwald, is the starting point for many mountaineering expeditions; it's only a dozen miles from Mount Cook. But the clerk at the backpacker's hostel told me it had now been raining for six weeks straight. "All the climbers have skedaddled," he said, "and the rest of us are starting to go a wee bit mad."

Allan had booked a helicopter to fly us into the mountains, but it wasn't to be. We considered walking in, but reports from climbers up in the alpine huts were dismal: No one had been able to move for two weeks.

After a few days of waiting, I abandoned Allan and Fox Glacier in search of sunshine. I drove down the coast, curled up over Haast Pass, and dropped into Wanaka, the Interlaken of New Zealand's Southern Alps.

New Zealand has made the most of its stunningly diverse geography. Canyoneering, mountaineering, trekking, sea kayaking, parapenting, skydiving—the place is a South Pacific Adventureland. (Bungee jumping was invented in New Zealand.) And the Kiwis have done such a bang-up job of marketing these attractions around the world that you can hear a dozen languages while strolling the streets of Wanaka. Disregard the cotton-ball sheep dotting the verdant hillside—they're picturesque, but that's it. Mutton and wool mean nothing: Tourism is what makes New Zealand tick.

I arrived in Wanaka (population 6,900) in the evening, ate dinner at a Turkish café where dreadlocked Lonely Planet travelers were humming along with a guitarist mangling Dylan, had dessert in an Indian restaurant crowded with noisy Spaniards, and drank beer in an Irish pub full of ornery British climbers.

And in the morning: By God, the sun was shining. I immediately called Allan. He claimed the sun was trying to sneak out in Fox Glacier, too, and if I drove directly back, we'd fly in and start climbing.

"The sun vanished right after you hung up!" Allan shouted from his porch as I drove up. Water gushed off the tin roof like a spillway. He pulled on his gum boots, and we tramped over to the Department of Conservation office to check the satellite weather reports for the umpteenth time. Climbers in New Zealand live by these weather reports. They have become meteorological masters at interpreting the concentric squiggles over the Tasman Sea. Studying isobars is as much a part of a Kiwi mountaineer's morning as coffee.

Allan divined that there was some chance of a momentary clearing early the next morning. For the third, maybe fourth time, we organized our gear, sorted our food, reloaded our packs, and went to bed with idiotically high hopes.

The next day it was raining spitefully hard. I hung around in Fox Glacier for two more days—still hoping, watching the trout spawn in the streets—and then left again.

To end up simply driving around in the rain after flying halfway around the world with the grand intention of climbing glaciated, blue-sky peaks is plain depressing. Perhaps if I were from Seattle or Portland, it wouldn't be so bad. They're used to rain. Some even claim they like it, although I suspect that had any outdoor veteran from the Northwest been advised between the isolines not to come over, as I had been, he or she would have wisely stayed home, knowing what interminable precipitation can do to a trip. Alas, if you hail from the Rocky Mountains, you tend to have this blind faith in the invincibility of the sun. Sure it'll rain or snow for a little while, but then the sun will pop out, just like it's supposed to. Right?

One thing I will admit: Rain does make one contemplative. You start thinking about things. In my case, if you're in New Zealand and have failed over and over to even get close to the mountains of your desire, you begin mulling over the other mountains you've failed on.

Like Everest.

• • •

I was on the 1986 US North Face Everest Expedition. There were eleven of us, and I was the youngest. Most of us had high-altitude Himalayan experience. The Great Couloir route on the North Face of Everest, a merciless mile-and-a-half-high wall of blue ice and rotten rock, had been climbed only once, two years before, by an Australian team.

This was back before Everest was actually famous. Remember? We paid for the expedition out of our pockets—$6,000 apiece, a whopping sum for dirtbag climbers. We brought our worn-out eleven-millimeter ropes to use as fixed line. Mail—handwritten letters on thin blue aerograms—was sent and received via yak. We were on the mountain for seventy-five days. We all came home. We came home with all our fingers and toes. And we all came home friends. But we didn't summit.

And this had stuck in my craw for fifteen years—until I was driving around in the rain in New Zealand. Which is perhaps no surprise. New Zealand and Everest are inseparably linked by the greatest triumph and the worst tragedy the mountain has ever witnessed. Sir Edmund Hillary is a Kiwi. So was climbing guide Rob Hall, one of the eight men and women who perished on Everest in May 1996.

Squinting through the rain-battered windshield, I replayed for the thousandth time our attempt at the summit. We had managed to fix lines from 21,000 to almost 26,000 feet, an exhausting, time-consuming job that had to be led one pitch at a time, most of it up solid ice. We'd fallen behind schedule, and by mid-May the monsoon began creeping into the Himalayas. Avalanches were starting to sweep the North Face. It was now or never.

This is my memory of what happened all those years ago: Four of us made the attempt—Dana Coffield, Sandy Stewart, Carlos Buhler, and me. Our high camp was at 25,000 feet, 4,000 feet from the top. Our only chance was to forgo establishing a final camp, carry minimal gear and supplies, and just start soloing beyond the last fixed line. One two-man tent for all four—one of us carrying the poles, another the tent body—and just a single stove—one of us carrying the stove itself, another the fuel. The plan: Climb from 21,000 to 25,000 the first day, sleep, summit the next day, pitch a one-night bivy at 27,000 on the descent, and then downclimb all the way to our 19,000-foot base camp the following day.

We set out in single file in the dark, jugging the lines up the face in the dim light of our headlamps. It was snowing hard, and we were soon lost to one another. Shove one ascender up the ice-coated rope, then the next, step up one foot, then the next. Do it again.

Spindrift avalanches began hitting us, plummeting from far above. Hearing one coming, we would brace ourselves—hunch our shoulders, flatten our bodies against the ice, clamp our mouths shut, and cling to our ascenders. When they hit, we would be blasted right off the steep ice, momentarily lifted out into midsky in a swirling, breathless maelstrom, then slammed back into the face as the gust of snow rushed on.

We had planned to regroup at 23,000 feet—a miserable camp on a precarious shelf surrounded by snow walls graffitied with urine and feces. Carlos arrived first, and I was second. We ducked into a tent, squeezed into our sleeping bags fully clothed, and waited, conserving energy, knowing Dana and Sandy were right behind us.

They didn't arrive. An hour passed, then another. After three hours we started to get worried. Carlos tried to raise someone on the radio. Nothing.

Careful not to drain the batteries, he began calling once an hour. It was after dark when we heard a scratchy, faint reply. It was Sandy.

"Where are you guys?" Carlos shouted.

The static was so fierce we could only make out snatches of what Sandy was saying.

" . . . glacier camp . . . "

"Are you okay?" Carlos yelled.

" . . . "

Carlos repeated the question.

" . . . yes, we are, but . . . "

More static and clicks. Then one complete utterance got through.

"We decided it was too dangerous," Sandy said. "We turned back."

I couldn't believe it. They'd turned back?!

The ramifications were clear: Without the crucial components of the tent and stove that Dana and Sandy were carrying, Carlos and I weren't equipped to continue. We couldn't go on.

The expedition was over.

• • •

During my second week in New Zealand, I decided to go for a walk. Technical climbing may be practically impossible in the rain, but hiking is not.

New Zealand has the finest hut-to-hut hiking system in the world. The huts themselves are immaculate wonders, featuring shimmering, stainless-steel kitchens with gas burners, heat-radiating coal stoves surrounded by benches, bunks as tidy as those at the finest summer camp, and head-shaking views you'd pay millions for in Jackson Hole or Zermatt. Paper, plastic, tin, glass, and organic waste are choppered out and recycled or safely disposed of.

Still, given the extraordinarily disagreeable weather, I assumed that even the most famous hut-to-hut tracks would be practically empty. Not on your life. New Zealanders apparently can't imagine anything on Earth more pleasant than hiking through freezing rain. They're worse than the Scots. They wear rough wool sweaters and heavy sailor's slickers and mushy boots and yet remain unyieldingly good-humored and eager. Many of the huts are booked up months, even years in advance. When I called the Department of Conservation, I learned that virtually every single bunk in every hut along the Milford Track was reserved until I become a grandfather.

The Routeburn Track, however, did have a few spaces left in one or two huts. One of the classic fjordland treks at the southern end of the South Island, it's meant to be a three- to four-day excursion. But when I added up the total distance, even with side trips, it was no more than twenty-five miles.

I hiked up the Routeburn Track the first day, spent the night in the Howden hut, and hiked out the Caples Track the next. It rained remorselessly. The New Zealanders I met on the trail were grinning and enjoying the hell out of their hike, and almost every foreigner was hypothermic and whining. In the shelter on Harris Saddle, I met a Kiwi wapiti farmer who said with pride, "'Tis indeed possible to drown just standing up in this gorgeous green land."

The hike was a respite from dwelling on an expedition that had long ago passed under the bridge. But back in the car, I found myself once again chewing on my Everest experience. I was stopped at one of the dozens of landslides that road crews were trying to clean up. A loader and a grader, working in methodical harmony, were trying to carve a path through an avalanche of mud and debris spilling across the highway.

That's when I had my epiphany.

For the first few years after the expedition, I'd harbored the sullen conviction that if Sandy and Dana hadn't turned back, we could have been the first Americans to summit Everest via the North Face. I was so strong, so self-confident. With more years of mountain experience, after the deaths of friends and fellow mountaineers, I'd come to accept that we probably wouldn't have made it, no matter what. But somehow I'd never taken it any further.

In New Zealand, staring through the foggy windshield at a deep river of mud that had cut the road in half and halted all traffic (no matter the dreams and schemes of man, simple bad weather can still shut it all down), my thinking took the final step. Suppose Dana and Sandy had come up and we'd all carried on. Above 26,000 feet we would each have been soloing, attached to the face only by the teeth of our ice axes and crampons. Had a spindrift avalanche hit any one of us, we would have been torn off the mountain, plucked into space a mile above the glacier. It would have been exactly like jumping out of a plane without a parachute. By turning back, our two teammates had made the right call.

• • •

I tried to get into the high peaks four more times while I was in New Zealand, twice by helicopter and twice on foot. It was a no-hitter, a shut-out. I drove back to Christchurch to fly home without ever even seeing Mount Cook.

En route to the airport, I stopped in to see Guy Cotter, Rob Hall's old partner and now the owner and operator of Adventure Consultants, Hall's guiding business. I knew that Cotter and Hall had been close friends. They had started climbing together as teenagers, became guides together. Cotter himself has led fifteen expeditions to the Himalayas. We had corresponded but never met, and I wasn't certain why I was going to see him. Sometimes we are guided by intuition we don't even know we have.

We hit it off immediately. We went out for breakfast, a great heap of eggs and bacon, and talked about kids and guilt and climbing and Asia. About loss and lessons. We talked straight into the afternoon. We left the café and went out to his house in the country and sat for hours drinking tea in a living room filled with mementos from Nepal. I told him about my own shadows of Everest. And Guy told me how, in 1995, he guided a client, Doug Hansen, up to the south summit of Everest before making the decision to pull the plug. Hansen died with Hall the following year.

It was a painful subject, and we quickly moved on. But the conversation eventually circled back. It had to. Guy Cotter had spent his entire adulthood trying to determine when to push on and when to turn around. One of his best friends had died on the crux of the dilemma. His wisdom was hard-won.

"To be a successful mountaineer," Guy said, "you've got to be very conservative. But also very pushy. You've got to be able to be objective about what's happening. A mountain is always giving you signals, and you have to have the knowledge to know what those signals are telling you. The mountain calls the shots. Not your sponsors or your clients or your emotions. I'm constantly thinking through the what-ifs. When all the conditions are favorable, that's when you push. If not, you must always, always be prepared to walk away."

It took him almost a half hour to itemize for me an expedition-honed checklist he uses to determine whether a summit push is safe: Snow conditions (neve is best, deep powder both difficult and dangerous), weather (past, present, forecasted), wind speed and direction, temperature (estimating windchill on the summit and calculating the odds of frostbite), team strength (are there team members he already knows can't make it), team attitude (even if they have the physical stamina, do they have the mental fortitude).

Guy set down his cup of tea and stared out the window at the drizzle.

"Mountaineering is the one sport in which you don't learn from your mistakes," he said. "If we're lucky enough to live through the ambition of our youth, one day we realize that it takes more guts to turn back than to push on."

• • •

We are fed heroic slogans from an early age. A quitter never wins and a winner never quits. Never give up. Never cry uncle. Never say die.

But encouraging kids to excel in schoolrooms and on soccer fields, in careers and team sports, doesn't impose mortal stakes. Mountains do.

Let me be hypocritical and blasphemous and honest.

The truth is, mountains aren't worth dying for. Democracy, social justice, the environment—these are causes worthy of your life. A mountain is not. Your death on a climb does nothing for the world. It merely scars your family and friends forever.

Yes, mountains are worth climbing, which admittedly entails risk, but the important thing is to clearheadedly recognize when the tables have turned and it's time to do precisely what we have all been brainwashed never to consider: accept defeat. Turn back. Give up. Go down. Go home.

Sleep with your beloved, play with your kids or your nieces and nephews, take your parents out to dinner. Accept that quitting was exactly the right move. I did, finally.

HEAD TRIP

Real alpinists know how to sleep. The night before a big climb I'm sure they eat heartily—slabs of bratwurst and chunks of blue cheese—put away a bottle of red wine, take a long, luxurious leak out the hut door, crawl under any old wool blanket on the bunk and fall asleep as contented as a Saint Bernard.

• • •

Not me, damn it. Here I am alone in the Empress hut, a breathtaking aerie perched above huge glaciers at the base of glorious 12,316-foot Aoraki/Mount Cook, the highest peak in New Zealand. It's almost 11:00 p.m., and I should be fast asleep, but no.

I know part of my insomnia is because this is a bit of a grudge match. Last November I came to climb in the Southern Alps and never even saw the bloody mountains. It rained biblical quantities. I drove around in a dark sluice, grinding through past failures. I have returned for redemption.

Now I have my chance, but I need some sleep; the moment my lids drop over my snowburned eyeballs, my mind's eye clicks open like the lens of a camera. I see the notorious Sheila Face, certainly named by some carnally dreaming mountaineer, looming like a succubus above the hut. I follow the lightning bolt of ice that jags up the stygian face, trying to discern the difficulties of every pitch. At the final 300-foot headwall of ice, I study its color and aspect and wonder if it will be hollow or mushy and suddenly see my ice tools plunging into depths of sugar snow and my feet slipping and then I'm sliding, dropping, cartwheeling through space.

See what I mean? I used to have a climbing partner—a redheaded Viking as psychologically sturdy and at ease as an oak couch—who could cheerfully sleep anywhere, anytime. No tent, no sleeping bag, no problem. "This spot here looks good pretty darn good to me," he'd say, and then proceed to lie down on a six-inch shelf of snow above a fathomless drop and be snoring away in five minutes. If only.

It's 11:30; I must be up in five hours. I rewind the scene I witnessed earlier this evening while I was reconning the route: a thumping chopper circling above the Sheila Face, lowering a cable, and plucking two stranded climbers off the peak. According to the hut radio report, they had bivouacked for two nights on the wall, then called in a rescue after almost getting killed by falling ice and rock.

Will that be me tomorrow? Again I slip into snapshots of ugly scenarios. Rock that is rotten or ice that is hollow or weather that sucker punches me partway up and I can't see shit for the swirling snow and . . .

Shut up.

Real alpinists know how to turn off their head. From years of experience, they realize that half the time the body knows better than the know-it-all mind. The mind is too fickle. Optimistic one minute, pessimistic the next, pitching back and forth like a rowboat on big seas. Not the body. The body doesn't exaggerate or self-deprecate or play mind games. The body is a machine, a realist. If it's hard and painful, well then it's hard and painful. If it's a cruise, why it's a cruise. The body doesn't make mountains into anything. The body is an animal. It moves and lives only in the present.

Now it's midnight. I wearily decide that the route will decide. It always does. I promise myself not to climb up anything I can't climb back down. I check the alarm on my watch, flick off my headlamp, finally drift off to sleep.

Alas, one side effect of an overactive imagination is that I do not sleep without dreaming. Tonight there is an elfin, fur-faced man in the hut. I don't understand what he's doing here, but even inside the dream, I realize this is all supposed to mean something. This old codger is supposed to be Death, of course, profound and portentous. So where's his rusty sickle and black cowl? Enough. I disavow all this Freudian hooey, the dwarf vaporizes, and I sink into sleep like a brick into a pond.

Just before the alarm goes off, I wake. 4:25. Piss out the hut door, pick up the pot of milk I mixed from powder the night before, gulp down three bowls of granola. (I only feel like having one, but I know better—big day ahead.) I check my ankles. They are mangled with blisters from the last five mountains. Days ago I bound them with pink antiseptic cream, layers of foam cut from a sleeping pad, and athletic tape.

Crampons on my boots, headlamp on my helmet. Ice axe in hand, ice hammer strapped to the pack—all by rote. I step out of the hut onto the glacier, gaze up at the stars floating like campfire sparks above the black monolith of the Sheila Face, and go.

Originally, I planned to climb with veteran Kiwi alpinist Guy Cotter, owner of Adventure Consultants. He suggested I come back at the end of January, midsummer, when the weather on New Zealand's South Island might be "a wee bit more predictable." Which I did, phoning him at his home in Wanaka from the Christchurch airport.

"Ah, mate, sorry," he said. "I'm just about to jet off to western Papua to lead a trip on Carstensz Pyramid."

I understood—work before play, even for a guide—but now I was on the other side of the world without a partner.

I drove straight to Aoraki/Mount Cook National Park and got a bunk in the Unwin hut, hoping to find a replacement ropemate. The New Zealand hut system is extensive, with a shelter in almost every major valley—from a fifty-dollar-a-night palatial lodge with fresh sheets and a chef to free cabins with fresh water and padded bunks. As in the European Alps, huts make the mountain experience a social, cosmopolitan affair—in contrast to the North American search for silence and solitude. On any given evening you're likely to be swapping stories and spirits with trampers and climbers from around the world. Invariably, the local Kiwi mountaineers are the most self-effacing. "Aye, 'twas a wee bit dodgy," they'll say, when in fact the smallest slip meant certain death.

There were trekkers in the Unwin hut but no mountaineers, so the following day, for a warmup, I decided to climb 6,699-foot Mount Kitchener alone—disregarding a rainstorm that was obviously growing into a gale.

"You don't want to be up there today," warned a dour female park ranger. "At that elevation, wind'll be 130 focking kmh."

Which it was. Clambering bullheadedly up the west ridge, I got knocked flat a dozen times. Strafing sleet stung my body like hornets. By the time I downclimbed off the summit and staggered into a high hut, I was so hypothermic I could hardly undress myself.

It was a humbling contretemps. Compared with other mountains in the Southern Alps, Kitchener is a mere pimple of a peak. After thawing out, wrapped in four wool blankets and sipping a tongue-scorching cup of cocoa, I wrote up the details of my baby epic—route, temp, wind speed, how much water I drank—on the back of the topo map, which is my habit.

I don't suppose many alpinists would have committed such a picayune ascent to paper, but I found the exercise useful. It is the simplest method

I know for imprinting lessons into the clay of one's mind. Like: heed the focking park ranger.

· · ·

I'm tramping up the Sheila Glacier in the dark, following my own frozen tracks by headlamp along the route I scouted yesterday. It is essential that I do this stretch during the coldest part of the night, when the ice is at its most stable. There are two tenuous snowbridges to catburgle across and perhaps twenty crevasses to cautiously end-run around.

I reach the bergschrund in less than one hour, only to find that I've miscalculated. The snow is treacherously soft and I can't cross where I had planned. I lose half an hour traversing left to a dubious bridge, from which I leap onto the face, metal-clawed hands and feet stabbing into the snow. At the top of the snowfield I chop a tiny ledge, precariously swap double boots for nimble rock shoes, and move upward on dry rock.

I cover 1,000 feet in an hour. It is still night, but day is coming fast. I don't want to be on this face in the sunshine. A little sun and things get nasty. The snow starts to melt, ice blocks begin to shear off, rocks start falling from the sky. But the sun won't hit the face until noon, and it's only 7:30. I remind myself to take my time and enjoy the climb. I stop, slide off my pack, eat a little, drink a lot. Check out that smooth sunrise turning everything a soft, deceiving pink. Little by little, last night's anxiety is giving way to a reassuring sense of calm.

· · ·

Although I relish scrabbling my way up almost anything, at the end of the day, I came to New Zealand to climb its highest peak, Aoraki/Mount Cook. But after Mount Kitchener, I knew I wasn't ready. I didn't know enough yet. So I drove south to Mount Aspiring National Park and hiked up to the French Ridge hut.

The most poignantly named peak on the planet, 9,931-foot Mount Aspiring is an aesthetic pyramid of snow and black rock, the one mountain on the tick list of every Southern Hemisphere climber. My objective was the Southwest Ridge, a classic ice arête. Two other teams in the hut—one American, one Aussie—had the same goal, and I was hoping to tie in with one of them. Unfortunately, they were both up and gone by one o'clock the next morning. Crunching across the Bonar Glacier around 8:00 a.m., I met the Americans coming back. They'd already turned around due to big wind.

"We just didn't feel like suffering," offered their team leader.

I carried on to have a look for myself. At the base of the ridge I met up with the Australians; they, too, were packing it in.

"'Igh winds and 'ard ice," said one of the threesome from Perth. "Another day per'aps."

Craning my neck, I eyed the 3,000-foot ridge. Plumes of spindrift were blowing off the top. Oddly enough, the scene reminded me of Wyoming in winter. Wyoming and wind are synonymous. After a decade or two, you have to be practically lifted off your feet to even notice. As for hard ice, I'd take that over gripless slush any day. All in all, the route appeared to be within my conditional comfort level.

Everybody has a CCL. For those born and bred on the coast, rushing seas are de rigueur, and they think nothing of a squall that puts their ketch over to port forty degrees. (Landlubber to the core, I get queasy in the bathtub.) For those from the desert, whether Bedouin or Bushman, 100°F heat is unnoteworthy. And people in the rainforest find one hundred percent humidity no sweat. It's all what you're used to.

I summited the southwest ridge of Mount Aspiring in two hours, maneuvering through easy rock bands and connecting ice gullies, staying on the leeward side of the arête, exiting through a narrow vertical chute of ice-rimmed stone reminiscent of something on Scotland's Ben Nevis. No room for mistakes, but then in the mountains, there never really is. It was a good romp and I never felt out of control. The key to determining your CCL is knowing yourself well enough to recognize the risks you can tolerate and those you can't.

The next morning the weather was so tumultuous, the French Ridge hut seemed to be cutting through clouds like a ship through swells. There were ten climbers aboard and only one—a square-jawed, twenty-two-year-old Australian sailor named Timmy Gill—was willing to climb. Gill hailed from Adelaide and had crewed on rough open-sea races all around Australia. Seaman Gill and I scaled the snowpacked cracks of 8,587-foot Mount Avalanche in a near whiteout, having a blast together.

"Three hours up, one down," I wrote afterward on the back of my map. "Rap route indiscernible beneath ice. Left four slings, two nuts. Just off glacier sky cleared like a blessing."

Times, speeds, conditions, thoughts—I write them down. These post-climb debriefings help me gauge the range of the possible. After a few mountains, I have a baseline of data. I can compare my own ascent rate and assessment of difficulties with whatever a guidebook may say, as well as with the subjective stream of beta from other climbers. In this way I begin to mentally relax and allow the muscle memory acquired in decades of climbing to carry me.

• • •

Higher on the Sheila Face, the rock is iced over. I delicately switch back to plastic boots and crampons. I also get out my second tool, the ice hammer. Now my pack is almost weightless.

A light pack is the *only* way to move fast. I have no tent, no bivy sack, no sleeping bag, no stove, no pot, no spare clothes. A coat, a headlamp, one can of tuna, and one liter of water are all that I have in my pack. I have learned how to live off the largesse of the New Zealand hut system. Most huts have a spare wool blanket or two and occasionally there's a box of free food left from some aborted expedition. It is a minimalist's dream. With small sacrifices in comfort, it's possible to move through this range as swiftly and lightly as a wolf. Speed is often safety in the mountains, but vigilance is vital.

• • •

After Mount Avalanche, I tried to solo 8,725-foot Rob Roy, a hoary, magnificent mountain also in Mount Aspiring National Park, but I went superlight and got caught out. After climbing 6,000 vertical feet in six hours, hunkering along the summit of Glengyle Peak just down from the helmet of Rob Roy, another gale descended. I tried to dig in, but without a stove or bag, I started to freeze. To save my bacon, I realized I'd have to turn back and descend through the maelstrom. I lost a glove and my footing several times in the course of twenty-one hours of continuous climbing.

Two days later I attempted the MacInnes Ridge of 9,557-foot Nazomi Peak with one of New Zealand's best ice climbers, forty-year-old Allan Uren. He'd tracked me down at the Old Mountaineers pub back in Aoraki/Mount Cook National Park. It took us two bivies, but we managed to summit Nazomi under blue skies.

Descending to the Gardiner hut, we were only a three-hour glacier walk from the lovely Empress hut and Aoraki/Mount Cook's stunning Sheila Face, but Allan wasn't interested.

"I rather feel like a spot of tea," he said like a true mountaineer.

I had not come to New Zealand to climb alone. I prefer to have a partner. Climbing with the right partner is much safer and more fun, leaving memories to share years later. But the weather was here now, and I was here now, and the most coveted peak in the Southern Alps was beckoning. I was going up.

Cramponing over the heavily-crevassed Hooker Glacier, I warily jumped each mortal gulf. Several times I stopped to glass the Sheila Face with the monocular, trying to commit every outcrop and ice runnel to memory. I'd met two alpinists, Matt and Pete, who had climbed the Sheila Face three weeks earlier. They told me it took them two hours to navigate up the Sheila Glacier and cross the 'schrund, seven and a half hours to climb the face, and thirteen and a half hours to descend— twenty-three hours total. I poured these numbers into the matrix of what I had learned about myself on the past five mountains. With no partner and no protection, on terrain that was not overly technical, I could climb 1,000 feet an hour. The Sheila Face of Mount Cook is 3,000 feet high.

• • •

I find I am in my element. Staying left, I climb snow and rock, locating the lightning bolt I'd spotted thousands of feet below. The ice is thin but grippy and I'm utterly focused. No world exists outside each precise swing of the axe, each sure crampon kick. I am my tools, accurate, unemotional, unapologetic. Where the ice runs out I stem, my picks hooking cracks, crampons scraping stone.

I don't know how fast I am moving. I don't know that I will climb the Sheila Face in four hours, or that in less than ten hours I will traverse the entire Mount Cook massif, Empress hut north to Plateau hut. At this moment, all I know is movement. I am not even thinking: I'm only climbing. Not thinking just like you don't think during sex. Shut down the brain and let the body be what it is: an animal.

Unbeknownst even to myself, somewhere high on the Sheila Face of Mount Cook, I unlatch the cage. You can't do this in civil society. It scares people. They think you're a savage. And they're right: You are. But the mountain doesn't mind; that's what it's there for. The cage door swings open and out steps the beast. It moves like a chimpanzee up glass-sharp jugs of rock, then along a rail of stone as stealthily as a catamount, then with axe picks and crampon spikes up the final headwall of ice, quick as a lizard.

Upward to the knife-edge crest and then, comfortable in its own skin, right to the summit, like a real alpinist.

THUS SPAKE ZARATHUSTRA

"The big day," John said.

"Yup," I replied, rubbing my eyes.

It was three in the morning. We were standing on the South Rim of the Grand Canyon, aiming the beams of our headlamps down the South Kaibab Trail—a mule-stomped trough of glistening ice running between snowbanks. The trailhead sign read ICY TRAIL: CRAMPONS REC-OMMENDED.

In the previous few days, with spring a week away, the South Rim had received a half-foot of snow; over on the North Rim, a foot had fallen. Crampons would have just slowed us down. We had light metal instep cleats strapped to our hiking boots, and trekking poles.

The trail descended into blackness. We looked out across the vast reservoir of cold night air toward the distant North Rim, distinguishable only as a horizontal line above which the stars were scattered. We searched the inky chasm for Zoroaster Temple, the formation we'd come to climb.

"Can you make it out?" I asked.

"Nope," said John.

Zoroaster Temple is a Grand Canyon landmark, an immense mountain rising inside the colossal rift. It's shaped like a pyramid and topped with a 700-foot, custard-colored sandstone tower that was first climbed by Dave Ganci and Rick Tidrick in 1958; before that, no technical rock climbing had been attempted in the Grand Canyon. After a pilgrimage to Yosemite had expanded the pair's conception of what was possible on big rock, Ganci and Tidrick, both in their early twenties, traded their clothesline for nylon rope and loaded their packs with World War II army angles and giant pitons forged by a Scottsdale blacksmith. Their epic ascent took seven days.

Geographically part of the North Rim, Zoroaster is more easily accessed from the South Rim. Although there are only six pitches of technical climbing, a round-trip climb of Zoroaster requires almost thirty miles of hiking and 20,000 vertical feet of elevation gain and loss—more than the trip up the south face of Everest and back from Camp II.

Just to reach the base of Zoroaster's final tower, Ganci and Tidrick had had to scout out the tricky passageways up through the shelflike layers of shale, sandstone, and limestone. Once the route had been reconnoitered, subsequent ascents cut the rim-to-rim time in half. It's still considered the grand prize of climbing in the Grand Canyon. According to John Annerino's 1996 guidebook, *Adventuring in Arizona*, 7,126-foot Zoroaster is "a remote, backcountry peak that requires at least three days."

We were going to attempt it in one.

• • •

There was half a moon, but its silver light was less useful than we had expected. Our headlamps illuminated the trail itself and nothing more, as if we were tromping down a mine shaft. On one side there were boulders; on the other, a black abyss. We didn't talk. We hiked, single file, John in front.

Right here, before we go any further, I must say that you don't march off on a mad caper with just anyone. Not if you want to succeed, or sometimes simply come home. It has to be someone whose bravery outstrips his banter. Someone whose strength and stamina are indubitable. Someone who has gotten himself into a hundred fixes and each time figured a way out. My forty-five-year-old partner, John Harlin—writer, editor, extreme skier, mountaineer, and all-around miscreant—is such a fellow. We had climbed on other continents together and knew each other well. More saliently, we were matched in skill, temperament, and speed.

A two-man team leaves little room for error. On the other hand, if you're a seasoned pair, there's no weak link. Add another person—or, God forbid, a few—and fast, clean, continuous movement becomes impossible. Somebody always has to stop to take a leak, tie a shoe, tighten a buckle—minor delays that burn precious moonlight. If you're in sync, two is the perfect team.

Before John and I walked into the Grand Canyon, we spent three days climbing in the Arizona desert together, working out the kinks, getting dialed. The night we dropped off the rim we felt ready. The temperature was 25°F, perfect for hiking. We sank into the cold, dark air as if it were a liquid. The season and the time of day were part of the plan.

In the desert, the two things most likely to kill you are heat and dehydration. Hiking at night, especially in March, neutralizes both factors. You don't overheat, so you don't get overly thirsty. Why do so few people hike at night? Perhaps it's a reluctance rooted deep in our psyches, a genetically imprinted trait that can be traced back for millennia to a time when humans were predators by day but prey at night. Today the saber-toothed tiger is gone, replaced by its shrunken descendant, the mountain lion, which is generally not up for taking on full-grown humans.

Nevertheless, "people have strange phobias about darkness," says Ken Walters, who teaches outdoor skills for the South Rim–based Grand Canyon Field Institute. "I tell them it's just deep shade. Hiking in the desert, you're always looking for shade—trying to get some chunk of rock between you and the sun. When you hike at night, you're putting a very big chunk of rock, the Earth, between you and the sun. It's always a huge breakthrough when people stop being hung up on daylight."

Thus our dark descent along the South Kaibab Trail. After we dropped 500 feet, the ice turned to mud and we removed our cleats. It was our only stop. Like two stones pushed off the rim, John and I rolled effortlessly down to the river. We crossed the suspension bridge over the quiet Colorado at 5:30 a.m. and followed the smell of bacon up to the Phantom Ranch mess hall. It was packed with people, light and noise streaming through the windows. We didn't go in. We stripped off our gaiters, changed socks, ate a bagel, checked the map, and chugged some Gatorade. As we were refilling our water bottles from an outdoor faucet, two cowboys stepped from the lodge into the darkness, their coffee cups steaming.

"What're you boys up to?" one of them asked.

"Hikin'," John replied.

They sat down on some rocks and looked up through the trees at the dwindling stars. Likely as not they'd been awake as long as we had. Three hours earlier, driving past the trailhead on the rim, we'd met a cowboy already loading his pack animals. We'd asked him if there was anyplace to park where we wouldn't get a ticket. "Don't s'pose there is," he'd said. After a long silence, he'd told us, "You boys look all right to me. Guess you could park up there beside my cabin."

Now these two cowboys watched us reload our packs and asked just enough questions to figure out what we were really up to.

"Sounds like some kinda endurance thang," one of them remarked, tossing the coffee grounds from his cup.

"We'll see," John replied.

"I, myself," the cowboy said slowly, "ain't into self-abuse. But good luck to you anyhow."

We tipped our baseball caps and galloped away.

A quarter-mile past Phantom Ranch we doglegged onto the Clear Creek Trail and began zigzagging up the north wall of the canyon. Light was pouring from the sky, washing out the night. The shapely buttes, scalloped slopes, and crenelated shelf lines of the South Rim glowed as red as a Mexican dancer's dress.

• • •

We arrived at Sumner Wash around 7:30 and stopped beside a tinaja, an ephemeral rainwater pool, to fill up our as-yet-unused two-quart water bags. We'd been forewarned to carry enough water for the entire climb from Phantom Ranch. But given the recent snow, we'd gambled on finding water at Sumner Wash, and did.

Lack of water is a hazard in the Grand Canyon.

"We do over 400 rescues a year," Ken Phillips, search-and-rescue coordinator for Grand Canyon National Park, told me by phone. "Most occur in June, July, and August." Around twelve people die every year in the park. "Half of these are preventable—people who die of dehydration, hyponatremia [critical loss of sodium], heat exhaustion, physical exhaustion, or some combination of the above."

Ganci and Tidrick nearly learned a fatal lesson themselves when they knocked off Zoroaster back in late September 1958.

"It was the first and only time I've ever experienced absolute thirst," Tidrick, now sixty-three, told me when I called him at his home in Colorado. "We had 100° temperatures. I lost fifteen pounds in six days."

"Rain was predicted," Ganci, sixty-four, said on the phone from Prescott, Arizona. "So we carried this five-gallon metal jerry jeep can and a tarp for collecting the rainwater. We had sixty-five-pound packs and looked like a couple of Sherpas."

But the rain came four days late, after they had completed the climb and were on their way down.

"We were in the red zone, advanced stages of dehydration, tunnel vision and euphoria, stumbling, floating along," Ganci recalled.

Impressed by their suffering, I'd started my own specialized training program: I quit drinking water. I'd go ice climbing or backcountry skiing and go the whole day without water. To compensate for the missing weight, I'd load my pack with useless climbing gear. Back at the house after a long, demolishingly parched day, I'd attempt to accurately mimic one of the mental side effects of dehydration (i.e., euphoria) by drinking only beer—a clinically tested diuretic. I found it to be one of the most enjoyable training programs I've ever attempted.

John and I filled our two-quart bags with green, insect-rich water and tossed in a few capfuls of iodine solution (later we would dump in a package of sweet-tasting electrolyte powder). We dried our socks in the sun, ate another bagel and surveyed the landscape. We were surrounded on three sides by a 500-foot band of limestone cliffs called the Redwall.

"Looks like there's only one way through it," said John.

He pointed to a dark slot halfway between the broad back of Sumner Butte and the squat, white steeple of Zoroaster. Our photocopy of the route description warned, "The climbing here is class 4. Use a rope if you feel at all insecure with a heavy pack."

A heavy pack. Make that the third thing that'll kill you in the desert, or anywhere else. If there's one good reason for doing something in one big day rather than several small ones, it's to avoid the utter misery of humping a heavy pack.

For some masochistic reason, John had been impressed by the huge loads that Ganci and Tidrick had carried, and his own training regimen reflected this. He lives on a farm in Oregon and is currently building a fireplace from river rocks. The river is 200 feet below and a half-mile away from his house. John took to loading a backpack with 120 pounds of rocks and hauling them up to his house. Your average washing machine weighs about 120 pounds. He'd make several trips.

For this climb, however, our packs were well under twenty pounds. We'd taken the lightest iteration of each piece of gear. Twin 145-foot ultrathin climbing ropes, featherweight wire-gate carabiners, Spectra slings, a frighteningly small rack of protection. We had no camping or bivouac gear whatsoever. Bring it and you'll use it—if only because the extra weight will slow you down so much that you'll be forced to stop.

The self-evident secret of going fast is to go light. To carry just enough. Too much and you fail, too little and you fail. Besides climbing gear, we brought insulated coats, fleece hats and mittens, sardines, bagels, M&M's, water, ibuprofen, and a pocketknife for compound fractures or field appendectomies.

Knowing how much to bring comes from knowing yourself. How far above your protection you can climb before you freak. How cold you tend to get. How much food and water you need to keep going. The answers are individual and acquired only through experience.

• • •

We dodged our way through agave and cacti, climbed the chimney sans ropes, and began moving up a ridge of sandstone shelves. Unlike Ganci and Tidrick, all we had to do was follow the route description and stride along in the sunshine, keeping one eye out for the next cairn. At 10:30 a.m. we contoured around to the shadowed north face of Zoroaster Temple.

"Back into winter," I whined.

"Ya sissy!" bellowed John.

There was a foot of snow on the north side of the tower, so the cairns were buried. We picked our way along, clambering up breaches in the bands of ice-cloaked sandstone, until we could posthole diagonally to the base of the northeast arête. It was below freezing. We pulled on caps and gloves, burrowed into our coats, and studied the route.

"Looks like some of the cracks have ice in 'em," exclaimed John, obviously thrilled.

We weren't sure of the route. A slab of rock had fallen out and changed the start. No matter. At noon sharp, John stripped off his gloves and coat and attacked the first frigid pitch. He climbed up to an overhanging 5.8-ish finger crack; clawed out the ice and snow, breaking off chunks of rotten rock; pulled over; scampered to a tree; and belayed me up. Then I led a wide, generously verglassed 5.7 crack. John got off-route during the next pitch and we ended up pumping through a drippy, peeling-off-in-our-hands 5.9 overhang and hauling into a two-foot snowdrift on top. The next two pitches were 5.8 stemmy chimney/hand cracks that would have been beautiful desert climbing had there not been ice or snow everyplace you needed to put your hands or feet.

Pitch five was supposed to be an airy, thirty-foot traverse protected by two bolts. John got out his monocular and searched the wall.

"Damn. Where are they?"

On any climb worth a story, it is axiomatic that there will come a point when the protagonists are confronted with something they really don't want to do. This, of course, is God giving you a chance to back off. You will lose face, but you'll save your ass. Wounded pride or peril, your choice. The mythic dilemma.

Infelicitously, it was my lead. I admit my pride is more sensitive than my flesh. I plugged in a little piece of dubious protection and moved out on a band of blank rock above the snow. The sandstone was wet, but the knobs were solid. I skittered sideways like a crab, only to discover that the last five feet of the traverse, invisible from the belay, were glazed with ice.

It was the predictable point of no return, the place where the fear of going backward outweighs the fear of going forward. A few easy moves (that's hindsight bravado talking) and I was through.

The final pitch was described as a "strenuous off-width, 5.9R." (*R* stands for *runout*, which means you can take a long fall if you slip.) It was John's lead. Even half-filled with snow it turned out to be not strenuous, not off-width, not 5.9, and thankfully not a runout.

Above the crack we plunged through two feet of snow, cut over to the summit block, scrambled up a chimney, and popped out into the sun atop Zoroaster.

"Four o'clock," said John, checking his watch. "Not bad."

We shook hands like men are supposed to do on summits, snapped photos, sat down, and ate the last of our bagels and sardines while soaking up the sun and the phantasmagorical view of the Grand Canyon.

"You know who Zoroaster was?" I asked John.

"Zorro's father?" John quipped.

Like Brahma, Buddha, and other divinely christened formations within the Canyon, Zoroaster was named after a sacred figure, in this case the Persian prophet who lived in the sixth century BC.

"Otherwise known as Zarathustra," I added. "Remember your Nietzsche? The Übermensch?"

"I remember Zorro the Gay Blade," wisecracked John.

"'Man is a rope, tied between beast and overman—a rope over an abyss.' Thus spake Zarathustra."

Much is made of summiting, but the fact is you're only halfway home. We started rappelling at 4:30 p.m., reached the base of the Temple at

5:30, hustled back across the snowy north face, trotted along the descending ridge to the Redwall gully, and were off the final raps by nightfall.

Hiking steadily, dreaming of cheeseburgers, we were back at Phantom Ranch by 8:30. The kitchen was already closed. As a consolation prize, the cashier offered us free Oreos and hot chocolate.

We recrossed the suspension bridge at 9:30 and methodically ground out the 5,000-foot ascent, reaching our car on the South Rim at one in the morning, twenty-two hours after we'd left it. We weren't sore, blistered, or exhausted, merely bushed. There had been no real drama. Drama happens when things go wrong. Drama happens when people make mistakes, when reach exceeds grasp. Ours was an epic non-epic.

On the way out, near the top, we noticed a large trail sign we had somehow cruised right by on our way down:

WARNING: DANGER! DO NOT ATTEMPT TO HIKE FROM THE CANYON RIM TO THE RIVER AND BACK IN ONE DAY. EACH YEAR HIKERS SUFFER SERIOUS ILLNESS OR DEATH FROM EXHAUSTION.

ICE IN THE BLOOD

Karl Ingolfsson is speeding through the whiteout, sanguine as a Viking in a longboat. The storm is swallowing us, but Karl is cool. He keeps the pedal to the floor, his large paws resting on the steering wheel, a rolled-up balaclava perched on his enormous shaven head.

"Never underestimate climate," he's saying, "or geography. Climate and geography are destiny. When Iceland was founded in 870, it was warmer, and the island was covered with trees. Then along came the little ice age."

We're crossing Langjökull—a 395-square-mile glacier in western Iceland, fifty miles north of Reykjavík—in a radically customized Nissan Patrol. It has balloon tires that float over the snow, monster-truck suspension, an extended wheelbase, and a low-gear tranny, not to mention leather seats and a killer sound system blasting Deep Purple. ("Glacier jeeps" are unique to Iceland. They're not off-road vehicles; in this environmentally sensitive country it is illegal to drive off-road except on self-healing glaciers.)

Veils of snow wash over the windshield, enveloping us in whiteness. Our depth perception has vanished. We are inside a mother-of-pearl continuum—everything behind us connected to everything ahead of us.

"It began getting cold around 1200, and the glaciers began to grow," Karl continues. "Snow covered the pastures, and the sheep were forced to eat tree branches. The winter of 1313 was called the Winter the Horses Died; 1405, the Great Snow Winter. Eventually, all the forests were cut down for fuel."

I'm listening but preoccupied. I glance at the speedometer: 90 kilometers per hour. I've always traversed glaciers in traditional nordic fashion: plodding on skis, dragging a sled. In a whiteout, it is considered prudent to move slowly to keep from plunging into a crevasse. Yet here we are, hurtling along. I imagine us shooting off the lip of a gaping gash in the glacier: Thelma and Louise go to Iceland.

"You know that the French Revolution was influenced by climate change," says Karl, looking over at me in his sunglasses. "The climate had grown much colder by the late 1700s, causing the crops to fail and the peasants to revolt."

"Are there any crevasses on this glacier?" I interrupt.

"Sure," Karl replies cheerfully, "but not here."

Karl, thirty-eight, is operations director for Iceland's Ultima Thule Expeditions. Built like a polar bear, he wears sandals year-round, snow be damned. Ragged trousers and a fuzzy Icelandic sweater are his work clothes. He is a mountaineer, ice climber, expedition skier, guide, father of three, and intellectual authority on the singular history and geography of his beloved Iceland.

"Changing climate can change people," Karl says.

I glance at the side mirror. Behind us is another hypertrophic glacier jeep, driven by Thorsten Henn, thirty-five, a dark-haired dead ringer for the young Rod Stewart. Thorsten is a German-born landscape photographer who transplanted himself to Iceland. "I was born in the wrong country," he told me when we met. "I hitchhiked here on a boat from Denmark when I was sixteen. Iceland has the most magical light on Earth."

Riding shotgun with Thorsten is tall, laconic Tyler Stableford, twenty-nine, photographer and former editor of *Rock and Ice*. He and Thorsten are taking pictures of our Mad Max mission across Iceland. We have just five days to explore the rarest and most ephemeral morphological features of a glacier: ice caves. Given that eleven percent of Iceland is covered with ice—some twenty glaciers—there could be no better place in the world for this operation. We've been driving since 6:00 a.m. Now it's night but still light, and our internal clocks are smashed.

Thorsten powers his rig up alongside ours, and Tyler motions for us to stop. Karl and I jump out into the blowing snow and crowd our heads through the window. Thorsten and Tyler are studying the screen of a laptop mounted on a rotating platform, Thorsten punching keys to improve the resolution.

"The caves are over here," he says, pointing to an X at the edge of the monitor. "We're here." He indicates a small arrow in the middle of an ocean of contour lines. "We've got to change course."

Off we go again, plowing side-by-side across the smooth, white-skinned back of the glacier. Thorsten is leading. I can see him inside the cab. He isn't looking out the windshield into the mesmerizing whiteout.

Instead, like a pilot flying on instruments, he's staring at the computer screen beside him.

Our arctic capsules eventually pass out of the ground blizzard and we find ourselves barreling across an endless expanse of undulating white. White extending to the horizon in every direction. Not until after midnight, in an eerie, luminescent twilight, do we sideslip around a medial moraine and discover two gigantic black holes in the silver glacier.

• • •

Iceland is an island the size of Virginia floating just below the Arctic Circle in the North Atlantic. Founded more than a millennium ago by Norwegian Vikings and Irish monks (whom the Vikings later enslaved), Iceland was isolated from the rest of the world for most of its history and consequently developed an iconoclastic, homegrown culture.

The 304,334 Icelanders still speak tenth-century Norse and revere literature. Young children can recite medieval literature: "The Saga of Ref the Sly," "The Saga of Gunnlaug Serpent-Tongue," and "Eirik the Red's Saga" ("Filth-Eyjolf killed the slaves near Skeidsbrekkur above Vatnshorn. For this, Eirik slew Filth-Eyjolf . . . ").

Hákarl (putrefied shark) is a national dish, chess a national sport, glacier driving a national passion, and the relentless weather a national conversation. Iceland contains Europe's most powerful waterfall, Dettifoss—which runs at more than 21,000 cubic feet per second during late summer—and its largest glacier, Vatnajökull, which covers 3,240 square miles (although, like glaciers around the world, it's shrinking due to global warming).

Such superlative geography has bred an adventure culture in which ice climbers outnumber rock climbers ten to one, and kayakers run pounding whitewater one week and the squalling Denmark Strait the next. In recent years, Iceland has become a coveted destination for active travelers of all stripes, including those who engage in one of the most idiosyncratic of sports: glaciospeleology.

By one romantic definition, glaciospeleology is "the line of research having to do with the exploration of a glacier's heart." In practice, this means climbing through bright shafts and dark tunnels inside a moving glacier—three-dimensional ice climbing in passageways that are constantly deforming.

Who would be up for such an undertaking? The Icelandic Tourist Board had one word for me: Karl. I e-mailed him two pages of questions—how big are the caves, how often do they collapse, do we need dry suits, oxygen tanks? He responded with two sentences: "You come over. We find out."

· · ·

"Looks like the mouth of a whale," Karl says as we stand outside the entrance to the first cave the next morning. The four of us spent the night camping on the glacier and are now cranking on our crampons after a breakfast of blueberry *skyr* (sour-cream-like yogurt) and muesli washed down with syrupy shots of cod liver oil, Iceland's all-purpose human antifreeze.

"Looks more like the devil's arse to me," says Tyler. The opening at the blunt terminus of the glacier is a massive black ovoid, twenty-five feet tall and forty feet across. We walk in together, Thorsten and Tyler armed with cameras, Karl and I with ice tools and ropes.

After our eyes adjust, we find the walls to be a gorgeous translucent blue, the surface scalloped into smooth, symmetrical wavelets. Moving farther into the cavern, we discover a short vertical duct passing straight up through the roof to a peephole of blue sky. As a warmup, Karl and I tie in and ascend this popsicle-colored mine shaft, poking up on top like two marmots, blinking in the brilliance, then scurrying back down our hole.

Deeper in the cave, the walls close in, darkness enfolds us, and we switch on our headlamps. It now indeed feels as if we're inside the throat—or perhaps the colon, depending on your perspective—of an enormous beast. Occasionally, basso profundo groaning, caused by the shifting ice, reverberates through the cave.

"This one could collapse soon," Karl announces as we crampon around freezer-size shards of ice that have calved from the ceiling.

There are two types of glacial caves: "warm" ones, created by heat from thermal activity beneath a glacier, and "cold" ones, like the Langjökull caves, carved by running water. A stream of meltwater flowing on top of a glacier (called a *bediera*) drops into its bowels through a hole, or *moulin*. Rushing water cuts a shaft through the ice until it reaches bedrock, then burrows out the terminus of the glacier. Both types have a life span of only a few months to a year.

After some distance, we can see light ahead and soon pass into a cavernous gallery with two cathedral-like vaults. Pale blue radiance bounces down from both shafts, flooding the main sanctuary. The architecture is astounding. Before us, hanging from the twin vaults, are gleaming white icicles—the stalactites of glacial caves—forming a semicircle of irregular pillars. Above us, both vaults swirl up for more than 200 feet.

"See those stripes of black?" asks Karl, pointing to dark seams embedded in the cross section of ice. "That's ash from volcanic eruptions, probably from Mount Hekla." He studies the lines like an arborist would study the rings of an ancient tree. "This ice is somewhere between 200 and 400 years old."

"What do you say we climb up and out?" I suggest, eyeing a route that ascends a narrow icicle into the right-hand vault, then disappears up into the nautilus.

Karl nods, seats himself in belay position, and begins telling me about Iceland's famous volcanic eruptions.

For eight months in 1783, lava poured from the Laki crater, in south-central Iceland, the largest lava flow in recorded history. Tephra shot ten miles into the sky, pumping the atmosphere full of volcanic ash and gas. "The temperature in the Northern Hemisphere was temporarily lowered by one to two degrees centigrade; seventy percent of Iceland's livestock and twenty percent of its population died."

The Askja eruption of 1875 was the third largest in history, Karl continues. "Southwesterly winds carried the tephra northeast and buried a few dozen farms."

I'm probing the brittle icicle with my hammer, trying to find a way up. "How far back can you trace your family history?" I ask him.

"Over a thousand years."

Above the icicle I find that the virgin blue ice, which looks ideal, is actually fickle and dangerous, tending to fracture wildly. At one point I'm certain the ice is about to shear off in a single slab—a dinner plate twenty feet in diameter—and provide me with the lead fall of my life.

Higher up, I discover something remarkable: The historically grim seams of spiraling dark matter provide the most secure purchase for my picks. This ice has a character different from the clear, unblemished ice, as if all the hardship of those periods had congealed to create a solid, imperturbable substance.

We ascend through the belly of the glacier like mountaineering Jonahs, passing up through the blowhole to the surface and sunlight.

• • •

Icelanders are Norsemen, so ice runs in their blood. But thanks to geographical circumstance, Icelanders are also hot-pool aficionados. You don't plan any adventure in Iceland without periodic steam cleanings in the countless hot springs that bubble up in the country.

The next evening, on a remote gravel road, Karl asks me if I've "ever wanted to swim from America to Europe."

"Actually, no," I reply.

He stops the jeep, gets out, and starts off down a path that leads through a tar black moonscape of pocked lava to a deep fissure. A series of ladders descend into the crack. Forty feet below the surface, a hot, deep, five-foot-wide river runs between walls of solid lava. Karl drops his clothes and slides in as easily as a big seal. He spreads his arms, one hand touching each wall.

"America. Europe."

Iceland straddles the Mid-Atlantic Ridge. Indeed, it is the spreading apart of the North American and Eurasian tectonic plates and the concomitant volcanic activity that created the island 100 million years ago. Karl explains that Iceland experiences more than 400 earthquakes a year, although most of them can't be felt. Geothermal heat warms eighty percent of the country's homes.

The four of us lounge in the Grjótagjá fissure until our muscles turn to jelly, then drive across the forbidding Askja landscape, one of the largest lava deserts in the world. It's two or three or four in the morning when we arrive at the Kverkfjallaskali hut. I'm dazed and bleary-eyed, but Karl seems unfazed. It appears that Icelanders have evolutionarily adapted to their high-latitude location—they get all the REM time they need during the long, dark winter, then go for weeks with little sleep in the sunsetless summer.

A catfish dinner/breakfast, a catnap, another shot of cod liver oil, and into the Kverkfjöll cave we stride.

This cave is nothing like Langjökull. One of the largest warm caves in existence, it lies on the other side of Iceland, along the northern edge of the mammoth Vatnajökull glacier. The entrance is A-shaped, the apex fifty feet above a steaming river, the sidewalls peeling off in gigantic seracs.

Karl and I walk into the cave. Within minutes, it's so dark and so saturated with steam that, even with headlamps, neither of us can see our boots. We clamber forward, allowing our feet to find their own footing along the bottom of the river. Sometimes we stumble into a waist-deep hole of whirling warm water, unable to see it, only feel it. Sometimes we use our ice axes to blindly tool up a bump of ice.

The roar of the river bouncing off the unseen walls of the cave makes it impossible to talk. We simply stay within arm's reach of each other, trading leads when we encounter an invisible barrier, allowing our senses of hearing and touch to guide us. We can tell the cave is constricting by the diminishing echo of the sound of the water.

Deep inside, we come upon a rock wall we climb by feel. At the top we hunch under a ceiling of ice. Warm water flows through a two-foot-high hole in front of us. I'm suddenly aware that something is wrong. My head is throbbing, and I can't catch my breath. My lungs feel like they're being flattened.

"Karl," I croak groggily, shaking his sleeve. "I can't breathe."

I can hear Karl gulping for air. "Mark, it's CO_2 poisoning. Perhaps we should turn back now."

The volcanic bedrock is off-gassing, producing high levels of CO_2 in the confined space. Our blood is filling with CO_2 rather than oxygen—a potentially fatal condition. Without another word, we scramble down the rock and begin splashing our way back out of the black tunnel of ice.

• • •

Iceland grew out of its warrior adolescence long ago. Today it's a nation committed to nonviolence. Icelanders have a higher standard of living than Americans, lower infant mortality, longer life expectancy, universal health care. There is hardly any poverty, no one is homeless, and most Icelanders have lived, studied, or traveled abroad.

And yet the enduring desire to experience the extreme lives on.

Staggering out of the Kverkfjöll cave, cloaked in steam, Karl and I plop down in the warm river, breathing deeply, surrounded by arching walls of ice.

The water is luxuriant, and as we strip off all our layers of wool and fleece down to the skin, Karl tells me of the Tindfjöll Games, a mysterious Icelandic event he says no foreigner has ever witnessed.

"It is something that happens in the mountains at night, usually in bad weather. It begins with a feast."

Karl says that, for this year's contest, his friend Tomas has already shot the reindeer, and the *hákarl* has been fermenting on the beach for weeks. Prodigious amounts of liquor will be consumed before and during the events, all of which will be performed buck naked.

First there's a race around the hut—barefoot, of course. Karl says it's only really interesting during a blizzard, when it's possible for someone to lose their way after the ninth or tenth lap. Then come games of strength, such as arm wrestling and its more bizarre offshoot, Inuit mouth wrestling.

But Karl's favorite is the snow-angel contest. "I have a friend, Magnus Gunnarsson, who holds the unofficial world record: 530 arm and leg movements," he tells me. "The snow was pretty frozen, and in the morning he had a hard time remembering why he lacked skin on his elbows, heels, and shoulders."

Karl and I absentmindedly eye our sopping pile of ice-climbing gear, the benign modern-day weapons of Vikings—and chance upon the same brilliant idea at the same moment.

"Shall we?" asks Karl.

We drag our plastic boots into the water and pull them on, snap on crampons, clip on helmets, tighten the leashes of our ice axes, stand up, and ascend an arching wall of blue ice, in the buff.

Naked ice climbing, it turns out, is a very delicate business, and I admit to eventually taking an embarrassing fall.

Afterward, we deice ourselves in the welcome, healing heat of the water. Floating on our backs, glacial liquid laps at our chins. Steam rolls out of the cave and drifts downstream. I'm surrounded by blue arctic ice, but I'm deliciously, equatorially warm. It feels both entirely natural and supremely foreign. I realize that this is what Icelanders have been doing for eleven centuries.

"Okay," Karl says. "Now you are welcome to the Tindfjöll Games." His big red face is one giant grin. "I just hope the weather is bad."

CLOSE ENCOUNTER

Seated in silence atop a broken column, halfway up the stone cathedral of Devils Tower, my feet dangling out over 400 feet of air, I'm entranced. Two tiny, white-throated swifts are chasing each other, deftly cutting left and right, up and down along the vertical walls of rock. Their dervishlike agility is astonishing. They buttonhook and corkscrew, wheel, reel, and twirl in the sky.

Screeching *jee-jee-jee*, the swifts buzz me from below, passing so close their feathers nearly brush my cheeks. They shoot straight up into the air, almost disappearing, then drop, twirling together, copulating, falling in a hundred-mile-per-hour death spiral, separating only at the last possible second.

The white-throated swift, *Aeronautes saxatalis*, is my favorite bird. One-ounce bullets, they are nature's miniature fighter pilots, masters of aerial acrobatics and one of the fastest birds in North America. They nest in remote cliffs, like here at Devils Tower, but spend their lives in flight.

My eyes follow the swifts skimming down the curtain of lichen green granite before I spot a kestrel floating just above the treetops. This surprises me; they usually hunt at twilight. Beyond the kestrel I spy three Canadian geese gliding along the surface of the muddy Belle Fourche River and a great blue heron flapping onto a nest.

Somewhere directly below me, hidden beneath an overhang, is my climbing partner, Patrick Fleming—thirty-three, punk rock drummer, PhD in mathematics, Devils Tower aficionado—inching his way up the 200-foot, 5.9 crack called Waterfall. Whenever I hear grunting I take in rope, but my mind is engaged in the gestalt of this place.

At dawn this morning, while quietly hiking to the base of this monolith, I saw three wild turkeys bounding through the underbrush, a dozen hightailing whitetail deer, and one mountain blue bird flickering from limb to limb. I felt as if I were entering a sanctuary. I couldn't believe it had been thirty years since I was last here.

A shadow rakes across my head and I peer up at the sun. A solitary turkey vulture is circling on the updrafts rising from the south face. Devils Tower has drawn all these different birds to its walls, sharing the same air space and nesting in the same sawed-off mountain.

It occurs to me that I have the same sublime, aerial perspective they have. From this vantage, the lay of the land is evident—the path of the past as circuitous as the Belle Fourche, the present as ephemeral as the wind, the view so clear I might almost see into the future.

• • •

This summer—2006—marks the hundredth anniversary of Devils Tower National Monument, named for a 60-million-year-old stump of intruded magma in the northeastern corner of Wyoming. (The nearest town is Hulett—feed store, lumber mill, bar, population 408.) Although it tops out at only 4,977 feet above sea level, Devils Tower rises a spectacular 1,267 feet from the valley floor; it's like a lighthouse above an ocean of prairie. In 1906, President Theodore Roosevelt, making quick use of the recently passed Antiquities Act—which gave the president power to grant national monument status to areas possessing significant historical, scenic, or cultural value—proclaimed Devils Tower America's first national monument. These days it's one of the most identifiable natural landmarks in the country, attracting some 400,000 visitors a year, and an enduring symbol of the conflicting nuances between the sacred and the profane.

Its name alone is controversial. Lieutenant Colonel Richard Dodge called the butte Bad God's Tower in an 1875 geological survey, but by the time Dodge returned east later that same year, it had become known as Devils Tower. Despite numerous protests, the name stuck. Various Native American tribes have their own names for the formation, although the most common is Mato Tipila, or Bear Lodge.

To Native Americans, the Tower has been a holy place for millennia. What the Wailing Wall is to Jews, Mecca is to Muslims, and Lhasa's Drepung Loseling Monastery is to Tibetan Buddhists, Bear Lodge is to northern Plains Indian tribes. According to anthropologists, Paleo-Indians, the ancestors of present-day Native Americans, were living in the Devils Tower region almost 10,000 years before the invention of Christianity.

"We look upon the land as female, a mother that nourishes us," explains Henrietta Mann, PhD, seventy-two, special assistant to the president at Montana State University in Bozeman. Mann is a Cheyenne and has a doctorate in American studies.

"We believe we come from the land, belong to the land, and that we are the caretakers of this land," says Mann. "For uncountable generations we went to Bear Lodge—we do not call it Devils Tower, even the use of that term is disrespectful for such a holy place—to pray, to seek guidance for the heart and spirit, and to maintain our sacred relationship to the land."

It's difficult to fathom the significance of Mann's statements without revisiting the savage history of the Devils Tower region.

In the spring of 1868 at Fort Laramie, on behalf of the United States government, civil war hero Lieutenant General William Tecumseh Sherman and three other generals signed a seventeen-article treaty with more than one hundred Sioux chiefs, including Sitting Bull, Red Cloud, One That Kills in a Hard Place, Rotten Stomach, and Whirling Hawk. The treaty ceded all of South Dakota west of the Missouri to the Sioux and designated those parts of Wyoming and Montana north of the Platte River and east of the Bighorn Mountains as Sioux hunting grounds, which "no white person shall be permitted to settle upon or occupy" without Indian consent. Both the Black Hills and Devils Tower, the two most sacred places for the Sioux, became officially and in perpetuity part of their homeland.

Six years later, in 1874, General George Custer led a large, illegal reconnaissance expedition into the Black Hills. Gold was discovered, and within months the Black Hills were mobbed with miners and homesteaders. In 1876 Custer was killed at the Battle of the Little Bighorn and the US government retaliated with ten years of genocide, methodically massacring or removing to concentration-camp-like reservations virtually all Native Americans.

"Even after we have lost everything, Bear Lodge is still there," states Mann, who participated in her last sun dance there in the nineties. "It is a powerful, sacred site, and we have a deep reverence for the place."

• • •

Devils Tower was first "climbed" in 1893 by two enterprising Wyoming cowboys, William Rogers and Willard Ripley. The handbill for the event declared that there would be "plenty to eat and drink," hay and grain for the horses, and "dancing day and night." Over the course of the previous month, Rogers and Ripley had driven two-foot wooden pegs into a crack on the south face, constructing a 350-foot ladder. On July 4, to the roar of more than 1,000 picnicking ranchers and farmers, Rogers climbed the ladder to the top in one hour and planted the American flag. (It was not recorded whether any Native Americans were present to witness this sacrilege.)

The first free ascent of Devils Tower was made by Fritz Wiessner in 1937. Wiessner, who'd pioneered climbs from New York's Shawangunks to British Columbia's Mount Waddington, made his 600-foot ascent in five hours, wearing rope-soled shoes and placing only one piton. Today there are more than 200 routes on the Tower, ranging in difficulty from 5.6 to 5.12 (there is no nontechnical route to the top). The Tower is most famous for its long, difficult, finger-size cracks, the likes of which exist nowhere else on earth.

As a mountaineer's tribute to the Devils Tower centennial, on our first day here Pat and I climbed a direct variation of the Wiessner Route. We swapped leads for four pitches and the climbing was spectacular. It was as though this hulking, fractured obelisk was made to be climbed. The cracks, squeezing my hands and feet, practically pulled me upward. Rising above the plains, I actually felt ashamed. Here was this gorgeous, world-class mountain right in my backyard, and I'd all but ignored it.

Clambering onto the top, Pat and I hiked across the circular plot of prairie to the summit cairn.

"The sign's gone," I said.

"Has been for years," replied Pat.

The only other time I'd climbed Devils Tower was in 1976, when I was seventeen. At that time there was a merry wooden sign sticking out of the cairn that read: NO CLIMBING BEYOND THIS POINT.

We were a rowdy group of high school athletes—two state champion swimmers, a state champion gymnast, and a nationally ranked downhill skier, all novice climbers—led by our swim coach, Layne Kopishka, a regular Clint Eastwood. The night before our big ascent, we'd camped at the Devils Tower campground, shoved down hotdogs around the campfire, and engaged in typical adolescent hijinks after midnight.

In the morning, to cool my jets, Coach had me carry the unwarrantedly heavy backpack. We climbed Durrance, the Tower's easiest route, and I struggled mightily in the chimney. Beneath a hot, cobalt blue sky, lacking any refinement whatsoever, shouting encouragement to one another, we gleefully muscled our way to the top.

On the summit we were wildly exuberant and parched.

"I feel like an ice cold soda," said Coach.

We all agreed, assuming he meant we should start descending. "Jenkins," he bellowed, "drinks on the house!"

I looked at him with a blank stare.

"Open the pack," he instructed.

It was a scene straight out of *The Eiger Sanction*. Beneath the extra rope and spare jackets and clump of metal climbing gear was a plastic sack the size and weight of a bowling ball; inside was a six-pack of root beer packed in ice.

As we rappelled from the summit, helicopters buzzed around the Tower with cameramen hanging out the sides. Far below we could see Hollywood sets and crowds of extras. Steven Spielberg was filming *Close Encounters of the Third Kind*, a sci-fi thriller starring the young Richard Dreyfuss.

Typical Hollywood, the plot is lame, but Dreyfuss does a superb job portraying Roy Neary, an ordinary dad who has a close encounter with UFOs and is subsequently driven bonkers by an inexplicable idée fixe. He shapes mountainlike forms out of shaving cream and mashed potatoes, and eventually sculpts a giant mountain of mud in the middle of his living room. (At which point his wife removes herself and the kids to her sister's.) Via a TV news bulletin about a dangerous gas that has exploded at Devils Tower—subplot: the government knows the UFOs will be landing at the Tower and is trying to clear the area of locals—Neary recognizes what has telepathically possessed him and madly drives the family station wagon right up to the base of Devils Tower, busting through military blockades, where he is finally, triumphantly, taken away by the little aliens.

Naturally, we all went to the movie as soon as it came out, absurdly hoping to see ourselves hanging off the Tower in one of the shots. We loved it anyway—it was an excuse for getting into the backseat at the drive-in.

For us, the climbing trip to the Tower had been a grand little adventure, nothing more. We came, we camped, we climbed, we scooted. Grounded in Judeo-Christian hegemony, informed more by Hollywood than history, we had no knowledge of the magnetic spirituality of the place. We were white, bright-eyed adolescents—naïve heirs of Manifest Destiny. That the Tower might actually be a sacred place didn't occur to us in 1977. It was a rock, not a church.

• • •

Fortunately, it did occur to the wiser members of government. In 1978, Congress passed the American Indian Religious Freedom Act. AIRFA acknowledged previous infringements on the rights of Native Americans to practice their religions and visit their sacred sites, stating, "It shall be the policy of the United States to protect and preserve for American Indians their inherent right to freedom to believe, express, and exercise the traditional religions."

Sites sacred to Native Americans exist all over the nation, but only a few—such as Shiprock, an 1,800-foot spire on the Navajo Reservation in New Mexico, and Spider Rock, in Arizona's Canyon de Chelly National Park, also on Navajo land—were off-limits to climbers. With AIRFA, government agencies were required to review their policies in consultation with Native American leaders. This mandate eventually forced Devils Tower National Monument to revise its management plan.

"Some Native Americans wanted climbing completely banned, and some climbers were offended by certain Native American rituals," says Deborah Liggett, fifty-one, the Tower superintendent from 1994 through 1997. "Devils Tower was unique in that it was the only park in the system that had recreational use in conflict with cultural use."

In 1994 Liggett formed a work group that included local Native Americans and representatives from two Native American advocacy groups, local climbers, and representatives from the Access Fund and the Sierra Club. Because so many of the Native American rituals—vision quests, sweat lodges, sun dances, the pipe ceremony, and other tribal and personal rites—are performed around the summer solstice, the National Park Service proposed banning climbing in the month of June. Hundreds of Indians make their pilgrimage to Devils Tower every year at this time. Interestingly, this offer was rejected by the Native American elders. Instead, they asked that the Park Service develop and educate visitors about a voluntary climbing closure for that month.

"The elders felt that making it voluntary would get climbers to think about their behavior," says Liggett, who instituted this request as part of the new climbing guidelines issued in April 1995. That first year, eighty-four percent of climbers chose not to climb in the month of June.

Pat and I climbed the Tower in May and stayed at homey Devils Tower Lodge, which is situated, unbelievably, inside the Monument's 1,347 acres—deer and rabbits are in the front yard every morning. Devils Tower Lodge is owned and operated by Frank Sanders. Sanders, a Washington, DC, transplant, is a climbing guide who helped put up dozens of new routes on the Tower in the 1970s.

Devils Tower fills the picture window in the lodge's dining room, and every night at dinner guests are encouraged to hold hands and share what they're grateful for. Sanders, seated at the head of the table with his long, silver hair under a purple handkerchief, his white Fu Manchu mustache, and his slow, solemn voice, ends the blessing with a soliloquy, which always includes thanks to "that indescribably beautiful tower of rock behind me."

Sanders clearly loves Devils Tower. Before he bought the lodge, it drew him back every year, just as it did Roy Neary and Henrietta Mann.

"To me, it's a sacred place. To climb it is to practice my religion," he says.

Sanders intentionally disregards the request of Native Americans and climbs and guides others on the Tower in June.

"June is a sacred month to me. It contains the summer solstice, a full moon, and my sobriety date," declares the former alcoholic. "Climbing is one of the things that makes me feel very close to my creator. In June, I climb on Devils Tower in an even more worshipful way than I do all the other months of the year. And unlike the Native Americans, I openly invite others to come and worship with me."

But Sanders is in the minority. According to Scott Brown, chief ranger at Devils Tower, of the 4,000 climbers who come to the Tower every year, only eight percent climb in June. Of those, more than half are guided by climbers like Frank Sanders.

"We live in a country where freedom of religion is enshrined in the Constitution," Mann, a former director of the AIRFA coalition, told me. "In the context of how and where we live today, the Devils Tower policy is a respectful attempt to recognize the rights of Indian spirituality."

Fatefully, in summer 2006, the path of the Tower's guardianship came full circle: In May, Dorothy FireCloud, a fifty-year-old Rosebud Sioux with a law degree and a long history with the Bureau of Indian Affairs, was appointed the new superintendent of Devils Tower National Monument.

•   •   •

In the afternoon of our last day on the Tower, Pat and I climb three classic finger cracks in a row, Carol's Crack, Rain Dance, and One-Way Sunset. My friends, the white-throated swifts, are nowhere to be found. Instead, two prairie falcons, the first we have seen and the only creatures with special privileges at the Tower, sail above us in a sky fading to lavender.

Because of my prolonged and now lamented absence from the Tower, we had hoped to finish our tour by climbing a notorious route called El Matador, but the entire west face is closed to climbing due to nesting prairie falcons. It is part of Devils Tower policy to protect the prairie falcon—its habitat and rituals—and every year some forty routes are off-limits all summer.

The irony isn't lost on the Native Americans, but they're remarkably realistic. For a hundred years, Devils Tower has been an emblem of both the spiritual and the secular, neither of which are absolutes: They're constantly overlapping and subject to personal interpretation and, ultimately, compromise.

On the hike back down through ponderosa pines, I discover a faded blue prayer cloth dangling from a limb. When I first climbed Devils Tower thirty years ago, prayer cloths might have been in the trees, but then I was too self-absorbed to notice. This time is different. Hidden in the branches like Easter eggs, the tiny bundles remind me of all the Tibetan prayer flags I've seen in sacred places across Tibet, Nepal, and Bhutan, where I've climbed during all the intervening years.

"Prayer cloths are pieces of calico of different colors—white, red, yellow, or blue—that carry our hopes and dreams, our sorrows and our misfortunes into the sky," Elaine Quick Bear Quiver, seventy-one, told me later by phone.

Quiver is from the Burnt Thigh clan of the Rosebud Sioux. Throughout her entire life, every June, she and her family have walked to Devils Tower from their home on the Pine Ridge Reservation in South Dakota. She made her last pilgrimage in 2005, at age seventy.

"It takes us five days of walking. We go there to pray. My ancestors are buried in the caves beneath the rocks there. I go to give thanks to the

Almighty Mystery for helping us through another year." She and her relatives camp at the Tower, worship on its flanks for four days, then walk back home.

Quiver was the interpreter for the Native American elders in Liggett's Devils Tower work group that suggested the voluntary June closure. Most of these sagacious elders are now dead.

"Bear Lodge is a place to sit and think, to reevaluate your life," she says. "To look at the past and the future. What can I do to make myself better? You sit quietly and ask for help. When you're isolated and alone, you just listen, and the wind will tell you."

Risk

FEAR FACTOR

We could hear the thundering roar of the falls before we could see them. The apprehension spawned little leaping frogs in my gut. The falls were beckoning, and the massive White Nile—bulldozing along at an unbelievable 45,000 cubic feet per second—was obliging, gliding us irrevocably forward. Jane Dicey, our veteran guide, knew our minds were haplessly entrained by the cannonade and was shouting instructions.

"Paddle *hard*. Right over the edge."

This class 5 wave train was called Total Gunga—total madness. We were aiming for a notorious hole called the G-Spot, a hydraulic so massive it could fling our raft and its eight paddlers into the African sky as easily as a kid flips a nickel into the air.

"When I say *drop*," Jane yelled, "grab the line and crouch on the floor of the raft."

I was in the bow of the boat, leaning forward, paddling with all my strength. Jane, a thirty-five-year-old South African who has guided all over the world, was in the stern. She was leaning sideways, her thick blonde ponytail flying out from beneath her helmet, her bronze arms steering the boat. Jane was one of those women born to be a guide: sangfroid formed into feminine flesh. The greater the chaos, the calmer she became.

She caught my eye and flashed a wide, here-we-go! grin.

Shooting off the falls, the bow was suspended over the drop. I snapped two futile strokes, catching only air; then we were nose-diving into a cataclysm of whitewater. Jane must have yelled for us to drop, but I was too caught up in the battle. I was stabbing my paddle into the back of the beast when a ten-foot wave walloped me out of the boat and sucked me under.

Suddenly I was tumbling like a doll in a hurricane, the flashing dark water pummeling my body. I held my breath and wasn't too scared. At one point I resurfaced and had enough sense to catch a quick breath before the river dragged me back under.

In river-guide parlance, I was being "Maytagged"—spun as if I were inside an enormous, violent washing machine.

"Don't fight the river," Jane had told us earlier. "There's absolutely nothing you can do to help yourself. Be passive—thrashing will only use up oxygen. Stay calm, curl up in a ball so that you're not twisted into a pretzel. Eventually you'll resurface."

Recalling her advice, I stopped struggling and tried to conserve my energy. I let myself be pulled and pushed like flotsam. It seemed to be working, but I couldn't hold my breath forever. My lungs were in flames. The poison of fear was dripping into my mind.

At that instant I surfaced, gulping and coughing, snatched half a breath, and was dragged way back under. I was shocked. I didn't have enough air to go under again! I opened my eyes and the whitewater had vanished; I was in a muscling vortex of black green liquid. My helmeted head smacked something, then I was slammed against a wall of rock and dragged along its surface. Jane had said that the Nile was comparatively safe, because the water was so big the boulders were far beneath the surface. Christ, I thought, I must be twenty feet underwater!

I was out of air and my lungs were spasming. I had been so calm before, but now I was doing exactly what you're not supposed to do: panicking full-throttle, my head thrown up toward the faded emerald light, my arms clawing desperately toward it, my legs writhing against the down-pulling current. My lungs had sucked my esophagus flat and my bulging eyes were rolling back in my head and I was almost ready to start breathing water like a fish. It no longer seemed like such a bad option, at least I wouldn't be in agony anymore and I wouldn't be terrified . . .

I burst through the surface, gagging and flailing my arms like a puppet. Jane merrily waved back from the raft. A minute, at most, had passed.

· · ·

A close call makes you think.

Three months later, I shattered my left wrist in a climbing accident in northern New Mexico. I fell twenty feet and hit the ground. It could easily have been much worse: I could have been paralyzed—or killed. As it is, I'm merely left with a left hand that doesn't work right.

Now, after a long recuperation, and as I prepare for my first major expedition since the accident—a remote trek in central Asia—I find myself thinking about my complicated relationship with adventure and risk.

Being held under the Nile is no picnic, and at the time I thought I was a goner. Yet the chances, in reality, were remote. I wasn't the first person to go for what Nile guides euphemistically term a "long swim." In fact, capsizing is so common that earlier in the day we had practiced it—intentionally flipping the boat in flatwater, going under, staying calm while our bobber-like life jackets returned us to the surface, then dog-paddling back to the raft. The African outfitter Adrift Adventure has been running the monstrous headwaters of the Nile in central Uganda since 1996 and has guided 16,000 people down some of the hairiest whitewater in the world—Bujagali Falls, Easy Rider, Total Gunga, Overtime, Retrospect, Bubugo, Itanda Falls, and, finally, the Bad Place. Although thousands of clients have swum, and a special few experienced the "long swim," no one has died.

This difference between what you fear will happen to you and what reasonably might—between the I'm-gonna-die! feeling I had deep inside the G-Spot and the statistical chances of actually dying—is what's known in the canon of adventure psychology as "perceived risk versus real risk." More than just a mind game, it's the keystone of modern adventure.

Your perceived risk in any adventure is based largely upon two factors—anecdotal and often apocryphal horror stories (grizzly eats entire Girl Scout troop) and personal inexperience (you have no firsthand information or knowledge). Real risk, on the other hand, is based on facts. In order to move from the subjectivity of perceived risk to an understanding of real risk, you need to take the leap and participate in the adventure. The more experience you have, the more acumen; the more acumen you have, the more competence, which is the prime mediator in any adventure.

Not surprisingly, risk—both perceived and real—is inversely proportional to competence. As your skill in any sport increases, your perception—or, more likely, misperception—of the danger decreases and, naturally, so does your fear. Once you learn how to roll your kayak, flipping over no longer freaks you out; when you can finally link telemark turns, steep slopes become inviting instead of terrifying. With this hard-won competence, real risk also decreases. If you know how to hand jam, you're less likely to fall from the overhang; if you know how to bunny hop your bike, you probably won't endo over the log.

The capability to accurately assess these two factors—your own competence and the real risk—is crucial for both safety and success. Disaster can strike when you overestimate your ability and underestimate the real risk. Conversely, undervaluing your skills and overestimating the risk—thereby amplifying irrational fear—can be so inhibiting that chances are good you won't give it a try at all, or you'll fail in your attempt, confirming what wasn't true in the first place. Between either extreme lies the sweet spot: that world-opening state where you have both an accurate understanding of your own abilities and a clear-eyed sense of the true risks.

This paradigm of risk is a recent development. For more than 70,000 years, humans lived outside, where life-and-death threats were a constant reality. To survive as a species, we had to adapt to adventure—physically, psychologically, and spiritually. Through much of the past millennium, adventure was synonymous with exploration or war, which meant you might not come back alive. In 1519, Ferdinand Magellan, bent on becoming the first man to circumnavigate the world, sailed from Spain with five ships and 270 men; three years later, only one ship and eighteen men listed back into port—Magellan was not one of them. On his 1778 voyage, Captain James Cook became the first European to set foot in Hawaii; he returned there a year later and was promptly killed. A month after becoming the first European to reach Timbuktu, in 1826, Alexander Gordon Laing was beheaded outside the fabled city.

Today, exploration and adventure have largely diverged in both meaning and substance. Apart from the deepest parts of some oceans, most of the world is mapped and explored, at least on the macro scale. A small core of adventurers are still attempting bold explorations—first ascents and descents, virgin BASE jumps, and mammoth waves—where the risks are truly unknown and death is a real possibility. But just one step back from the mortal edge lies the expansive kingdom of modern adventure, where the chances of dying diminish dramatically but the thrill of the challenge thrives. Genetically programmed for risk but now living in warm houses and paying fat health-insurance premiums, we still crave adventure—we just don't want to die doing it.

• • •

No wonder, then, that the optimal adventure experience for many enthusiasts is one in which the perceived risk is high but the actual risk is acceptably low. Running rapids is a good example.

"People look at big whitewater and their perception is that it's very dangerous," says Pamela Dillon, former executive director of the American Canoe Association. "But the stats tell a different tale. In sheer numbers—including canoeists, kayakers, and rafters—the most common way someone dies boating is in a canoe, on flatwater, with no PFD [personal flotation device], drinking alcohol.

"Fifty percent of people who die in canoes and kayaks are out fishing," Dillon continues. "They're not tuned in to the skills and information they need to participate safely."

Charlie Walbridge, longtime board member of the American Whitewater Safety Committee, has been tracking whitewater accidents for three decades. Like Dillon, he believes a failure to take sensible precautions is responsible for most deaths.

"The number-one reason people get killed on whitewater is because they're not wearing a life jacket," explains Walbridge, who began boating in the 1960s, when everyone made their own fiberglass kayaks and sewed their own spray skirts.

"Today the gear is much better and much safer, and there's so much instruction available that there's really no excuse not to do the basic things right. What's wonderful is that, unless you're doing an exploratory expedition, you get to choose your level of challenge. Almost every adventure sport can now be participated in at a level that's just plain fun."

• • •

I've been climbing for thirty years—squeaking through first ascents on snow and rock from Utah to Greenland, Tibet to Bolivia—and this busted wrist is the first serious injury I've sustained while actually climbing. Which isn't to say that there haven't been times when luck alone saved my ass. Still, the activity of climbing, like river running, has evolved dramatically in the past half-century.

In 1966, American alpinist John Harlin II was making the first ascent of the direct route of the Eiger's north face when the rope snapped and he plummeted 3,750 feet. It was a horrific death that became the subject of numerous articles and inspired the 1975 Clint Eastwood thriller *The Eiger Sanction*.

But four decades later, modern climbing ropes, unless they're corroded with acid or cut by a knife blade or sharp rock, simply don't break (although they do wear out and need to be replaced). Equipment failure in rock climbing and mountaineering is extraordinarily rare. According to the American Alpine Club's *Accidents in North American Mountaineering 2004*, of the 5,840 reported accidents and 1,304 reported deaths from climbing in the United States between 1951 and 2003, a mere thirteen (about one-quarter of one percent) were attributed to malfunctioning gear.

Nonetheless, I instinctively check my ropes, my harness, my knots, my partner's knots, my equipment, the anchors. Never forget: Our hardwired fear of death is an extremely healthy and useful survival trait. It's what makes us cautious, careful, and thorough. On the other hand, too much fear is paralyzing. Finding your own balance—between legitimate concern and irrational worry—is part of the path of adventure.

Hitting the ground has also made me think about the fear of falling. It's one of the few innate human fears, an evolutionary adaptation passed down in our genes from the time we lived in trees. The gush of adrenaline when you're clinging to rock, toes trying to smear onto a dime-thin ripple and sweaty fingers losing their grip, is precisely what makes climbing so alluring. It creates a high perceived risk while the actual risk is typically pretty low—as long as you and your partner are following basic safety procedures. This, of course, is a critical caveat. Climbing is one of the few sports in which you literally put your life in someone else's hands.

Mountaineering, on the other hand, carries with it significantly higher, very real risk. This is usually attributed to objective dangers—unpredictable acts of God such as avalanches, icefalls, rockfalls, and hellish, flesh-freezing weather.

The last conversation I had with alpinist Alex Lowe, in August 1999 in Salt Lake City over a tumbler of single-malt, was about how many chin-ups a climber needed to do to stay fit for the mountains. We agreed it was between 100 and 200 per day. But in the end it was irrelevant. Several months later, Alex died in an avalanche on Shishapangma, a 26,289-foot peak in southern Tibet. I'd climbed that same peak, fortuitously without incident, in 1984.

So objective dangers are real, but are they really common?

Wyoming climbing rangers George Montopoli and Renny Jackson, collaborating with University of Wyoming statistician Ken Gerow, analyzed all ninety backcountry deaths in Grand Teton National Park between 1950 and 1996. Only three percent were caused by rock- or icefall, one percent by lightning, nine percent by avalanches. A whopping seventy-three percent were due to slips and falls on snow or rock. Half the people killed rock climbing in the park were unroped.

"The reality is that the biggest producer of accidents here is unroped slips on snow," says Jackson, fifty-two, coauthor of *A Climber's Guide to the Teton Range*. "With an ice axe and sturdy boots, if you have the ability and skill to execute an instantaneous self-arrest, you're going to be fine. You can go a lot of places, climb a lot of peaks. Without this skill, you run a risk of being one of the statistics."

Jackson maintains that even objective hazards are not absolute and can be minimized through behavior and knowledge—taking an avalanche course, a first-aid class, a seminar in weather, and then applying what you've learned in the mountains.

"Ultimately, the perceived risks are not what normally kill people," he says. "What kills people is pilot error: poor judgment and lack of basic skills."

• • •

During my final hand examination before leaving for Asia, Colorado surgeon Ken Duncan, a climber and kayaker, told me my wrist might never heal one hundred percent, but he cleared me to "go for it." No restrictions.

Just in time. My partners and I plan to attempt an unclimbed 20,000-foot peak. We've been told that the most serious risks we'll face are avalanches, land mines, Russian helicopters, shoddy buses, and rabid dogs. On the bright side, at least I won't have to worry about bears.

I've had close encounters with grizzlies in Alaska, Canada, and Wyoming, and they always scare the hell out of me—for good reason. I'm slower than every other prey species in the woods, from deer to ducks, and would make a fine, if stringy, meal. I'll undoubtedly have future opportunities to be reincarnated as a large pile of steaming bear scat, but what are the chances, really?

In a word, slim.

Between 1980 and 1994, Yellowstone National Park recorded more than 600,000 backcountry overnights and hundreds of thousands of day hikes. In this period there were twenty-one grizzly-related injuries—fewer than three for every 100,000 visits. Since 1895, more than 130 million people have visited Yellowstone; five have been killed by grizzlies, the last one in 1986. Grizzlies do kill people now and then, but—as it turns out—they are pathetically ineffective compared with more contemporary murderers, like cars, cholesterol, and cigarettes.

But what about the risks of being mauled by other backcountry predators?

While elk hunting this past year in the Beartooths, I came upon mountain lion tracks in the snow. They were so large I thought at first they were bear tracks, and I spent the rest of the day anxiously glassing the cliffs above. I needn't have bothered. Since 1890, fewer than one hundred people have been attacked by a mountain lion in the United States, and eighteen of them died. In short, the chances of being killed by a mountain lion while out hiking, biking, climbing, camping— you name it—are statistically insignificant.

So, out in the wilds, what are we worrying about? The wrong stuff.

Not that we shouldn't acknowledge, even relish, perceived risks. What would climbing be without the threat of falling? What would the wilderness be without lions and tigers and bears? What would rivers be without whitewater? Go ahead, revel in your fears. Just as long as you understand and are prepared for the real risks. Just as long as you don't forget that, in the end, it's not rockslides or rapids, avalanches or animals, icefalls or equipment that are going to get you. It's you.

On an adventure of any kind, you are the greatest risk to yourself.

ELEMENTS OF STYLE

In the spring of 2005, after sixteen years of effort, Ed Viesturs became the first American to climb all fourteen of the world's 8,000-meter peaks. Fittingly, the forty-six-year-old Seattle-based mountaineer's quest ended with Annapurna, the first 8000er ever climbed.

"I was in high school when I read *Annapurna*, and it really inspired me," Ed said when I called to congratulate him. *Annapurna*, by Maurice Herzog, is the romantic (if misleadingly one-sided) account of the first ascent of the 26,545-foot Nepalese peak by a 1950 French expedition.

"It had everything," Ed continued, "camaraderie, bravery, sacrifice, perseverance. That's the book that got me into climbing. I grew up in the great mountaineering state of Illinois and moved to Seattle right after high school. I could see Rainier out my dorm room window. That was my Annapurna then."

It took Ed three tries before he summited Annapurna, just as it had taken him three attempts to summit Everest. He is only the twelfth person to climb all 8,000-meter peaks; this accomplishment alone would not be that notable, but for one salient point: Ed climbed all of them without supplemental oxygen, and most in alpine style with little or no help from Sherpas.

"From the beginning I made a decision that if I couldn't do it without oxygen, I wouldn't do it," Ed told me. "It was a personal choice. Could I train myself to meet the demands of climbing at high altitude? Could I train my mind? It wasn't just about getting to the top; I wanted to experience what it felt like up there. Going without oxygen was more interesting, more challenging—technically, physically, and mentally."

Ed is first to acknowledge his debt to Tyrolean alpinists Reinhold Messner and Peter Habeler, who pioneered the first oxygenless ascent of Everest in 1978. (Messner in 1986 became the first person to climb all fourteen 8000ers.) At the time, the naysayers were legion, predicting that Messner and Habeler would suffocate to death or suffer brain damage. Apparently none of these pundits had read their history.

Reams have been written about the 1924 Third British Everest Expedition, in which George Mallory and Andrew Irvine vanished into thin air, leaving unresolved the possibility that they had summited. And yet the most significant achievement of that climb has been all but overlooked: Four days before Mallory and Irvine made their fatal, oxygen-assisted attempt, expedition leader Lieutenant Colonel Edward Norton climbed to within 900 feet of the summit of Everest without oxygen.

Norton and his partner Howard Somervell left their high camp on a windless morning. Climbing steadily—through the Yellow Band, traversing across the upper North Face—they reached the final summit pyramid by noon. Somervell's throat was so raw he could barely breath; he couldn't continue, but he encouraged Norton to press on. Norton was wearing hobnail leather boots, a tweed jacket, wool knickers, and a felt hat. He wielded a single wood-shafted ice axe; he didn't have a rope, crampons, a down coat, Sherpas, or oxygen. Because he had removed his snow goggles to cross the black rocks of the North Face Norton's eyes were sunburned—nonetheless, he climbed upward without Somervell.

"The whole face of the mountain was composed of slabs like the tiles on a roof . . . ," Norton later wrote. "[I]t was a dangerous place for a single unroped climber, as one slip would have sent me in all probability to the bottom of the mountain."

At 28,126 feet, exhausted from the delicate, perilous climbing and realizing that he was going snow-blind, Norton turned back. No human would go higher until Edmund Hillary and Tenzing Norgay, using supplemental oxygen, climbed Everest twenty-nine years later. No human would go higher without oxygen for more than half a century, until Messner and Habeler in '78.

But what if Edward Norton had summited Everest in 1924, solo, without oxygen? Not only would it have changed the history of Himalayan mountaineering, it would have set an entirely different precedent for the style in which high mountains are climbed.

• • •

In a now-famous 1964 article in *Ascent* magazine, "Games Climbers Play," American climber Lito Tejada-Flores defined climbing as a game "precisely because there is no necessity to climb." Tejada-Flores outlined a hierarchy of the game consisting of seven basic forms: bouldering, cragging, continuous rock climbing, big-wall/aid climbing, alpine climbing, super-alpine climbing, and expedition climbing. After more than forty years of evolution, today we would have to add at least five more forms—ice climbing, sport climbing, sport ice climbing, gym climbing, and speed climbing. Each of these climbing games has a distinct set of rules.

According to Tejada-Flores, bouldering is the most complex game in the hierarchy, because it has the most rules—no rope, no rack, no belayer. On the other end of the spectrum, expedition mountaineering, "although complicated to organize and play, is, formalistically speaking, the simplest of all, since virtually nothing is forbidden to the climber. The recent use of aeroplanes and helicopters exemplifies the total lack of rules in the pure expedition-game."

I've always admired Tejada-Flores's explanatory essay, and even more the anthology of climbing articles it inspired—1978's *The Games Climbers Play*—but I think Tejada-Flores had his hierarchy upside down. Certainly to most of us it seems that the more players, the more equipment, the more money, the more logistics, the more risk—the more complicated the game. Isn't bouldering—which requires merely a rock, rock shoes, and a chalk bag—the simplest, even purest form of climbing? The polar opposite is four unshaven, unwashed guys stormbound for the thirteenth day in a two-man tent on a ledge at 26,000 feet wondering why the hell they never took up golf.

Still, Tejada-Flores's larger point stands: Climbing, at heart, is a kind of game, even if it is sometimes mortally dangerous. Precisely because climbing can kill you, many people—including me—flinch at the frivolity implied by the word *game*. Is bull riding a game? Is BASE jumping a game? Perhaps this is elitism, or simply semantics. All these activities have rules, and rules are essentially a code of honor created to protect the spirit of the game. In BASE jumping you must leap from something on earth, rather than from the safe height of a plane; in bull riding you must hold on, but only with one hand, for eight seconds.

Of course, you can always break the rules. It's your conscience. In the mountains, there are no referees or spectators. The freedom to make your own choices is one of the main reasons we climb.

As Tejada-Flores wrote, "Ethical climbing merely means respecting the set of rules of the climbing-game that one is playing."

Which isn't to say that the rules never change. When I started rock climbing in the mid-seventies, the sport was in the midst of an environmental and ethical revolution. Pitons—metal nails hammered into the rock—were being replaced by stoppers and hexes, devices that could be placed in cracks and easily removed without scarring the stone. Today, "pins" are used only as a last resort, when none of the less invasive forms of protection will work. The shift from pins to hammerless equipment improved the sustainability of a finite resource—some cracks were becoming nothing more than a series of pin scars—and, consquently, improved the sustainability of the sport itself.

The evolution of rules to preserve the integrity of a game is commonplace. Hunting is a good example. In 1738, to protect the dwindling deer population, the colony of Virginia banned the harvesting of does. In 1878, Iowa became the first state to initiate bag limits on game. In 1934, the Migratory Bird Hunting and Conservation Stamp Act established a requirement that waterfowl hunters purchase a federal duck stamp; proceeds were used to finance the purchase and management of waterfowl refuges. The list of hunting regulations intended to preserve the resource, and the experience, goes on for the next fifty years.

In 2002, nearly one hundred of the world's top climbers collaborated to produce the "Tyrol Declaration on Best Practice in Mountain Sports." It was distributed to eighty-nine alpine clubs in sixty-seven countries and published in the *American Alpine Journal* in 2003. If you haven't read it, do. (The text is widely available online.) It is a pivotal manifesto that outlines in plain Strunk-and-White English the accepted rules of the climbing game. It presents a hierarchy of values, with human dignity at the top, followed by life, liberty, and happiness; the intactness of nature; solidarity; self-actualization; truth; excellence; and adventure. There are ten articles in the Tyrol Declaration, each one addressing a different aspect of climbing, from conservation to responsibility, first ascents to sponsorship.

Article 8 is about style. It ends with one far-reaching sentence: "Good style on big mountains implies not using fixed ropes, performance enhancing drugs, or bottled oxygen."

• • •

So much has been made of *why* we climb. As David Roberts notes in his climbing memoir, *On the Ridge Between Life and Death*, "From Victorian days onward, climbing writers have spilled flagons of ink shaping transparently lame answers."

Why do we climb? For the challenge. Climbing is an act of hubris, a psychological-cum-physical defiance of the most fundamental earthly power: gravity. Some people enjoy participating in this; others enjoy reading about it. And yes, it's a risky, nakedly narcissistic business—precisely why it's a good read—but here's the catch: The proximity to death can brilliantly illuminate life itself, but with one slip, this brilliance is instantly extinguished and your death becomes a black hole for those left behind.

Why we climb is personal, but *how* we climb—a question hardly ever asked—is communal. How we climb defines the spirit of our sport. How we climb directly impacts not just the practice and future of mountaineering, but the health of the mountain environment.

Last year my good friend Keith Spenser went to Everest. He spent ten grand and two months on the North Col route, the climb Norton attempted, and did not summit. Back home in Laramie, he gave us a slide show and a synopsis of the experience.

"There's no leading to do on this route. There's a fixed line at the base of the North Col that goes all the way to the summit. Guide companies hire Sherpas to put up the ropes. For the average client—oxygen, tent, fuel, stove—it's all carried up by Sherpas. You couldn't climb the mountain by the standard routes on your own anymore even if you wanted to. You'd be six inches from a fixed line and the Sherpas have already staked out all the tent platforms for the clients. It's not mountaineering. It's not even an adventure. At best, it's an endurance event."

Last year was also the fiftieth anniversary of the first ascent of K2, which, at 28,250 feet, is the world's second highest peak. Steep and technical, with a reputation for taking lives, K2 has always been considered a mountaineer's mountain. But the Everest contagion reached K2 in 2004. More than 200 people were on the peak, a greater number than ever before; six climbers and six porters died. Fixed lines—ropes attached to anchors at the top and bottom that essentially act as a handrail—were set almost all the way to the summit on the Abruzzi Ridge. Sherpas were imported from Nepal to hump up dozens of bottles of oxygen. There were more than forty ascents, almost every one on fixed lines, more than half oxygen-assisted.

Oxygen and fixed lines are being used on 26,906-foot Cho Oyu, the sixth highest peak, as well. How long will it be before all the 8,000-meter peaks are morbidly ill? Five years? Ten? There's been a fixed line between 15,000 and 16,000 feet on the standard route up Denali for years. How long before this line is extended up to Denali Pass, or right to the summit? How long before there's a fixed line up the Exum Ridge on the Grand Teton or Liberty Ridge on Rainier?

This is ersatz mountaineering. When the technology, techniques, knowledge and precedents of a sport evolve, so must the rules.

• • •

For an increasing number of mountaineers, winning the game has become more important than how you play it.

Richard Salisbury, a former computer programmer at the University of Michigan, and Elizabeth Hawley, longtime Kathmandu journalist and expedition archivist, recently collaborated to publish the *Himalayan Database*, a statistical record of all expeditions that have climbed in the Nepal Himalayas from 1905 to 2003 For the first time, we can study the act of mountaineering using science, rather than anecdotes.

From 1950 to 2003, of the 11,734 people who went above Everest Base Camp, 2,251 reached the summit. Of these, 2,120, or ninety-four percent, used oxygen; 131, a mere six percent, did not.

What does it really mean, physiologically, to use oxygen at high altitude?

"Inhaling oxygen at two to four liters per minute—a typical flow rate for climbers—reduces the height of Everest by 5,000 to 9,000 feet," explains San Diego high-altitude physiologist Brownie Schoene, MD. In other words, climbing Everest (or K2, or any other 8,000-meter peak) with oxygen brings the peak down to around 20,000 feet at rest and 24,000 feet while climbing. That's lower than dozens of other Himalayan peaks.

"Oxygen is a performance-enhancing substance," Schoene states. "Using oxygen in high-altitude mountaineering is like blood doping in cycling. It could be said that climbing Mount Everest with oxygen is cheating."

John Harlin III, editor of the *American Alpine Journal*, says using oxygen is a form of aid climbing, relying on gear more that your own ability.

"The reality is, Hillary and Norgay did not make the first true ascent of Everest," Harlin says. "It had been a race for years—a nationalistic, no-holds-barred competition to see who would be the first to the top. In fact, it wasn't until Messner and Habeler summited Everest that the mountain was really climbed."

Today, in the twenty-first century, using oxygen in the mountain-climbing game is bad style. Furthermore, in my opinion, it is unethical. Why? Because if you didn't carry it up (and scarcely anyone does), a Sherpa did. Unlike using porters to pack gear into a basecamp, getting oxygen tanks up to a high camp is hazardous work: According to the *Himalayan Database*, in the past half-century, 119 climbers have died on Everest, along with sixty porters and Sherpas, more than two-thirds of whom were putting in fixed lines and hauling oxygen and supplies for clients. Enlist a Sherpa to carry your oxygen and you are paying someone else to assume your risk.

In order to safely move bottled oxygen and other supplies up to high camps, Sherpas put in fixed ropes. Clients subsequently clip into these lines and march up the steps kicked in the snow by Sherpas. Wouldn't this be considered unsportsman-like in other games? Imagine using a step ladder to dunk a basketball, or racing a tandem with a partner but never pedaling. More important, by jugging a fixed line, you're missing the opportunity to lead a pitch with ice axe and crampons, skill and resolve. You're missing out on the very joy of climbing.

Fixed lines contribute to the despoiling of our mountains. They allow an excess of equipment—extra food, oxygen bottles, computers, iPods, etc.—to be carried to high camps, some of which is never brought back down. Even the fixed lines themselves are often not removed, leaving yet more debris high on the peak. *Leave no trace* has been a maxim for backpackers for decades, and yet this basic principle is still frequently ignored in mountaineering.

I realize that eliminating the use of supplemental oxygen, and all it entails, on 8,000-meter peaks would have serious consequences—but the very integrity of the sport, as well as the beauty and majesty of the mountains, is at stake. Because oxygen increases the margin of safety, climbing without it might increase the death rate. Everest guides often use oxygen to help them make clearheaded decisions, Sherpas use it to accompany clients, clients use it just to keep moving—so perhaps, sans oxygen, Everest and K2 could no longer be commercially guided. Certainly, at least in the short term, this would financially stun a handful of Everest guiding companies, their several dozen guides, and several hundred high-altitude Sherpas. But look, these outfitters guide on many other peaks. All the other 8,000-meter summits—Nanga Parbat, Shishapangma, Makalu, Dhaulagiri, etc., most of them more technically challenging than Everest—would still be there, not to mention the rest of the world's splendid mountains.

• • •

At the end of Tejada-Flores's prescient "Games Climbers Play," he writes that he can "visualize the day when, with ultra-modern bivouac gear, a climbing party of two sets off to do an 8000m. peak just as today one sets off to do a hard route on the Grand Teton or Mont Blanc."

Eleven years later Messner and Habeler did just that. Others have followed in their footsteps, but not many. Such climbing demands deep outdoor acumen, technique that has become instinctual, steely mental stamina, the legs and lungs of a locomotive, and heart—all of which require years of apprenticeship in the mountains. When you substitute oxygen for training, fixed lines for technique, and Sherpas for personal responsibility, you've not only diminished the great, mortal game of mountaineering, you've diminished yourself.

And yet if your dream has always been to climb a big Himalayan peak, you can still do so ethically and thoughtfully, even with a guide. Use porters to help you get your gear to basecamp, but hump everything above there yourself. If you must fix a line or two, do so yourself, then remove it—along with all your gear and garbage—when you depart. Finally, face the mountain and its glorious, rarified ambiance on its own terms, without oxygen.

Why we climb is made manifest by how we climb. We have choices. The Tyrol Declaration is not enforceable. There are no penalties. The mountains are still free and we're all at liberty to climb them largely as we desire. Let the best of your character be your guide.

But forget not: We are what we do.

And style *is* substance.

FUTURE ROCK

We are moving through a mystery. Whiteness envelops us. We can't see where we're going, or what lies to our left or right. Our only guide is ascent: We climb the fall line, crampon points and ice-axe picks skittering on verglas-glazed rock.

There are just two of us on this expedition: quiet Louisiana man Ross Lynn, twenty-six, and yours truly. We're in a cirque with no name in China's Daxue Shan Range, at the far eastern edge of the Tibetan plateau. It has been my dream to come here and climb. There are no rescue choppers or Sherpas, cell phones don't work, the nearest hospital is days away. Ross and I are on our own.

We can't see them, but from the map we know there are four unclimbed 20,000-foot summits looming above us. We're hoping to climb just one, 20,059-foot Nyambo Konka.

A squall swoops in, hail rattling upon our helmets like gravel.

"Can't see a damn thing!" I shout.

But the higher we go on the mountain, the more sunshine breaks through. Within an hour, the 4,000-foot visage of Nyambo is staring down on us. Blind to the terrain above, we've managed to climb right up beneath a deeply fractured, quarter-mile-long hanging glacier— something like wandering into a building that's about to be dynamited.

Ross and I make an abrupt right turn, hustle across a vast, telltale fan of avalanche debris, and descend via a safer route on the north side of the cirque.

"Let's not do that again," I say on the way down.

"Scratch plan A," Ross agrees.

In the morning we move our camp higher. Plan B is to climb the central couloir (a steep ravine of snow), which we discover, to our alarm, is running with avalanches. On to plan C: Ascend another couloir farther north.

We dig out a tent platform at the base of the face we believe to be safe from avalanche. Erect the tiny tent, eat cubes of yak gristle, drink

Chinese tea, load our packs for the morning attempt, scootch into our sleeping bags, talk.

Ross is regaling me with tales from his ascent of Lurking Fear, a notorious route on Yosemite's El Cap, when an ominous roar drowns out his voice. Suddenly our tent is being pummeled and bashed in and Ross and I are screaming and tearing at the tent zippers, diving out into the darkness clawing bare-handed and sock-footed to safety. After the avalanche passes, we find our tent partially flattened, a softball-size rock having sliced through the fly.

"Perhaps we should move camp," Ross says in his calm Southern drawl.

We spend the next two hours digging out a new tent platform by headlamp, only to have an avalanche sweep by on the opposite side the moment we're back in our bags.

"Busy place," I quip.

Neither of us sleeps that night. We listen, like infantry soldiers in a trench, ears straining to interpret the portent of each explosion. We wait to see if we survive. We wait for dawn and plan D.

Climbing mountains is an act I happen to love, but it is only one form of adventure. There are thousands. In fact, there's one for every human with the passion to push personal boundaries.

Recognizing this, W. L. Gore and Associates, the manufacturer of Gore-Tex, began awarding grants in 1990 to "small, unencumbered teams of friends with daring and imaginative goals," teams that would attempt their projects "in a self-propelled, environmentally sound, cost-effective way." The Shipton/Tilman Grants, as the program is known, have supported a wide array of explorations—caving in Thailand, crossing the Gobi on foot, sea kayaking around Tierra del Fuego, kite skiing across the Yukon. Our plan to climb Nyambo Konka earned a grant as well, in part for its imaginative simplicity: one rope, two guys, three weeks, four ice tools, and an unclimbed peak in an unexplored amphitheater.

Eric Shipton and H. W. Tilman were two British mountaineers a half-century ahead of their time. From the 1930s into the 1960s, they explored mountains in Africa and Asia with an elegant, prescient style. While most expeditions of that era were enormous, nationalistic undertakings, Shipton and Tilman usually chose to move quickly and lightly, at low cost and with low impact. Together they were the first to traverse the West Ridge of Mount Kenya, the first to break through the Rishi Gorge into Nepal's Nanda Devi Sanctuary, and the first to explore and survey the northern approaches to K2 and its subsidiary glaciers.

The duo epitomized the best of what adventure can be—exploratory, gallant, seeking higher truths—which, frankly, made them historical anomalies. Although it hasn't been a linear progression, exploration has evolved profoundly over the past half-millennium. In his encyclopedic *Great Adventures and Explorations* (1947), Vilhjalmur Stefansson, twice president of the Explorers Club of New York and a legendary polar explorer in his own right, bluntly characterizes the "self-confessed greed for riches, lust for conquest, and bigotry in religion" that motivated many early explorers.

Prior to the 1700s, expeditions were generally military forces with the dual purposes of imperialism and religious conversion. Francisco Pizarro, the conquistador who conquered Peru, had the native inhabitants burned alive or torn apart by dogs if they couldn't help him in his search for El Dorado. The early exploration of Africa was motivated almost entirely by the slave trade: tracking down humans, capturing them, and selling them. It wasn't until the Enlightenment, with its emphasis on knowledge, ethics, and aesthetics, that the nature of adventure changed. Science, rather than gold, slavery, or religious coercion, became integral to exploration. Alexander von Humboldt (1769 to 1859), the father of modern geography, was perhaps the quintessential scientist–explorer of this period—climbing mountains to take barometric pressure readings, recording the interaction between the ocean and geography—and the Humboldt Current off the coast of South America is his namesake. Humboldt's writing inspired a young naturalist by the name of Charles Darwin (1809 to 1882), who, through his own world travels and intellectual synthesis of what he saw, changed the very foundation of biological science.

By the twentieth century, imperialism had been largely replaced by nationalism, science was being conducted as much in the lab as in the field, and only the farthest corners of the earth were left unexplored. American naval officer Robert Peary reached the North Pole in 1909; Norwegian explorer Roald Amundsen made the South Pole in 1911.

Shipton climbed the first 7,000-meter peak, Kamet, in the Indian Himalayas, in 1931. A four-man American team made the first ascent of 24,790-foot Minya Konka, the highest peak in the Daxue Shan Range, a year later. Frenchman Maurice Herzog nabbed the first 8,000-meter peak, Annapurna, in 1950; Hillary and Norgay summited Everest in 1953.

In the past two generations, all fourteen of the world's 8,000-meter peaks have been climbed. The Amazon, the Nile, the Niger, the upper Tsangpo—all have been run. Everest has been skied, Angel Falls BASE jumped, the sky itself surfed. So what's left?

Nothing, according to some fin de siècle defeatists. You've likely heard the lament: Africa has the Internet, the Silk Road is a highway, the Inca Trail a tourist trap—time to play *Dragon Quest VIII*.

Columnist John Tierney, in a 1998 *New York Times Magazine* critique titled "Going Where a Lot of Other Dudes with Really Great Equipment Have Gone Before," promoted this sort of fashionable jadedness by coining the word explornography: "the vicarious thrill of exploring when there is nothing left to explore." According to Tierney, the "Age of Exploration has been succeeded by the Age of Explornography." Even Italian alpinist Reinhold Messner, who should know better, declared last year in London's *Guardian*, "Mountaineering is over. Alpinism is dead. Maybe its spirit is still alive a little in Britain and America, but it will soon die out."

They're both wrong.

It's self-evident that the age of grand geographical exploration—with the enormous exceptions of deep space, deep earth, and the deep sea—is over, but as I see it, the age of adventure has only just begun.

• • •

The moment there is even a semblance of light, Ross crawls out of the tent and through a monocular studies the wall of Nyambo above us.

During the night, using a Russian 1:200,000 topo, altimeter readings, and GPS coordinates, I had pinpointed our location. But these are just numbers. They establish our position, but not the conditions—the hollowness or hardness of the ice, the depth or danger of the snow, our fatigue or faith. These, the actual exigencies of a mountain, can be ascertained in only the old-fashioned way.

"Which couloir looks good?" I ask.

"None," says Ross, handing me the monocular.

There is a hundred-foot-deep cornice hanging over the breadth of the face. Our best option appears to be angling northward, crossing avalanche chutes, trying to climb largely on the rock ribs.

The first few hundred feet are a scramble, then the face steepens and we are confronted with the appalling insecurity of the rock—thousands of feet of sharp, irregular blocks stacked one on top of the other and held together only by the mortar of ice. Pulling out any chunk might bring down a million tons of rock.

Plan E: Forget the cornice, climb yet another couloir.

Had Nyambo been previously ascended, we would have already known what to do, and for me, much of the mountain's magnetism would have been lost. What enthralls me most about entering unknown country is that you have to make it up as you go. There's no rule book. Improvisation is imperative.

And yet there's something even deeper, something even more seductive, about exploring one of the millions of slivers of terra incognita left all across the planet: If no one has been where you're going, you have no idea whether what you want to do can be done. The reason to go is to find out. To discover firsthand whether you have the nerve and craft, the resilience and resourcefulness to think on your feet and dance on your fears.

Unroped, swinging ice tools, Ross and I gradually ascend a web of interconnected couloirs. It's sometime in the afternoon when we stop at a insecure belay. Spindrift is flying around our faces.

"We're moving too slow!" I shout over the roar of the wind. Ross nods. Yelling back and forth, we discuss our options. Continuing upward, whether we reach the summit or not, will guarantee an exposed, bagless bivouac. Hypothermia certain, frostbite probable. I reluctantly stab my finger downward, and we turn around.

We rap off several frighteningly small rock fragments frozen into the wall before finding a gully we can downclimb. It's a long haul back to the tent, where we both collapse.

• • •

It's true that the most obvious adventure icons, the Everests and the Amazons, have been done. But there's still so much left, and it's accessible to more of us than ever before. Airplanes and the Internet have democratized adventure. It took the 1932 Minya Konka expedition three months to get to the Daxue Shan from the United States; it took Ross and me less than a week. You no longer need special contacts or sponsors to pull off a world-class trip. You need only a good partner, a few weeks, and a fistful of desire.

According to the International Union of Alpine Associations, there are 144 unclimbed 7,000-meter peaks (those rising to between 22,965 and 26,246 feet). At a recent Alpine Club symposium in Penrith, England, Japan's Tomatsu Nakamura, the leading authority on the mountains of eastern Tibet, estimated that there are 200 to 250 unclimbed 20,000-foot peaks in this region alone. And even after all the peaks have been climbed, there will still be beautiful routes left to find.

"As technical standards continue to increase, people look at things with different eyes and see new possibilities," says renowned alpinist Kelly Cordes, thirty-seven, assistant editor of the *American Alpine Journal*. Cordes has put up unrepeated first ascents in Alaska, Peru, and Pakistan, most recently scaling the 7,500-foot face of Pakistan's Great Trango Tower in a stunning four-day sufferfest.

"The potential for adventure is limited by your imagination," explains Cordes, "not by geography."

This evolution—from planting the flag to a more subtle, primal focus on the personal how and why—is the future of adventure.

"From a kayaker's point of view," says Asheville, North Carolina, river rat Daniel DeLaVergne, "there's an endless supply of places to go get lost and get in trouble, an uncountable number of unrun rivers in Alaska, Canada, New Guinea, China."

DeLaVergne, twenty-eight, would know. In 2005, he and his pals did the first descent of Mosley Creek, in the Coast Range of British Columbia, a deadly three-day carnival of class 5+ rapids.

"But you know, it's not really all about first descents," says DeLaVergne. "It's about how you paddle. It's about keeping your shit humble and making good decisions. You can do the same river everybody else has done but try to do it in better style. No matter what happens, every time, you learn something."

And it's more than just technical prowess and physical risk. A friend of mine has journeyed to Nicaragua and El Salvador to monitor elections, and his tales match those of any adventurer.

Ecologist Michael Fay's 1999 to 2000 Megatransect, a 455-day foot traverse of central Africa's Congo basin, is a perfect example of modern exploration at its best. Fay's goal was to "go as deep into the last wild place on earth as possible" in order to help conservationists and governments identify the most vital places to protect. He walked 1,243 miles, used twelve rolls of duct tape on his blistered feet, and filled thirty-nine yellow waterproof notebooks with everything from accounts of thousands of elephant sightings to descriptions of plant species. In 2002, due in large measure to Fay's journey, the government of Gabon created thirteen national parks, setting aside more than ten percent of the country's land area.

Adventure, then, is no longer simply about exploitation or adulation; it's about the quest for understanding. You don't need a mountain or a river or a jungle—you need only an open mind. Your goal does not have to be a first; it need only be something that takes you to a new place and challenges you physically or mentally, emotionally or spiritually.

• • •

Ross and I back off all the way to base camp, sing Johnny Cash songs around the campfire for a couple of nights, then attempt Nyambo's south ridge.

The first 2,000 feet are an unbelievable briar patch of thorns. Imagine a jungle gym of cactus reaching into the sky, then imagine trying to climb it with a fifty-pound pack on your back. I manage to fall backward and impale my forearm. When we finally emerge onto the alpine slopes above, we're so scratched and bloodied, we'll be pulling spines out of our hands for a month.

We dig camp into the rocks at 15,000 feet. The wind is fierce, and we resort to lining the inside of the tent with brick-size rocks to keep it—and ourselves—from being blown into the sky.

The next morning, on our second summit bid, we encounter a series of intricate, unsafe gendarmes—castlelike towers of friable rock guarding the snowy ridge to the summit. We dislodge boulders that career frightfully through space. We climb sideways and down and over and sometimes, when we're lucky, up. The weather is splendid and, despite my badly bruised arm and a nasty wind, I think we have it made.

Then, somewhere above 17,000 feet, Ross slumps to the ground. His legs refuse to go any farther. He has altitude sickness.

I ask him to sit tight and rest while I recon above. I climb up the arête, crisscrossing through a maze of stone turrets, entranced by the terrain. My progress is eventually stopped by an overhanging stone face I can't scale without a rope. I climb back down to Ross, hoping he might have recovered, but his face is ashen. We have no choice but to descend.

I don't say anything to Ross, but I'm burning with that agonizing, compulsive need to stand on the summit. I secretly, perhaps foolishly, decide I'll solo it.

Once Ross is safely back in the tent, I march off along various spurs to inventory my options. I sit in the buffeting wind and move the tiny, circular window of the monocular up and down every possible route. All the rock is rotten, the glacier a spiky ocean of seracs, the summit a minefield of hidden crevasses.

Ten years ago, little of this would have mattered. Ten years ago, my drive and ambition would have gotten the best of me and I would have gone on regardless. But something inside me has changed. I sit on a frozen promontory and study the lines of Nyambo Konka, and somehow the risks just don't seem worth it. Thoughts of my daughters and my wife, my friends and my community and my climbing partner, overlay my view of the mountain. This has happened to me before, but usually I've been able—for better or worse—to put these considerations aside. This time I can't. I seem to have lost my single-mindedness of purpose, and I feel disappointed in myself.

Right up until sundown, I desperately search the south side of the mountain for a route to the summit that I can justify soloing, but I find none. On my first visit to Tibet, in 1984, I was willing to do whatever it took to reach the top. Now, I've learned, I'm not.

Our climb is over, but not our adventure. We're in Tibet, for God's sake, surrounded by magnificent mountains and an unfathomably rich culture. Enough with mirthless ice and snow.

During our final week in Tibet Ross and I just follow our noses. We trek through stone villages and drink cups of traditional yak butter tea, but also find solar panels and satellite dishes on the roofs. We hire a Tibetan yak driver to clean up all the garbage along a stretch of trail. We listen to a chanting monk methodically thump a six-foot brass drum deep inside a yellow-walled monastery, then later see him chatting away on his cell phone.

Adventure has always been about discovery, but because we and our world are constantly evolving, what we discover is, and forever will be, something new. The Tibetan culture is changing rapidly, and, due to global warming, the ice on Nyambo Konka is melting. When I come back, it will be a different place and a different adventure.

Striving for superlatives is part of human nature—the highest, the longest, the deepest. But now that many of these goals have been reached, the future of adventure lies in more subtle, more discriminating endeavors: the most beautiful, the most technical, the project accomplished with the most style. Adventure will be less about simply surviving and more about performing with grace and virtuosity. More personal, more internal, just you and your dream.

The golden age of adventure is upon us. Now go.

•   •   •

Postscript: On March 7, 2007, Daniel DeLaVergne was struck by a train and killed near Asheville, North Carolina.

Mortality

PART I

The sound resembled that of a large limb being broken off a tree. One second I was pounding down the trail on my bike, enveloped in the myth of my own immortality, artfully dodging rocks and sagebrush, and the next I was sprawled out on my back in the dirt. It happened so fast I don't remember going over the handlebars, flying through the air like a man somersaulting off a trampoline. (Forensic evidence would later reveal that I hit a deep, cleverly concealed gopher hole at approximately thirty-five miles per hour, came off the bicycle headfirst, and rammed my right shoulder into a boulder.) All I remember is that sound.

When I sat up my right arm didn't bother to come with me. I lifted the arm like a chunk of firewood, set it in my lap, and inspected the top of the shoulder. Sticking out was a protuberance somewhat larger than a doorknob, the skin stretched so taut it was about to tear.

Cradling my right arm with my left, I stood up. I was out in the prairie. I didn't feel my finest. I remember looking up into the azure late-afternoon sky as if an airplane, or perhaps the gods, might have witnessed my little accident and would now consider coming to my rescue. No such luck. I abandoned my bike and set off cross-country. I could walk only so far before I had to sit down for several minutes to keep from passing out. Sweat was seeping through my pores, soaking my clothes, dripping into the dirt; I was racked with spasms of shivering. Peripheral vision disappeared, the sky turned black. It was as if I were walking through a tunnel.

At some point I reached a house on the edge of town and rang the doorbell. By now the muscles in my neck and back had convulsed and distended. I must have looked like Quasimodo, for the woman who opened the screen door took one look at me, turned pale, and declared, "We have to take you to the emergency room." She got me into her pickup, ran every stop sign on the way to the hospital, moved me past the receptionist into a room, took my phone number, and left to call my wife.

The room was burning white. I sat on a white bed enclosed by white walls. The fluorescent lights were hot white. A nurse in white started asking me questions, and I answered, although I could barely hear my voice. It came from someplace far away. He said the doctor would be in any moment. "Thank you," I said, attempting to sound normal and chipper. "I'm going to pass out now."

When I came to, struggling up out of whirling confusion and nausea, several people were moving swiftly around me. I had no idea who they were or what was going on. Someone was shoving a needle into my arm, someone else was cutting off my clothes, and a man had his face right up in mine, examining my eyes.

"Where am I?" I demanded.

"The hospital," he said.

"Why am I here?"

"You basically tore your arm off your shoulder."

• • •

The next morning, Michael Wasser, MD, master bone carpenter and shoulder specialist at Gem City Bone & Joint, the local orthopedic clinic, studied the x-rays excitedly. "A-C separations are usually graded one through three," he said. "You have a five."

I opened my well-thumbed copy of the *Atlas of Human Anatomy*, an intimately detailed medical textbook. I bought it a decade ago and take it to doctor's appointments after every wreck. Pointing to various illustrated body parts, Wasser explained how I had torn my clavicle from my acromion, shredding the trapezoid and conoid ligaments and ripping apart the fascia between the deltoid and trapezius muscles. To put it back together would require sawing off the ends of the acromion and clavicle, drilling holes, slicing the vestigial coracoacromial ligament, and using the ligament like a hose clamp to reattach the joint.

"Procedure's called a Weaver-Dunn," said Wasser, manipulating my arm and shoulder into surprising positions as I jumped. "Looks like you also tore your labrum. I'll nail it back on. There's other damage as well, but we won't find it until we're in there."

Translation: shoulder reconstruction. An orthopedic surgeon's wet dream.

Wasser grinned. "Want me to repair that torn joint capsule while I'm at it?"

I smirked. "Might as well."

Wasser knew me as a steady customer. Eighteen months earlier I had dislocated my shoulder doing a contortionist move on a 5.11 off-width crack climb. Although I had managed to pop it back in while hanging from the rope, I'd also torn my joint capsule. The MRI revealed damage to the rotator cuff and the labrum, but I'd chosen several rounds of rehab over surgery. "Up to you," Wasser had said at the time. "You'll be back in here soon enough anyway."

And here I was, nothing if not punctual.

The following morning I was being prepped for surgery by a nurse who was as friendly as she was frank. She deftly slipped in the IV, read the lengthy preoperative diagnosis, and pooched her lovely lips.

"They have a lot of work to do," she said. "I don't want you to misunderstand: You're going to be in a lot of pain for a long time. Have you ever been hurt before?"

• • •

I couldn't help but smile. My list of wrecks was like that of a car at the demolition derby. I'd broken or smashed, wrenched or ripped, sliced or gouged almost every cubic inch of my body. I'd been into the lovely Gem City Bone & Joint facilities so many times they were considering naming a wing after me.

There may be some serious outdoor athletes who have never been hurt, but I don't know any. All my friends have scars and the stories to go with them. If you've never hurt yourself, you've likely never pushed yourself. Climb enough mountains, mountain bike enough miles, kayak enough rivers, and you will get injured. This is not a probability; it's a money-back guarantee. Wrecks come with the territory. The world is one giant garden of cliffs, canyons, and cacti, and if you're out there exploring it for any amount of time, you'll discover that flesh is softer than stone, weaker than water, and highly vulnerable to velocity.

Hence we veterans of the outdoor life all have our proud lists of injuries, which of course make for some fine tales of struggle and heroism. But don't be fooled. Injuries are mistakes made manifest. Rare is the accident not due to pilot error. You can't blame the world—it is what it is. The nature of nature is fundamentally merciless. You can't blame ice for being itself, transient, capricious, unfaithful; or rock for being existentially rock-hard and immobile; or water for being fluid, fast, and reckless.

This is the first lesson of injury: Take the blame.

• • •

The nurse was right. I came out of the operation looking and feeling like someone had tried to cleave my shoulder from my body with a broadsword. For the first week I could do nothing more than lie in bed and moan pathetically. Any movement was excruciating. Even in sleep I was sheathed in agony. I was rich with self-pity.

(A note about the difference between doctors and nurses. Doctors do not care about your pain. Don't expect them to. They know pain will pass. Doctors care about the ends, not the means, the destination, not the journey. If you are capable of getting back to the life you had before you messed yourself up, they have done their job. Nurses, on the other hand, care about the means. Listen to them closely. Heed their advice.)

It is common to curse the thunderstorm of pain, but it often brings forth that most rare and delicate of flowers: humility. It is difficult and peculiarly unbecoming to be puffed up with pride when you are too weak to sit up. Machismo melts when you need help going to the toilet. If it hurts bad enough, you will break. This is very useful self-knowledge.

To become an invalid is to pass through perhaps the most important veil of life, the veil of compassion; to be just like the people you might ordinarily ignore—the old, the weak, the disabled, the sick. All those gray-faced people, thin and fatigued, suffering some imperious malady that you, purely by the whim of the gods, do not have to face. One twist of fate and you're just like them. Hurt, hurting, in need of help.

This is the second, albeit greatest, lesson of injury: be humble.

• • •

A week after the surgery, friends began dropping by and leaving gifts. Ed, a philosophy professor, my bicycling compadre and intellectual foil, left *It's Not About the Bike*, by Lance Armstrong, and *Seven Pillars of Wisdom*, by T. E. Lawrence (the redoubtable Lawrence of Arabia). Wade, my climbing partner, left *Camp 4: Recollections of a Yosemite Rockclimber*, by Steve Roper. Ken and Carol, skiing companions, gave me a glossy dreambook of photographs of Patagonia. Richard, my college mentor and also a philosophy professor—a Woody Allen humor omnibus. Bill, an old history professor—the obscure and brilliant works of Patrick Leigh Fermor. Annie, fellow scribbler—*The Immortal Class*, by Travis Hugh Culley. John, colleague and expedition partner—a bottle of Captain Morgan rum and the current issue of *Playboy*. My mother—a tape of a lecture, *Choosing the God Who Answers by Fire*, by the Rev. Dr. James A. Forbes Jr. Vicki came by with a vintage bottle of tequila. Rick slipped a six-pack of Guinness into the fridge. My daughters drew me entire books' worth of get-well pictures.

Sometimes, all you have to do is fall off your bicycle—something seven-year-olds manage without getting hurt—and you find you are connected to the souls of others by a thousand invisible cords. This is lesson number two in reverse.

• • •

On the ninth day after surgery I shaved, left-handed, almost taking off my head. Day eleven, I typed the whole day, left-handed. Day thirteen, I walked three blocks, had a relapse into incapacitating pain, and spent the next twenty-four hours back in bed.

The third week, the grand horror of rehab began. My physical terrorist was a man named Jim Scifres. Big Jim. He was soft-spoken and easy-going. Jim had once been a football player. He'd busted his own shoulder. He weighed 260 pounds and could have ripped my arm off. Instead, he bent it, bit by bit. He told me to let pain be my guide, which I found hilarious. If you walk through a physical therapy clinic you will hear people screaming behind the curtains. Were you to literally let pain be your guide, you'd never go to physical therapy. You'd stay home, eat popcorn, watch old movies. Alas, if you want to get better, it's gonna hurt. Big Jim serenely denied the validity of this philosophy and then blithely proceeded to put the hurt on me.

I showed up for my second appointment barely able to move. Jim asked me what I'd done, and I admitted that I'd tried to do a pushup.

"Time somebody told you the truth," he said. "Four to six months for seventy-five percent recovery, a year to full recovery. You won't be doing pushups anytime soon."

He showed me some stretching exercises I should practice at home. I did them more religiously, more rigorously than a Tibetan monk does his straight-backed recitations. The next time I saw Jim I was almost paralyzed. He put my shoulder in one of his Greco-Roman holds and asked me what I'd done this time. I admitted I'd done 200 reps for each rehab exercise. He shook his head and suggested I try twenty.

And so it went. Jim would put the hurt on me, then I'd go home and hurt myself on my own. All those years of mountaineering, one of the more masochistic endeavors, stood me in good stead. Jim complained that I was the most noncompliant patient he'd ever had, but I don't believe it. I did everything he said—every stretch, every exercise—500 percent.

Thus the third lesson of injury: be patient.

Except I don't think I really learned it. I wanted to, I tried to, I fully recognized that this wreck was my propitious opportunity to work on one of the outstanding inadequacies of my character. And I gave it my best shot—but in the end I think I was mostly pretending. I don't think the true ennobling nature of patience really sank in. Every time I had a slight bit of improvement, I'd idiotically come to the conclusion that I was healed, go out, and scrabble up an easy pitch or two or enter a bicycle race.

Then pay for it.

• • •

After two months I couldn't stand it anymore. I had to do a trip. I couldn't yet come close to doing a pullup. I couldn't do a pushup. But what of it? All that meant was that I couldn't climb or kayak or mountain bike or ski or carry a heavy pack. I still had legs. I could still hike. A mountain with maximum elevation gain but minimal technical requirements would be just what the doctor ordered. (Ha!)

It occurred to me that if injuries are little clues that we are mortal, there's at least one mountain in the world that mortals were once not permitted to ascend: Mount Olympus. In Greek mythology, Olympus was the exclusive abode of the immortals—Zeus, the forever philandering god of the sky; Hera, goddess of marriage, his jealous and cruelly conniving wife; the ugly but good-hearted Hephaestus, god of fire; Aphrodite, goddess of good sex; and the rest of that fractious pantheon. Nothing pleased the Greek gods more than good, old-fashioned adventure (consider the struggles of Prometheus or Hercules). For a recovering invalid, climbing Mount Olympus seemed an appropriately hubristic first foray back into the backcountry.

Not any partner would do. It had to be someone who had suffered from his own stupidity as much as I had, and preferably more. Stephen

Venables—friend, colleague, renowned British alpinist, and author of humorous books about Himalayan climbing—came immediately to mind. Stephen had lost most of the toes on his left foot after bivouacking high on Everest in 1988, and yet he claimed that "losing the little piggies wasn't really an injury at all, just occupational wear and tear—or, shall we say, unfortunate erosion." In 1992, at the end of an otherwise safe, successful expedition to the Indian Himalayas, a piton popped during a rappel and he took a 300-foot fall, breaking both legs. In his book *A Slender Thread*, Stephen describes this episode with such characteristic British understatement and wry comedy that you almost forget he nearly died.

Stephen responded to my first e-mail with "sounds like good fun" and to the second with "deification imminent." A week later we met in northern Greece on the shore of the emerald-blue Gulf of Salonika.

Mount Olympus rises 9,570 feet above sea level. We started our hike in the village of Litóchoron, not far from the topless beach, giving us a healthy 9,000-foot ascent. Penetrating the Enipeus River gorge, which cleaves the eastern flank of the massif, we passed through terrain seldom associated with Greece—a deep, mossy forest of giant beeches, walnuts, and holly oaks, matchless terrain for Artemis, goddess of the wilderness and the hunt.

Not one hour into the woods I knew the gods were with us. We had stopped for some bouldering on a pristine block of limestone. I set my sunglasses aside and they promptly vanished. After spending forty-five minutes scouring the hillside, we abandoned the search. But, just as we were walking away, I spotted them, crushed into the gravel in a spot I had probed ten times. Hermes, the mischievous god of thievery, was up to his old tricks.

High in the cleft we passed the ruins of the Monastery of Saint Dionysus (splendid to think of the god of wine and debauchery transformed into a chaste Christian icon), switchbacked among Balkan pines with trunks four feet in diameter, and spent the night in the Spilios Agapitos hut.

Zeus was out carousing well into the wee hours, bellowing with lecherous laughter, tossing thunderbolts left and right, apparently chasing every virgin nymph and maiden this side of the Acropolis.

We set off for the summit at dawn, passing beyond the timberline into jagged alpine country. Stephen, formed of equal parts madness and wisdom, stopped so often to admire, name—"*Campanula oreadum, Jankaea heldreichii*"—and photograph the alpine flowers that I took to calling him The Gardener. The night before, Zeus had left an inch of new snow on the last thousand feet of the climb. It was no more than a steep scramble up into dark shrouds of mist, but the snow made the limestone slick and treacherous, giving my rebuilt shoulder a good test.

Aeolus and his four chiefs of the cardinal points—Boreas, Zephyr, Notus, and Eurus—were wrestling ferociously when we reached the sharp summit, throwing us one way, then the other. Clouds were springing to life on the leeward side of the peak, obscuring the view down, but off in the distance the Aegean Sea shimmered like the Golden Fleece.

We humans are not immortal—we fall, we break, we die—and yet, to fulfill our own mythic dreams, we must live as if we are.

Stephen and I, two gimps at the top of Greece, shook hands.

PART II

I'm falling. Horizontal in midair, face toward the empty sky, back toward the rocky ground twenty feet below. Nothing comes from my mouth, but my mind is electric, hurtling faster than my body. This can't be happening.

What takes place next I don't remember exactly—like sinking into a deep sleep while watching a violent movie, dreaming, awakening, the movie still playing. I will only piece it together later from the accounts of the six friends who were climbing with me in New Mexico's Rio Grande Gorge that bright October day.

Midflight, I curl into a ball as if doing a gymnastics maneuver, hit the ground on my back—somehow missing the jagged rocks all around me—roll backward into the sagebrush, bounce to my feet, and ridiculously ask my belayer if she's all right. Her face is as white as marble.

"I'm okay," I tell her. "I'm not hurt." And I believe this, because my body is surging with adrenaline.

Then I follow her eyes and look down at myself. My left hand is facing the wrong direction, the wrist unnaturally lumped.

"I have to walk out," I say.

I don't remember how I got my climbing harness off. I remember cradling my left arm with my right hand and determinedly scrambling up a large boulder and down the other side. Ten feet along the trail I am flooded with nausea and know I'm about to pass out. I drop onto the dirt path and try to put my rushing head between my legs, but it's already swirling away. Lightning explodes inside my closed eyelids and everything is flying off inside me. If this were the first time, I would think I was dying. Instead, at the very center of the maelstrom, I recognize what is occurring: I'm going into shock. Later I will be told that my body was convulsing.

Next thing I remember, Rob is looking into my face, but I can't see him. His face is at the end of a long black tunnel. He is talking to me but I can't make out the words. They sound like glue. I study his face and can see he is worried and I try to unstick his words.

"Mark, stay with me. Mark, stay with me. Mark."

I know I have to respond but I don't have a tongue. So I grow one, like a plant in my mouth.

"I'm okay."

"Mark, you may have a head injury."

I am burning up and shivering uncontrollably. I know this is shock and it shall pass.

Two things will stand out above all else. The first is Rob holding my head in his hands, talking to me, reassuring me. Rob, I'll learn later, is a certified wilderness first responder. He knows what to do, and though gravely concerned, he does it with stoic composure. He feels the back of my head and neck with his fingers, then dribbles water into my parched mouth. He removes the sharp rocks from under my ribs and thighs. He covers my chest and arms with fleece jackets; tells Gordy to run to the top of the cliff with the cell phone. But I don't recall these acts. I remember this: Rob right there talking to me, his voice very calm: "You're gonna be fine, just fine."

Then Janine is by my side, holding my good hand, and Ki is on the other side, wiping the hotcold sweat from my forehead, and they both look so scared I try to tell them a funny story about a past wreck, but I can't do a decent job of it.

The flight-for-life helicopter comes into my slice of sky, and somehow a moment later the flight nurse has a morphine IV in my right forearm and an air splint compressing my left arm. I don't have a head wound after all, just a badly broken wrist. Do I think I can walk out? I can try. The chopper disappears over the dusky gorge without me.

Walking turns out to be difficult. The steep, switchbacking trail is loose underfoot, and I have to concentrate on each step. I have no balance. I am moving so slowly, the paramedics and parade of climbers behind me. It is cool in the shadow below the cliff. The far rim is flaming, ebony depths below. The sky is the color of blue you see only in dreams. I understand that everything is the way it should be.

It takes me half an hour to walk half a mile. I'm being helped into the back of the ambulance. Evening sunlight, warm and quiet as air, is cutting across the red desert. Friends encircle me. Hal shakes my hand and says Katie is going with me, and I have to smile.

The jeep road is rutted and I groan when we hit bumps but none of it really matters now because we're on our way across northern New Mexico and Katie is at my side stroking my hair. This is the second thing that will stand out above all else: Katie knowing it is not necessary to speak, only to be there. Her touch like gentle, slow-moving river water touches the bank.

It is dark outside the ambulance windows now. The EMT is trying to get my medical history, which makes me laugh.

• • •

I have been my life's private guinea pig. I can't count all the wrecks. A bad concussion from a rockslide climbing a mountain in the Black Hills when I was five years old. A broken collarbone fighting with my grade-school nemesis atop a fence. Multiple concussions and a broken back in gymnastics, Mom always there, nursing me through some rough nights. Broken toes in karate. Broken hand and cheekbone bicycling across South Africa, my brothers laughing at the pumpkin sound my head made when it hit the pavement. Separated ribs alpine climbing. Broken leg telemark skiing, which required a plate and six screws to put back together. A torn biceps tendon ice climbing. A triple hernia from carrying too many heavy packs in the Himalayas. A shattered shoulder mountain biking, two bones sawed off and cobbled back together.

Not to mention all the frostbite, altitude sickness, and diseases, the punctures, incisions, and stitches, the number of times I went too far in northern Burma, eventually splitting my mind into unidentifiable pieces. (The truth is: physical injuries are a walk in the park compared to mental injuries. When your mind is broken, it is impossible to recognize that the pain and terror you are experiencing is temporary. Sometimes this can be too much to bear. Hope *is* healing. Without it, everything goes unspeakably black.)

Now, a mangled wrist.

I deserved it all. In every case, I was inattentive to something critical. I realize this is a failure of character, but I have not been able to correct it.

Most people do not deserve their afflictions. The daughter with AIDS. The mother with Alzheimer's. The brother crippled by a drunk driver. The father with inoperable cancer. The sixteen-year-old girl in Iraq, legless from one of our "smart" bombs. They are all victims of the unfathomable cruelty of fate.

But me, I have deserved every accident that has felled me. They have been good for me, every single one. An accident can be a cryptic message, your body merely the messenger. It's up to your heart to decipher the meaning.

• • •

The dislocation is reduced in Taos but there are so many broken bones I will need surgery. I fly home to Laramie to have my orthopedic surgeon, Michael Wasser, nail me back together. He's done it before. The carpentry takes three hours—anchoring ripped ligaments, tweezering out bone fragments, running in a long screw. My wife, Sue, calmly reads in the waiting room, as she has many times before—worried but you'd never know it—her faith in my indestructibility a fathomless ocean that buoys me.

General anesthesia and I have long-standing animosities and I take time to come to. The post-op nurses say I was kicking so hard I rammed my legs through the hospital bed rails. When I at last return from this expedition of the mind, Sue gets me home and into bed. She patiently spoon-feeds me a bowl of soup while my daughter Teal reads me her report about African elephants: "Did you know that elephants poop eighty pounds a day?" With narcotics paralyzing my insides, I'm just hoping to go at all.

I awake at night in agony. My wrist feels as if it is being smashed in a vise. At 4:00 a.m. I finally admit that this can't be right, and Sue bundles me off to the emergency room. Dr. Wasser is there in minutes. I have the beginnings of compartment syndrome—pressure from the stitches is restricting the blood's circulation and could permanently damage the muscles and nerves in my hand. He gives me two options: go back into surgery immediately or snip the deep sutures without anesthetic so I can tell him whether the pressure has been relieved. He suggests that Sue leave the room. I almost puke when he starts cutting, but it works.

"You're getting your MD the hard way," he says after finishing up, "one limb at a time."

I am readmitted to the hospital and intravenously plugged into a bag of Dilaudid—hospital heroin. I depress the self-administering plunger again and again. Soon I'm surfing my hospital bed like an out-of-control ten-year-old. Nurse Jeff is grand. I believe the other nurses rotating through the night to be the most beautiful women on earth.

I'm quite certain it would be best to spend another month or two here; alas, after two days, I'm heartlessly taken off drugs and released upon the shoulders of my wife. My surefootedness is gone, and Sue must support me. She already has our bedroom set up for my recovery, a bouquet of sunflowers, cattails, and red berries blossoming atop the dresser. Both daughters start to cry when they see me. They have made get-well cards. Addi's is poster-size and double-sided, a poem of word-pictures: "whenever you want a huge scoop of ice cream let me know . . . you are somewhat free, so lean back and have fun . . . this accident is just another one of your memories . . . "

Janine sends me a bouquet of sunshine: brilliant yellow daises, lilies, and roses. Katie mails me a new world of music in CDs and poems. Megan leaves a mountain of date cookies in the house. Sarah makes us a spinach quiche, and Craig makes us spaghetti and meatballs. Ken drops off a gyroscopic wrist rehabilitator device. John mails another torture device from Hood River. Pat pulls me out of the house and we drive up to the mountains to take photographs of the snow-rimed walls we intend to climb together.

I need to eat protein, so Sue is making the most magnificent sandwiches for lunch: grilled pastrami, turkey breast, provolone on black rye. Yogurt full of fresh fruit. My mother comes over with a book about fathers and daughters. Alyson drops off two volumes of hip short stories and a novel.

I've done nothing to deserve all this kindness. Getting hurt is like dying without having to go that far. Those you care about unselfconsciously show how much they care about you.

Tomorrow, next month—sometime—someone close to me will be hurt. Then it will be my turn. Will I give back all that I have been given? But why wait for an accident? Why can I not develop the humility to show compassion without the need for pretext?

• • •

Everybody asks about the pain as if it were a bad thing. Actually, I made friends with it years ago, and now Ms. P. and I have an intimate relationship. We don't see each other for a while, then we meet again and it's like no time has passed. I have learned so much from her. She shares truths I prefer to ignore. For instance, I have a tendency to live as if I am not mortal. She won't put up with such arrogance and sets me straight. And when I forget how many people are suffering all over the world, she reminds me. With her help, after every accident, I am humbled. Without her I would be a compassionless ass.

Spending time with Ms. P. is just one gift of an injury. There are many.

Any injury worth the time will slow you down—precisely what we all desperately need. An injury will make you do one thing at a time. You'll re-remember that multitasking only means you're doing several things poorly. Injured, you must focus on one thing for it to happen at all. With this singularity of focus comes happiness, for you have been released from distraction, the most corrosive disease of twenty-first-century life.

With only one hand, it takes me minutes to button up my jeans. Try it yourself. For the first few days I can't do it at all and have to wear sweats around the house like an incontinent old man. I can't squeeze toothpaste onto my toothbrush; instead I squeeze it onto my tongue. Like a kindergartner, I can't tie my shoelaces; my daughters did it for me, giggling.

I start using my mouth again, like a dog. To pull on my shirt. To pull it off by the sleeve. To unscrew the ketchup bottle cap. To lick food off the side of my face. Our tongues, lips, and teeth really are so useful and yet so underutilized.

By necessity, I learn how to do two things surprisingly quickly: popping open the childproof bottles of painkillers with one hand and typing swiftly, without pecking, with that same hand.

If challenge is something we all need—and I believe it is—then all of this has been quite good for me.

• • •

One morning about a month after surgery, I decide to remove the splint, snip out the sutures from the three incisions, and try moving my fingers. First just wiggling them, then little squat thrusts. The swelling has gone down and I can almost cup my fingers.

My wrist, however, is as rigid as wood. It's swollen, deformed, and still faintly yellow. Any wrist movement at all makes me jump. Doc Wasser is concerned that it might not be healing properly. My first second opinion recommends another surgery, a radical procedure that involves slicing me open from little finger to elbow, sawing off bones, drilling holes—a surgeon's wet dream. My second second opinion thinks that advice unwise and pronounces that I can expect eighty to ninety percent recovery of mobility and strength, plus arthritis. Translation: permanent disability. Given that my physical life is not only my passion but also essential to my livelihood, this doesn't exactly set my one hand to clapping. My third second opinion comes from a hand surgeon who also happens to be an accomplished climber and kayaker:

"No surgery and no predictions," he tells me. "Mark, do your rehab like your life depends on it. Expect recovery to take six to twelve months."

I know the drill, and it's going to hurt. Rehabilitation, conducted with monklike discipline, is the only way to get back to doing what you did to get hurt in the first place.

I already have every wrist rehabilitator ever made: two sets of grips, two finger grips, rubber webs, a set of small weights, a climber's rubber squeeze ball, a golfer's twistable grip stick. They are strewn around the house—in the office, in the bathroom, in the bedroom, in the kitchen.

My physical therapist says, "Compliance is usually the problem. It hurts so patients don't do it. You have the opposite problem." She tells me to only do one session a day. I do my best to keep it down to three.

I use the whirlpool at the gym every other day. I hold my injured appendage under the surging hot water and slowly twist, rotate, and spell the alphabet. It is not tedious; it's therapy. Another chance to calm down, take time, breathe.

Some days my wrist appears to be improving and I am exuberant. I see myself in the future: rock climbing again, jamming big, strong hands into wide cracks, swinging ice tools into frozen waterfalls, pushing my girls on the tree swing, hugging my wife. Some days I know I've overtrained and must stop exercising, and doubts about my recovery emerge from the shadows like boxers I can't possibly beat with just one hand.

These are the emotional ups and downs of rehab. I try to accept it. Acceptance—particularly accepting the present just the way it is—is one of the greatest lessons a serious injury can teach. Unfortunately, it will probably take a few more wrecks before I learn it.

My mountaineering partner, John, and I have had to cancel our expedition to Tibet. That's fine—the mountains won't go anywhere. In lieu of Tibet, he's invited me to do the Eiger later this year, slyly giving me a rehab goal.

Pat has gotten me over to the indoor climbing wall. I can barely hang on, of course, so we work the wall for only half an hour. Then we do hundreds of situps, preparing for a summer climbing project that will require repeatedly hanging upside down.

During the first month after the surgery, my neighbor Reed took me out walking almost every day. We do this whenever one of us is injured. A fast clip for an hour or two to get the blood pumping. We talk about everything under the sky.

Over the winter we skate skied together in the Medicine Bow Mountains, without poles. We'll keep doing that right through May here in Wyoming. I may have twigs for arms, but I'll have Apolo Ohno thighs.

Sue is running stadium stairs with me. She talks, I try to keep up.

And I'm back to bicycling to school with Teal and Addi. Simply riding beside them is a rediscovered joy.

They say it's the circulating blood that causes the healing, but I believe it's the circulating love.

Vanishing

IN DENIAL

We'd heard rumors that the Alps were decomposing, but we ignored them. Europeans can be so querulous, so theatrical, waving their arms as if the sky were falling. John Harlin III and I had been planning this trip for half a dozen years, and we weren't about to change our minds.

Any mountaineer worth his weight in crampons eventually visits the Alps. It is the climber's hajj—a pilgrimage to the birthplace of the sport. But for John, this particular journey meant considerably more.

John's father, John Elvis Harlin II, died on the north face of the Eiger in March 1966 when his rope snapped and he fell 3,750 feet. He was thirty, and John was ten. Harlin II is still remembered in Switzerland for his California charm and his many bold first ascents. Not surprisingly, the north face of the 13,025-foot Eiger has long haunted Harlin III, an accomplished climber and the editor of the *American Alpine Journal*.

After many other trips together, we'd finally come to climb the macabre Mordwand, or Death Wall (a play on Nordwand, as the Eiger's north face is called). It would be a first for both of us. But we were too late.

"The Eiger has changed completely," Nicho Mailänder told us upon our arrival in Geneva. A peerless climbing historian, Mailänder is one of the authors of the Tyrol Declaration, a pioneering manifesto on mountaineering ethics and environmental responsibility that was adopted by the Union Internationale des Associations d'Alpinisme in 2002. "It is not the mountain it used to be. To climb it this summer would be very, very dangerous.

"The Eiger per se no longer exists," he continued. "There used to be three main icefields on the Eiger. Over the last five years, they have all but vanished. In their place are slick, fifty-degree limestone slopes covered in rubble. Rubble which tends to slide off. Who wants to climb rubble? No. I'm sorry, but nowadays, the Eiger can only be safely climbed in winter."

Given that more than forty-five climbers have died on the Eiger, "safely" is a relative term. So much for the Eiger. It was almost a relief.

John and I went directly to plan B: a new route on the Fréney Face of Mont Blanc. Rising to 15,771 feet and straddling France and Italy, Mont Blanc is the highest peak in the Alps, and the Fréney Face is its most difficult wall. Free of the shadow of John's personal tragedy, however, it seemed to us a comparatively easy alternative.

But when we got there, the news was the same. *"C'est suicide!"* announced the French caretaker of the Franco Monzino hut, a fortress-like hostel on the Italian side of the mountain. *"Mont Blanc est ruiné."*

The crevasses were hanging open like the mouths of a thousand dragons. The summit snowfields were running with water and setting off torrents of stone. Couloirs that alpinists had used to reach the massif's climbing routes for generations had melted out.

With balmy obstinancy, John and I decided to go up and have a look for ourselves. Despite a foul-weather forecast, we departed the Monzino lodgings laden with more than a week's worth of food and fuel, a complete wall rack of climbing gear, and Jacques Barzun's 900-page history *From Dawn to Decadence: 500 Years of Western Cultural Life, 1500 to the Present.* We hated our heavy packs within the first five minutes.

Throughout the day, scrambling vigilantly toward the Eccles hut, we heard rockslides thundering all around us. Ice and snow had been the glue that held the crumbling layers of rock to the substrata. Without it, every hand- and foothold was appallingly loose, balanced at the angle of repose. Pull out or nudge off one rock and thousands of tons of jagged blocks could begin slipping downward like a calamitous escalator.

Still, we kept climbing. Denial is a powerful thing.

• • •

In Europe, the summer of 2004 was the hottest in recorded history. New highs were set north to south, east to west. In England—where people are accustomed to wearing tweeds in July—the mercury shot above 100°F for the first time ever. In Switzerland, the temperature spiked at a Saharan 107°F. From the Netherlands south to Italy, at least 35,000 people, many of them elderly, perished from dehydration and heatstroke. France, which was hit the hardest, attributed some 15,000 deaths to the six-week heat wave. More than 500,000 acres of forest went up in flames in Portugal, 75,000 acres in Spain.

In the Alps, several massive rock towers collapsed on the 14,691-foot Matterhorn in mid-July, stranding some seventy climbers and temporarily closing the mountain. In early August, a series of enormous rockslides swept down the usually climbable west face of 12,237-foot Le Petit Dru, knocking out a chunk of the legendary Bonatti Pillar. By mid-August, the three customarily safe snow marches up the Mont Blanc massif had become death traps: the Grands Mulets route was threatened by collapsing ice cliffs, the Traverse route menaced by a labyrinth of yawning crevasses, and the Goûter route plagued by rockfall. After two hikers were killed by falling rock below the Goûter route in mid-August, alpine guides stopped taking any bookings for Mont Blanc, effectively shutting down the peak for the first time in its 217-year climbing history.

Mont Blanc is the indisputable geological father of mountaineering. In 1760, Professor Horace-Bénédict de Saussure of Geneva offered a reward of twenty gold talers for its first ascent. The prospect of climbing this behemoth of groaning glaciers was so intimidating that no one took him up on the offer for fifteen years. It would require ten more years and ten attempts before Frenchmen Michel-Gabriel Paccard and Jacques Balmat reached the summit on August 8, 1786. They had neither crampons nor rope, and they bivouacked in the snow wrapped in wool blankets.

The first woman to summit Mont Blanc was Marie Paradis, from Chamonix, in 1808. The world's first recorded climbing catastrophe occurred on the mountain in 1820, when an avalanche swept five guides into a crevasse, killing three. Ascents of all the satellite summits—Grandes Jorasses, Les Droites, Petit Dru, Aiguille Du Grépon—were accomplished before the turn of the twentieth century; the innumerable difficult routes were put up on these same spires during the last century.

Today, the vast, intricately incised Mont Blanc massif remains an icon of mountaineering.

As long as there's snow.

• • •

Following a snug night in the Eccles hut, John and I scampered up the slag heap of steep talus to a knobby pinnacle called Punta Eccles. The entire southeastern side of Mont Blanc, in all its intimidating splendor, rose before us. To the left was the Brouillard Face and to the right, the Fréney Face; the two are separated by the jagged Innominata Ridge.

Rivers of stone were cascading down the Brouillard Face, but the Fréney Face appeared pacific. Then the sun pulled itself above the morning haze and, minutes later, rockslides began ricocheting down between the Fréney's four main rock pillars. The top of Mont Blanc seemed to have been hit with a mortar. Stones came rumbling down the face—one the size of a Volkswagen van, bouncing like a rubber ball.

The roar diminished. "Guess that clinches that," John said.

As the hut keeper had predicted, fusillades of rockfall made climbing the Fréney Face out of the question. Desperate, we began glassing the Innominata Ridge, directly above us, our eyes drawn to a red granite pillar split by a gorgeous dihedral.

"It's never been climbed!" I enthused. This I knew from a visit to the Office de Haute Montagne, in Chamonix, a constantly updated library of Mont Blanc climbing routes.

"Might be because of that ten-foot icicle dangling from the first overhang," John replied.

Two hours later we were at the base of the pillar.

"I wouldn't waste time when you're directly below the icicle," John remarked, his way of saying that if it broke off at the wrong time, I might be cleaved in two.

After sixty feet, I was below the icicle, fist jamming in the overhang right beside it, when the back of my shoulder accidentally glanced against the monster tooth and the whole thing let loose.

Miraculously, all the head-crushing junk missed John.

"Good work!" he bellowed.

In less than two hours we were standing atop the 200-foot pillar, talking big about our new route.

It was late, 4:30 p.m. There were only two easy chevals and two shorter pillars above us, and then our first ascent of the Super Directissima—as we had modestly named it—would be complete. But heavy clouds and buffeting winds were rolling in; the foretold winter weather was arriving right on schedule. If we continued, we'd have to rappel down—or, worse, bivy high—in the snowstorm.

John had a different idea: "Leave most of our rock gear up here, snow blows through, then we come back up and knock this baby out."

It seemed to make perfect sense, so we bailed. All the way back down to the Eccles hut.

We shouldn't have. We had just snatched defeat from the jaws of victory.

• • •

"The world's climate is getting warmer," professor Andreas Kääb, a glaciologist at the University of Zurich's World Glacier Monitoring Service, tells me. "There has been a one- to two-degree-centigrade increase in the past century, and much of this occurred in the past fifty years."

What's a couple degrees? Plenty. It turns out the alpine glaciers in Europe and the Himalayas, as well as most of them in North and South America, are "temperate"—the ice hovers right at freezing—and therefore extremely sensitive to changes in temperature. The air warms just a degree or two and it's like moving an ice cube from the freezer to the fridge: It'll melt—slowly but surely.

"Glaciers in the Alps are receding at unprecedented rates," says Kääb, his office walls papered with grainy satellite images of the world's glaciers. "We have also documented dramatic downwasting"—a shrinking of ice thickness—"of the large glaciers. At the present rate of global warming, it is probable that all the small glaciers in the Alps will disappear entirely in the next one hundred years."

Within twenty years, he predicts, the Alps' few remaining summer ski areas will likely close, as will many low-elevation winter ski areas. Only the upper reaches of the larger winter ski areas will have dependable natural snow, and lodges and lifts built on present-day permafrost will begin to collapse. Warmer temperatures are also the most salient reason for increased rockfall in the mountains.

"Formerly, the ice in the joints held these immense slabs of rock in place," explains Kääb. "Now that the ice is melting, rockslides are inevitable."

Therefore, climbing routes and their approaches will continue to change, rendering older guidebooks frustratingly inadequate at best, dangerously inaccurate at worst.

Meltwater will obviously increase, swelling rivers and temporarily generating abundant hydropower. The permafrost line will rise, unleashing ice avalanches and landslides. Glacial lakes—water where there used to be ice, held in place only by loose terminal moraines—will burst their tenuous natural dams and flood the valleys below. Dozens of towns and cities in Europe lie in the line of fire.

"The Alps as we know them," Kääb says, "are disintegrating before our eyes."

· · ·

As if to convince us otherwise, the storm clamped down on Mont Blanc that night. By morning the incessant thunder of rockslides had stopped. A small drop in air temperature, a fresh coat of snow, and the mountain suddenly went silent. When we cracked open the troll-size door of the Eccles hut, brilliant white light and snowflakes sprayed into the room. Back to bed.

The next morning, ditto.

The morning after that, ditto.

So much snow had fallen that going up or down would have been tricky. But we were safe in our tiny cliff dwelling, and happy (John) or claustrophobic (me), as the case may be.

John began reading aloud the best bons mots from Barzun's *From Dawn to Decadence*:

"Dessert without cheese is like a pretty girl with only one eye."

"We cannot be wrong, because we have studied the past and we are famous for discovering the future when it has taken place."

While the snowstorm railed, Barzun revealed to us through numerous examples how persistently and valiantly humankind has been grappling with the tough issues—equality, poverty, liberty, and justice—and how discouragingly slow we have been to devise and implement solutions.

The storm broke late on the fourth day. John and I plowed up through one to two feet of fresh, wet, surprisingly stable snow to Punta Eccles to determine the possibilities of completing the Super Directissima.

"Doesn't look that bad," I said.

"No, it really doesn't," replied John.

Somehow, patently ignoring the obvious, we still believed things had not changed enough to warrant a change of plans.

• • •

If the Alps are transmogrifying so radically, what about the other mountain ranges of the world?

An August 2001 United Nations report cited "a rapid retreat of nearly all glaciers" in the Himalayas and the Karakoram from 1860 to 1980. A UN team dispatched to Nepal's Everest region found that compared with fifty years ago, when the peak was first climbed, the area is now "unrecognizable as ice has retreated up the mountain." The glacier that was once at the foot of nearby Island Peak is now a mile-long, 330-foot-deep lake that is imperiling villages downstream—just one of the twenty new glacial lakes in Nepal that the UN identifies as being "in danger of burst-ing its banks."

In Africa, Ohio State University geologist Lonnie Thompson has found that thirty-three percent of the ice on Mount Kilimanjaro has dis-appeared since 1980, eighty-two percent since 1912; last January, a chunk of the mountain's Furtwängler Glacier dislodged and rained down on the summit crater. Mount Kenya's famous Diamond Couloir ice route, put up in 1977 by Yvon Chouinard and Mike Covington, is now nothing but an ugly rock gully.

In the Snowy Mountains of Australia, the tree line has jumped one hundred feet, after 300 to 500 years of stasis. John Morgan, a botanist at Melbourne's La Trobe University, believes Australia could lose its pre-cious alpine ecosystem entirely within the next seventy years.

In the south-central Peruvian Andes, the Quelccaya ice cap has shrunk by twenty percent since 1963. Eight mountaineers were killed in July 2003 when a giant block of ice near the summit of 19,511-foot Alpamayo broke loose. Thirty-five climbers have died in the Andes in the last five years, almost twice as many as in the previous five-year period—a jump locals attribute to unstable conditions.

Of course, it's not just glaciers and tundra that are feeling the heat. Sea levels have risen four to ten inches in the last hundred years and could rise another two to three feet in the coming century, threatening coastal cit-ies from New York to Shanghai. With rising global temperatures, the mosquito has extended its range, bringing malaria, dengue fever, and West Nile virus to previously unafflicted regions. Other species, such as North America's pika—a rabbitlike mammal deftly adapted to alpine ter-rain—are on the decline: In the February 2003 issue of the *Journal of Mammalogy*, Erik Beever of the US Geological Survey cited a twenty-eight percent reduction in the animal's population across the West between 1898 and 1999, due largely to warmer temperatures.

As for the much-debated cause of global warming, the answers are becoming obvious. Even the United States, one of only fifteen nations that has not ratified the fundamental 1992 Kyoto Protocol, has conceded the predominance of scientific proof. "Greenhouse gases are accumulat-ing in the Earth's atmosphere as a result of human activities, causing global mean surface air temperatures and subsurface ocean temperatures to rise," states the Environmental Protection Agency's 2002 US Climate

Report, which identifies automobile use, oil refining, and electrical power generation as primary offenders. Furthermore, the United States is the worst offender: while we constitute only four percent of the world's population, we contribute twenty-five percent of the planet's greenhouse pollution.

· · ·

John and I were up before our alarm went off and out before we were awake. The steps we'd postholed the night before gave us confidence until we began scratching our way up the granite arête. The rock was thickly glazed with multiple layers of ice and snow. The new route we'd begun five days earlier in the heat wave of summer was now a winter climb. We were forced to use crampons and ice axes to reascend what we had originally climbed with rock shoes and bare hands.

We reached our gear, buried beneath two feet of snow, at dawn, but the sky was black with fresh storm clouds. The consequences of continuing would likely be severe: a cold bivouac, frozen toes, perhaps worse. We had been defying and denying the conditions on Mont Blanc from the start, but such impertinence was no longer tenable.

Sometimes, when you have all the evidence you need, you just have to accept it—and then change course. After ten days of ignoring the obvious, it was time to cut ourselves loose.

"We've got to go down," yelled John through the swirling snow.

So we did.

LAST STAND

I'm crawling on my hands and knees through a labyrinth of limbs when it occurs to me that a hundred years ago, this was the haunt of the Tasmanian tiger. The striped, doglike, carnivorous marsupial would have slipped easily through this crisscrossed deadfall of myrtle, sassafras, and musk. Six feet from nose to tail, two feet high at the shoulders, sixty-five pounds of muscle, it would have crouched motionless beneath the twenty-foot fronds of a tree fern, eyes glued on a doomed wallaby. The Tasmanian tiger was cunning and shy and had astounding stamina, often pursuing its prey until the quarry was exhausted.

I'm hunting, too. I've come to the inconceivably dense north slope of the Styx River Valley, in the heart of the heart-shaped island of Tasmania, to find the tallest hardwood tree in the world, the *Eucalyptus regnans*, or swamp gum. The mightiest swamp gum so far discovered is 321 feet tall, just shy of the California redwoods, which top out at about 375 feet.

"We'll have to take off our packs to go any further," says Matt Dalziel, my fleet-footed Aussie partner. It's the first day of our four-day trek through the valley and already the undergrowth is so thick we can barely squeeze through. Matt disappears into the sylvan maze.

We're not on a trail. There is no trail. Beyond the thicket we come upon what we've taken to calling a *gangplank*—a downed tree so enormous it creates an elevated walkway through the forest. We clamber atop the behemoth and step carefully along its moss-slick back.

"Check 'er out, mate," exclaims Matt, pointing to a tree exploding into the sky. "Now that's a rippah!" Finding a tree of such magnificent proportions is like catching sight of a dinosaur—a primordial creature that somehow survived here at the edge of the earth. At the end of the gangplank we jump back down into the ocean of verdure; waves of foliage close over our heads as we half walk, half swim toward the giant.

"Who knows what you'll find out there!" Geoff Law, campaign coordinator for Tasmania's Wilderness Society, had exclaimed as he spread out

119

the maps in his Hobart office three days earlier. Law, forty-seven, a dogged, inexhaustible environmentalist, has been fighting full-time for twenty years to protect Tasmania's wildlands. In the process, he's hiked more of the Styx than anyone. "To my knowledge, no human has actually done what you intend to do: cross end-to-end through one of the last contiguous stands of giant old-growth *E. regnans*." His voice caught. "Now's the time to go: It could soon be gone forever."

When I find Matt, he's standing beside a finlike buttress root taller than he is. It would take six people holding hands to encircle the base of the trunk. I crane my head back and stare. The mammoth, ancient tree, the tallest flowering plant alive, shoots up and up and up, disappearing into the sky like Jack's beanstalk.

• • •

Tasmania, the smallest of Australia's seven states, lies 150 miles south of Melbourne across the Bass Strait. Aboriginals had lived on the West Virginia–size island for 20,000 years before Dutch seafarer Abel Tasman arrived in 1642. Like the rest of Australia, Tasmania was first settled by British convicts. In 1803 a penal colony was established on the southeast coast near present-day Hobart and within one lifetime all full-blooded aboriginals were extinct.

Tasmania's economy was originally based on sheep ranching, agriculture, and extractive industries like mining and logging. But this frontier mentality was openly challenged in 1979 when the Labor-led state government announced plans to dam the Franklin River, one of the island's last large, free-flowing rivers. This galvanized a small cadre of proto-environmentalists, who in 1976 formed the Wilderness Society, Australia's first high-profile environmental organization. In 1981 their Franklin River Campaign stopped the dam project, a watershed victory for Australia's nascent environmental movement. In 1983 the Franklin River, along with several other wilderness areas in Tasmania, was listed as a World Heritage site by the United Nations. Through one battle after another over the next two decades, the Wilderness Society secured environmental protection for almost twenty-five percent of the island.

One-tenth of the Styx catchment became part of a national park, but the rest was left in the hands of Forestry Tasmania, a for-profit state corporation charged with managing all of Tasmania's forests outside the parks and World Heritage regions. Many of the tallest hardwood trees on earth, 400-year-old *E. regnans*, lie in the Styx Valley of the Giants, a proposed national park composed largely of an unprotected section of the middle Styx Valley. Roughly one-third of the entire Styx Valley has already been clear-cut.

"It's goddamned heartbreaking," said Richard Flanagan, internationally acclaimed novelist, author of *Death of a River Guide* (1994), *The Sound of One Hand Clapping* (1997), *Gould's Book of Fish* (2001), and *The Unknown Terrorist* (2007). "To be here, and from here, and watch your own country being systematically destroyed. The soul of the land sold for nothing, clearfelled, napalmed, poisoned."

Flanagan lowered his close-shaved, bouldery head, studied me with unwavering eyes, then took a swallow from his pint. It was my first night on the island, and I'd gone to Knobwood's, a notorious harbor pub in old Hobart, where Flanagan and his pals—all accomplished kayakers—hang out. He introduced me to his friends: Matt Newton, landscape photographer; Craig "Swarz" Chivers, fireman; and Matt Dalziel, four-time Australian Wildwater kayaking champ and marketing director for Sea to Summit, an Australian outdoor-equipment company.

On this island drenched by storms and surrounded by seas, all of these men had done first descents or first crossings: when Flanagan was sixteen, he became the first to kayak the twenty-five-mile class III to IV Styx River. They know water and weather, tides and trees—and politics. It was here, in 1972, that the world's first political Green party was formed. Bush walkers and boaters, environmentalists and literati coalesced into a single, vocal force. In the last state election, some 51,000 Tasmanians—eighteen percent of the island's population—voted Green. Forestry, fishing, farming, and mining today represent just seven percent of the economy; tourism now employs twice as many people as logging. Tasmania is poised to become the next New Zealand, luring adventure travelers to its rugged shores and giant trees—if they're left standing.

"Industrial logging is ugly business," Flanagan continued. "Tasmania's natural heritage—our last giants that exist nowhere else on earth—are logged and sold to Japan as wood chips. It's obscene. People are wiping their asses with paper made from Tasmania's 400-year-old trees."

Flanagan is known as an outspoken advocate for Tasmania's wildlands. In December 2003, the Australian magazine *The Bulletin* published his lengthy exposé "The Rape of Tasmania," which carefully documented fifteen years of corrupt connections between big forestry and big government in Tasmania. Although vilified by Tasmanian politicians, Flanagan went on to publish two international articles on the subject in 2004, one in the *Guardian*, the other in the *New York Times Magazine*. With the help of Flanagan's campaign and thousands of volunteers, the Wilderness Society made saving Tasmania's old-growth forests a major issue in Australia's 2004 elections. Prime Minister John Howard declared that, if reelected, he would protect an additional 425,000 acres of Tasmania's forests; Howard's conservative-coalition administration has yet to make good on this promise.

Flanagan hunched his thick shoulders and looked at me hard. "But the only way you'll really understand what's going on is to go out there and have a look for yourself."

It was my shout. When I brought back a round of pints, Dalziel, thirty-four, the smallest and quietest of the men, with high cheekbones, a strong nose and penetrating blue eyes, offered to go with me.

"I could use the exercise," he said, and the table cracked up.

Two days earlier, Dalziel—a classical scholar and father of a baby son—had won the Cradle to Coast Ultra Challenge, a fifty-three-mile mountain race that takes hikers four days to complete. As Tasmania's mountain-running champion, he'd run it in eight hours, twenty minutes. Ten days from now, he planned to run the length of the Western Arthurs, another fifty-mile mountain run.

"A wee bit of bush bashing is just what I need," Dalziel said.

"Bush bashing?" I'd never heard the term.

"Tasmanian specialty," he replied.

I've hiked all over the world—from the slide alder thickets of British Columbia to the bamboo jungles of Burma to the rainforests of West Africa—but I had no idea what I was in for.

•   •   •

Balancing on my belly like an uncoordinated opossum atop a trapeze of branches ten feet above the ground, my pack suddenly slips over my head and I plunge forward. In midfall, my ankles miraculously hook between the slingshot-shaped crook of a leatherwood limb. I swing upside down for a few seconds, snared, before the bough breaks and I drop onto my head.

Success! I have circumvented a nasty patch of stinging nettles. I get to my feet and continue pushing through the fray.

This 10,000-year-old woodland is nothing like a typical rainforest with a lush, sunlight-blocking canopy, luxuriant understory, and a permanently shaded, relatively open forest floor. Here the dominant trees, mature *E. regnans*, stand fifty yards apart and rise as smooth and straight and pale as the Washington Monument. The forest floor receives abundant sunshine and rain and thus supports a healthy plant community, including twenty-five-foot-deep briar patches.

"Over here!" Matt shouts. I follow his voice, zigzagging inside a matrix of biodiversity so dense I can never take more than three steps in one direction.

He's standing near the base of another enormous eucalyptus. Beside it, he looks like a Lilliputian leaning on the foot of a one-legged giant: Its buttress roots grip the soil like prehensile toes; its leg, blistered with burls the size of bathtubs, rises twenty stories into the sky before molding into a slim torso. Another ten to fifteen stories higher, small limbs with twisted elbows sprout out.

"A noble creature, eh," yells Matt joyously. "How tall you reckon she is?"

"Taller than Gandalf's Staff."

"Think?"

Matt and I drove into the Styx Valley (only a couple hours from Hobart, the capital) two days ago and spent our first night at the Global Rescue Station, a volunteer eco-commune. In late 2003, determined to stop the destruction of ancient trees, the Wilderness Society and Greenpeace erected a base camp beside a fresh old-growth clear-cut. Choosing Gandalf's Staff, a 279-foot *E. regnans* as their mascot, they suspended three platforms from the tree, 200 feet above the ground. For five months, volunteers living in these precarious nests beamed out SOS messages via satellite, an act of courage that eventually saved Gandalf's Staff from chainsaws.

A dozen volunteers were at base camp the night we arrived: Bell-bottomed Japanese college escapees, dreadlocked Aussies, gorgeous granola girls with nose rings. Penniless but passionate, they were clearing foliage and building trails to the colossal trees.

"The forest is so dodgy and dense and slick, we're putting in tracks to give ordinary people a chance to get close to the big trees," said camp coordinator Peter "Peck" Firth, twenty, a blond-ponytailed grape grower from Western Australia who's been working in the Styx for fourteen months, without pay, to save what's left. "We want people to come here and feel their beauty and presence and sacredness. When you've been in this forest and stood beside these trees, they change you."

What changed me more was the macabre graveyards of the clear-cuts. To reach the start of our bush walk, Peck drove us through an ongoing, apocalyptic clear-cut: Charred logs lay like corpses across a battlefield; blackened stumps sat among funeral pyres of unmarketable trees.

Clear-cut logging in the Styx Valley is a four-step process. After all trees in a selected area are felled, the straightest and most easily trans-ported are removed. Everything else—millions of board feet of lum-ber—is left as waste. Eucalyptus seedlings require fire for regeneration, so logging contractors spray jellied petroleum (also known as napalm) from the air, igniting the debris and creating plumes of air pollution. Next, the area is sown with *E. regnans* and other native hardwood seeds and any animals—wallabies, kangaroos, wombats, opossums, bandi-coots, sugar gliders, quolls—that might eat the seedlings are fenced out, trapped, or shot. (Until recently, the despicable practice of scattering poisoned carrots was used to kill animals.) This new tree farm is regu-larly sprayed with herbicides and pesticides (poisoning streams with atra-zine) and harvested after eighty years, two centuries before the trees reach maturity.

• • •

Matt and I had started our bush walk in another clear-cut, this one beside Diogenes Creek, a small tributary of the Styx. Diogenes was a fourth-century-BC Greek cynic who eschewed material wealth and rejected government, reputation, and convention, focusing instead on moral self-mastery. He was nicknamed the Dog by Aristotle and is said to have walked in vain across Greece searching for an honest man.

We spent that first day picking our way through an unspoiled swath of forest on the north side of the Styx. At natural openings we could see cadaverous clear-cuts across the river. We made five miles in seven hours before deciding to camp. The forest floor was far too overgrown for a tent, so we waded out to a rocky island in the middle of the Styx and pitched up there. South of the river it was all clear-cuts, and northward were the last stands of old-growth eucalyptus. In Greek mythology, the River Styx is the boundary that separates the land of the living from the land of the dead.

In the morning, we continued our tour of the wildest forest I'd ever explored. We climbed as often as we walked. It was a literal jungle gym. At one point, while pulling himself up onto a ten-foot thick gangplank, Matt looked over his shoulder and proudly said, "Now this is true bush! It's not made for man."

Often the going was so slow that we covered less than 500 yards an hour. But we were among the titans, and that was all that mattered. We had no way of measuring the trees, but we guessed that some of them were larger than anything yet discovered in Tasmania.

"They're the whales of the forest," said Matt. "Cutting them down is like whaling. It's the same mentality."

By the morning of the third day we'd passed back into the land of clear-cuts.

• • •

"Let me first say that there are no plans to clear-fell any more of the north side of the Styx," Steve Whiteley, a district manager for Forestry Tasmania, tells me in their offices a week after our hike.

"We're also not going to clear-fell where the Wilderness Society set up its Global Rescue Station," Whiteley said.

(This is news to the Wilderness Society. When I relay it to Geoff Law later that day, he leaps up and gives me a hug. "They've never said that before!" It's a small victory for the activists, but no guarantee for the rest of the Styx Valley.)

"But we will keep harvesting approximately 300 hectares [740 acres] of forest from the Styx per year," Whiteley continues. "The Tasmanian parliament has set a quota of 300,000 cubic meters of quality eucalypt sawlogs and veneer for Tasmania. Our approach is to have a relatively small level of activity over a larger area. The last thing we want to do is to put undue pressure on any particular area."

At this rate of harvesting, essentially all of the Styx giant trees, the largest on earth, will be gone in fifteen years. (In the United States, ninety-six percent of all redwood forests are now gone.)

According to Whiteley, Forestry Tasmania is trying to balance industry needs with conservation. Consequently, it has decided that any tree more than 279 feet tall will be spared. Yet a survey published in the December 2000 issue of *Tasforests* found that the vast majority of Tasmania's giants have a height just below this figure.

So what percentage of harvested old-growth forest is turned into sawlogs?

"Twenty percent," says Whiteley. "The rest is just residue and is wood chipped."

Weeks after the interview, after considerable Diogenes-like searching, I learn three profound facts. First, in 2003 to 2004, Forestry Tasmania harvested 357,088 cubic meters of quality eucalypt sawlogs and veneer, twenty percent above the mandated quota. Second, the Styx provided only 27,862 cubic meters of this wood, so if the quota was exceeded, why was the Styx logged at all?! Finally, the quota itself was set in 1920, and the logging industry has managed to keep it unchanged for eighty-five years.

Back in 1920, the Tasmanian tiger was still alive.

• • •

On the last day of our bush walk, Matt and I decide to climb 4,085-foot Mount Mueller at the head of the Styx Valley. After tramping one depressing logging road after another, we need an overview of the landscape. But as we rise above the clear-cuts, the section of unmolested old-growth that we first passed through looks small and imperiled.

We thrash up to the rocky crest of Mueller and for our effort are rewarded with an expansive view northwest into the Florentine Valley. Like the Styx, only the upper Florentine is still blanketed with old-growth forest; the rest was clear-cut over the last fifty years. But there aren't enough volunteers to erect a global rescue station to let the world know about the majestic singularity of the upper Florentine—and Forestry Tasmania knows this. Like bulldozing the Parthenon to make tract homes with the stones, logging is scheduled to begin on the upper Florentine in 2007.

After an hour on the summit, sitting, watching, wondering, we head back down. Just below the rocks, hidden in a pocket of heath, we discover a small, silvery pool—-the source of the Styx. Matt and I cup our hands and drink from the fountainhead. In Greek mythology, the Styx was said to be poisonous.

I imagine the Tasmanian tiger stopping here en route from one primeval forest valley to the other. Lowering its head to lap up the cool water, it would have seen its own doomed reflection. In 1888 parliament placed a bounty on the Tasmanian tiger, and by 1936 it was extinct.

PAGAN PILGRIMAGE

To propitiate the gods, as soon as we reach camp, Sonam the cook builds a *sang*—a small votive fire of fresh juniper bows sprinkled with buckwheat flour. The smoke purls up like a blue ribbon between the black canyon walls while Sonam says a prayer. Jon Miceler, a tall, bespectacled reed of a man in a conical Asian hat, and I stand in the muddy yak meadow, watching from beneath sodden umbrellas.

It has been raining ceaselessly since we began this trek five days ago. This may be a sign from various tutelary deities that we are unwelcome here.

"No *cheelips* [foreigners] have ever entered this place," says Sonam gravely, perhaps implying that Jon and I, two American interlopers, are distressing the gods that inhabit this Himalayan valley deep in northern Bhutan.

Earlier today, hiking up through a narrow gorge on a trail so heavily overhung with flowering rhododendrons that it was like a secret passageway, we stopped at a *chorten*, a primitive Buddhist shrine. A moss-covered cairn topped with a faded prayer flag tied to a branch, it had been carefully garlanded with flowers by passing nomads. Sonam collected a handful of fuchsia blossoms and placed them at the base as an offering. When I asked him why he'd done this, he shrugged. Later, walking a crooked path carpeted with dark blue rhododendron petals, he whispered that we needed protection as we entered the sanctuary of mountain gods.

The rain douses the *sang*, but our group—Jon and I and seven Bhutanese—is already ensconced inside several nomad huts. They are built of stacked river stones with a roof of wide planks split from a nearby tree. You crawl in through a hole in the rocks. Inside there is a fire pit, and fir boughs are spread over the dirt floor. The leaking roof is so low you have to crouch, and the boughs are infested with fleas. Still, once a fire is crackling, it is a snug shelter.

During the night, the rain stops for the first time in a week. We awake in a different world, almost as if we've passed through a sacred portal. On

128

both sides of the valley, frosted mountains, formerly hidden by curtains of mist, rise sharply into a cold blue sky. Looking northwest, up the valley, we see a sawtoothed ridge of brilliant white. Jon and I scramble along the side slope to get a better view.

The spine, one valley west and still at some distance, is the east ridge of the highest mountain in Bhutan and the highest unclimbed peak on earth—Gangkar Punsum. Its immensity is staggering: 24,836 feet of intimidating, swordlike arêtes. Like one of Bhutan's many animistic gods, Gangkar Punsum has a fierce, even savage, visage. The summit is not some benign hump, but a point of frost blue ice as threatening as the thunderbolt of Chana Dorje, Tibetan Buddhism's wrathful deity of power.

"No wonder it was never climbed," I say.

"And never will be," Jon replies.

Gangkar Punsum lies at the border of Bhutan and Tibet, 300 miles east of Everest. At least four expeditions attempted it in the mid-1980s—the Americans and the Japanese in 1985, the Austrians and the Brits in 1986—and all failed. The American team, which included Rick Ridgeway, Yvon Chouinard, and John Roskelley, never even found the mountain. Then in 1987, following reports from villagers that the gods, furious at this trespassing, were taking revenge by sending crop-flattening hailstorms, Bhutan banned mountaineering across the kingdom. To the Bhutanese, mountains are sacred citadels, no more meant to be climbed than the dome of the Sistine Chapel or the minarets of Mecca.

Jon Miceler and I had come not to poach the peak, but to pioneer a route along its southern flank. Jon is a Buddhist himself. He lived in Chengdu for eight years and has spent almost two years in retreat—in Ladakh, in France, in the Himachal Pradesh. He speaks and reads Chinese and Tibetan and knows more about the colorful, twisted history of the various forms of Himalayan Buddhism than anyone I've ever met.

Jon owns High Asia Exploratory Mountain Travel Company, an outfitter that guides custom expeditions in China, Bhutan, and India. He is also the founder of Inner Asian Conservation, a nongovernmental organization devoted to helping governments develop sustainable methods for handling tourism and trekking in the last pristine places in the eastern Himalayas. His conservation work in Arunachal Pradesh, India, was recently awarded a John D. and Catherine T. MacArthur Foundation grant. Jon had been invited by the government of Bhutan to scout a route to the base of Gangkar Punsum from the southeast; the goal was to determine the feasibility of creating a Himalayan "haute route" that would traverse directly below the peak, perhaps eventually connecting to Bhutan's epic, twenty-five-day Snowman Trek.

We stare at the craggy hulk of Gangkar Punsum until, inevitably, clouds begin to engulf it. First the summit disappears in a suffocating white scarf, then the adamantine shoulders, then the mountain vanishes altogether.

. . .

Bhutan is a mountainous kingdom the size of Switzerland in the heart of the Himalayas. Bordered on three sides by Indian states—Sikkim, Assam, and Arunachal Pradesh—and by Tibet to the north, it remains one of the most inaccessible countries on earth. There is only one airport, in Paro (west of the small capital of Thimphu), served by one airline, Druk Air; and only one contorted highway, sometimes no wider than a bicycle lane, that crosses the country.

Until the 1950s, Bhutan, a nation of only 700,000 souls, existed in self-imposed, self-contained isolation. The Bhutanese bred their own animals and wove their own clothes. Serfdom was not abolished until 1956. There were no roads prior to 1961. The first bank was established in 1968; before that the Bhutanese bartered. Television and the Internet were allowed into the country only in 1999. Archery is the national sport.

The state religion is Mahayana Buddhism, a form tuned to ecological balance. In dramatic contrast to the rest of the Himalayas, almost seventy-five percent of Bhutan is covered with virgin, mixed-tree forests, and roughly twenty-five percent of the nation has been designated an ecological preserve of some kind. Clear-cut logging and hunting are banned; fishing is severely restricted. In 1995 Bhutan's National Assembly passed a resolution declaring that the "country must maintain not less than sixty percent of the Kingdom's total area under forest cover for all times to come." In 1999, almost ten percent of its landmass was officially protected as a system of biological corridors. In sum, Bhutan is the most environmentally progressive country in the world.

This commitment to ecology is matched by a thoughtful concern for human well-being. In the late 1980s, Bhutan's leader, King Jigme Singye Wangchuk, forty-seven—an Aristotle and philosopher-king if there ever was one—declared that "gross national happiness is more important than the gross national product." The gross-national-happiness concept was adopted as government policy and described in a 1999 report as a plan that "cannot be found in the conventional theories of development, but resides in the belief that the key to happiness is to be found, once basic material needs have been met, in the satisfaction of non-material needs and in emotional and spiritual growth."

Although a number of travelers penetrated Bhutan over the past few centuries, including several incorrigible British botanists, official tourism didn't begin until 1974. Fearful of the hippy counterculture that quickly Westernized Nepal, the Bhutanese originally set an annual quota of just 2,000 visitors. Today the government keeps tourist numbers low by pricing excursions into the country well above a shoestring traveler's budget. Foreign visitors pay a minimum of $200 a day for meals, lodging, guides, and transportation ($65 of which goes directly to the government to fund education and health care). Less than 15,000 travelers visit Bhutan each year, most of them on packaged bus tours. Fewer than 1,000 are trekkers, and none are allowed to visit unauthorized places.

Jon managed to obtain our permit because Bhutan's Ministry of Tourism recognizes the popularity of trekking and, in a country where the annual income is only $1,000 and eighty-five percent of the population are still subsistence farmers, also understands the low-impact, high-revenue economics of hinterland travel. That is, as long as it doesn't deleteriously affect the sacred traditions of Bhutan.

· · ·

We start our trek in the central province of Bumthang with nine woolly horses; three old mule skinners with the seamed, sun-burnished faces you can find only in the mountains; three young camp cooks; and our wiry guide named Karchung.

Not one of them has ever been where we want to go—very close to the Tibetan border. Twice we are turned back by the military, the officers scoffing at our government permit. Tensions with China, Bhutan's arch enemy ever since it crushed Bhutan's sister theocracy, Tibet, in 1959, still run high. But Karchung does what a good guide is supposed to do, assess and solve (or circumvent), and we're eventually allowed to continue northward.

After our first glimpse of Gangkar Punsum, we hike to the head of the valley, setting up tents in freezing sleet at 15,000 feet. It is a barren place.

Gray rocks rise into clouds on both sides of us; the dirty snout of a glacier can be seen up-valley. Only to the south is there the welcoming green of life.

This high and deep into the mountains, our team has become tremulous and agitated. Karchung has blistered feet and insomnia and can't eat. The cooks all have altitude headaches and brooding malaise. Jon and I have such impressive cases of dysentery we've each lost ten pounds. Even the packhorses are mutinous.

To our Bhutanese companions, these are clear warning signs. Centuries ago, Buddhism in Bhutan became inextricably entwined with indigenous animism. Humans have lived here for more than 4,000 years, so the cosmology of Bhutan is populated with more temperamental deities than Italy has saints or ancient Greece had mercurial gods. There are specific spirits who inhabit rivers, lakes, and marshes (Lu, Dued, and Tsomen); a deity who inhabits ridges, glaciers, meadows, and forests (Nyen); a deity that dwells on mountain passes (Zhidag); one who lives like a snow leopard in the cliffs (Tsankhang); and the particularly dangerous gods who abide in the white mountains (collectively called Lha). These divinities are almost all fearsome and vengeful, riding tigers or horses or yaks or snakes, and armed to the teeth with thunderbolts, tridents, sickles, and swords.

According to sacred scripture, most of these maleficent gods were subdued by early Buddhist saints, including Guru Rinpoche, founder of Tibetan Buddhism. However, a few of these native divinities remain powerful enough to menace humans, particularly the gods who dwell in the mountains. According to ethnologist Christian Schicklgruber, coeditor of *Bhutan: Mountain Fortress of the Gods*, "For the peasant population the protection of the mountain gods presents the most important underpinning of daily life. As long as they receive proper veneration and offerings, these deities guarantee fruitfulness and protection against the powers of evil and natural calamities. But should someone disturb their peace or the requisite offerings fail to appear, they may threaten the livelihood, and even the lives of their believers."

After a long night, Jon and I have a palaver with Karchung. He informs us that everyone wants to pack up and head down.

Jon is incensed. "We've only just begun!"

We pressure Karchung to allow us to continue on alone. Foreigners are not allowed to move unaccompanied, so Sonam the cook and his assistant are reluctantly pressed into service.

At noon the four of us shoulder heavy rucksacks, abandon our bedeviled entourage, and set off. We cross a swirling glacier-fed river and zigzag for hours up rock shelves. At 16,500 feet we reach a tundralike basin and are surprised to find several abandoned yak herder's cabins—the roofs half blown away, snowdrifts inside. The young cooks burrow desperately into one hut, Jon and I camp inside another.

We spend the next few days tramping through deep moats of snow amidst gorgeous castles of rock and ice searching for a pass that cuts west over to the Mangdi Chu valley, the main drainage of Gangkar Punsum. The two cooks dutifully trudge along behind us, scared to death of this savage landscape. The effort exhausts us all, but is rewarded. High above frozen blue tarns, Jon and I find a breach in the cirque.

"Can it be crossed?" Jon shouts, almost invisible in a flurry of biting snowflakes, "and where do you go from there?"

"We'll find out tomorrow," I yell back.

The next morning, following a night of Cheyne Stoking—the medical term for when the body, already starved for oxygen, absurdly stops breathing—I'm so excited I blow a fire to life at 4:00 a.m. I stay in my bag, writing, graupel hissing through the walls. When Jon wakes I melt snow and we have yak butter tea.

Sitting cross-legged inside his bag, Jon holds his cup with both hands as if he is meditating. Firelight glances off him like the statue of an emaciated bodhisattva. His fingers are skeletal and his cheekbones protrude. He is too sick to go on.

Because I cannot go alone, Sonam is drafted. Outside the stone huts, standing in the desolate cold, Sonam says good-bye to the other cook as if he is marching off to war. I take the 1:200,000 Russian topographical maps and Jon lends me his GPS. I have one week to complete the tramontane reconnaissance of Gangkar Punsum and find my way back to civilization.

"*Tashi delek*," says Jon, wishing me good luck in Tibetan.

Jon and the assistant cook head down, Sonam and I head up. We will not meet again until we're all back in Thimphu.

• • •

Late that day, at 17,300 feet, Sonam and I cross a cleft between colossal walls of ice-sheeted rock. We find an ancient cairn but, ominously, no prayer flags flapping out prayers for us. The shrunken carcass of a blue sheep lies in the rocks.

From the pass, I see one black, jagged ridgeline after another. Rows of them, like the teeth of a shark.

"That's where we're going, Sonam," I say.

"No, Mr. Mark, sir. I not go."

"Why not?"

Sonam's back hurts and his head hurts and his feet hurt, and this is all because we are penetrating the domain of the gods.

"I am kook," says Sonam dolorously, "not mountain man."

I assure Sonam that I'll look after him. He smiles faintheartedly and we carry on.

It begins to snow. We laboriously jump talus all the way into the Mangdi Chu valley, where Sonam spots, from a thousand feet above, a collapsed stone hut at the end of a spatulate lateral moraine. We arrive just before dark, spread our tent over the windward wall, build a fire inside, and watch it snow from our sleeping bags.

Once again, the sky clears during the night. In the morning it is so bright I can scarcely open my eyes. I fumble for my sunglasses. Four inches of snow have fallen, and the majesty of Gangkar Punsum is peering down on us. Sonam slits one eye and instantly crimps it shut.

We don't see the same thing. The immense white face of Gangkar Punsum is merely a mountain to me, a beautiful, inanimate object composed of stone and snow, created by the Indian tectonic plate slamming into the Eurasian plate and governed by the largely predictable rules of science. Sonam sees a living being with capricious supernatural powers. The snow is a bad omen, he says. Gangkar Punsum is angry. "We must leave at once! Go down!"

A heathen mountaineer, I go up, in search of the pass that will connect our new route with the Snowman Trek. Sonam stays by the fire. He says he will build a *sang* and pray for me and wait for my return, if I return.

• • •

Some days in the mountains are so transcendent that you feel you are the luckiest human alive. Inexplicably, after everything, you're in the exact right place at the exact right time. The very air resonates with your good fortune. That is the kind of day I have. Just the snow, the mountain, and me.

Alone, free from the fearful burden of the faithful, I feel myself slip back into my natural, easygoing relationship with the world. Oh, what magnificent, swashbuckling liberty there is in agnosticism. A warm emancipatory joy wells up inside me. Unbound from ancient strictures, my heart is free to revel in the magical aesthetic of the material, physical world.

I trot along the right lateral moraine for several miles. At the glacier, I put on crampons, wield my ice axe, and push straight up the middle. I am below the névé line, so all the crevasses are obvious and easy to jump. In the center of the glacier I enter a maze of slot canyons made of pale blue ice. I navigate through sculpted corridors, leap silver streams, and sidestep moulins all the way to the base of Gangkar Punsum, where I shot a whole roll of film of the ice-armored peak.

From there I turn westward and travel up a spur glacier for hours. Eventually, I find what I am looking for: a pass at 18,000 feet that cuts west between two sharp summits on the left shoulder of Gangkar Punsum. Mission accomplished. I am jubilant, and then instantly, profoundly fatigued.

I sit down. I put an X on the Russian topo, take a GPS reading, take a bearing on the forbidden pass—all by rote. I eat and drink and try to regain my strength, but I feel unbelievably weak. I stare dumbly at my watch. It is late afternoon. I look up at Gangkar Punsum, noting nonchalantly that it is once again being swallowed by clouds. I am so exhausted that my mind is drifting. In a split second of clarity, I realize I am in trouble. I force myself to stand up and start moving.

Going back down, I stay off the glacier, stumbling along the left moraine, often catching myself with my arms just before slamming into glacial erratics. I try to will my body to do the right thing, but it is spent. I try focusing my mind, but it feels loose and floppy. I hope to stay ahead of the snowstorm, but it laughingly catches up and pisses all over me. I hope to outpace dusk, but it, too, easily catches me, throwing a dark cape over my head.

At some point I realize I have gone too far south and will have to cross the roaring Mangdi Chu river to reach camp. I struggle over the slick boulders along the bank in snowy twilight, searching for a place to ford.

Impatient and dull-witted, I mindlessly plunge in, thinking the water will be thigh deep. When it churns up to my waist, the cold slicing straight to the bone, I can barely keep my balance. Just before reaching the far bank, I step in a hole and the solid, frigid water rushes up to my chest and sweeps me off my feet.

I am abruptly lucid, the fog of fatigue and sickness stripped away by the power and paralyzing cold of the water. I think about how arrogant and presumptuous I was to have insisted on pushing into these holy mountains. I think about how stupid it would be to drown. Most of all, I feel the deep stab of fear, the conviction that the river is intentionally trying to kill me.

Then my flailing, outstretched fingers grasp an overhanging clump of ice-crusted willows and I barely haul myself out of the river.

I know I am mortally hypothermic. My hands and feet are numb and my clothes are swiftly hardening into a cast of ice. I hike furiously, but it is pitch dark and snowing heavily. I am lost and everything is icy and I keep slipping and falling. I can feel the presence of the mountain. It feels alive and malevolent, out to get me.

Until I see Sonam's fire.

• • •

Sonam and I eventually make it out. We take game trails along sheer gorges and cross snowy passes, once actually following the footprints of a snow leopard to find our way out of a blizzard. In spite of several more close calls—or perhaps because of them—the chance to find Gangkar Punsum's hidden pass is a dream expedition for me.

Because the Bhutanese have held fast to their ancient form of Buddhism, which enshrines the spirituality of nature, Bhutan is what Nepal must have been like before the rapaciousness of capitalism, what eastern Tibet must have been like before the rapaciousness of communism. With no hyperbole, the kingdom of Bhutan is the most beautiful country in the world.

I tell Sonam this when we are back in Thimphu. He agrees, but tells me he will never go into the mountains again. We were trespassing, he says, and it was only through the mercy of the gods that we survived. He is quite happy to stay in town. He wants to open a cybercafé or a pizza joint.

MAROONED

"They escaped into the jungle," says Marvin, lifting his paddle from the hazel water and pointing toward the tangle of verdure. "Just running and running. Not knowing where to go. Not knowing what to eat. Lost and day by day starving and cut all over from the thorns, and the soles of their feet bloody but still running because to be a slave is worse."

Marvin lays his slim blade inside the dugout and starts rolling a joint in his lap. He stops paddling whenever he tells a story, as if in deference to the primacy of the tale. Frankie and I keep pulling the boat downstream, plunging our long, fish-shaped paddles into the warm Suriname River.

"They slept hiding beneath big leaves and then ran more," continues Marvin in his vaguely Rastafarian lilt. "They ran for weeks. All the way to the top of this river. So deep into the jungle only the jaguar knew where they were."

Marvin learned his stories from his grandmother in the bush camp at night, after the men and boys had spent the day clearing a plot and the women and girls had planted rice or cassava. Most of Marvin's yarns were humorous allegories involving clever monkeys or parrots or caimans with human weaknesses. But this one was the tale of his people, his forefathers, the Saramaka Maroons, so he was uncharacteristically grave.

"They knew they were not safe even this far back in the jungle," he says. "They were escaped slaves. Escaped slaves that never come back give other slaves ideas. They maybe start to think they could be free themselves. This is impossible for the white people. So they sent out hunting parties. Men with muskets and swords guided by Indian trackers who knew the trails of the jungle."

Marvin smokes, contemplating the passing wall of impregnable green. There is no hurry. He passes the cigar-size joint back to Frankie and exhales.

"They were hunted like animals. My grandfathers' fathers. Sometimes they were killed in the jungle, but this was bad, because no one saw them die. Mostly they were beaten and whipped and had iron shackles locked around their necks and their ankles and were dragged back to the plantations. Then the tortures began. All the slaves on the plantation were forced to watch. Tortures so cruel it is impossible to imagine. You can't believe what they did to us . . . "

We are now gliding between islands of flat black rocks, the river pouring through channels like chocolate. I can hear rapids. Marvin lifts his paddle and in one sweeping, powerful stroke turns our dugout toward a tiny island cove. He will take the unstable craft through the rapids singlehandedly, while Frankie and I hopscotch over the rocks. We step out and Marvin twirls the canoe back into the current, yelling, "This story is not finished!"

Then he disappears. A lone black man in a small burnt-black dugout against white water.

• • •

I'd come to Suriname, a country slightly larger than the state of Georgia on the right shoulder of South America, to canoe through the homeland of the Saramaka people. Descendants of escaped slaves, the Saramaka have, for centuries, sustained a remote wilderness civilization in the country's jungle interior.

As with most Saramaka, Marvin's family history is based on fact, not folklore. Runaway slaves were called Maroons, a term derived from the Spanish word *cimarrón*, which means "wild one" and originally referred to feral cattle. The first Maroon absconded just as the slave trade was beginning, in 1502, into the mountains of Hispaniola, the island that today comprises Haiti and the Dominican Republic. Thousands followed, banding together and creating fugitive settlements.

"The wilderness setting of early New World plantations made marronage and the existence of organized Maroon communities a ubiquitous reality," writes Richard Price, a leading authority on Maroon culture, in his book *Maroon Societies*. "Throughout Afro-America, such communities stood out as an heroic challenge to white authority and as the living proof of the existence of a slave consciousness." Between 1672 and 1864, more than fifty Maroon settlements were established in North America, with hundreds more in the Caribbean and Central and South America.

Suriname operated perhaps the most savage slave system in the Western Hemisphere. From 1668 to 1823, more than 300,000 slaves were shipped into the country, yet at the end of this period, the total black population was only 50,000. Slaves were deliberately worked to death. John Stedman, a Maroon hunter in Suriname in the late eighteenth century, describes a planter who flogged a slave until he was flayed open and died. "It being a Rule in the Colony of Suriname that by paying a fine of 500 florins per head you are at Liberty to kill as many Negroes as you please."

Today, Suriname is home to the largest extant Maroon population in the world. Like many emerging postcolonial states—Suriname received its independence from Holland in 1975—this nation of 460,000 citizens has slogged through military coups, guerrilla wars, colossal corruption, land settlements, and embryonic parliamentary government. Of the six distinct Maroon peoples living in Suriname today—the Saramaka, Kwinti, Matawai, Ndjuka, Paramaka, and Aluku—the Saramaka, 20,000 individuals residing in some 70 settlements along the Suriname River, have arguably been the most successful survivors.

• • •

To reach Saramakaland, I'd taken a one-hour bush flight from Paramaribo, the port capital of Suriname, to Bendekonde, a pleasant village on the banks of the upper Suriname River where cashew and palm trees are planted along the footpaths but there is no electricity, telephone, or running water. There I'd spent days searching for a boat and boatmates.

I wanted to canoe from Bendekonde to Atjoni, a village on the edge of Saramaka territory, where the first dirt track wriggles out of the rainforest. It was a distance of fifty river miles, past about forty villages and down dozens of small rapids.

There are no roads in this region. The one highway is the river, so the Saramaka are expert canoeists and canoe builders. Until the present generation, it was incumbent upon every husband to carve a dugout for his wife so she could paddle to and from the fields. Every family still owns a dugout—it's the vehicle of choice and is used daily. But since the introduction of gas engines in the 1960s, no one paddles great distances anymore. Now there are bigger dugouts fitted with outboard motors that, like shuttle buses, transport people and goods up and down the river. I met one eighty-nine-year-old man who had canoed all the way to Paramaribo—"a difficult, eight-day journey"—but he'd done it half a century ago.

"Canoe to Atjoni! It's very crazy, my friend," Marvin Pansa shouted gaily the first time we met. He was tall and tattooed, his long limbs glistening with sweat. He was in the midst of a ferocious soccer match in a pasture. Word had gotten around that there was a white man looking to canoe the river.

"Who knows how long it could take," Marvin said. "Three, four, five days." Frankie Pansa, Marvin's short, non-English-speaking sidekick, appeared behind him. "Me and Frankie will have to paddle the canoe back upriver."

Marvin grinned, revealing a gold front tooth. "You pay for both directions?"

I met them on the riverfront at half past six the next morning. They were in shorts and flip-flops, Marvin sporting a Nike visor, Frankie wearing a Giorgio Armani T-shirt. Each had a sealed five-gallon plastic tub with his belongings inside—hammock, pants, extra shirt, toothbrush—and a hand-carved paddle. Their supplies for the journey consisted of one bottle of ninety-proof Mariënburg white rum, a bag of homegrown ganja, a machete, and a shotgun.

Marvin, twenty, lives in Bendekonde. He has a wife and young child and a girlfriend who is pregnant. (Traditionally, the Saramaka are a polygamous, matrilineal society; most people in a village have the same last name—as Marvin and Frankie do—even if they are only distantly related.) Marvin knew he needed money, which is why he volunteered for this trip. Besides, he had experience with *bakaa* (Saramaka for *whites*). His father owns a tourist camp in the bush, and Marvin had guided Dutch *bakaa* on rainforest ecotours.

Frankie, twenty-two, had borrowed his grandmother's dugout. The intricately carved upturned bow and stern that Saramaka boats are known for (often reinforced and decorated with hammer-patterned metal fittings) had both broken off, and the normally smooth, elegant clapboard gunwales nailed to the hull were battered. But it floated. Almost.

We pushed off into cobwebs of mist, and within an hour the dugout, christened *Oma*—Grandma in Dutch—was sinking. Marvin and Frankie were unperturbed. Marvin started bailing with an oil can while Frankie stood up, machete in hand. Hiking up his shorts and pulling down his boxers, he sliced off a strip of fabric and plugged it into a bubbling crack in the hull. Then he cut off a second strip and sealed another leak.

Over the course of the journey, Frankie would use up his underwear chinking old, cracked Oma.

. . .

Outside of total insurrection, marronage was what most frightened planters. They called it "the chronic plague." Runaway slaves threatened the very structure of the New World economy during the sixteenth, seventeenth, and eighteenth centuries. Without slave labor, the sugarcane, tobacco, and cotton industries would collapse and rich, aristocratic planters would become paupers. Thus, the most demonic punishments were reserved for recaptured runaway slaves.

According to Suriname criminal court records from 1730, "the Negro Joosie shall be hanged from the gibbet by an Iron Hook through his ribs, until dead; his head shall then be severed and displayed on a stake by the riverbank, remaining to be picked over by birds of prey. As for the Negroes Wierrie and Manbote, they shall be bound to a stake and roasted alive over a slow fire, while being tortured with glowing Tongs. The Negro girls, Lucreita, Ambira, Aga, Gomba, Marie and Victoria will be tied to a Cross, to be broken alive, and then their heads severed to be exposed by the riverbank on stakes."

Maroon outposts were fortresses in the wild, located in the most inhospitable terrain. Paths leading to a village were concealed and booby-trapped with pits of sharpened stakes. The only way into or out of some villages was either through an underwater tunnel or by passing through a narrow defile; most communities were surrounded by wooden palisades.

To feed, clothe, and defend themselves, Maroons became masters of outdoor survival, domesticating jungle plants, concocting medicines, fishing, hunting, wood carving, and weaving.

Always outnumbered and outgunned, Maroons also developed guerrilla warfare tactics. Using ambushes, night maneuvers, and hit-and-run attacks, Maroons sometimes managed to vanquish European mercenaries trained in regimented fighting. The most powerful Maroon societies regularly raided plantations—stealing slaves into freedom—which eventually forced their former masters and colonial governments to sign accords granting them not only their freedom but also land ownership and trade opportunities.

Peace treaties with nascent Maroon governments were inked in Hispaniola, Panama, Venezuela, and Ecuador in the 1500s; Mexico, Colombia, and Brazil in the 1600s; and Jamaica and Suriname in the 1700s. Despite these treaties, most Maroon communities were eventually destroyed by colonial troops. And yet some—through a combination of intelligent diplomacy, fierce courage, and wilderness resourcefulness—survived. The Saramaka are one such group.

In 1762, they signed an agreement with the Dutch colonial administration granting them land rights along the Suriname River from fifty miles inland south to the headwaters. Remarkably, for the next two centuries this treaty was largely respected. During those many generations, the Saramaka built a world in the rainforest, creating their own language, their own animist religion, their own architecture, and their own cuisine.

• • •

We camp on the banks of the river or in small villages. I set up my tent; Marvin and Frankie string their hammocks. One morning I awake at 4:00 a.m. to rhythmic thumping and laughter. It is a sound I haven't heard since my last journey to Africa, and it gives me enormous pleasure. I lie there listening, drifting through dreams, until dawn. When I unzip my tent I find a group of women using heavy, baseball-bat-size pestles and tree-trunk mortars to pound palm nuts into mush, which they will boil over wood fires to transform it into palm oil.

That afternoon, we buy three catfish from a boy fishing with a string from a listing dugout. Frankie, being a quiet bachelor, turns out to be something of a chef, acquiring onions and tomatoes and rainforest vegetables I don't recognize to produce an inspiring fish stew for dinner.

On the second evening, we paddle through a thunderstorm, a warm rain that explodes the surface of the river. Marvin and Frankie just keep paddling and singing. I think it might be some ancient African-American river song.

"Hah!" Marvin shakes his head. "It's a Saramaka rap tune, mon."

One glassy morning I foolishly decide it is my turn to sit in the stern and steer. The dugout doglegs radically right, then left, then right again. I can't get the boat to go straight to save my life. Marvin and Frankie peal with laughter.

When we stop to rest on rock islands, Marvin tells me about the Saramaka government. The Saramaka are divided into twelve matrilineal *lôs*, or clans. The *gaanman*, the king (currently Songo Aboikoni), holds office for life, and each village is administered by a *kabiten*, or captain. Crimes and disputes are settled through a *kuutu*, an oratory governed by elaborate rules and often conducted by captains and other village elders.

Near the end of the trip, I ask Marvin if he would like to boat on, past Atjoni, and cross W. J. van Blommestein Lake.

"It is not possible," he replies flatly. "This boat would sink and we would be eaten by piranhas."

I chuckle, but Marvin is serious: "That part of Saramakaland is gone forever."

Blommestein Lake is actually a 600-square-mile reservoir created by the Afobaka hydroelectric dam, built by Alcoa and the Suriname government in the early sixties. The reservoir, one of the largest in the world, flooded roughly half of the riverine land of the Saramaka, forcing the removal of 6,000 villagers.

"What you have seen is all we have left," Marvin says.

• • •

In 1997, the Saramaka discovered a large Chinese logging camp in their territory. Without notifying them, the Suriname government had sold logging concessions to their land. Suriname military personnel guard these logging operations and prohibit the Saramaka from entering. The clear-cutting, like clear-cutting the world over, is devastating the land— destroying wildlife habitat, causing erosion that silts the streams and kills the fish, and gutting a rainforest ecosystem that the Saramaka, through swidden agriculture and hunting and gathering, have maintained as a sustainable resource for 300 years.

According to witnesses, the majority of cut timber, much of it cedar, is simply bulldozed into piles and left to rot. Only the old-growth trees are trucked out, the ancient wood to be sawed into floorboards for shipping containers.

The Saramaka filed formal complaints with the Suriname government of president Ronald Venetiaan in October 1999 and October 2000 and never received a reply. In August 2002, the Inter-American Commission on Human Rights issued a request to Suriname's government, including the attorney general and the minister of natural resources, asking that it "take appropriate measures to suspend all concessions, including permits and licenses for logging and mine exploration and other natural resource development activity on lands used and occupied by twelve Saramaka clans."

Cognizant of their dire situation, the Saramaka presented a detailed map of their territory (surveyed by GPS) to the government in October 2002, requesting that they be recognized as the legal and rightful owners of this land.

To date, the government has not responded. And so the logging continues, devouring, acre by acre, Saramakaland.

· · ·

During the last hours of paddling before we reach Atjoni, the river is as smooth as syrup. White-skinned, baobab-like trees reflect upon the dark water. The air is still, warm, wet. We have found our rhythm and paddle in harmony. Each stroke hits the water at a slightly different moment, like synchronized drumbeats.

We're gliding downriver almost in a trance when Marvin starts to sing: "One love, one heart. Let's get together and feel all right."

Marvin wails out the whole song, Frankie and I doing the refrain.

Together we sing all the Bob Marley anthems we can remember: "Buffalo Soldier," "Exodus," "Get Up, Stand Up."

We sing "Redemption Song" two times through, and then we begin to hum it, the melody sailing over the water and into the jungle.

From the Saddle

WHERE THE DEER
AND THE ANTELOPE PLAY

Once we were cowboys. The vast prairie began at the end of the block. It was like living next to the ocean—all this boundless adventure waiting just beyond our backyard. That was back when parents would give boys of eight or nine as much freedom as they would take. And we'd take it all. In cutoffs, a sandwich in the pocket of our windbreaker, we'd leap into the saddle and head out into the red dirt hills for another day of heroic deeds and dangerous riding.

Bikes were our steeds. To us a bicycle was better than a horse. It was patient and wouldn't kick and never needed feeding or brushing. It was boy-size and built like we were—lithe, light, invincible.

We'd ride dirt trails from sunup to sundown, from one make-believe shoot-out or showdown to the next. When the sun sank over the horizon, we'd take one last, longing look out into the beckoning prairie, then wheel around and canter back to town. We'd crawl into our bunk beds covered in red talcum, exhausted, glowing with the grandness of the day.

And in our dreams? What else: We dreamed of just riding off across the plains like a sailboat glides out to sea. Of riding into the sunset.

• • •

Thirty years later.

Reed's brother, Buzz, was in town. Reed Zars, a zealous, take-no-prisoners environmental attorney, is my cycling and skate-skiing companion. Buzz, like many younger brothers, turns out to be the antidote to Reed. A Caterpillar mechanic living in Tenino, Washington, Buzz is easygoing and imperturbable.

Reed and Buzz grew up on a remote ranch near Hayden, Colorado, running sheep and cattle, pitching hay bales. Although they make light of it, it was a difficult, cold, lonely childhood—a hardscrabble upbringing that turned them into tall, leanly muscled men with wry, resourceful minds. Physically and psychologically, both are built for endurance—like all cowboys. And both are serious cyclists. Buzz had brought his mountain bike to Laramie.

That night, through the potion of beer, we regressed back to boyhood and hatched a homemade adventure: At sunrise, we'd ride out of town.

• • •

Over the past decade, the word "adventure" has mistakenly become synonymous with "expedition." Thus it has become common wisdom that any real adventure requires extensive planning and preparation. Plane reservations made months in advance, pages of lists, stacks of guidebooks, duffel bags stuffed with new gear, and mountains of money. We all need to reread *Huckleberry Finn* and find two friends like Reed and Buzz.

"No tent, no stove, no panniers, no sleeping bag," Reed decreed.

"No itinerary," Buzz averred.

Sticking to trails and dirt roads, we would pedal a four-day lariat loop through the mountains and high plains of Wyoming and Colorado.

Ten hours later I crammed a rain jacket, a sweater, two 1:100,000 maps, a patch kit, a few bike tools, and a wallet into my front bag and met up with the brothers Zars at the end of the block. We took the first gravel road going west, gliding out across the prairie with the sun at our back.

• • •

There are few things in life more joyous than lighting out on an adventure. To do so in good company on a bicycle—the most elegant and elemental of conveyances—with little more than the clothes on your back and a couple of warm brownies in your pocket is heaven.

There were antelope everywhere. Frantic and fleet-footed, they raced beside the barbed wire as if they'd been shot at, which they had. It was hunting season in Wyoming. We chased our own telephone-pole-tall shadows across dry swales and swells until the road hooked south. On the spur of the moment we decided our first stop would be Albany, a settlement consisting of little more than a saloon at the base of the Medicine Bow Mountains. We cut west and began following a straight-shot trail that parallels a buried water line.

Pretty soon we had to start jumping fences.

"We should get permission," Reed, the lawyer, said nervously.

I shrugged.

"From who?" said Buzz.

We topped a bluff and spotted a tiny ranch house out in the ocean of brown.

"Them," said Reed.

"We'll be off their property and onto someone else's before they even know it," said Buzz.

But Reed was already gone.

Buzz and I kept riding along the pipeline, lifting our light bikes over one fence after another. The ranch house was a long way off. When Reed finally reached it, Buzz and I stopped and waited. After a few minutes we saw Reed on his bike tearing across the horizon, hell-bent-for-leather in the wrong direction. Moments later a blue pickup spun away from the ranch and went ripping after him down the same dirt road.

It didn't look so good.

"Best if we just keep going, I'd say," said Buzz, raising his eyebrows and grinning. We'd meet up with Reed in Albany. Hopefully. Buzz and I hopped back on our mountain bikes and continued onward across the new frontier.

$$\bullet \quad \bullet \quad \bullet$$

The big-armed waitress slid our hamburgers onto the bar. "There's enough grease to keep you going," she said.

Buzz and I ate as if we'd just pedaled fifty miles over terrain as rugged as the Gobi Desert in a teeth-gritting headwind. Which we had. Several times I'd looked down at the speedometer to find us moving at a humble seven miles per hour.

"Saddle sore?" I asked Buzz. He was wearing plaid cotton shorts in lieu of padded Lycra, a wool cap instead of a helmet. He shook his head.

We were the only guys in the bar not wearing fluorescent orange, the fall fashion color of choice for hunters everywhere.

We'd just finished our burgers when Reed strolled in, his face flushed and eyes jumpy.

"What the hell happened?" Buzz asked.

"I about got myself ventilated!" replied Reed, and proceeded to tell, or rather to act out, the story.

The rancher must have seen him coming. After weaving past the usual assortment of clutter—cars sunk in sagebrush, a rusted bailer, tilted outbuildings—Reed dismounted and started walking toward the front door. That's when the rancher stepped out from around a shed with a shotgun.

He was wearing overalls, an oily baseball cap, and red sneakers. Reed introduced himself and extended his hand but the man waved it away. Reed, realizing he was at somewhat of a negotiating disadvantage, nevertheless asked permission for us to cross his land. The rancher grimaced, reached down and shifted his balls, brought his hand back to the shotgun, and said, "No."

Reed politely explained that we were simply following the pipeline trail and would be off his property in a matter of minutes.

"No," he repeated. "You'd hurt the grass."

Reed looked out at the rancher's land. It had been a fall so dry spit evaporated in midflight. That and a century of overgrazing had transformed this short-grass prairie into tumbleweeds and dirt.

He tried charming the man with the details of our youthful outing. We were like modern-day cowboys, really—riding the range, traveling light, searching for a saloon to wet our whistle. But of course the last Wyoming cowboy to spend more than an hour in the saddle was Jimmy Stewart in *The Man from Laramie*. Cowboys haven't ridden anywhere for ages. Cowboys are American icons so, naturally, they drive. Big American pickups, four-wheelers, snowmobiles.

"Ya'r an environmentalist!" the man sputtered, a label that, for certain ranchers, means someone more evil than murderers and rapists.

"I am not!" Reed emphatically replied—his lie an act of apostasy so outrageous that Buzz and I almost fell off our stools laughing. As a lawsuit-slinging lawyer, Reed has forced utility companies across the nation to spend millions on clean-air equipment.

"Ya'r too!" the rancher insisted astutely. "You're one a them goddamn environmentalists!" He brandished the shotgun. "Git! Git off my property!" So Reed got, as fast as he could.

Buzz and I were snorting so hard we raised the ire of the orange-clad men in the bar, all of whom had their rifles in the gun racks in their trucks out in the corral. We decided to step outside.

A banner from the BlueRibbon Coalition was cracking in the wind above the Albany bar. This is the fascist arm of the wise use movement, redblooded Americans hoping to repeal offensive, rights-abusing legislation—like the Wilderness Act and the Clean Water Act and the Clear Air Act—so that all public land will be open for righteous, God-fearing down-home fun—monster-truck mud-digging.

"Don't think we're all that welcome 'round here," said Buzz.

Time to hit the trail.

• • •

We doglegged north along Highway 11, riding single file through a valley of hay fields and irrigation ditches, each caught up in our own thoughts. I found myself smiling. We weren't more than an hour's drive from home, and already it felt as if we'd entered another country. We were strangers in a strange land.

A corollary to the adventure-equals-expedition fallacy is that adventure exists only someplace else: Namibia, Nepal, New Zealand, New Hebrides. To experience the exotic, to meet memorable characters seemingly from another epoch, to expect and ultimately find the unexpected, you must fly halfway around the world. Don't buy it.

It was late afternoon and a cold wind was churning dirt in the air when we rode into Centennial, population one hundred.

There were three motels in this one-street town. It could have been Mongolia. The first, a squat cinder-block bunker, had beds so swaybacked and Lilliputian that when we tested them, our butts hit the floor and our feet stuck out in midair. The second had its door wide open, but no one was around. The gas-station attendant told us to check at the bar for Suzy.

Suzy, a vision in Tammy Faye Bakker eyelashes and a gaudy Western shirt that didn't quite hold her all in, sat on the last bar stool in a long line of bar stools filled by guys in flannel shirts. Buzz and Reed graciously let me do the talking.

"Do you have any rooms available?"

"I do," she cackled.

"How much are they?"

"Sixty smackeroos, boys."

"How many beds in a room?"

"Now what do you think?" She was so tanked she could hardly stay upright on her stool. "But we have ourselves a problem." She cast an eye down the bar and the men grinned. "The beds haven't been made. All the sheets are dirty." She let out a cachinnation you wouldn't think could come from a woman.

"Tell you what, I'll give 'em to you for half price."

"Thirty dollars."

"I said half price. Forty dollars."

"Forty dollars per person for each of us to enjoy the luxury of sleeping in somebody else's soiled sheets."

She slapped her knee and crowed.

We ended up in the last-chance motel in a room with two beds whose log frames could have been used to support a mine shaft. We ate in the attached restaurant, a prohibitionist establishment packed wall-to-wall with country kitsch.

Outside, the wind was carrying off sheep and small cows and trying to uproot a sign that said WYOMING: LIKE NO PLACE ON EARTH.

• • •

At daybreak we rode into the Medicine Bow Mountains, up along Gold Run Creek, then east along a jeep track next to Jim Creek. Beyond Four-log Park the track dissolved into mud. Gloriously technical riding followed: deep mud holes with ice still riming the edges, stumps, roots, boulders, branches right at neck height.

On the backside we flew down French Creek (pronounced *crick*) to where it debouched into the shallow, rocky North Platte. We stopped for a late lunch in the willows along the bank on the wrong side of a PRIVATE PROPERTY—NO TRESPASSING sign. From the map, it was obvious this "private property" was actually public land. Like all signs in Wyoming, it was perforated with bullet holes.

We ate everything we had and drank all the water in our water bottles and thus had no choice but to ride on through the uneven plains.

That evening, we sidled into Riverside, population eighty-five. There were two bars and a huddle of log cabins for rent. We booked ourselves into Muleskinner, a diminutive hut subsiding into a cottonwood meadow. A handwritten note on the wall read: "We do not dispose of animal carcasses."

Riverside is actually a suburb of Encampment, population negative 1,500. From local postcards we learned that Encampment is the home of the two-story outhouse. (When the snow gets too deep, you use the second floor.) In 1902 Encampment experienced a copper rush. A sixteen-mile aerial tramway, at the time the longest in the world, was constructed to transport ore to the smelter. Houses, hotels, and brothels were built. Then, in 1907, the copper ran out and the town went bust. The three of us pedaled up and down every empty street. As far as we could tell, about all that was left was a sawmill, a post office, and two bars.

"Not a grocery store in a thousand square miles," commented Reed when we returned to our cabin, "but four bars within stumbling distance."

Lying on my bunk that night, musing on our progress so far, I realized another salient truth about adventure: It doesn't matter where you go. It's not what you see, but how you see. To the jaded eye Paris is dull, Everest a sham, Africa stuffed with animals already seen on the Discovery Channel. But if you think of your mind as a microscope and take a close look, there is not a chunk of earth on this planet—maybe even right around the corner—that isn't original, even inexplicable.

That night we rented a TV, a VCR, and a movie, all for three dollars, from a gas station and drank a six-pack watching *O Brother, Where Art Thou?*

• • •

The third morning we pedaled south into Colorado over Independence Mountain. Along the way we stopped to visit some natural rock baths that Native Americans once used, and later wandered around inside the roofless guts of an abandoned homestead, hope and hardship still in the walls papered with yellowed newsprint.

We spent the day surmounting a 10,000-foot pass on a mining path and broke out of the aspens just before sunset. Below us lay the sweep of North Park, a well-watered expanse of golden grassland cradled by mountains on all sides—the Mount Zirkel Wilderness Area to the west, the Rawah Wilderness Area to the east, the Rabbit Ears Range to the south, and the Medicine Bow Mountains to the north.

After one flat tire and two hours of serene, resplendent riding, we glided into Cowdrey, Colorado. Cowdrey is so small it doesn't even have a bar. It does, however, have the Cowdrey Trout Camp, on the bank of the Canadian River: ten dollars a bed and all the heat you can trick out of a leaky propane heater. Just lay the cash on the table in your bunkroom when you leave.

Famished but foodless once again, we hitched a ride in the back of a pickup ten miles south to Walden. There we found an old, dimly lit pool hall half-converted to a pizza joint. It was a cavernous space, with the heads of elk shot long ago peering down from the walls, a thick coat of dust on their antlers. Off in the corner was a young mother, a crying two-year-old clinging to her apron and a crying three-month-old fastened to a rocker on the counter. She was making pizzas by herself. There were no other customers. She had the radio tuned to a country station and was humming along. It was a song I didn't recognize in a world I'd forgotten.

•   •   •

It was below freezing the next morning, so cold the mud puddles in front of our cabin were frozen solid.

"The joy of going superlight is that one is always unprepared," Reed said cheerily.

Buzz found some plastic bags and we wrapped our feet before stuffing them inside our cycling shoes. We pulled our sleeves over our hands and sank our faces into our windbreakers and set out.

After one hour we were each wondering how many fingers and toes would eventually have to be amputated. When the sun rose and the road reared up, blood began to burn its way back into our appendages.

We were over our last 10,000-foot pass before we even knew we'd started. After only three days on our bikes, miles were nothing. Distance was merely space. Had we the time, we could ride right across the continent.

That afternoon, skimming down through the forest, the trees shuttering by as if we were in a passenger train, we floated into a small clearing suspended in sunlight. In the center of the numinous glade stood three deer: two big four-point bucks and a doe. Their statuesque heads were turned toward us as we slowed to a stop.

They seemed so calm, so poised. I rummaged in my front bag for my camera but kept my eyes on the deer. I couldn't believe they hadn't spooked.

"Wait a minute!" Buzz yelled.

The three of us pedaled over to the deer, and they never twitched an ear or blinked an eye. They were decoys, placed in the meadow by the Colorado Division of Wildlife to catch poachers.

We took a close look. The taxidermist had carefully stitched hide over hollow, lifelike plastic forms.

Each was riddled with bullet holes.

THE ANSWER

As we ride up to the fish farm, a mob of women crushes against the tall metal gates. They have walked here through suffocating heat and humidity from mud huts dotting the Western Sahara veldt, carrying tin basins on their heads. Packed together, they are desperate, determined, on the verge of breaking down the fence. Workers inside are wielding sticks to keep them from clambering over the top.

Brad Schroeder, my unflappable guide, squeezes his yellow bicycle straight into the fray. I follow on his heels. The gates crack open just long enough for us to slip into the compound beyond, the surge of humanity attempting to follow us inside.

A tall man in sunglasses, his shaven head glistening with sweat, greets us. "What's going on?" yells Schroeder as they smoothly execute the Ghanaian handshake: white-man clasp, brother clasp, white man, brother, mutual snap of the fingers.

"Giving away free fish," replies Mark Amechi, smiling broadly.

Amechi, thirty-three, is the Nigerian-German owner and operator of Tropo Farms, a fish company he founded here, near the banks of the Volta River, in the West African nation of Ghana. He has a master's degree in aquaculture and raises tilapia, a one-pound white-flesh fish he sells to the markets of Accra, Ghana's capital of 2 million. This morning, Amechi traveled to the nearby village of Asutsuare to announce that he would be handing out 3,000 pounds of undersize stock. That's roughly seven pounds of perfectly good fish per person, worth about two and a half dollars—more than a day's wage for a rural Ghanaian. By the time Amechi got back to the farm, word had spread and a throng of villagers had arrived to claim their share.

"Might as well help out the local families," explains Amechi. "The fish would rot otherwise." He invites us into his un-air-conditioned office and proffers a bottle of ice water and some oranges. Schroeder and I have just bicycled sixty-five brain-baking miles north from Accra, across rolling farmland, and we're dripping profusely in the equatorial heat.

Schroeder slugs back a quart of freezing liquid in one go, hands the bottle to me, rips open an orange and swallows it in two bites, then peals up his shirtsleeves to reveal a serious, flaming-red sunburn.

"Bit warm," he laughs, "but at least the Harmattan hasn't arrived yet."

Schroeder, a twenty-seven-year-old from Charlotte, North Carolina, is the Ghana program officer for the Institute for Transportation and Development Policy (ITDP), a nonprofit, nongovernmental organization (NGO) based in New York whose mission is "to promote environmentally sustainable and equitable transportation worldwide." His current goal is to make bicycling in Ghana more economically feasible and reliable by importing well-built bikes designed for the rugged conditions in Africa. Until now, Ghana's bike market has consisted primarily of new and used single-speed city bikes from Europe and shoddily built imitation mountain bikes from Asia—which sell for between forty and a hundred dollars.

In 2002, Paul White, ITDP's Africa regional director, spearheaded a plan to create an affordable bicycle that would combine the dependability of European bikes with the versatility of mountain bikes. He then teamed up with bike giant Trek to create just such a product. "The challenge," Trek president John Burke told me, "was to build a durable, high-quality bike that was actually affordable for Africans."

Manufactured for Trek in China, the so-called California Bike—named, according to White, to give bicycling a successful, upscale image—is a banana-yellow, six-speed hybrid mountain bike with a chrome-moly frame and fenders, sturdy rear rack, and puncture-resistant tires. To date, ITDP has imported 600 of the bikes to Ghana and sold them to local companies and dealers at cost.

Schroeder is irreverent, inexhaustible, realistic yet irrepressibly optimistic—the kind of guy who solves problems with an élan born of directness. He works like a dog, drinks like a fish, and pops beer bottle caps off with his teeth. He and I have spent the last three days wheeling through the thickly polluted, impossibly congested, blaring, sweltering, treacherous streets of Accra.

Today's ride is our first into the bush—it's Schroeder's mission to deliver the California Bikes we're riding to a village in the north and to check in on Amechi's recent acquisition of twenty-six bikes for his employees. The bikes cost seventy-five dollars each; Amechi picked up thirty percent, and the workers will pay off the rest with deductions from their paychecks over the next seven months.

"So how're the bikes working out?" Schroeder asks Amechi, speaking clearly even with an entire orange in his mouth.

"Brilliantly," Amechi says. "Already they've become something of a status symbol. The men are quite proud of them. Some of my guys were walking five to ten miles to work, so I've seen a significant decrease in tardiness. They have so much more freedom now. A few even ride home for lunch. There's a newfound self-esteem." Glancing out the door to the front gate beyond, he pauses. "Would you excuse me for a moment?"

Amechi springs to his feet, races into another room, then flies past us and out the door, shoving shells into a shotgun as he runs. The villagers have burst through the gates and are rushing helter-skelter toward the ponds to get their fish. It's bedlam. Amechi raises the shotgun and fires into the air. They freeze. He fires again, and then, shotgun in hand, charges the mob, bellowing at the top of his lungs. The crowd spins about en masse, hightailing it back out through the twisted gates, where Amechi will have them wait to be let in, ten at a time.

I'm stunned, but Schroeder merely shakes his head: "Giving anything away for free never works."

•   •   •

There are two Africas: the bush—ancient, agrarian, slow to change—and the city—vibrant, dissonant, evolving by the minute. This dichotomy is especially vivid in Ghana, an English-speaking country of 20 million, roughly the size of Oregon, on the Gulf of Guinea. Nicknamed the Gold Coast in the seventeenth century for its lucrative precious-metal trade, Ghana was the first country in sub-Saharan Africa to gain independence, in 1957. Today, it's a relatively stable democracy with one of the most prosperous agricultural economies in West Africa.

In Ghana, as in the rest of the continent, life in the bush often revolves around basic human needs: food, water, shelter. Services remain so spread out and transportation options so few, many villagers walk enormous distances every day—to their fields, to the well, to market, to school, to medical clinics. Unimaginable hours of productivity and education are lost for lack of efficient transport, let alone the suffering endured because of too-distant health care. In rural Africa, less than one percent of the population owns a car. A staggering seventy percent of freight, from bricks to buckets of water, is still transported on the heads of women.

The problem is just the opposite in the city. Africa's inexorable rural-to-urban migration—at 4.9 percent, its annual urban growth rate is the highest in the world—has turned metropolitan centers into sprawling, toxic messes. Too many cars, too many taxis, too many tro-tros (private minivans used for public transporation). Traffic accidents occur with alarming frequency, and the number of deaths per vehicle are fifty times those in the United States. In the major urban areas of West Africa, seventy-five percent of commuters live within six miles of work; in Accra, however, thirty-five percent take a taxi or tro-tro, at a cost of about one dollar round-trip—this despite the fact that incomes can be as little as three dollars a day. The result is a country—and continent—in desperate need of alternative transportation.

Enter ITDP and Brad Schroeder. A rock climber, Appalachian Trail through-hiker, and competitive water-skier with a bachelor's in environmental science, Schroeder joined the Peace Corps in 2000. He was stationed in Volivo, a village in southern Ghana with no electricity and no running water. Over the course of two years, he learned to speak Dangbe (one of Ghana's seventy-five tribal dialects), drilled five potable-water boreholes, built a canoe that sank in the Volta, came down with malaria, and developed a taste for *akpeteshie*, palm-wine moonshine.

At the end of his hitch, the sounds, smells, and tastes of Africa had so permeated Schroeder that he decided to stay in Ghana, took a job in Accra with ITDP, and began work on the California Bike program.

"The bikes aren't free—that would only put the local bike dealers out of business," Schroeder tells me over lunch at a restaurant the next day, back in the welter of Accra. He explains that he's organizing Ghanaian bike dealers into a co-op that will have the financial resources to buy and sell California Bikes on its own: "So many well-meaning NGO projects have devastated local business and replaced it with a welfare economy. That's unsustainable. Besides, it robs people of their pride." He fires down his de rigueur double shot of gin, stands up, and swings his leg over his bicycle.

"C'mon," he says. "You can see how it's working." And back into the fray we fly.

Our first stop is Latex Foam, an Accra mattress factory that employs 300 workers and has just purchased California Bikes for twenty of its top employees. As we arrive, the workers are wheeling around, getting acquainted with their new rigs.

"They are too good to be true," says Eric Nayanyi, thirty-five, the union chairman at the factory. "The workers with the California Bikes will no longer be stuck in traffic, missing wages."

Down the road, a powdered-milk company called Promasidor is awaiting delivery of sixty California Bikes. Managing director Dirk Laeremans tells us, "The price of gasoline doubled recently. These bicycles will save our employees considerable commuter money. My guess is that, in five to ten years, many, many people will be bicycling here."

Last on our agenda is Accra's city hall: We have an audience with Mayor Solomon Darko.

"Bicycles are an obvious transportation solution," says Darko, speaking from behind foot-high stacks of paper on his desk. "They're inexpensive, often faster than a car in the city, cost the government nothing, and are pollution free." Darko is a city planner by profession, educated in the Netherlands and Great Britain. He and the Accra city government, in consultation with ITDP, are developing a master plan to build a system of bike lanes throughout the capital. "People will bicycle if they feel safe," he adds. "Why not? It's a healthy, beautiful thing. We already have excellent examples of this in our country. Have you been to Tamale, in the north?"

"We're flying up there tomorrow," Schroeder says.

The mayor listens carefully as Schroeder outlines our itinerary: First, a tour of the progressive, bike-friendly city of Tamale, followed by a three-day, 250-mile test ride of the California Bike through rural Ghana's roughest terrain. We'll pedal from Tamale to Yendi, Bimbila, and Salaga, then back up to Tamale, where we'll drop off our bikes at a dealer—the first in the area to join the ITDP program. When Schroeder finishes, Darko looks at us gravely and says: "That is no small thing."

• • •

On the flight to Tamale the next day, Schroeder and I are joined by Ben Gherardi, twenty-six, a six-foot-four jock from Fort Collins, Colorado, who works for Right to Play, a Toronto, Canada–based NGO that promotes health through sports. Brad and Ben are boon companions, having done everything there is to do within a 300-mile radius of Accra: rock climbing in the Volta region, kite surfing off Cape Coast, road trips to

Togo and the Ivory Coast. We assemble our bikes at the airport, then ride the twelve miles into town.

Tamale, a thriving northern commercial hub of about 150,000 surrounded by savanna, is indeed a bicycling wonder. In the early 1990s, the World Bank funded the construction of fifteen-foot-wide paved bicycle paths that parallel the main streets on both sides, as well as low concrete barriers that separate motor vehicles from bicyclists and pedestrians. A decade later, more than fifteen percent of trips in Tamale are made by bicycle.

We spend all day cruising around town, marveling at the efficiency and pleasantness of it all. Not surprisingly, people on bikes are everywhere: men in billowing blue caftans, schoolgirls in brown-and-orange uniforms, farmers with hoes tied to the top tube, village women with towering loads of firewood roped to the rear rack.

The next day, we ride to Yendi, bouncing along a rutted mud track through hand-tilled yam and cassava plots. Over the course of sixty-five miles, only two groaning trucks and an occasional courageous car pass us, but cyclists are numerous, with people of all types wheeling from one village to the next on typical Ghanaian bikes: heavy, slow, jury-rigged contraptions.

An hour into our second day, the rough road takes its toll: Schroeder's seatpost, raised high to accommodate his lanky legs, buckles under the pressure. His only options are to sit on the rear rack, as if he were on a recumbent, or to pedal standing up. So he reclines on his panniers, singing a riff from *Easy Rider* and spinning like a circus bear.

"Sure you can ride like that?" I ask.

"No sweat," Schroeder replies, although he's drenched and straining. "Just a minor design flaw. We're still tweaking the bike to find the right balance of strength and weight."

By the time we straggle into Bimbila, Schroeder has ridden twenty miles on a bumpy dirt track without a saddle without complaining once. We go straight to the village blacksmith, a stick-thin, barefoot man sitting cross-legged amid a pile of scrap metal. His scrawny, big-eyed son hunches beside him in the dirt working a bellows sewn from a car tire tube. The man studies the problem, then goes to work with his tongs, tiny forge, and anvil (a chunk of railroad track). Using a one-inch-diameter piece of solid rebar he's found at his feet, in less than ten minutes he manages to cut, fashion, and fit it inside the hollow seatpost. The homemade heavy-metal splint works perfectly.

Schroeder beams. "God, you gotta love Africa!" he says. "Improvisation is what it's all about."

• • •

That afternoon we pedal around Bimbila, a dusty place with a roadside bike shop on nearly every corner, looking for lunch. We're famished, but as fate would have it, it's Ramadan, the month in which Muslims abstain from all food and drink from dawn 'til dusk. Eventually, we're directed to a clapboard hut on the edge of town—I believe it was called The Infidel's Fish Shack—where a pair of women in bright turbans stir two large cauldrons with paddles. Inside one is *fufu*, yams pounded and then heated to a rubbery, mashed-potato consistency; in the other is a gruesome fish-head gruel. We pull up a couple of benches and are served.

Fufu turns out to be one of Schroeder's favorite dishes; he wolfs down his plateful heartily, as does Gherardi. I'm three-quarters of the way through my slimy, foul-tasting chowder when I feel something curious in my mouth and spit it out: a fat, white, wriggling maggot.

"Say, Brad, mind having a look at this?" I ask, figuring he'll just tell me to munch it down.

Brad and Ben peer into my bowl, and blanch.

"Well," Schroeder says, "I'm finished. How 'bout you guys?"

We saddle up and ride on. And on. It's another forty-five miles of burning, leg-leadening, sweat-sucking dirt to Salaga. In villages along the way, our yellow bikes attract considerable attention from passing cyclists. To Schroeder's delight, several young men ask where they can buy one.

At a bridge thirteen miles outside of town, we halt from sheer fatigue. It is almost dark. Twenty feet below, brown water is swirling beneath the bridge. Ben and I are on empty, but Brad strips off his shirt and shoes, climbs up onto the railing, and jumps.

Now there might be anything hidden just under the opaque water—a floating tree, rocks, a sandbar—but of course there isn't. Brad comes bobbing back up with a mischievous grin, swims around a bit, then pulls himself out of the river as happy and cool as an otter.

It is pitch dark when we finally reach Salaga, a thriving slave-transfer station in the nineteenth century, but now simply an isolated village. The only rooms available are concrete cells with cold water and buckets for bathing. In these dismal surroundings, Gherardi becomes violently sick. Could have been the fishhead-and-live-maggot stew, could have been something else. Regardless, he shows off some impressive projectile vomiting. By morning, he's so weak and pallid that we put him on the bus back to Tamale. He will eventually wind up in the Accra hospital with something nasty but unidentifiable.

• • •

Schroeder and I manage to pedal the last seventy-five miles of packed red dirt back to Tamale. To avoid drinking the dubious village water, which might expose us to guinea worm (you don't even want to know), we pour hot Fanta and Coke into our water bottles. Every seven or eight miles, we fall off our bikes and crawl beneath the shade of a baobab tree to hide from the heat.

Each time, while I lie there sweating, trying to decide if I'm actually dying from heatstroke, Schroeder falls right to sleep and then wakes up twenty minutes later, cheerfully bellowing, "Doesn't get more African than this!" and hops back on his bike.

As we roll into Tamale, Schroeder tells me his dream for the bike program: "Make myself and ITDP obsolete. In our place, independent California Bike corporations in Kenya, Senegal, and South Africa owned and operated by Africans with the money and muscle to lobby their own governments and influence policy."

Africa is a peculiarly obdurate part of the world, a continent where idealism can be worn down by brutal circumstance. But dreams are the wheels of hope, and I sense that Schroeder will stick his out until at least some of it comes true.

And that would be no small thing.

BIKING VIKINGS

Rolling through a majestic fjord along a sun-splashed bike path—that's the way we were supposed to begin our ten-day tour of Norway. Cobalt ocean, azure sky, and soaring granite walls, the two of us boldly pedaling forth inside this picture postcard.

Ah, well. It was pelting cold rain when we bounced our bikes off the train at a remote station in southern Norway. We'd intended to take the bus down to the coastal village of Flekkefjord, but a baby-Thor-size stroller filled the storage compartment. My partner, Harald the Fairhair, wanted to cram our bicycles inside, but the bus driver shook his head, closed the doors, and drove off.

According to our map, Flekkefjord was only ten miles away. We climbed into rain suits, threw panniers on our bicycles, snapped ladies' shower caps (courtesy of Harald's wife) onto our helmets, and wobbled innocently onto a deserted two-lane highway called E-39.

Soon enough traffic was zooming by, headlights yellow smears in the miasmic downpour. There was no shoulder, merely a slick white line beside a drop-off into forested oblivion. By then we'd realized that E-39 is the autobahn of southwestern Norway. The rain was so dark and heavy I was certain that motorists, their windshield wipers batting back and forth, couldn't see us. I feared for Harald.

Harald the Fairhair—a nom de guerre I bestowed on him in homage to the first king of Norway, a ninth-century Viking longhair—is a close friend in publishing, a large, good-humored, deskbound man. Harald can elucidate the subtexts in Pynchon or Roth and is an aficionado of detective novels. Ex–New Yorker, cynical optimist, audiophile, he is a cycling enthusiast but is forthright about his physical reality. "I'm built like a fuckin' Shetland pony." Which he is. Broad shoulders, stout legs, huge heart.

I'd been trying to get him on an adventure for years and finally forced the issue by buying plane tickets. Norway was his idea—"someplace civilized yet still connected to nature." (Harald is of pure Norwegian stock, with mayonnaise skin and wispy blond hair, all four of his grandparents having unaccountably emigrated from this perfect little country.) But he'd agreed to go only under one condition:

"No Jenkins sufferfest. I mean it, Mark."

Harald was familiar with my unique ability to turn even the most innocuous outing into an epic.

"And no camping. This is a vacation, not an expedition. You do understand the difference?"

So here we were, hour one, wearing women's shower caps in public and defying death by riding bikes on a perilous mountain highway in a sheeting downpour. And that was before the tunnels.

The first one was short but dark—and so terrifying that we pulled off to the side immediately afterwards.

"This is just the kind of thing my wife said you'd get me into!" Harald shouted. "If I die, which appears extremely likely, she will track you down and kill you, you know this."

Around the next bend we slid unwillingly into another tunnel—long, and black as blindness. Tractor-trailers roared by inches from our mortal bodies. This time it occurred to me that we could indeed become road-kill.

Beyond the tunnel I stopped along the guardrail and waited in the torrential rain. Ahead, I could just make out the maw of the next dreaded tunnel. It took exceptional sangfroid, not to mention bicycling technique, to hold your line in the slick subterranean darkness. I peered nervously behind me.

Out of the hole Harald came as if blasted from a cannon, shoulder to shoulder with a barreling semi, his wet brakes squealing as he closed in on me.

"All right. All right! I've had quite enough!" He was apoplectic, his red face steaming. "This is deeply insane! It's like a very bad acid trip!"

• • •

People make much of ominous beginnings. Not me. The first day could be great, could suck—either way, it portends nothing about the rest of the trip. It's a shakedown. You make a mistake or two, things go wrong, you get in a fix, you get out of it. That's adventure.

We took the first exit and with boundless gratitude escaped E-39. (The term became part of our private trip lexicon: "E-39, noun: anything ghastly, deadly, or outrageously stupid.") In Flekkefjord, we fortified ourselves with hot chocolate in a cozy wharfside café, watched a white-bearded sailor repair his nets in the rain, then set out north along the crenulated coast of Norway.

Harald and I had chosen to travel by bicycle because it was where our disparate physical worlds overlapped—and because bicycling is a singularly sensory form of exploration. You roll through geography, unhurried and immersed. Smell the rain, feel the voluptuous ground, hear its whispers and groans.

Our plan was to link together three epic Norwegian bicycle trails—the North Sea Cycle Route, the Rallervegen, and the Numedalsruta—on a 500-mile arc through some of the most stunning landscapes in northern Europe.

Staying in hotels was part of my compromise with Harald. All my previous bike tours—across the United States, Europe, Africa, Russia—entailed "stealth camping": riding till dark, then pitching a tent wherever I was. I'd slept illegally in New York's Central Park, the Bois de Boulogne in Paris, cornfields, vineyards, and town parks, and on beaches and fancy estates with low fences. Alas, Harald wasn't interested in roughing it. Instead we would be wallowing in elegant Scandinavian hospitality—hotels with blond-wood floors, ergonomic faucets that separately adjust volume and temperature, large windows that actually open, fluffy down comforters, chocolates on the pillows.

That first night on the coast, we had reservations at the Sogndalstrand Kulturhotell, 50 miles southeast of Stavanger. We wheeled in just at dusk, having climbed over Jossingfjord Pass, and were met by one of the hotel's hosts, May. She was expecting us. I'm afraid May was the woman you dream of when you dream of Norway: blonde, piercing blue eyes, athletic physique. She showed us to our private house, once the shop of the village tailor. When we asked where we could lock up our bikes, May was amused.

"There is no criminality here," she said, smiling gaily. "Leave them there."

That night we had a traditional Norwegian dinner: delicate boiled monkfish and heaps of peeled potatoes with a robust bottle of Leon Galhaud chardonnay. For me, accustomed to bread-and-cheese bike fare, it was a feast. Later, Harald slept like a baby—through the wall I could hear him melodiously sawing logs—but I got so hot under the comforter I had to open all the windows and pace around naked to cool down.

The next morning was wet and blustery, and we had another big pass to climb. Without a load of camping gear, my bike danced uphill. It was glorious. I shot straight to the top of the pass, thought, Why the hell not? and then spun around and rode back down to where Harald was grinding away.

"Please, Mark, noble as it may seem to you, do not come back for me."

I tried pedaling at his pace, but Harald clearly found this annoying, so I blasted back up the pass, pulled out my journal, and scribbled this note: "Perhaps it's worth suffering through sleeping in a capacious down bed in a beautiful room in exchange for flying a bike light as a kite."

Over the pass, our little highway turned first into a bicycle path and then, just as we entered a dark, damp coastal woodland, into a muddy two-track. It was the kind of otherworldly place where you might spot a pointy-eared elf: boulders blanketed in teal moss; small, gnarled trees; scarves of mist wafting over emerald ponds.

"I christen this the Troll Wood," announced Harald, adding another phrase to our trip lexicon.

I said nothing, not wanting to break the spell, and we glided on in silence.

"Cycling is such an intimate way to see the country," said Harald miles later, while deftly negotiating a slippery one-log bridge.

I agreed. The method of passage is the message.

"You know, traveling by train or car is like watching a movie from some great distance," he mused. "There's detachment. An invisible glass wall between you and the world. But bicycling, you're in the movie."

• • •

Our bike path passed through the Troll Wood by design.

Since leaving Flekkefjord, we'd been spinning along the North Sea Cycle Route (NSCR), the longest signposted cycleway in the world. Linking 3,729 miles of trafficless trails, paths, and paved bikeways, the route circles the North Sea and passes through eight countries: Scotland, England, Belgium, Holland, Germany, Denmark, Sweden, and Norway. One of the founders of the NSCR, a fifty-three-year-old professional city planner named Vicky Hartland Gramstad, happened to live just north of the Troll Wood. She joined us later that day.

"Piecing it all together took years," explained Vicky, riding just ahead of us into a fierce headwind. "It required the cooperation of sixty-eight regions and some 700 municipalities."

The NSCR opened in May 2001. Half a million bicycle maps were printed in six languages, and thousands of small bicycle signs were planted at the junctions. Costs for developing the cycleway are split fifty–fifty between the European Union and local communities. As secretariat for the NSCR, Vicky receives half her salary from the government of Norway and the other half from the EU.

"The goals of the North Sea Cycle Route are multifarious," Vicky continued, still wheeling blithely into the wind. "Naturally, to encourage bicycling, the healthiest form of travel. But also to promote economic development in remote villages. And to promote transnational cooperation. And to recognize and strengthen the ancient connections between the countries of the North Sea.

"But I should let you two go," she said, as if she were holding us back rather than pulling us along. "You still have three hours to go to the Sola Strand Hotel." With that she whirled around and waved good-bye like the Good Witch of the North.

Harald and I pushed onward. I thought we'd sadly seen the last of Vicky, but she must have gotten home and then realized that the Sola Strand Hotel, on the coast just outside Stavanger, was much farther than we'd calculated.

Three hours later, still far from our hotel, dusk ready to pounce and the wind now blowing so hard we were just barely riding faster than we could walk, we watched as Vicky and her husband, Egil, pulled up beside us in their compact Mercedes. I had no idea what was going on, but Harald did. He dismounted at once and popped off his front wheel.

"What're you doing?!"

"What do you think?" said Harald, accepting what was, for him, a heaven-sent ride. Egil was already hefting the bike up onto the car's rack.

I was aghast. "You're kidding, right?!"

Harald gave me his are-you-really-that-stupid look.

"What happened to the intimacy of cycling?"

"The wind ate it whole."

"I'll ride in."

"Remember your promise."

Frankly, getting into that car was one of the hardest things I've done on any bike tour. I would have gladly ridden into the headwind right through the night. But this was my part of the bargain.

Humming along in the warm glass-and-metal capsule, spared from the knuckle-freezing cold and howling wind, Harald the Sweatyhaired was slumped in the front seat looking like a tattered Winnie the Pooh, a contented, sleepy smile on his face.

"I christen this the Ride of Shame," he said.

•   •   •

Harald and I pedaled north along the North Sea Cycle Route for three more days, spinning lightly and effortlessly through undulating farmland and along the rocky coastline. It rained most of the time, but it didn't matter, because we weren't camping. Each morning we awoke beneath clean sheets, rode no more than fifty miles, and then dined on something exquisite—salmon, minke whale, giant prawns.

It was decadent. Harald loved every minute of it; problem was, I was secretly starting to enjoy it myself. This could gravely endanger my reputation, not to mention my equanimity on my next spartan, one-hundred-miles-a-day-camping-in-the-dirt tour.

From Bergen, the NSCR leaps westward via ferry to the Shetland Islands, but Harald and I took a train east to ride the heralded Rallervegen—a 152-mile bicycle path through the 5,000-foot Hardangervidda Mountains. We'd been told that some 15,000 Norwegians pedal it during the two-month period each year when it's not buried in snow.

The rain was hammering us again when we lifted our bikes off the train in Finse. At least thirty other cyclists were already there, all in full-body rain suits, their mountain bikes equipped with fenders and mudflaps, bike lights, and giant waterproof saddlebags. A tall, attractive brunette appraised our mounts and said, "Your tires look a bit thin for this ride."

The Rallervegen is a narrow, hundred-year-old gravel supply road that parallels the Bergen–Oslo railway line. We flatted more than once over the next two days, but the cruise through the austere alpine landscape was so overwhelming we hardly noticed: tarns reflecting a gray-blue sky, glacier-polished granite walls—just like in the postcards.

That afternoon we took a spur trail, caroming down two dozen or so gravel switchbacks on our way to the too-quaint tourist hamlet of Flåm (think cruise-ship Japanese tourists buying heavy Norwegian sweaters they'll never wear), where we ate another rich meal in the company of the brunette and her girlfriend.

In the morning we had to ride right back out of Aurlandsfjord, up all of those switchbacks. I admit I reveled in the pain. We are what we are, and pushing myself is, unseemly as it can be, part of my nature. Harald dismounted, plugged in his iPod, cued up a playlist he'd ripped specifically for this trip ("The Wheel," by Jerry Garcia; "America Is Not the World," by Morrissey; "Roland the Headless Thompson Gunner," by Warren Zevon; and a dozen others), and walked up every last switchback, humming.

At the town of Geilo, we joined the 174-mile Numedalsruta, a three-day downhill run all the way to Oslo. Feeling fit and fast, we spun ourselves eastward out of the mountains into pastoral Norway—verdant meadows with round milk cows and log farmhouses so tightly built they're still standing after more than 500 years and coniferous forests where selective cutting has maintained the resource for centuries.

Riding side by side, Harald and I, like all American rubes who visit Norway, couldn't help but discuss the country's astounding progressiveness. In 2006, Norway was ranked first in the world on the UN Human Development Index—a matrix that measures poverty, life expectancy, literacy, and education level—making it the most livable place on the planet. You honestly feel as if you're viewing the next century. Here is a nation with well-paid bicycle-path designers and citizens who take cycling vacations in the mountains, in the freezing rain, and love it.

• • •

It was the weekend when Harald and I rolled into Oslo, our big smiles catching bugs. One of the greatest gifts of a bicycle tour is a new body. We were both leaner and stronger than when we'd started our ride. But saddle sore. So in the evening we went downtown on foot, searching for and finding the acclaimed jazz bar Herr Nilsen in the heart of the city. We drank a hundred dollars' worth of booze—which in Norway is only enough to make you pleasingly warm—listened to some of the finest jazz you can hear anywhere in the world, and didn't budge from the bar 'til the wee hours.

Outside, Saturday-night revelers—the ubiquitous kissing couples, the purple-hair/pierced-cheek/black-leather crowd, the clogs-and-wool-sweater guys—were walking arm in arm or twirling by on bicycles.

"Something's strange," said Harald.

It took us a minute to figure it out: There were no cars. Here we were, out late on the weekend in one of the most cosmopolitan cities in the world, and no one was driving. Each and all were afoot or asaddle.

A block before our hotel, we came across a flatbed truck parked beside a long bicycle rack. Painted on the truck in Norwegian was *Healthy and Fast*. All the bicycles in the rack were identical: sharp four-speed commuters with fenders and a front rack—part of a citywide bike program. For ten dollars a year, you can ride one of these impeccably maintained bikes anywhere at any time. The truck driver told us he was returning most of the bikes to the suburbs so residents would have them in the morning.

At that moment, a ridiculously gorgeous woman with flowing blonde hair and very long legs in purple tights swiped a magnetic card, pulled out a bike, and rode away, her locks lifting in the cool night air.

Harald the Fairhair stared at me in wonder and said, "I don't know. All this humane innovation. All this forward thinking. All this relentless nubility. I really don't know if I could live here."

Oh, but I could. At least until the next expedition.

LAISVÉ

It is one of the great regrets of travel: You meet someone on a journey, come to know them intimately in just a few hours, then never see them again. You promise to keep in touch, but it seldom happens. When you return home, your own life takes over and so does theirs, and the bond begins to fade.

This summer, while researching a family trip to St. Petersburg, Russia, I happened upon a story in *City Paper*, a Baltic-states online zine, about a new theme park in Lithuania called Stalin World. Surrounded by barbed wire and guard towers, with a replica of a human cattle car and a collection of hypertrophic Soviet-era statues, it was said to combine "the charms of Disneyland with the worst of the Soviet gulag prison camp." I couldn't imagine a more macabre, yet twistedly appropriate, post-twentieth-century tourist attraction. Reading the article, I flashed back to the five months I'd spent cycling across the USSR in 1989 and a man I'd met on that trip: Saulius Kunigenas.

I was part of a seven-person team—three Americans, four Russians (three women, four men). We rode from Vladivostok to Leningrad, sea to shining sea, 7,500 miles across the largest country on earth. It was the hardest journey of my life—not physically but spiritually.

Two months into the trip, I met Saulius on the shores of Lake Baikal. I remember it was sleeting. We spotted a ribbon of smoke in the forest and veered off the road to a campfire, around which huddled six Lithuanian cyclists. We shook hands, and they shared their meager food and pushed our shivering bodies toward the warmth of the snapping birch fire. We were kin, members of the fellowship of the wheel.

Saulius was the smallest of the Lithuanians, a sinewy, birdlike man with a hawk nose and burning, white-blue eyes. He and I had an immediate, inexplicable connection. It was as if our friendship were already there, like a set table, just waiting for us to come from the far corners of the world, sit down, and renew a conversation we'd been having for years.

172

We talked of the surreal Soviet nation we were experiencing: villages where there was no food but every man, woman, and child was drunk on rotgut; cities with monolithic concrete tenements, but only a dirt road leading into and out of town. Bread lines, vegetable lines, vodka lines, but no telephone lines, no newspapers, no magazines. The countless hagiographic statues of Saint Lenin. The Big Brother billboards extolling the virtues of communism. The KGB trailing us in black Ladas. People so oppressed they'd lost their dignity.

That evening we all rode together for a stretch, and Saulius and I exchanged bicycles—me struggling along on his heavy, antique veloci-pede and him piloting my light, modern machine as if it were a glider. While I cranked to keep up with him, Saulius explained to me in broken English the real reason he had come to Siberia: to find the work camp where his wife, Palmira, had been interned as a child.

Deportations of Lithuanians began immediately after the Soviet Union occupied the country in the summer of 1940. Between 1940 and 1953, Stalin sent some 350,000 Lithuanians to Siberia. Many never returned.

On May 22, 1948, the KGB set a one-day record in Lithuania, arrest-ing 35,766 citizens—10,897 of them children—packing them into cattle cars, and shunting them off to work camps in Siberia. Palmira and her family were victims of this purge. Her grandfather was a small but suc-cessful farmer. He owned potato fields, beehives, and a few head of cattle, and was therefore a capitalist, a criminal. Palmira was three and her brother, Remigijus, two. Their father eluded capture, but Palmira and her mother, uncle, grandfather, and brother were deported to the shores of Lake Baikal.

Palmira's father, living under an assumed name, managed to send them food, and they gardened with fervor, at night, on small secret plots. But they had to be careful. If they were found to be improving their lives above the lot of others, they would have been sent even deeper into Siberia.

Nine years later, on April 24, 1957, Palmira and her family were released and allowed to return home. Their stone farmhouse had been seized by the government and was now the residence of a Soviet oligarch, so they lived with friends in Kaunas, a small city in central Lithuania.

Riding beside me, Saulius relayed this story with quiet gravity. The next morning, we exchanged addresses, then he and the Lithuanians rode east along Lake Baikal and my team and I rode west.

It would take us three more months to reach Leningrad and become the first people to bicycle across the USSR. It was such a long journey it wasn't a journey at all; it was just life. We rode and we ate and we slept, and then we got up and rode and ate and slept. Our bikes became our friends, and we gave them Russian names. Tom Freisem, the leader of the trip, named his *Blagorodnaya Sobaka*—Noble Dog. Torie Scott, the only American female, called hers *Zavtra*—Tomorrow. I named my bike *Svabodny*—Free.

By the time we dipped our front tires into the ice-cold Baltic, fall had come to Russia. It was snowing and we were so exhausted we could have slept for a year. Instead we threw a party, each of us inviting someone who had meant something special to us during our ride. I invited Saulius. We sang hard and drank hard and danced hard, as if it were our last night on this earth. And in a way it was. It was the end of 1989, and the Soviet Union was imploding.

In the melancholy hours of the morning I gave Saulius my bicycle, *Svabodny*.

•   •   •

That was the last time I saw Saulius, but I wrote about him in a book about that trip, *Off the Map*. Now, remembering our friendship, I pulled it from the shelf and read the opening passage about Saulius:

> Sometimes you meet someone you know. You have spent nights together. You've camped together beneath the sky and sung songs together and drunk beer in each other's homes. You have hugged and cried and laughed together. And you've never met. There are few such people in the world, but they are the ones you will always know and who will always know you. They are living in parts of the world where you haven't been. They are living lives you cannot know. They have kitchens with bright windows you can't imagine, where you had coffee. These are the people you meet, and know, before you speak.

Sixteen years later, my words sounded presumptuous. How could I have felt that I really knew this man? We'd spent so little time together. Were we really that close, or was it just the circumstances?

My wife and I were leaving for St. Petersburg in two weeks on a pianist exchange program for our two daughters. On the off chance they could help, I dialed the University of Wyoming's international-students office and asked if they knew of anyone in Laramie who spoke Lithuanian. They did: Rimvyda Dreher, a Lithuanian-American who worked as a business manager at the school. Lithuanian was her native tongue.

I explained the task to Rimvyda. I had only his name: Saulius Kunigenas. I didn't know where he was or even if he was alive. She was eager to help—her father had been in the Lithuanian Resistance before escaping to the United States in 1951. Amazingly, after multiple online searches and a half-dozen dead-end phone calls, Rim found Saulius.

The connection was so staticky she could barely hear him, but she managed to catch an e-mail address. E-mail didn't exist when I first met Saulius. I wrote immediately and got a response from Laima Kunigenas, his daughter. I hadn't even known he had a daughter. She was twenty-four, spoke English, had worked in California, and had just finished her master's in economics at Kaunas University of Technology. Laima wrote that of course her father remembered me.

"He says for you to come to Lithuania. Bring your bicycle. He will be waiting for you."

A month later I was on the night train south from St. Petersburg to Vilnius, the capital of Lithuania, then west to Kaunas, Saulius's hometown. As I rumbled through flat pine forests in a sleeper, watching the sun sink at midnight then bounce annoyingly back up at 2:00 a.m., the enterprise suddenly seemed mad.

Would we even recognize each other after so long? And if we did, what would it be like to see each other again? I remembered an agile, athletic man, but what is memory? Mostly what you want to remember, heedless of reality. I'd imagined that perhaps Saulius and I could bicycle across Lithuania, a country the size of West Virginia on the Baltic Sea. But was he even still cycling? So much happens in sixteen years. Unnervingly, it occurred to me that I actually knew very little about Saulius. I never knew how old he was or what his profession was. We'd just clicked on an emotional level. Our shared landscape had been the brutal, irrational Soviet empire, but now the USSR was dead.

· · ·

Saulius spotted me, and I him, the moment I stepped off the train. He ran to me, gripping my hand and hugging me at the same time. He looked just as he had a decade and a half ago—Roman nose, deeply tanned, the wiry body of a Tour de France rider. In the strength of his handshake alone, I knew that our friendship was still alive. We threw my collapsible bicycle into the backseat of his car and drove to his home.

The awkwardness I'd feared lasted only moments, then we were excitedly shooting questions back and forth, trying to catch up on each other's lives. He was fifty-five now, had survived stomach cancer, and was still cycling hard, having logged more than 125,000 miles. He and Palmira had traveled through Australia, Brazil, Iceland, and much of Western Europe. He was delighted to learn that I too was still cycling, and surprised to discover that I was a journalist, had a wife and two daughters, and had also traveled extensively.

"Everything!" Saulius said happily, practically shouting. "Everything different now."

Even with the rise of computers and the Internet, even with 9/11, Afghanistan, and two Gulf wars, in the past two decades life for ordinary Americans has hardly changed at all compared with life in Lithuania.

The solemn intensity Saulius had exhibited when I met him in Siberia had been transformed into the energy of hope. Pre-independence, he'd worked for a Russian construction firm as a poorly paid mechanical engineer. Post-independence, he went back to school, got an MBA, became a general contractor, and began building small, efficient custom homes in Kaunas. After five years he and Palmira had saved enough to leave their dismal Soviet block apartment and build their own house next to a forest on the outskirts of the city.

As we pulled up to his modest brick home with cherry trees and a barbecue grill in the backyard, I couldn't help but wonder whether he'd kept *Svabodny*. Back in 1989, along with the bike, I'd given Saulius a crate of spare parts, so he could have kept it rolling indefinitely—but perhaps it didn't mean to him what it had meant to me.

Yet there it was, hanging in the garage, perfectly maintained.

"No bike like this in all Lithuania before independence," said Saulius, explaining that he used to ride *Svabodny* through Kaunas to show people what was happening beyond the Iron Curtain. After independence, Saulius rode right across the borders, touring through Finland and Germany and all the Baltic states. "I ride and ride. It's a special bike—your gift to me."

He reached for *Svabodny*, I assembled my folding bike, and we went for a ride. It felt natural to be on bikes together, cruising the streets of Kaunas.

That night, in a kitchen with bright windows, I met his wife, Palmira, a retired professor of textiles, and his daughter, Laima, a fledgling economist. Over after-dinner coffee, conversation inevitably fell to geopolitics.

"The only way to enslave a country," said Palmira in German, "is to cut off the head. Stalin understood this; that's why he deported the teachers, the engineers, the government officials, the officers, the successful farmers, the businessmen—all of us."

More than 20 million people died in the gulag. The post-Stalin decades were less violent, but the intellectual foot-binding continued. In 1986, Mikhail Gorbachev began the process of liberalization that quickly gave eighteen Soviet states their freedom. The new constitution of the Republic of Lithuania, a parliamentary democracy, was ratified by referendum in 1992.

"But that is all past," Palmira said, smiling at Laima, who will never be sent to Siberia. "Tomorrow you shall see Lithuania today."

• • •

The next morning, just as I'd imagined, Saulius and I rode off on what he dubbed the Democratic Tour of Lithuania. We planned to pedal from Kaunas to the sea and back, a 400-mile loop, camping wherever we found ourselves at the end of the day and living off local markets. From the start, there was an ease to the trip that made me feel as though we'd been touring together since childhood.

That first day we slid west along the Nemunas River, Saulius showing off the medieval castles and Gothic cathedrals that overlook the sleepy green waterway.

"Lithuania was independent country for 500 years," he stated proudly from the top of one castle turret.

Under the reign of the Grand Duke Algirdas (1345 to 1377), the borders of Lithuania had extended from the Baltic Sea to the Black Sea. The geographical center of Europe lies in Lithuania, and it has always been a Western-leaning country. Unlike Russia, Lithuania fully embraced the

Renaissance. The first book written in Lithuanian was published in 1547, and Vilnius University was founded in 1579.

That night we pitched our tent in a cow pasture. In the morning, we cycled along narrow, tree-lined roads, through brilliant yellow fields of rapeseed, all the way to the coast. A motorboat, owned by a father and son who had started a ferry business after independence, took us out to the Curonian Spit, a 61-mile arm of sand dotted with summer communities. We beach-camped on the Baltic, sand in our gears, the sound of the waves in our ears.

On day three we winged north along the spit from the seaside resort town of Nida (loaded with thick-calved Germans), through the port city of Klaipeda, and on to Palanga (loaded with pale-skinned Finns). The tourism industry was clearly buoyant as a beach ball.

In the years since independence, Lithuanians, industrious and entrepreneurial, have made their country the most successful former Soviet republic. Privatization of once-nationalized companies is almost complete. Business is thriving, from banking to bioengineering; exports are robust; and in 2004 Lithuania was accepted into the European Union.

On our fourth day out, we circled back inland, visiting the farmhouse of family friends who had also been sent to Siberia in the late forties. When I asked Saulius if any of his family had been deported, he said, "No. My uncle was shot."

After World War II, during the early years of Soviet control, an armed underground resistance formed in Lithuania. Eventually numbering 100,000 partisans, the movement fought a guerrilla war against Soviet occupation until 1953, when it was finally crushed. Saulius's uncle had joined the resistance in 1948, at the age of twenty-four, was caught by the KGB, and was executed in the forest.

That afternoon, Saulius guided me to another remote farm he felt I must see: the gardens of sculptor Vilius Orvidas (1952 to 1992), a deeply religious, mystical man who devoted his life to opposing the occupation. His farm was a strange labyrinth of gargantuan logs and monumental religious and communist sculptures, the antithesis of the Stalin World theme park. On one heavy slab of black granite, Orvidas had depicted the USSR as a giant spider, its hairy legs reaching into Europe, Asia, and Siberia. Across the top of the rock was inscribed COMMUNISM IS THE SORROW OF THE WORLD.

On the last day, looping back into Kaunas, we rode together without talking, mile after mile. We were in unison, and words were redundant. Just riding together again, after so many years, was enough.

Outside of Kaunas, Saulius took me by the fortresslike home of a mafia boss, explaining that prostitution, corruption, and drug use have increased in Lithuania in the past decade.

"It is one small bad side of capitalism," Saulius said exuberantly. "But at least we have independence!"

●　●　●

The night before I left Lithuania, Saulius and I stayed up talking. I invited him to the United States, to my home in Wyoming. I told him about Yellowstone and Devils Tower, the mountains and the deserts.

"Finally," Saulius said softly, "I can come."

After we went to bed, I sneaked into Saulius's garage and took down *Svabodny*. With yellow, green, and red paint—the colors of Lithuania's flag—I painted a new name along the top tube: *Laisvé*—*Freedom* in Lithuanian.

I wish this story ended here.

The next morning, Saulius had a stroke. I found him in the garage lying on the concrete below *Laisvé*. I cradled him until the ambulance came. Palmira would not let me stay. I had a plane ticket back to the United States, and she insisted I return home to my own family. Saulius is in rehab now, and it is uncertain whether he will bike again.

Even deep friendships are fragile. Someone you met on a journey years ago is out there. The friendship is not lost, only dormant, waiting for the spark of contact. Go. Find that person.

Into the War Zone

POLES APART

I was leaving for Afghanistan. I had my plane tickets for Kabul and the perfect travel companion waiting for me: Greg Mortenson.

Greg is the founder of the Bozeman-based Central Asia Institute (CAI), a nonprofit humanitarian organization that builds schools and health clinics for the remote mountain people of Pakistan and Afghanistan. He has spent much of the last eight years working in Baltistan, a region in far northern Pakistan bordered by Afghanistan, China, and Kashmir. Few Americans know more about this area, an intricate geopolitical knot as jagged and confusing as the landscape itself.

Greg and I had been planning our trip for six months. We intended to spend six weeks walking across the almost unknown mountains of far northern Afghanistan, living village to village. Greg had obtained promises of safe passage from various military commanders and warlords, including the leader of the anti-Taliban Northern Alliance, Ahmad Shah Massoud.

I knew a bit of the region's history—tales of the Raj, the wars and diplomatic skirmishes of the nineteenth-century's Great Game that pitted the British against the Russians as both countries sought influence in Central Asia, the lore of K2 and the Karakoram. Greg undertook the task of bringing me up-to-date via a correspondence course in realpolitik. Among the books he sent me were Eric S. Margolis's *War at the Top of the World*, Ahmed Rashid's *Taliban: Militant Islam, Oil and Fundamentalism in Central Asia*, Inayatullah Faizi's *Wakhan: A Window into Central Asia*. I learned about the centuries-long history of fractious Afghan warlords; about the British spies trickling through the country as far back as 1810; about the forty-seven British military expeditions, every one of which failed; about the Russian troops sent to conquer this graveyard of armies; about the inexhaustible intrigues of the CIA, the KGB, Pakistan's Directorate of Inter-Services Intelligence, and Afghanistan's KHAD state information service; about the collusion and contradictions of the mujahideen, the jihads, the madrassas. Even on the most remote mountain trek, you never simply traverse the landscape; you pass through politics and history.

Then, on September 11, 2001, nineteen hijackers turned four US passenger planes into missiles and massacred 3,000 innocent people. I immediately spoke to Greg, who was visiting CAI projects in northern Pakistan, via satellite phone.

"Massoud has been assassinated," he said somberly. "Some of our military clearances have been compromised, and I'm no longer certain we have safe passage. Our exit in Faisalabad is particularly problematic."

Greg and I discussed our options, both of us in shock and overwhelmed by a sense of loss.

"This is not only a horrific tragedy, it's a taunt," Greg said. "These terrorists want the US to overreact. They want us to lash out indiscriminately. They want us to ignite a global jihad."

We decided to suspend any decision about our journey for a few days, to see what changes time might bring.

I was gravely conflicted. Like all Americans, I was aflame with the desire to do something, to help, a frustrated passion whipped by the emotional winds of helplessness after so much evil and so many deaths. The uncertainties and complications of war had suddenly trumped the simplicity of adventure. We had planned to trek through remote valleys along ancient trade routes, dreaming of history and of a better future for the inhabitants of those mountain outposts; now we would be passing through nervous, disconnected fiefdoms bristling with tension and bracing for the battles to come.

· · ·

Like most of my generation, I have never served in the military. I've seen the raw borderlands of hot and cold wars, however, in South Africa and Burma, in Sierra Leone and Tibet. I've been arrested, interrogated, and detained by guerrillas and by "legitimate" military forces. I've sidestepped land mines, crawled under barbed wire, and ducked bullets with soldiers and mercenaries. And most importantly, I've met their victims. This tenuous trip to Afghanistan was now forcing me to confront the contradictory relationship between war and adventure.

For much of human history, from the imperial triumphs of Alexander the Great to the conquests of colonialism and our own ultimately world-altering revolution, adventure and war have been virtually synonymous.

Boys, be they Vikings or Greeks or Mongols or Brits, were taught the fundamental skills of warfare. Swordsmanship, archery, and wrestling were the educational prerequisites for the great test of manhood: war. The same flags that flew at the vanguard of expeditions of discovery flew over the smoke and carnage of battlefields.

Some of the world's greatest explorers were military men: Sir Richard Burton, Major John Wesley Powell, Captain Robert Falcon Scott. Yet many others were not: Ibn Battuta, Marco Polo, Fridtjof Nansen, Roald Amundsen. All were driven as much by an inextinguishable curiosity as by a sense of national duty. In our own culture, Theodore Roosevelt might be considered the quintessential soldier–adventurer. He hunted, fished, climbed the Matterhorn, explored Africa and Brazil; he also served as assistant secretary of the navy and commanded troops and fought in Cuba.

"War always does bring out what is highest and lowest in human nature," Roosevelt wrote in his 1913 autobiography, just before the outbreak of World War I. A decade later, veterans of the Great War, for one of the first times in history, would speak candidly about the conundrum that Roosevelt had acknowledged. Yes, in war there were untold thousands of heroic, self-sacrificing acts, but there were also untold horror and thousands of acts of cruelty and sadism. To those who had not seen it, war remained a grand and mysterious opportunity for adventure—but few who had seen its unspeakable depravity spoke of it that way.

• • •

Two days passed, and when Greg managed to get through via sat phone again, the situation had further deteriorated. Radical clerics in Pakistan had called for a fatwa against their own government, and there was rioting in Peshawar.

"It might be difficult to travel right now," he said. "Things are rather fluid."

This was Greg's laconic way of saying the region was a mess. We discussed our misgivings about adventuring through the fields of war: Our journey could potentially jeopardize the lives of those who had sworn to protect us, and yet the urge to go was still keen.

Greg, who is fifty, came to his life's work through mountaineering. He grew up in Tanzania and served in the US military in Germany from 1975 to 1977. In 1993, already a veteran of several Himalayan expeditions, he went to climb K2. After a grueling seventy-five days on the mountain, during which time his team managed to rescue two men, he stumbled down into a Balti village, emaciated, exhausted, spiritually drained. Nursed back to health by the villagers, he vowed to return not to climb, but to build a school.

That promise took three years to fulfill. He wrote nearly 600 letters asking for donations and twelve grant proposals, and got nothing. He had sold his climbing gear and his car, and was about to head back to Pakistan when the phone rang. It was Jean Hoerni, a Swiss physicist who had made a fortune in the microchip industry. Hoerni established the endowment that created CAI in 1996.

CAI has since built fifty-eight schools, twenty-four water projects, and fourteen women's vocational centers in Baltistan and has launched several dozen community health programs that provide such services as cataract surgery and midwife training. It also supports refugee camps for women and children who have escaped the Taliban.

In doing CAI work, Greg has repeatedly put himself on the line. In 1996 while visiting water projects in Waziristan, 200 miles south of Peshawar, he was kidnapped by a group of warring clansmen.

"Eight men with Kalashnikovs burst into my room at 2:00 a.m., blindfolded me, and drove me off into the hills," Greg told me when we were first planning our trip. "I was held in a windowless mud room. At first I became deeply depressed. On the fourth day, I decided I needed to at least try to understand why I was a captive."

He asked his guards for the Koran. They brought the Koran as well as a teacher. "I studied the Koran with this man, attempting to gain a deeper understanding of their point of view." Greg ultimately learned that there was a dispute between two local tribes and that he was being held hostage as a potential bargaining chip.

"I told them I was expecting the birth of my first son," said Greg. "This is a big deal in their culture. "

Greg believes that it was only through his willingness to reach across the cultural and religious divide that he escaped execution. "It was a useful lesson for survival."

· · ·

Where does adventure lie within the range of human endeavor? Somewhere between sport and war.

Any great adventure is a physical challenge. A marathon may last three and a half hours; a Himalayan expedition is seldom shorter than three weeks; an ocean voyage may require three months. And yet it's not simply stamina that is required, but technique developed through years of practice—the gymnastic ability to pull through a difficult move on rock, the uncoiling precision of a kayaker's Eskimo roll. But adventure moves beyond the realm of pure sport at the point where sport moves into the realm of mortal consequence.

In most sports, if you make the wrong decision you probably won't pay for it with your life. You may twist an ankle or break bones, but you won't die. Make the wrong call climbing a big mountain or kayaking a big river, and it could be your last.

Furthermore, unlike other sports, adventures have objective hazards. The jaws of an icefall, boat-swallowing holes, flesh-freezing cold. The secret of getting good at adventure is to develop the skills needed to accurately assess and circumvent these deadly traps. Some of us are still randomly picked off by rockfall, lightning, and storms, but most deaths can be attributed to bad judgment.

Not so in war. The risk of death, along with the crucial relevance of teamwork, esprit de corps, and trust, are where war and adventure overlap, but there are at least three fundamental distinctions.

First, the obstacles in war are other humans (and their manufactured hazards—booby traps, bombs, bullets) who are incomparably more clever and unpredictable than water or rock or weather.

Second, in war, innocent people always die along with the soldiers. When adventure goes wrong, innocent people are not killed. Adventurers risk their own lives, not those of others.

Third, in war, participants are not allowed the freedom to make consequential decisions; they must face danger without holding authority over their own fate. To maintain discipline amid the terror of war, the chain of command must be rigidly hierarchical. In adventure, the individual almost always must decide his or her own destiny, to turn back or go on. This freedom of will is the very embodiment of adventure.

• • •

Three days later Greg called again. He had just hitched a ride around K2 in a Pakistani military chopper, on the way back from visiting one of CAI's schools.

"It was gorgeous!" he said, his voice faint with the distance. "I don't think there is a more beautiful place on the planet. I wish everyone could trek into this part of the Karakoram. But maybe right now's not the time."

I told Greg I'd been concerned about the prospect of reporting from a war zone after months of preparing to write about adventure, and that I was wrestling over the distinction between war and adventure.

"They're poles apart," he responded. "Adventure is a building-up process. It's about appreciating beauty, nature, and people. War is a tearing-down process."

He launched into an explanation of all he'd learned about himself and the world through adventure, from climbing Kilimanjaro in 1969 at the age of eleven to his life-changing attempt on K2 in 1993. Like the rest of us, he still has a list of hoped-for journeys: following in the footsteps of nineteenth-century British Great Game spies across the Himalayas; ascending a number of unclimbed peaks north of the Hindu Kush; walking across northeastern Afghanistan, as we had planned.

"Adventure is touching the fringes of your own physical, mental, and spiritual dreams. Adventure is connecting with other people. You know who are the best ambassadors for America? Not diplomats: adventurers. Villagers over here have seen the *Rambo* movies. But the ones who actually meet Americans suddenly see us as humans, not villains. And these same travelers return home capable of seeing 'the enemy' as human. It sounds so trivial, so simple. . . . "

The line started popping, his voice grew faint. "Mark, I'll call you back. We have to make a decision."

• • •

On an adventure you are self-selected, a volunteer; you participate of your own free will. This is seldom the case in war. Even in a volunteer army, many young people sign up simply for a free education, not to kill somebody. And yet in war, the challenge is to overcome the enemy, which directly or indirectly means killing. On an adventure the challenge is not to take life, but to enrich it, to test one's will and skill and stamina against the immutability of the earth. Yes, there is sometimes pettiness, selfishness, and pride, but the gestalt of adventure is still the antithesis of war.

Fascists and fetishists of war have smugly described adventure as an adolescent surrogate for war—as if war were the apogee of human engagement. But even with all the staggering acts of heroism that warfare can engender, even if giving your own life so that others may live is the highest sacrifice a human can make, anyone who has been through a war knows the mendacity of such thinking. The boy I'd met on the border of Sierra Leone who'd had his hands chopped off by the rebels knows. The legless soldier in Russia knows. The nine-year-old girls in northern Burma who had been raped by government soldiers know. To all the victims, war—even when morally obligatory or politically unavoidable—is the zenith of human failure.

Adventure opens doors to some of the highest human instincts—courage, camaraderie, patience, tenacity—without simultaneously opening a Pandora's box of atrocities. I remember Andy Lapkass, retching with pleurisy, warming soup for me on the north face of Everest when I was too weak to even light the stove. I remember Belgian hang gliders rescuing me and my brother Daniel after he broke his leg deep in Morocco. I remember the maroon-robed Buddhist monks hiding me from the police in Arunachal Pradesh.

Adventure is largely a luxury of peace. And when peace fails, the spirit of adventure is inescapably twisted into the martial form of war.

• • •

Greg got through five days later. He was calling from Islamabad, where rumors of an imminent US attack on Afghanistan were flashing through the streets.

"There are nearly 27 million Afghans and probably no more than 45,000 Taliban," Greg said. "That's one Taliban for every 600 Afghans. We helped create the Taliban. We funded them, we trained them, we used them in a proxy war to stop the Soviet Union from marching down to the Arabian Sea—basically to keep them away from our oil. Then, after we got what we wanted, we abandoned Afghanistan and its people to the Taliban radicals."

Greg was appalled at the prospect of more killing in a country that was already "nothing more than a land of starvation, mutilation, and oppression.

"The Afghans know war better than any people," he said. "They have had two decades of hatred, executions, torture. The long-term solution to terrorism is to help them. Feed them, clothe them, help them create a viable economic infrastructure. If we ever want to reduce terrorism, we will need the support of the Afghans.

"We have to show them that the world can be a better place. We have to show them love."

. . .

I spoke to Greg one last time before he escaped to the refuge of the mountains. I told him I wouldn't be coming over, at least not in the next few weeks. At this stage, any trip through Afghanistan could only focus on the crisis. The beauty, the history, the culture would only be footnotes to a story of death and destruction. Journalists from around the world were rushing to Pakistan and Afghanistan to cover the brutal play-by-play. I would not be one of them.

"Mark, it's the right decision," Greg said sadly.

I asked him what he was going to do.

"Stay here. Go back up to Baltistan. Work on the schools. You know, it sounds absurd, but perhaps none of this would have happened if women were allowed to go to school."

In some fundamentalist Islamic cultures, women are forbidden even a basic education. The Taliban, who have imposed an unrecognizably distorted form of Islam on Afghanistan, deny women the right to learn to read and write. From the start, CAI has focused on education for girls and on the empowerment of women; each time CAI funds the building of a school, the villagers must agree to increase girls' enrollment by ten percent annually. The CAI refugee camps for Afghani women and children focus not simply on food, clean water, and shelter, but on education.

"Girls' education has a major influence on a region's quality of life," Greg said. "Educating girls reduces infant mortality and overpopulation, which in turn reduces ignorance and poverty—the most fertile grounds for extremists."

Greg Mortenson, like Sir Edmund Hillary before him, is a climber who came down from the summit with a conscience. In a ravaged part of the world, he is one man who has severed the Gordian knot entwining adventure with war, and instead has bound adventure to acts of kindness.

"No matter what happens," he said, "the schools, the children, the mountains—everything that really matters—will all still be here next spring. You can come then."

SEMPER FI

"Suffering is mandatory," Captain Clinton Culp shouts, an egg-size plug of chewing tobacco in his mouth. "Misery is optional!" He spits in the snow and grins.

It's meant to be a joke, kind of, but the marines, twenty of them, are too cold to laugh. They're standing in a foot of snow in a clearing in central Alaska. It's 3:00 p.m.—already dusk, the sky and the snow an ice-pale blue, another endless arctic night descending. The temperature is −15°F, with a scalpel-like breeze, and the marines are doing everything they possibly can to stay warm: stamping their white skis, clapping their heavily mittened hands, turtling their balaclava'd heads into their hunched shoulders. The men aspire to become instructors at the Marine Corps Mountain Warfare Training Center. After months of classes and exercises at the center, about twenty miles north of Yosemite, they've been flown up to Alaska to find out if they have what it takes to teach at the toughest school in the corps.

Culp, thirty-five, a lean, tall Texan, could pass for a country singer. Now Captain Justin Anderson—twenty-nine years old, 215 pounds, with flat eyes and a redbrick corner of a nose, the reincarnation of a nineteenth-century Scottish boxer—steps forward. Anderson comes from a military family—one uncle took shrapnel to the head in Korea, one uncle was gut shot in Vietnam. Anderson would have joined the Marines right out of high school if his parents hadn't insisted he go to college. So he did, at the Citadel.

"Marines! If you're cold it's your fault!" The clouds of Anderson's breath swirl in front of his face. "Now fucking pay attention, this is how it's supposed to be done! Sergeant Tooby."

Colour Sergeant Steven Tooby, thirty-four, is a British Royal Marine with a scarlet face who refuses to wear a hat no matter how damn cold it is. Instead, Tooby wears an indomitable, elfish smirk. He can ski like a Swede, telemark like a Norwegian, and curse like a sailor, and he gladly informs any marine at any time how "'orribly foken bahd" he's fucking up.

Tooby raises an arm and four skiers in white arctic camo come gliding into the clearing in single file. Even the M-16s strapped across their chests have been carefully wrapped in white tape. Suddenly the lead skier is firing—crack-crack-crack-crack-crack—the ejected shells arcing into the snow. The second skier has already veered right, dropped to one knee, swung his poles forward, planted them in an X, set his M-16 in the notch, and started firing. In seconds the team is fanned out and advancing; three skiers provide cover fire while one bounds forward, kneels, and starts shooting. The fighters hopscotch forward, swiftly skiing and shooting their way toward a line of green cardboard targets—silhouettes of enemy soldiers—at the far end of the clearing.

It's a deadly display of precise choreography. This is a live-fire immediate-action drill; if any of these guys were to trip, slip, or miscalculate, they could instantly execute a fellow marine.

They start retreating. Again, three skiers provide cover fire while one drops back, kneels, makes the ski-pole X, and begins firing while another marine is falling back. They retreat all the way back into the trees; silence returns to the snow-laden landscape.

I'm standing to the side with thirty-five-year-old Major Craig Kozeniesky—"Major K," the boss—and Captain Mike Andretta, twenty-seven, his second in command. I peer through my monocular at the cardboard soldiers. In their chests are ragged holes the size of a silver dollar.

Culp, Anderson, and Tooby stare dourly at the huddle of marines. The four who just performed are their finest instructors. They created them. Someday a few of the men gathered before them might be that good, and thus qualified to teach other marines how to fight in the mountain cold.

"So!" Anderson says, cocking his square head, "Sergeant Tooby and I don't care if your tits are frozen solid! Your job is to do what they just did."

•   •   •

The Marine Corps Mountain Warfare Training Center (MWTC) was founded in 1951 in response to the losses suffered by ill-prepared US forces in the Korean War, where more than 3,000 soldiers sustained severe frostbite during the Chosin Reservoir campaign alone. Over the last half-century the MWTC, headquartered near Bridgeport, California,

has trained nearly half a million members of the corps, other branches of
the US military, and armed forces from other nations. Every year approximately 10,000 marines undergo training at the MWTC. By comparison,
the army's Northern Warfare Training Center in Fort Wainwright,
Alaska, sees fewer than 500 servicemen annually, and the Army Mountain Warfare School, in Jericho, Vermont, trains several hundred soldiers,
guardsmen, and reservists each year. The army's Tenth Mountain Division, despite its name and history, has not trained units in mountaineering, avalanche work, or cold-weather survival since World War II.

When the US-led campaign against the Taliban and al Qaeda forces in
Afghanistan was launched in October 2001, the relevance of mountain
warfare was thrown into sharp relief. The withdrawal of the Soviet military from Afghanistan in the 1980s was attributed not only to the ferocity
of Afghan guerrilla fighters, but to the region's vast, rugged, and remote
mountain landscape. Despite the antiterrorism coalition's overwhelming
air superiority and the panoply of new technology available to American
forces, the prospect of US soldiers helping to hunt down Osama bin
Laden and his Taliban allies in harsh winter conditions across some of the
most difficult terrain on Earth suddenly became very real.

In the past, it was widely assumed that civilian mountain guides, rock
climbers, and avalanche specialists were far more advanced in technique
and equipment than their military counterparts. "Military climbing" has
sometimes been used as a term of ridicule. Today, however, a strong liai-
son exists between adventure athletes and soldiers. In recent months, for
example, Exum Mountain Guides in Jackson Hole, Wyoming, has been
training military personnel who are on their way to the front line in
Afghanistan.

Among the members of the Fifteenth and Twenty-Sixth Marine Expe-
ditionary Units deployed near Kandahar in late November were a number of "mountain leaders" and assault climbers who received advanced
training at MWTC; hundreds of other marines who were sent to Afghanistan have also been trained at the center. But according to Major General
Thomas Jones, the Quantico, Virginia–based commander of training and
education for the Marine Corps, the mission of MWTC goes beyond
preparing units to fight in places like Central Asia.

"Training in a cold, mountainous environment is the closest thing we
have to approximating the stress a soldier undergoes in combat," Jones

told me. "If a marine can learn how to fight in the cold in the mountains, he can fight anywhere—desert, jungle, anywhere. Severe cold and rugged terrain force soldiers to work together, to share and eventually overcome incredible adversity. It builds cohesiveness.

"You can't simulate humping a seventy-pound pack up to 11,000 feet," he continued. "You can't simulate climbing or skiing. You can't simulate cold. You can't simulate fear. You have to experience these things—experience them and learn from them. That's how to make a soldier. Even if we never fought another day in the cold or the mountains, we would still train in Alaska, because it teaches marines how to handle extreme conditions. That's the real power of the Mountain Warfare Training Center, and the brass know it."

I arranged to visit MWTC in California and then accompany about sixty marines to winter maneuvers at a training site south of Fairbanks, Alaska. In addition to the ten battalions that receive summer and winter mountain warfare training at MWTC each year, some 300 marines come annually in hopes of either becoming MWTC instructors or mountain leaders for their own battalions. One purpose of the trip to Alaska is to evaluate the program's would-be leaders. Nearly a third of these hopefuls don't succeed.

"It's the most physically intense program in the military," Captain Andretta told me when I first spoke with him by phone. "It's an elite posting. You have to want to come, and you have to pull strings to make it happen. Those marines who survive to become instructors are the cream of the crop: the strongest, the toughest, the smartest in the corps."

● ● ●

MWTC lies in the belly of the central Sierra Nevada, on 46,000 acres leased from Toyaibe National Forest. Elevations range from 6,000 to 11,500 feet, and the terrain rises from creek-bottom brush to towering ponderosa forest to sheer granite walls. Much of the alpine portion is buried beneath six feet of snow for half the year. The base itself resembles a community college—a cluster of brown and tan buildings cradled by mountains. The day I showed up, a foot of new powder was on the Sierra crest.

Captain Andretta is the OIC of the IQC for MWTC. In civilian-speak, that's the officer in charge of the Instructor Qualification Course.

He showed me around, starting with a gleaming, state-of-the-art fitness center and weight room.

"Instructor candidates spend a month straight in the field," he said, "and are taught and then tested on such subjects as advanced avalanche skills, rock climbing, ice climbing, mountain navigation, cliff assaults, cold-weather weapons operations, survival, water procurement, wilderness first aid—everything that fighting in the mountains entails."

Passing into the gymnasium, Andretta flicked on the lights to reveal a thirty-five-foot-high climbing wall with radical overhangs, cracks, pockets, and chimneys stretching the length of the basketball court. He asked if I'd like to climb. We spent the next several hours on the wall, climbing one route after another.

Andretta is a kayaker and a vegetarian, drives a hammered Toyota pickup with the radio locked on National Public Radio, and has a degree in civil engineering. He loves the satire of the *Onion*, and the furniture in the house where he rooms with a marine helicopter pilot has been arranged according to the principles of feng shui. His dad was a marine. "Antiquated as some may think it sounds," he told me, "I joined because I wanted to serve my country. My mom keeps asking me when I'm going to use my degree, but to me, I already have: I used it to get a commission in the Marine Corps."

In the morning I worked out with the mountain instructors and then showered with a bunch of muscled guys—clean-cut military men who, naked, turned out to be inscribed with tattoos: barbed wire, battle cries, babes.

I spent the afternoon with the quotable Captain Culp, a seventeen-year career officer who's been deployed in Korea, Somalia, Norway, and the Philippines. He loves the life: "Hey! If it doesn't give you a woody, you're in the wrong fuckin' business."

Culp drove me up toward Sonora Pass, pointing his bulging cheek full of chaw at a snow-caked peak. "Every morning the men run, ski, or snowshoe four miles straight up from the base, a gain of 3,000 feet."

I must not have seemed appropriately impressed.

"With an assault load, of course," Culp added. "Daypacks, full canteens, full magazines, M-16s."

Culp took me to the granite cliffs where the marines practice rock climbing.

"Thirteen different knots, twelve different rope systems. To pass the course you have to lead 5.7."

Well, I thought, 5.7 isn't that difficult.

In standard-issue combat boots, Culp went on, again with an assault load and loaded weapon.

At night.

"With a headlamp?" I asked.

Culp shook his head. "Nice big target smack-dab on your forehead."

For downhill-skiing instruction, the marines are shuttled to Kirkwood, a nearby ski area to learn and then practice telemarking. This, too, must eventually be done with a full load, in the dark.

"All the flat-ground training we teach right here," Culp said. "Diagonal stride, V–1, V–2."

Back at the base he loaned me a set of manuals and textbooks. The avalanche material, I saw, came from the most recent edition of *Snow Sense*, the best book on the subject; the alpine-climbing sections featured the latest information from *Mountaineering: The Freedom of the Hills*, sixth edition; the river- and canyon-crossing procedures reflected the most sophisticated canyoneering techniques in use anywhere. The gear, too, is first-rate: Patagonia's Capilene long underwear, Polartec fleece, Gore-Tex jackets and bivy sacks, Alico three-pin boots, The North Face tents, Mountain Safety Research WhisperLite stoves.

Culp has one implacable expectation, and it is not simply to create skilled outdoorsmen. "We teach them how to climb and ski, and most of them love it," he said. "But those are just the means to an end. After they ski up through a pass or climb to the top of a cliff, they still have to have the capability and the strength and the will to fight. To hunt down the enemy and kill the bastards."

• • •

We flew in a C-130 transport plane to Alaska, sitting in nylon-strap seats in plane-length rows. The engine was too loud for conversation. We wore earplugs. Several guys played chess. Most of the men read. Andretta: *'Tis*, by Frank McCourt. Anderson: *The Trial*, by Franz Kafka. Culp: *The Bear Went Over the Mountain: Soviet Combat Tactics in Afghanistan*.

We landed after dark at Eielson Air Force Base and were bused south to the Fort Greely Military Reservation and its absurdly named Texas Range. It was −10°F.

The marines unloaded their gear, set up tents in the snow, and began what would become a ceaseless struggle against the cold. Every hour a new shift of sentries would crawl out of their sleeping bags, take up their M-16s, and stand guard in the cold.

The weak dawn illuminated a forbidding landscape. To the south was the Alaska Range, its thousands of peaks and valleys eternally encased in ice. To the north stretched a black, primeval forest. And all of it was as silent as Siberia, as if the cold itself had strangled all attempts at communication.

Forty of the sixty instructor candidates were ranked Tier Two—experienced, proven men. Twenty of them were Tier One—beginners struggling to pass the Instructor Qualification Course.

On day two, Tier Ones practiced flat-ground skiing exercises while Tier Twos were trucked up to the Black Rapids Training Site to practice telemarking. That night both groups did long, exhausting, lightless forest recons.

On day three both groups spent the day doing live-fire drills. They practiced skiing and shooting. They practiced snowshoeing and shooting. They practiced wearing seventy-pound packs and pulling sleds and breaking through willows and shooting. That night they practiced tracer-fire ambushes.

Everybody camped out in the snow, snatching what sleep they could between night maneuvers, night watches, and the never-ending winter-camping necessity of boiling snow for water and meals. I shared a tent with Captain Andretta and Major K, both of whom brought tiny black electric razors and, every morning, shaved sitting up in their sleeping bags.

Major K does everything his men do. When they ski, he skis; when they snowshoe, he snowshoes. And when they boot across some endless snaggly creek bottom with a seventy-pound pack he follows right behind—bearing his own load, observing, listening, saying very little. General Jones described him as "tougher than a woodpecker's lips," adding, "He's precisely the marine to train our marines."

Major K has been in the corps for thirteen years and has a degree in political science from the University of New Mexico. He has a wife and two sons and doesn't know what he would do if he weren't a marine. "My mom and my old man were marines," he says. His father lost both legs in

Vietnam. "He used to say that he had six good years and one bad day and that he'd still be 'in the suck' if he could be."

On day four, maneuvers are supposed to begin at one in the morning and include ice climbing, but there have been several "environmental casualties" among the novice instructors. One marine got his hands severely frostbitten and may lose several fingers; one scalded his hand while boiling snow water; one went down with vomiting and dehydration. And another was struck in the eye by an M-16 shell casing that burned his cornea during a midnight live-fire ambush. At 5:00 a.m. the remaining sixteen or so novices, some of whom have frostnip on their fingers or toes or are obviously hypothermic, are once again standing in the black cold, shivering, waiting for their orders.

Andretta is glowering. He looks furious—it's a side of him you might never know existed.

"What time is it?" he screams.

"0500, sir!" the marines shout, their breath instantly freezing.

"What time were we supposed to move out?"

"0100, sir!"

"I gave you four extra hours to unass yourselves. Why?"

"Safety, sir!"

"That's right. Goddamn it, pull your heads out of your asses! You're fucking up! You have to take care of yourselves. You have to take care of each other. You haven't even met the enemy yet, but already, one by one, you're going down!"

These men have hardly slept in four days. They've been skiing with a pack and firing their frozen M-16s and moving all day and deep into every night. They don't have the experience of the seasoned instructors. You can see the fear of the cold in their glazed eyes and rigid bodies.

Their orders: to attack an observation post (held by Tier Two veterans), rout the enemy, and consolidate the captured terrain. The observation post is on a bluff above the brush-choked, mile-wide Delta River. With a bare, windswept ridge at its back, birch draws buried in deep snow at either side, and an eagle's-eye view of the entire ice-coated river valley, the post commands a devastating 360-degree view.

The attack takes all day. The marines are exhausted and chilled to the bone and thus extremely slow. Some of them are carrying almost one hundred pounds. The snow varies from six inches of powder to thigh-killing crust. The marines trudge up through the hellish deadfall of the forest. They trudge across boggy open meadows. They trudge through pack-snaring willows. By the time they finally straggle up to the observation post, each of them has been "killed" by the enemy a dozen times.

Major K takes pity and allows them into the hut for their debriefing. Too often, he says, they were moving out in the open—directly in the enemy's line of sight—rather than utilizing the microterrain. Too often they were bunched together, ensuring mortar fire from the enemy. They attacked uphill rather than circling around and attacking downhill.

They also made simple winter mistakes. They didn't eat enough. They didn't drink enough. Worst of all, they failed to layer and unlayer properly. Terrified of the cold, most of them wore their heavy fleece throughout the movement. Sergeant Tooby is outraged.

"You know why you're all so foken exhausted? You foken sweated too much! You're totally dehydrated." He picks up one of their fleece jackets and wrings a torrent of sweat out of it. "It's absolutely foken mad!"

That night three more soldiers are pulled out of the squad. All have potentially severe hypothermia and will require warm-fluid IVs and a night in the heated operations trailer to recover.

High winds are predicted for sometime in the early hours. The howling begins at 2:00 a.m. By 3:00 a.m. the sixty-mile-per-hour gale has snapped the poles of many of the tents, including ours. Major K and I dismantle the wreck, pack it away, and crawl back inside our bags.

· · ·

I awake sometime later and sit up. A sentry is standing watch beside me. He is motionless, rifle shouldered, staring out into the night.

I don't know this marine. It occurs to me how little of themselves— their individuality, their singularity—these would-be instructors have revealed in the past few days. Each of them has volunteered to live in a world where personalities are less important than the task, and the task can only be accomplished by a team. They have subjugated their own egos in order to work together, to stay focused, to forge a unified fighting force. They don't whine. They don't psychoanalyze. They don't obsess. They do.

This absence of self-dramatization is a rare phenomenon. I've been on dozens of expeditions. Whenever one fails we blame it on the weather, the avalanche conditions, the rockfall. And sometimes such objective factors are decisive. But often it's about failing to figure out how to pull together.

Before I fall back asleep, I remember asking Captain Culp to define, in one sentence, what it means to be a marine.

"It's all about discipline," he replied, and his smile seemed to acknowledge that, imbedded in this cliché, there was life-or-death truth.

The next night—our last—after a day of patrols and ambushes, the final stage of the Instructor Qualification Course begins: another grueling cross-country attack.

"Men," says Major K, "I know you're cold. I know you're exhausted. Sometime tonight you may feel so whipped that all you want to do is stop and lie down in the snow. Well, listen up, marines, that's what this field exercise is all about! This environment is enemy number one. You have to whup the cold before you can whup the enemy. You have a mission. The mission is to attack the objective. That means to kill somebody who's trying to kill you. Don't fucking forget it."

He stops and looks for a long moment at his haggard men.

"Suck it up."

The squad is under noise-and-light discipline. Signals are passed along by hand; no one is allowed to use flashlights or headlamps.

Starlight reflects faintly off the boundless snow as the marines fan out on snowshoes behind scout skiers who have already vanished ahead. The soldiers are all but invisible in their overwhites—huge, hooded jackets and baggy pants—and their bulbous white vapor-barrier boots, white mittens, and white backpack covers. It's a squad of ghosts.

After four hours of continuous movement, they reach the edge of a forest. They slip into the woods, then stop. A message is whispered back from man to man: "Overwhite top off." The men are staggered through the dense forest in a wedge formation, each man kneeling behind a tree. Every other man silently drops his seventy-pound pack and strips off his monkish cloak while the rest stand watch. In minutes the squad is retailored to match the black-and-white terrain.

Once again the scout skiers are sent ahead to recon the approach. As they have a half-dozen times during this night attack, the rest of the marines wait. Kneeling in the snow, acutely alert, wordless, they're as motionless as ice sculptures. Something has coalesced inside these men. They seem to have regained their strength and confidence. You can feel it.

When the scout skiers return, another message is passed back through the men: "Ranger file." The marines slide laterally into a strung-out line, ten meters between each soldier, and begin walking through the forest, M-16s in their arms.

Twenty minutes later, barely enough time to get the icy sludge of blood flowing again, the patrol halts. The men wait. And wait. No word is passed. The marines kneel in the snow beneath their giant packs with their weapons on safety and stare into the darkness.

Finally word comes: "Column file, five meters."

The men form two lines with five meters between each soldier and advance. They halt again in less than ten minutes. A string of commands and information gradually moves back through the platoon. The objective is fewer than 150 meters dead ahead. Drop the packs. Have weapons and magazines ready.

Major K touches me on the shoulder and we walk up through the heavily armed men crouched in the snow. To the right is a clearing. We step to the edge and Major K hands me a pair of infrared night-vision goggles. Instantly the cover of night is obliterated. Black is transformed to a ghoulish green, all lighter colors to shades of orange. Everything is fuzzy but visible. Through the pines I can clearly see the objective: a group of metal buildings. There is a chain-link fence around the compound. The platoon commander's navigational skills are impeccable. After moving for miles in the dark, sometimes through open country with no landmarks, sometimes through thick forest, he has hit the objective precisely.

I turn and study the soldiers. They are all kneeling beside their packs, rifles up, eyes burning blindly in the dark. I can see the tension in their bodies, their predatory anticipation, their primal desire to fight.

Major K and I move back to the rear of the squad and wait. He leans over and whispers, "By God, they pulled themselves together."

The scout skiers have breached the chain-link fence. The marines remove their snowshoes and begin advancing very slowly, carefully stepping in the snow holes of each other's footprints, ducking beneath branches.

In what happens next, the bullets and mortars are blanks. And yet, stripped clean by exhaustion and suffering and their shared ordeal, the men become what they've trained to become.

Somebody snaps a trip wire and the entire forest explodes. The detonation sends a concussive wave slamming through the air and burning flares light up the night. The noise is shattering: machine-gun fire and mortar rounds. The marines are rushing forward, plunging through the trees, the whole scene lit up by a shifting incandescent glare, orange muzzle-flashes popping everywhere. The squad leader is standing knee-deep in snow screaming, "*Go! Go! Go, fuckers, go!*" and the men are charging the breach in the fence firing their machine guns and screaming and smoke is obscuring the passage and men are tripping and falling in the drifts and pulling each other up and firing and running into the blackening breach into the breach into the breach.

BLOOD ROAD

Duck off the road, run. Down dark passageways, right at one corner, left at the next, no idea where I'm going. On a main street in the town of Namsai, I spot three armed Arunachal Pradesh border policemen up ahead. They're hunting for me. I'm in this northeastern Indian state illegally. I slide into the flow of tasseled trishaws, pedestrians, clicking bicycles.

A vintage white Ambassador—that lumpish, fifties-era sedan still found throughout India's hinterland—creeps along within the bright human throng. Behind it a young tribal girl carries two buckets of water on a bamboo pole. I step up alongside her. She smiles, then covers her face. I snap off my baseball cap and place it on her head. She laughs and unwinds an orange cotton wrap from around her shoulders and hands it to me. I knew she would do this; it's not possible to give a gift in this part of the world without receiving one in return. I dive both hands into one of her buckets, slick back my shaggy hair, and whip the orange fabric into a turban around my head. Then I wink at her, step to the rear passenger door of the Ambassador and jump in the backseat.

I find myself sitting beside a large Buddhist lama in maroon robes. I adjust my disguise and scan the crowd outside.

"You are being chased," says the lama.

"I am."

The lama speaks to the chauffeur. The chauffeur taps his horn, maneuvers around a Brahma bull seated in the road, speeds up. At the outskirts of town, we roll onto a long grassy driveway, pass a freshly gilded stupa, and stop in front of a group of wooden buildings. The lama lifts his frock above polished black shoes and steps out.

"My name is Aggadhamma," he says in British-accented English. "This is the Namsai Buddhist Vihara, a monastery for boys. You are safe here."

That evening I have dinner with the lama and a dozen shaved-headed acolytes. We sit on the floor around circular tables. The walls are Easter-egg blue. A tin plate heaped with rice, dal, vegetables, and burning-hot, fuscous curry is set before me. I eat with my right hand.

After the meal, the boys slug back a last tin of water and scatter into the warm, lampless dark.

"Now," says Aggadhamma, "please tell me, what brought you to this distant corner of our earth?"

I don't have any reason not to be truthful. "I want to travel the old Stilwell Road and cross into Burma."

I outline my obsession. Six decades ago, during World War II, American soldiers under the command of recalcitrant General Joseph "Vinegar Joe" Stilwell carved a 1,100-mile road from Ledo, in the Indian state of Assam, to Kunming, China, through a wilderness of dripping mountains and leech-infested jungles in northern Burma.

No one even knows if this old military road still exists. Perhaps it has vanished entirely, consumed by the jungle like a snake eaten by a tiger. It's a mystery I've been hoping to solve.

"This is your plan, despite the fact that Arunachal Pradesh is in the midst of civil unrest—car bombings, assassinations, and the like—and therefore closed to foreigners," responds Aggadhamma. "I take it you are here without government permission."

I admit that I do not have a restricted area permit.

"It's not as serious as it sounds," I add. "Mostly just a game of cat and mouse with the border police."

Aggadhamma eyes me. "You can get away with this in India," he says. "India is the greatest democracy in the world. The government here is like an old elephant: vast, but slow and avoidable. Clever people can keep from being stepped on."

I don't tell him that I have already been arrested, and escaped, a half-dozen times, but he already seems to know.

"You are clever, then," he continues, "and yet you wish to sneak into Burma and play this same game?"

I just nod.

For the next three days I hide out in the Namsai vihara. I help spade black soil in the vegetable garden and teach the eager pupils American slang in their English classes.

On my last night in the monastery, Aggadhamma tells me he has someone for me to meet. After supper, he introduces me to a nine-year-old boy named Myin. The boy is as beautiful as a girl, with brilliant eyes and a perpetual grin. He is also an amputee, his left leg vanished at the hip.

"Myin is from Burma," says Aggadhamma, and tells the boy's story as Myin stares at me with a guileless smile.

Myin is a Jinghpaw, or Kachin. The Kachins are an ethnic group whose homeland includes most of northern Burma; they are one of seven major ethnic minorities—along with the Karen, Karenni, Mon, Chin, Shan, and Arakanese—that make up about thirty percent of the country's population (sixty-eight percent of the fifty million citizens are Burmese), each with its own state. All told, there are some 140 ethnic groups and one hundred dialects in Burma.

Two years earlier, soldiers under the military regime burned Myin's village to the ground and took all the boys. They were tracking pro-democracy Kachin guerrillas through the jungle. The soldiers knew the trails were booby-trapped, and they used Myin as a human minesweeper, forcing him to walk alone in front of the soldiers. He was seven years old and couldn't have weighed forty pounds when his leg was blown off.

"We have several boys from Burma here," says Aggadhamma. "Each has been maimed in one way or other. This is what Burma does to humans."

After dark I leave the Namsai Buddhist Vihara. Aggadhamma shakes my hand with both of his hands, holding on tightly even after I release my grip.

• • •

During the late eighties and early nineties, I went to the Himalayas on a mountaineering expedition every two years. When I was stormbound at high altitude, the best escape was always a good book, so I blame historian Barbara W. Tuchman for my original fascination with the Stilwell Road. Deep inside my sleeping bag at 23,000 feet, with waves of graupel slamming the tent, I read her Pulitzer Prize–winning 1970 book, *Stilwell and the American Experience in China, 1911–45,* and was transported to another world and another time.

By the time the United States entered the Second World War, imperial Japan had been penetrating ever deeper into China for more than a decade, gaining control of nearly one-third of that weakened giant. In the first five months of 1942, Japanese forces rapidly subjugated much of

Southeast Asia: the Philippines, Hong Kong, Singapore, Malaysia, Indonesia, and a large swath of Burma. If China fell, all of Asia was threatened, from the rice fields of India to the oil fields of Baghdad.

America had been attempting to bolster the Chinese Nationalist forces of Chiang Kai-shek by supplying his forces via the back door, through India. Pilots were flying ordnance and ammunition from India to China over "the Hump"—the dragon's tail of the Himalayas that hooks south into northern Burma. But China was still losing. General Stilwell, commanding general of the China–Burma–India theater, believed these supply flights weren't enough. A tough, wiry West Point graduate who had spent years on clandestine missions in China, Stilwell was a military traditionalist. He was convinced that to adequately supply the Chinese, an all-weather military road had to be created from India through the unknown mountains and swamps of northern Burma. This 478-mile road, dubbed the Ledo Road, would connect with the old Burma Road, a convoluted 717-mile mule track built by the Chinese that ran northeast from Lashio, Burma, to Kunming, China—creating an 1,100-mile supply route called the Stilwell Road. (Today, it's popularly, if erroneously, known as the Burma Road.)

British prime minister Winston Churchill characterized Stilwell's endeavor as "an immense, laborious task, unlikely to be finished until the need for it has passed." Stilwell was undeterred.

Completing the road cost $150 million and required the labor of 28,000 American soldiers, almost all of them black, and 35,000 ethnic Naga and Kachin workers. It was a dangerous job; casualty rates were so high that it was dubbed the Man-a-Mile Road. Japanese snipers, monsoon floods, malaria, and cholera took the lives of 1,100 American soldiers and untold numbers of Asian workers before the Stilwell Road was completed in January 1945. Over the next seven months, 5,000 vehicles and 35,000 tons of supplies traveled it. Then the atomic bombs were dropped on Hiroshima and Nagasaki, and the Japanese surrendered.

In October 1945, the United States abandoned the road. Churchill had been right.

In the following decades, the old Burma Road across southwestern China remained in use, but the stretch of Stilwell's highway that crossed the remote fastness of northern Burma reverted to a blank on the map, an enigma that became my obsession.

Detouring on the way home from various mountaineering trips, I managed to travel the entire Chinese section of the road by the early 1990s. I would sit on the roofs of listing, overloaded trucks grinding up and down hundreds of switchbacks across the gorge-scarred Yunnan province, and read obscure classics of Asian World War II history—Jack Belden's *Retreat with Stilwell*, Ian Fellowes-Gordon's *The Magic War*, Shelford Bidwell's *The Chindit War*. It was my own private adventure. I didn't talk about it, didn't write about it.

And yet minor triumphs gradually set the foundation for great expectations. Over the years, my desire to get into Burma and traverse whatever was left of the Stilwell Road began to displace my passion for mountain climbing. Mountains were simple, predictable beasts compared with nations. I knew the unknowns—the brutal cold, the avalanches. I knew how to suffer, how to summit, and how to fail. What I didn't know was Burma, a different kind of impossible challenge.

In late 1993, during an expedition into eastern Tibet, I tried to enter Burma from the north with a partner. We were caught by the Chinese border patrol, interrogated, and jailed for a couple of nights. We signed a confession and were released.

In the spring of 1996, I traveled to the Indian state of Assam to write a magazine article about wildlife poaching, then veered off to Ledo to try my luck again. Two weeks after leaving the Namsai monastery and traveling most of the twenty-mile stretch of the Stilwell Road through Arunachal Pradesh to the India–Burma border, I was nabbed. I was detained for three days in Tezu and politely interrogated (tea and scones were served) by Indian army officers, all of whom assumed I was a CIA agent. On the fourth day I was placed in a jeep with two armed guards, driven to the banks of the enormous, mud-brown Brahmaputra, put on a leaky tug dragging a mile-long raft of timber, and deported downstream to Assam.

Still, I felt that I'd successfully completed my apprenticeship in duplicity. I knew how to operate alone, how to lie, how to stay calm while looking down the barrel of a gun. I had completed the Chinese and Indian sections of the Stilwell Road. All that remained was the 458-mile ghost road in Burma.

• • •

Back home, I wrote to the Myanmar embassy in Washington. (Since 1989, Myanmar has been the military government's name for the country.) In

1996, with great fanfare, Myanmar launched a campaign to promote tourism, and visitors could obtain a visa to travel in the southern part of the country, but northern Burma, including the region the Stilwell Road passed through, was off-limits to foreigners.

After pestering the embassy for several months, I was referred to Jefferson Waterman International, Myanmar's public relations agency. Waterman published the *Myanmar Monitor*, a propaganda rag that pasted a smiley face on the Burmese military government. Waterman managed to get me an appointment with U Tin Winn, Myanmar's ambassador to the United States. I did my political homework before our meeting.

General Aung San, leader of Burma's Anti-Fascist People's Freedom League, demanded independence from Britain in 1947. While writing the constitution, Aung San, along with six of his ministers, was assassinated, igniting a series of bloody coups and bringing Prime Minister U Nu into power when independence was granted, in 1948. In 1962, General Ne Win overthrew the civilian government and abolished the constitution. A gallows hood was dropped over the face of the nation. Through coercion, repression, state-sponsored murder, and Stalin-style domestic terror, Ne Win maintained control for nearly thirty years.

By 1988, conditions were so unbearable that prodemocracy demonstrations erupted throughout the country, led by returning exile Aung San Suu Kyi, daughter of Aung San and head of the National League for Democracy (NLD). These demonstrations were brutally crushed by the dictatorship—between 3,000 and 10,000 peaceful protesters were killed—and the State Law and Order Restoration Council (SLORC), a cabal of Burmese generals, was created to run the country.

In 1989, SLORC declared martial law and placed Aung San Suu Kyi under house arrest. Diplomatic pressure and agitation by the NLD forced SLORC to hold general elections the next year. When the NLD won a landslide victory, the generals declared the results invalid and subsequently imprisoned hundreds of NLD members. In 1991 Suu Kyi was awarded the Nobel Peace Prize—perhaps the main reason she is still alive. In short, Myanmar has the dark distinction of being one of the last totalitarian regimes on earth.

At my meeting with Ambassador Tin Winn, I outlined my plan for traveling the Stilwell Road across Burma, tracing the route on a WWII-era US Army map. Ambassador Tin Winn was enthusiastic about my "daring historical journey" and introduced me to an embassy official named Thaung Tun, who was to arrange a special visa and assist me in navigating the Myanmar bureaucracy.

On the phone and in a series of letters, Thaung Tun was invariably gracious and upbeat. "Everything looks good—we're on course. Proper papers are assembling," he told me. "Things take time only." At first I believed him, but as the months passed, I came to recognize this behavior as classic puppeteering. After more than a year of strategic confoundment, Thaung Tun suggested I break the impasse by seeking permission in person. He knew who I should talk to. I flew to the capital, Rangoon (renamed Yangon), in the fall of 1997.

For three days I sat in a hot, dank hallway waiting to meet Thaung Tun's government colleague. Making you wait is how bureaucrats exercise dominance. I took to bringing bread crumbs for the rats that scurried along the walls. When I finally met the man, a pinched homunculus with nervous eyes and no eyebrows, he pushed me right out of his office.

"Stilwell Road gone!" he screamed. "Disappeared! No possible!"

This only served to incite me. Stilwell and his men had faced countless obstacles, too—torrential rains that raised rivers twenty feet, titanic mudslides, jungle diseases—and Stilwell had been repeatedly told that it was impossible to build a road across Burma. I began to envision defying the Myanmar junta as not merely just, but obligatory. I was still young enough to believe—bewilderedly, arrogantly, passionately—that through sheer force of will, I could bend the world to my ambition.

• • •

In February 1998, I return to Assam and the town of Ledo, the beginning of the Stilwell Road. After several weeks of bureaucratic wrangling, I manage to sidestep obtaining a restricted area permit and inveigle permission to travel the road up to the border of Burma. A platoon from the Twenty-Eighth Assam Rifles garrison, led by Commander Y. S. Rama, is enjoined to escort me on foot from Nampong, the last Indian outpost, up to Pangsau Pass, on the border, and then directly back. It is illegal to cross the border in either direction.

The night before our hike, I pull out several bottles of whiskey and start pouring drinks. The soldiers regale me with tales of the horrors unfolding nearby in Burma. There is a command post somewhere past

Pangsau Pass, and the soldiers there are almost starving. Many have malaria. Rice is in short supply, and they never have salt. Salt is worth anything to the Burmese soldiers. They sneak over the border with something they have taken from the Naga or Kachin tribes—a bearskin shield, a wooden mask—and trade it for salt. Pangsau Pass, they say, is a punishment posting for Burmese soldiers who have run afoul of the military leadership.

Commander Rama, in his blue uniform and white ascot, sits ramrod stiff after polishing off most of a bottle of whiskey by himself. "Across the border is the end of the world," he declares. "You can go backward in history, Mr. Mark. Americans want to believe that everything goes forward. But if you went forward on this road, you would go backward."

When I leave at five the next morning, the platoon is fast asleep, as if the warm night air were an anesthetic. The men lie limp and sweating in their unclean underwear, dreaming of the women in the pictures taped to the walls above their heads.

I glide stealthily past the barracks and up onto the Stilwell Road. I know I have a head start of only a few hours at most. The road hooks uphill, disappearing into the black Patkai Range, taking me with it.

My intention is to cross over into Burma, alone and illegally. I don't think I'm delusional; I have a plan. I also know that my plan might fail. The difficulty itself is no small part of the appeal. If success is a certainty, where is the challenge? I am still entranced by the road, but now the seeds of something darker have taken root inside me.

The Stilwell Road was built to stop the spread of totalitarianism. For 2,000 years, from Caesar to Stilwell, building roads was how one nation conquered another. That ended with the rise of air power: Planes in the sky, not trucks on a road, would thenceforth largely determine the course of warfare. Some generals could envision this not-so-brave new world, but Stilwell was not one of them. It was an airplane that dropped the atomic bomb and pushed us across a new rubicon of technological morality.

The Stilwell Road is a paradigm for failure, another one of humankind's grandiose exercises in futility. I know in my heart that this means my own attempt at traveling the Stilwell Road is stained with the same futility. But of course this doesn't stop me. On the contrary, I charge forward, carrying through with my complicated, contradictory convictions. Is this not what all humans sometimes do? We deftly lay out snares and then proceed to walk right into them.

• • •

I leap the tropical trees that have fallen across the track and move between the moss-sheathed embankments. The road narrows to a tunnel. I step through spiderwebs larger than me, strands clinging to my face.

In two hours I reach Pangsau Pass, a road cut through mud walls. There is a rotting concrete sign atop the pass. I snap a photo and walk into Burma.

Just over the border the road begins to disappear. Light and sky are closed off by vines thick as hawsers, leaves large as umbrellas, bamboo stalks rooted as densely as prison bars. I begin to wonder if the trail might be booby-trapped.

A queer uneasiness comes over me: I'm being watched. It makes me want to stop, but I don't. I keep walking. When I finally look over my shoulder, two soldiers, as if on cue, part the jungle with the barrels of their rifles and step onto the road. Two more soldiers appear in front of me.

They are small men in dark-green fatigues and Chinese-issue camou-flage sneakers. They have canteens on their belts and AK-47s and bando-liers of rounds across their shoulders. One wears a large knife on his hip, another a black handgun in a polished black holster.

I wave to the two soldiers ahead of me and move toward them eagerly, as if I am a lost backpacker. Their jaws tighten. I hold out my hand, talk-ing and smiling. The soldiers train their weapons on me, their faces flat and strained.

The soldiers behind me begin to shout. One soldier starts prodding me with the barrel of his rifle, as if he's trying to herd me back where I came from, but I won't move. A soldier behind me grabs my pack and starts to pull me backward. I spin around and he lets go.

This is the moment—they know it and I know it. The soldier in charge, the one with the black handgun, steps forward and holds my eyes in a cold, searching stare. I stare back. I know what he's looking for: fear. Fear is what he most wants to see, what he is accustomed to seeing.

But I have a secret weapon: I'm white. My whiteness protects me. My whiteness is a force field around my body. I know it is unjust, immoral even, but my whiteness means he can't act unilaterally. White people can cause trouble. He knows this.

The soldier shouts in my face but drops his eyes. His men begin to march me down the road, deeper into Burma, barrels at my back. Eventually we arrive at a burned-out building in a clearing. Laborers in rags are squatting in the mud in front of the building. Using machetes, they're hacking long bamboo poles into three-foot spears and hardening the points over a campfire.

From the color of their sarongs and the way they wear their machetes in a shoulder scabbard, I know they are Naga tribesmen. The Nagas were headhunters until the early twentieth century (British colonial authorities outlawed the practice in the 1890s); although the Nagas have their own language, architecture, religion, and customs, the junta lumps them in with the Kachins.

As I come close, the squatting men do not look up. Soldiers are all around. The soldier with the handgun continues up steep stairs cut into the mud embankment, while the other three remain to guard me. I drop my pack and lean against the roofless building and watch the laborers. Their machetes make muted hacking sounds, the sounds you hear in a butcher shop. The men themselves are silent, as if their tongues have been cut out.

I realize that this is exactly what I was not supposed to see. This is why northern Burma is closed, why so many remote regions of Burma are closed. According to the Free Burma Coalition, an international alliance of activists dedicated to the democratization of Burma, most ethnic minorities across the nation have been viciously persecuted; more than 600,000 have been removed from their villages and forcibly relocated. By interviewing refugees, Amnesty International has documented forced-labor camps hidden throughout the country.

Anytime a country closes its borders, it has something to hide. History is clear on this point. National security is always a ruse. Governments that close their borders are doing something unspeakable that they don't want us to see. Russia under Stalin. China under Mao. Nicaragua not long ago. Sudan today.

• • •

I wait for seven hours, tearing engorged brown leeches off my legs and watching the blood run down into my boots. Late in the afternoon, the soldier with the black sidearm comes down the embankment, grabs me by the hair, and jerks me to my feet. I knock his hand away. He wants to hit me so badly the muscles in his cheeks quiver.

I am pushed up the mud steps. Seated against the building, I could see only the laborers and the rolling jungle. When I reach the top of the mud steps, I truly confront the world I have entered. It is medieval, something from the Dark Ages.

Before me is a 400-foot-high hill, stripped naked. Cut into the base of the slope, circling the mountain, is a trench, twenty feet wide and ten feet deep. Two-foot bamboo spears, sharpened punji sticks, stab upward from the bottom of the trench. Just beyond the punji pit is an eight-foot-high bamboo wall. The top and outer face of the wall are bristling with bamboo spikes.

Past this is a strip of barren dirt too smooth and manicured to be anything but a mine field. Beyond that is another lethal bamboo wall. There are five walls and four strips of mined no-man's-land ascending the hill in concentric circles. The only break in the stockade is a narrow passageway that zigzags up the middle.

I am dragged over the first punji pit on a bamboo drawbridge and through the first wall via a small, heavy door with bamboo spikes. We enter a tunnel, the walls and stairs dug out of the wet mud, the ceiling roofed with logs. Passing through the tunnel, I try to imagine some purpose for this surreal jungle fortress. It lies on a forgotten, forbidden border and would be a ridiculous target for any combatant. It can only be protecting the Burmese soldiers from the local people they have enslaved.

After passing through four doors, the mud steps rise back up to daylight. We are on top of the hill. I am taken to a table set in the red dirt beneath a canopy of leaves, behind which is seated a fat man with a pockmarked face. Underneath his sweat-stained fatigues, which have no insignia, I can see red pajamas. He is wearing green flip-flops.

There are four armed soldiers standing behind the man. He says something to them and my pack is torn from my back and a bamboo chair forced against the back of my knees. I sit down. One of the soldiers dumps the contents of my pack onto the dirt and starts rummaging through my stuff. I stare at the fat man, wondering who will interpret, when he speaks for himself.

"Passport. Give."

I take my passport out of my money belt and hand it to him.

His eyes don't leave my face. Without looking down, he flips through the pages, then throws the passport back, hitting me in the face.

"Visa. Show visa."

I open the passport to the correct page and hand it back. He studies the stamp. I make every effort to appear bored. I have an official visa for Myanmar. It is a large stamp that fills one page of the passport. At the bottom of the page, in blue ink that matches the stamp, I've blotted out the words "all land entry prohibited."

He shakes his head and shuts the passport.

"Not possible. No one come here. Border closed."

I expected this. I am already unfolding two other documents from my money belt. I hand them to him. One is a personal letter from Ambassador U Tin Winn, written and signed on embassy stationery, inviting me to Myanmar and urging all officials to help me travel along the Stilwell Road. The other is an official Myanmar Immigration Department Report of Arrival. My photo is affixed to this document, and it, too, has an official stamp from the Myanmar government. Along with my name, passport number, and visa number, there is a list spelling out my itinerary and the towns in Burma I have permission to travel through: Pangsau Pass, Shingbwiyang, Mogaung, Myitkyina, Bhamo.

These are all forgeries, but I have confidence in them. He has no way of checking their authenticity.

The documents make him angry. "Where you get?" he demands.

"From the embassy of Myanmar. I had lunch with Ambassador U Tin Winn. He invited me to your country." I surprise myself with the calmness of my voice. I tell him I have brought gifts. I gesture for one of the soldiers to bring over a sack from the pile of my belongings. Inside he finds a five-kilogram bag of salt, a package of twenty ballpoint pens, and three lined notebooks. Each notebook has a $100 bill paper-clipped to the cover.

The commander looks back down at the documents. All of his fingernails are short and dirty, except for the nail on his right pinkie, which is clean and long. I can only assume that he is the warlord of this lost jungle fiefdom—beyond civilization and beyond the fragile wing of morality—and that there is no law here, no God. He is God.

But I have these troublesome documents. I can see his mind working. Someone must know I am here. Why wasn't he informed? If these documents are real, he would've been notified of my arrival. I would've had a military escort.

He raises his small black eyes, stares at me, and says something in Burmese. Two soldiers leave. A few minutes later, a boy, perhaps thirteen years old, is dragged up to the commander. He is clearly a prisoner. Skeletal, wearing nothing but torn trousers, he has an angular head, protruding ribs, legs so thin his knees are larger than his thighs.

The commander barks at him and the boy cringes, then speaks to me.

"Why are you here?" His English is catechism-perfect.

"I told him already," I reply, feigning weariness. "I have been invited by the Myanmar government to travel the Stilwell Road."

The boy translates this.

The commander stands up and slowly walks toward me. He stops with his face in front of mine. Then he walks over and stands like a bear next to the emaciated boy and says something.

"He doesn't believe you," the boy tells me. "Why have you come here?"

When I give the same answer, the commander turns sideways and slams his heavy fist into the boy's rib cage. The boy screams and crumples to the ground.

The commander looks at me and laughs. The message seems to be: You may be someone it would not be prudent to harm. But this boy, this boy is perfectly expendable. This boy could easily disappear without a trace.

I am sickened by my naiveté. I've been willing to imperil my own life to travel this road, but not the life of someone else—that's why I chose to go alone. I should have known better.

When I refuse to answer any more questions, my audience with the warlord is abruptly terminated. I'm hustled back down through the mud tunnels and out of the compound. At dusk, my pack and my passport are returned to me, but my forged documents have disappeared. The film has been ripped from my camera, and all pages with writing have been torn from my journal.

I am marched back up to Pangsau Pass. Commander Rama and his platoon are waiting for me at the border. Rama stares at me with his old, oily eyes but doesn't say a word.

• • •

This should have been the end of it. But what began as a private passion I now twist into a professional goal. I secure a contract with a publisher to write a book about the Stilwell Road. This, I think, will legitimize my bewitchment. Although my editor believes I already have enough material for the book, I insist that I have to complete the route.

I return to India in the fall of 1999, hell-bent on finding a way around the Pangsau Pass military compound. The Naga tribesmen I manage to speak to refuse to guide me. No amount of bribery will change their minds, and I can't do it without them. I briefly consider bushwhacking my way into the jungle in a parallel traverse of the Stilwell Road, or whatever is left of it.

Instead, I decide to attack the problem from a southern approach. I'll take a train from Yangon to Mandalay, then another train up toward Myitkyina, a city of 75,000 on the Stilwell Road. Recently opened to foreigners, Myitkyina is accessible only by plane or train, and the region between it and Mandalay remains closed. I intend to secretly hop off at the closed city of Mogaung, twenty-five miles southwest of Myitkyina, and light out from there, to the west and north, along the Stilwell Road.

I buy a black backpack and a dark-green bivy tent and dark Gore-Tex raingear. I conceal a knife and cash in the sole of one of my boots and obtain declassified Russian and American maps.

This all somehow seems appropriate to me. I have only one crisis of confidence.

While studying the maps on the flight to Bangkok, trying to guess where the military checkpoints along the road will be, I suddenly experience a visceral foreshadowing of my own death. It isn't a vision, just a profound blackness, a terrifying emptiness. My body goes cold, and my mind feels as if all the synapses are short-circuiting and exploding. Then I begin sweating profusely, soaking my seat. It is such a powerful presentiment of my own death that I begin to cry.

For several hours I convince myself that I will get on the next plane home. Instead, I write farewell letters to my wife, Sue, my eight-year-old daughter, Addi, my six-year-old daughter, Teal, and my parents. I mail the letters from Bangkok, but they never arrive.

• • •

Heading north from Mandalay, I climb onto the roof of a passenger car to avoid the conductor. The train lumbers along, stopping at every rice–pig–child village, then chugging slowly back into the country. Water buffalo chest-deep in black mud. Women bent in half in green rice pad-dies. Deep teak forests. Bicyclists on dirt paths. Asian pastoral—just like the brochures.

Twenty-four hours later, as the train slows outside Mogaung, I hop off, run down a dirt road, and leap into the first trishaw I see. The driver ped-als me through Mogaung, but there is a roadblock on the far side of town. He wants me to get out right there, in front of the soldiers. Wagging cash, I get him to pedal down a side street before I step out. Not five minutes later, the police pick me up off the street. They don't say a word. They are very young—adolescents with weapons, driving a souped-up Toyota Corolla. The driver flips on flashing lights, plugs in a bootleg tape of an Asian girl singing Cyndi Lauper songs, and flies north out of Mogaung.

We're on the Stilwell Road, heading toward Myitkyina. After half an hour, we pull into a compound across the street from the railroad tracks, at the edge of town. I peer out and shake my head in surprise and relief. They've taken me to the Myitkyina YMCA.

I register and am given a spare, clean room with a high ceiling. I shave, drop the key off with the clerk, and go back onto the street to explore. I hike muddy cobblestone streets between squat, nondescript buildings. I try to speak with people here and there, but no one will say a word to me. They ignore me, their eyes darting left and right. I end up in an outdoor market where wide-faced women sit under umbrellas amid a cornucopia of brilliant, alien fruits and vegetables.

Back at the Y, the desk clerk asks me how I enjoyed the market.

The next morning I hire a trishaw driver to take me out to the Irrawaddy River. When I come back, the clerk asks me how I enjoyed the river.

In the afternoon, it rains and I go for a walk alone, zigzagging ran-domly and speedily to the outskirts of town. At a wet intersection, I find one of the trishaw drivers who usually hangs out in front of the YMCA waiting for me. I yank a handful of grass from the side of the road before accepting his offer to give me a lift back to the Y.

Early the next morning, I repack my bag, folding tiny blades of grass into my clothes and equipment. I leave and walk the streets of the town, returning to my room at noon. I find my pack right where I left it, every-thing folded precisely the way it was, but blades of grass are scattered on the floor.

That night I slip through the window of my room and steal away, carefully climbing over a block wall with pieces of broken glass embedded along the top. I find an unlocked bicycle and take it, pedaling through the darkness to a corner where several old women, perhaps lost in opium dreams, sleep on the street. I lift a conical hat off the head of one of the women and slip a wad of bills into her shirt pocket. Now I'm disguised.

For the next five nights I leave my room and ride right past the roadblocks, with their sleepy sentries, and pedal out to the villages around Myitkyina. At dawn I return the bicycle and sneak back into my room at the Y.

In these neighboring villages, under cover of darkness, I finally find people who will talk to me. They are Kachins who are dying to speak to someone. A deluge of stories, always told behind closed doors, beside candles or oil lanterns that are frequently doused—and always in whispers.

A shopkeeper who says that everyone is an informer here: "Trishaw drivers, businesspeople, teachers," he says. "Even good people are informers. This is the only way to protect their families: to give up someone else. It is poison."

This shopkeeper takes me to see a former government official who was tasked with beating tribals used for road gangs in the Karen state, in far eastern Burma.

"I was expected to hit them with a club," he says. "Not systematically, because then they could plan and train their minds to resist, but randomly. This works very well. It maintains the fear of the unknown. This is how to create terror in a human heart."

Sometimes I ask questions about the Stilwell Road, but they have stories of their own. What happened to me at Pangsau Pass is happening again: Traveling the Stilwell Road is becoming irrelevant, almost insignificant—a profoundly selfish misadventure, compared with chronicling these stories of suffering and struggle. On the third night, an interpreter is provided and people are brought to me at a secret location, an outbuilding at the edge of an old teacher's enormous vegetable garden.

A truck driver who uses the Stilwell Road delivering construction materials: "My wife washes clothes in the river for the bribe money," he says. "I must pay the soldiers every time I pass through a roadblock; otherwise they will take a part from my truck."

Two ancient soldiers tell me about fighting for the Americans during the construction of the Stilwell Road, traveling ahead of the bulldozers and clearing the forest of snipers: "We knew the jungle," one says. "We could kill the Japanese. The Americans were brave but did not know the jungle, so we helped them. Then they left us. Now we are in another war against our own government, but America has forgotten what we did for them."

The son of a father who was imprisoned for friendship: "The bravest of all, Aung San Suu Kyi, came here in 1988," he says. "My father knew her; they were schoolmates. Just friends. When she left, my father was taken away. He managed to get letters out to us. How they tortured him with electricity. How they used an iron bar rolled on his shins. How they used snakes with the women. Put snakes inside the women's bodies. He was released after five years, and then he died."

A middle-aged woman who tries to speak but can only cry and wring her hands.

I write pages of notes, hiding them in a jar in the grass behind the YMCA.

On the fourth night, the woman who could only weep brings her daughter. The mother sits quietly in the shadows while her daughter speaks. She tells me she is nineteen years old. She learned to speak English from Christian missionaries. She has dense black hair braided into a long ponytail.

"My mother came to tell you my story, but she could not do it," she says. "We have heard you are interested in the Stilwell Road." She tells me that, except in the far west, between Shingbwiyang and Pangsau Pass, the road still exists. She knows—she has been on it. Junta warlords have been logging in northern Burma and, in places, are rebuilding the road in order to transport the trees to China. Kachin households must provide one family member for the labor.

She was fourteen when she was taken away in a truck and put in a work camp with thirteen other girls. At night they were locked in a large bamboo cage in the compound. Nearly every night, she says, a different girl was dragged out and gang-raped by the soldiers. One of the girls in her crew bled to death. Another girl went mad. After a year, she was set free to find her way back home, walking barefoot back down the road.

She does not pause or weep as she tells me this, but her lower lip trembles.

"We have heard you want to travel the Stilwell Road. It could be done, but it would be very dangerous. I mean, not for you. For the people who would want to help you. But we would do it."

She tells me that since Myitkyina is now open to foreigners, tourists are coming. She believes someday there will be tourists on the Stilwell Road, and she wants them to know the truth. That it is not a road built by Americans. That was history. History is over. It's a road built by the Kachins.

"Do not believe it is a noble road. It is a road of blood. A road of death."

With both hands, she wipes away the tears now in her eyes, stands up, bows, and leaves with her mother.

My hands are trembling too much to write. I cannot listen to anyone else. I ride the bicycle around in the dark for the rest of the night, looking up at the cloudy Burma sky, asking myself, What am I doing here?

• • •

The next morning the desk clerk asks me how my night was.

I look him in the eyes. He looks at me. He's on to me. I realize I've been endangering the people who shared their stories with me.

That night, to reduce suspicion, I decide to go drinking with the trishaw drivers. We end up in a bar, a dark, low-ceilinged place where women walk out on a little stage and sing pop songs under a ghoulish red light. When I'm ready to go back to the YMCA, my companions insist I have one more drink. A toast. It doesn't taste right. I drink some and spill the rest down my neck.

Something starts to happen with my eyes. Things begin to slide. My glass glides off the table and I reach out to catch it and knock it onto the floor. It shatters into little pieces that turn into cockroaches that scrabble away. I can't move my feet properly; they spill and flop like fish. Someone is slapping me, and I stand up swinging, screaming, spinning around.

I open my eyes. Nothing. Darkness everywhere. There's a bird over me in the dark, flapping.

I wake. My head is sideways. I try to focus. Lift my head. I'm naked, bloody, and filthy, covered with feces and dried urine. It's broad daylight.

Two wide-eyed little boys are looking down at me. I sit up. I'm in the alley behind the YMCA.

I make it back to my room and fall asleep on the floor. The next time I wake up, I crawl into the shower, wash off the blood, and look at my bruises and cuts. Just beat up. Then I notice the words written in black ink on the palm of my right hand: Leave or die.

· · ·

Push far enough, and you will encounter the world the way it is, not the way you imagine it. Your body will collide with the earth and you will bear witness. In this way you will be compelled to grapple with the limitless kindness and bottomless cruelty of humankind—and perhaps realize that you yourself are capable of both. This will change you. Nothing will ever again be black-and-white.

In total, I spent a year of my life trying to complete the Stilwell Road, but I gave back the advance and didn't write the book. I wasn't ready. To this day, my arrogance, ignorance, and selfishness appall me. Adventure becomes hubris when ambition blinds you to the suffering of the human beings next to you. Only at the end of my odyssey did I fully accept that traveling the road didn't make a damn bit of difference. That wasn't the point. It wasn't about me. It was about Burma and the struggle of its people.

Since 1989, Aung San Suu Kyi, the leader of the National League for Democracy and winner of the 1991 Nobel Peace Prize, has spent more than thirteen years under house arrest in Burma; according to Amnesty International, more than 2,000 peaceful demonstrators have been taken into custody, interrogated, and, in many cases, tortured as political prisoners.

In May 2002, Suu Kyi was released by the junta. She immediately picked up where she'd left off, guiding the nonviolent democracy movement in Burma as much through her defiant, selfless bravery as through her words and speeches. Suu Kyi is Burma's Nelson Mandela. "In physical stature she is petite and elegant, but in moral stature she is a giant," Archbishop Desmond Tutu said, in 2001, on the tenth anniversary of Suu Kyi's Nobel Peace Prize. "Big men are scared of her. Armed to the teeth and they still run scared."

On May 30, 2003, while Suu Kyi was on a lecture tour with members of the National League for Democracy near Mandalay, her small convoy was ambushed by members of the government militia. Four of her body-guards and some seventy supporters were reportedly killed, and hundreds were injured, including Suu Kyi herself, who suffered face and shoulder lacerations. Suu Kyi was arrested and held incommunicado at an undisclosed location. In late July 2003, Red Cross officials met with her but were not permitted to give any details of her detention. Aung San Suu Kyi was then placed under house arrest by the junta, where she remains to this day.

"Courage means that if you have to suffer for something worth suffering for," Suu Kyi has said, "then you must suffer."

A SHORT WALK
IN THE WAKHAN

The old Wakhi horseman sucks deeply on his pipe, the opium glowing scarlet in the darkness, and blows smoke in my face. We're lying side by side on pounded wool mats in a cavelike hut in far northeastern Afghanistan. The stone walls and stick ceiling drip with black tar from decades of burning yak dung. A goat is butting its horns against the crooked door. Outside, the sheep are shuffling nervously inside the stone corral, waiting for a wolf to take one of them.

The fire is almost out and everyone is asleep—pressed together for warmth like the animals—except the horseman and me. His wind-shot eyes are shut. He inhales, his craggy face relaxing, then exhales, the psychoactive smoke swirling around my head.

Another long day done. Our team of eight—three Americans, our Pakistani guide, and four Wakhi horsemen—is walking the Wakhan Corridor, Afghanistan's ancient, forgotten passageway to China. We are more than halfway through, en route to Tajikistan. Marco Polo passed this way 734 years ago. It was medieval then, and it still is.

It was late afternoon today when we climbed out of the dark canyons up onto the treeless, 13,000-foot steppe. Two vultures, with their pterodactyl-like six-foot wingspans, were circling above a yak carcass. Our day's destination, a place called Langar, turned out to be this solitary hut out on the vast brown plain. A gaunt woman in a maroon shawl invited us into the smoke-choked shelter and gave us salt tea in a chipped china cup. Her name is Khan Bibi. She is thirty-five, but, weather-beaten and missing teeth, she looks twice her age. She began making flatbread, wetting handfuls of flour with water from a pail. She sent her youngest child, a four-year-old girl whose nose was running with green snot, out to collect disks of fuel. With blackened hands the woman slapped the slabs of dough against the horseshoe curve of the clay hearth. As they finished baking and fell off into the fire, she reached into the flames and passed them to us.

We all went back outside when we heard a chorus of baaing. Khan Bibi's husband, Mohammad Kosum, forty-five, and their seven-year-old son, both in black Russian fur caps with earflaps, were bringing the sheep and goats into the corral. Together this family of four began lifting lambs and kids from a cellar, placing them with their correct mothers, allowing them to suckle, then dropping them back down into the two-foot-deep hole where their combined body warmth would keep them alive. With 800 animals to move, the process lasted 'til dark.

Khan Bibi returned to the hearth and squatted there for the next three hours, making us rice and more flatbread and more salt tea. There was no electricity, no lamp, no candle. Dim orange firelight and a shaft of blue moonlight cut down through the whirling smoke from a square hole in the roof. The tiny girl fetched water from a snowmelt creek running through the reeking carcasses of yaks that had died during the snowy spring. When we were all fed, Khan Bibi curled up on the shelf above the fire with her two children and pulled a yak-hair blanket over the three of them.

Now, hours later, the old horseman is next to me, blowing smoke in my face. He's on his fourth or fifth bowl. I can't keep track anymore. I'm floating on secondhand smoke, back to my first day in Afghanistan.

I'm running up Aliabad, a mountain in the middle of Kabul. Tilting dirt streets with runnels carved down the middle by sewage. I pass two faceless women, heads trapped inside helmets of blue mesh. In the rocks above the flat roofs, I pass a shepherd girl shooing sheep along the mountainside. I reach the top and begin to run along the ridgetop in pink light. Up and down through trenches, stepping on piles of rusty four-inch-long bullet casings, skirting a blown-apart artillery gun, leaping an ordnance dump.

Below me, Kabul is brown. Everything in Afghanistan is brown. Smog obscures the city, but there's not much to see anyway: mud-brick houses and miles of ruins. Supposedly in the seventies there were paved, tree-lined streets and outdoor cafés and a university and women with faces who wore flowered skirts. Today it is apocalyptic—the destroyed capital of a country that has been at war, with invaders and itself, for twenty-five years. Make that twenty-five centuries.

I'm running along thinking about baby-faced, flak-jacketed American soldiers in their armored convoys when I glance at the ground and stop dead in my tracks.

I'm surrounded by rocks painted blood red. I know what this means— it's the first thing you learn upon arriving in Afghanistan: land mines. My eyes shoot side to side, searching for the rocks painted half red, half white. Cleared paths through minefields are lined with such bicolored rocks, the white side indicating safety.

But there is no path. I hold myself motionless. Try to breathe calmly, look over your shoulder. I am twenty feet into the minefield. Very carefully, step backward. I place one foot precisely in its own footprint. Do this with the other foot. Delicately, imagining myself as weightless as the ghost I could become, I retrace my steps.

I rub my eyes. Beside me, the horseman is still smoking. I'm slipping.

A few days ago, on the road outside Kabul, I met a man whose eleven-year-old son, Gulmarjan, was killed by a land mine while tending a flock of goats. Now, in a hazy, smoky dream, I see Gulmarjan running through red rocks, chasing a goat. Suddenly he's up in the air, his face stricken, blood splattering the brown sky and the brown earth and his feet still in his boots but not attached to his knees. My friend Greg's voice floats back to me, saying, "Three million land mines in a country of 25 million— that's at least one for each family. . . . The Russians made ones that looked like little butterflies. Curious children still pick them up . . ."

The horseman is asleep, his face smashed against the wool mat, the pipe still glowing. Gathering up my sleeping bag, I escape the hut. The air is ice-sharp, the sky buckshot with stars, the walls of the encircling mountains black, the snow along their crests as luminescent as a crown. I walk out into the pale blue steppe and find a spot among the slumbering yaks.

I slide into this distant night in no-man's-land. Lie back, look up, breathe. Safe and sound in this eternally unsafe, unsound country.

• • •

In 2000, Greg Mortenson and I hatched the idea of traversing the length of the Wakhan Corridor, the thin, vestigial arm of northeastern Afghanistan that extends eastward to the border of China, separating Tajikistan from Pakistan. As founder and director of the Bozeman, Montana–based Central Asia Institute (CAI), a nongovernmental organization that has built more than fifty schools in the tribal borderlands of Pakistan and Afghanistan, Greg has plenty of experience navigating the region's dicey political landscape.

We were planning to go in the fall of 2001. Then, on September 9, Ahmed Shah Massoud, commander of Afghanistan's anti-Taliban Northern Alliance, was assassinated by al Qaeda suicide bombers. Two days later, 9/11. A month later, American cruise missiles were detonating on Taliban positions. Within half a year, the war in Afghanistan was putatively over, but it wasn't. It's never over in Afghanistan.

Afghanistan is a palimpsest of conquest. The Persians ruled the region in the sixth century BC, then came Alexander the Great 200 years later. The White Huns in the fourth century AD, Islamic armies in the seventh, Genghis Khan and the Mongols in the thirteenth. It wasn't until the eighteenth century that a united Afghan empire emerged, then came the British, then, in 1979, the Russians. And now the Americans and their allies.

In October 2004, Afghanistan elected President Hamid Karzai, but his control barely extends beyond Kabul. As it has been for centuries, the Afghan countryside is ruled by tribal warlords with their own militias. It's a complex power network fraught with shifting allegiances. In the eighties, Afghan mujahideen ("freedom fighters") were armed and funded by the CIA to resist the Russians. After the Soviet occupation ended, in 1989, Afghanistan plunged into a state of internecine fighting: Warlords clashed, and the country fractured into a patchwork of fiefdoms. In 1996 the Taliban, a generation of Afghan Islamic fundamentalists who had grown frustrated with civil war, seized control of Kabul. They subsequently gave safe haven to Osama bin Laden and his al Qaeda fighters. Today, despite the presence of 33,000 NATO and coalition troops, Afghanistan remains a violent, dangerous mess.

If any region of the country stands apart, it's the remote, sparsely populated Wakhan Corridor, which has been spared much of the recent bloodletting. Carved by the Wakhan and Panj rivers, the 200-mile-long valley, much of it above 10,000 feet, separates the Pamir mountains to the north from the Hindu Kush to the south. For centuries it has been a natural conduit between Central Asia and China, and one of the most forbidding sections of the Silk Road, the 4,000-mile trade route linking Europe to the Far East.

The borders of the Wakhan were set in an 1895 treaty between Russia and Britain, which had been wrestling over the control of Central Asia for nearly a century. In what was dubbed the Great Game (a term coined by British Army spy Arthur Conolly of the Sixth Bengal Native Light Cavalry), both countries had sent intrepid spies into the region, not a few of whom were caught and beheaded. (Conolly was killed in Bokhara in 1842.) Eventually Britain and Russia agreed to use the entire country as a buffer zone, with the Wakhan extension ensuring that the borders of the Russian empire would never touch the borders of the British Raj.

Only a handful of Westerners are known to have traveled through the Wakhan Corridor since Marco Polo did it, in 1271. There were sporadic European expeditions throughout the second half of the nineteenth century and the beginning of the twentieth. In 1949, when Mao Zedong completed the Communist takeover of China, the borders were permanently closed, sealing off the 2,000-year-old caravan route and turning the corridor into a cul-de-sac. When the Soviets invaded Afghanistan in December 1979, they occupied the Wakhan and plowed a tank track halfway into the corridor. Today, the Wakhan has reverted to what it's been for much of its history: a primitive pastoral hinterland, home to about 7,000 Wakhi and Kirghiz people scattered throughout some forty small villages and camps. Opium smugglers sometimes use the Wakhan, traveling at night.

In 2004, American writers John Mock and Kimberley O'Neil crossed much of the Wakhan, exiting south into Pakistan. As far as Greg and I could find out, for decades no one had traversed the entire length of the Wakhan, following the old Silk Road from its entrance at the big northward bend of the Panj River all the way across to Tajikistan. We had no idea if it could even be done.

• • •

By the time our schedules matched up, four years later, Greg was so busy running CAI that he no longer had time to attempt the Wakhan traverse. But he was still passionate about the journey, and delighted to help make it happen. In his former life he'd been a climber and adventurer—it was the path that had led him to aid work.

Greg believed that the only way to truly understand Afghanistan, with all its contradictions and complexity, was total immersion. Excited about the trek, he found a partner for me: Doug Chabot, director of the Gallatin

National Forest Avalanche Center in Montana and a longtime Exum mountaineering guide. In an e-mail, Greg described Doug as "a tough, hardworking, easygoing, non-ego guy." Since we planned to attempt at least one virgin peak in the Wakhan, Chabot's avalanche experience "would be good life insurance." Our plan was to cross the Wakhan from west to east, using a four-wheel-drive van as far as we could, then going on foot or by horseback.

The first time we all assembled was in Greg's dingy room in the Kabul Peace Guest House, a small hotel in central Kabul, in late April 2005: Greg, forty-seven, comfortably attired in a dirt brown salwar kameez; Doug, forty-one, tanned, trim, with big green eyes and an inimitable laugh; and Teru Kuwayama, thirty-five, a New York–based photographer who had previously shot in Pakistan and Iraq.

We'd be relying on Greg's contacts with regional warlords to secure safe passage through the Wakhan, but the real uncertainty was getting out of Afghanistan. Although we had visas for Tajikistan (and China, just in case), none of us knew anything about the borders at the eastern end of the Wakhan. We could be stopped by Tajik guards and sent back, forced to retrace our journey in reverse. Or we could be arrested.

The corner of the Wakhan where Tajikistan, China, Afghanistan, and Pakistan meet is sensitive territory. On the China side, the Uighur, a Muslim Turkic population of 8 million, are clamoring for independence. In Kashmir, Pakistan and India have yet to resolve their decades-old dispute over borders and ethnic governance. To the north, the former Soviet republic of Tajikistan is run by an unstable, authoritarian government, and the country is an integral part of the global opium pipeline. (As much as half of all opium produced in Afghanistan is exported via Tajikistan.) Islamic fundamentalist guerrillas have been known to infiltrate the region; if we encountered them—or were mistaken for guerrillas ourselves—it could get ugly.

Greg couldn't go with us. He said he'd try to meet us within ten days in Sarhadd, in the middle of the Wakhan. He introduced us to fifty-year-old Sarfraz Khan, his right-hand man.

"Sarfraz will be going with you," he said.

A tall, dark, mustached man stood up and extended a crippled hand toward me. "I am very pleased to meet you," he said.

Over the years Greg had told me stories about Sarfraz. Born and based in the Chapurson Valley, in northern Pakistan, Sarfraz had served as a commando in Pakistan's elite mountain force; while stationed in Kashmir, he was wounded twice by Indian troops. One bullet passed through his palm and paralyzed his right hand. He speaks English, Urdu, Farsi, Wakhi, Burushashki, and Pashto. He'd spent years traveling the Wakhan as a yak trader. In a land where everything is impossible, Sarfraz would be our indispensable, indefatigable fixer.

We spent several days in Kabul before heading north, shopping for supplies and exchanging dollars for bricks of Afghan banknotes at the Shari Nau market. We bicycled out to the now abandoned blue-domed Ministry of Vice and Virtue, whose Taliban enforcers had patrolled the city, whipping women for infractions as minor as revealing their ankles.

While the Afghan government has ratified treaties to increase women's rights, the country still has a long way to go to meet the standards it has set. A few days after we arrived in Kabul, the BBC and other international news sources reported that a twenty-nine-year-old woman named Amina had been buried up to her chest and stoned to death near Faizabad, the capital of northern Afghanistan's Badakhshan province, for alleged infidelity. According to the reports, seventy people from the community, including her husband and father, participated in the murder. In early May, 200 women gathered in Kabul to call on the post-Taliban government and Islamic leaders to oppose acts of violence against women, a first step on a very long, dangerous journey.

One day we visited the village of Lalander, south of Kabul, for a tribal meeting at a CAI school. It was a brand-new whitewashed, plumb-walled building amid helter-skelter mud homes. CAI schools are joint projects: The costs of construction and teachers' pay are split between CAI and the village. (Most of Greg's work is financed by private donations; CAI receives no US government funding.) With few exceptions, its schools are coed.

At the Lalander school, boys and girls were lined up in their Friday best to present Greg with wreaths of paper flowers. After the welcoming ceremony, he spoke at the *jirga*—the council of elders—which met inside the village mosque. Forty stone-faced, bearded men sat cross-legged on worn Afghan rugs. Greg asked for Allah's blessing, thanked the greatness and wisdom of Allah, asked Allah to guide the judgment of the *jirga*. Lalander, he said, would be recognized as the most powerful village in all of Afghanistan because it had the courage to build a school that both boys and girls could attend.

Later, Greg told me that some of the men at the *jirga* were Taliban. "My dream is to build a school in every village from Kabul to Kandahar right to Deh Rawood, the village of Mullah Mohammed Omar, fugitive leader of the Taliban."

As we were driving out of Lalander, Greg saw a man standing on a hillside near a pile of rocks and stopped our van. We walked over to talk to him. He was Gulmarjan's father; in June 2004, the boy had been blown to pieces by a land mine just a hundred yards from the half-completed school. According to the International Committee of the Red Cross, leftover land mines and ordnance killed or wounded some 847 people in Afghanistan in 2004; despite determined de-mining efforts, the carnage continues.

The man told us how excited Gulmarjan had been about going to school with his younger sister. As he spoke, he raised his arms in the air, as if expecting his son, alive and whole, to drop back into them.

• • •

It took us three days to drive to Faizabad, home to the northernmost American military base. En route we passed dozens of stripped Russian tanks, most of which had been repurposed as bridges, retaining walls, storage units, playground equipment, even art installations: In a field beside the road we saw a row of three half-buried tanks sticking out of the ground like an Afghan version of Cadillac Ranch.

In Kunduz, a jovial Afghan teacher helped me order charcoal-grilled sheep shish kebab from a street vendor, and we struck up a conversation. "It took the Russians only a few weeks to take Afghanistan—just like you Americans," he said. "And I believe the regret began immediately."

We spent a night in Faizabad, then drove a few hours east to Baharak, the last town in which we could buy provisions. Doug, using his avalanche forecaster's waterproof pad and clear script, was our quartermaster. A veteran of extended climbing expeditions to Pakistan, he knew exactly what we needed. He'd announce the acquired item, then mark it off his list.

"Ten kilos rice: check. Ten kilos potatoes: check. Two kilos salt: check. Aluminum pot: check. Plastic pail: check. Fifty feet nylon cord: check."

In Baharak we stayed with Sardhar Khan, a powerful leader in the Badakhshan province. We'd been told we needed his blessing to pass through his territory and into the Wakhan.

Khan, forty-eight, is a small ethnic Tajik with a creased chestnut face who calls himself a former warlord. One of the most feared and respected commanders in Afghanistan, he spent fifteen years bivouacking in the mountains with his militia—ten years fighting the Russians, five years fighting the Taliban. His village had been bombed more than eighty times. Among his tiny, lethal volunteer militia, disloyalty, disobedience, and cowardice all had the same punishment. Khan would have the man tied to the back of a jeep and then dragged until he was skinned alive.

But the Sardhar Khan I met was polite and soft-spoken. He personally laid out the silverware for a picnic in his tiny apricot orchard and told us about the school he'd built with Greg last year. It was CAI's largest—a fortresslike structure with stone walls four feet thick and a wood-burning stove in each of the eight classrooms. More than 250 kids would be attending the school this fall.

With his wars over for now, Khan was writing poems. Greg sent me a sample of his verse after our trip:

You may wonder why I sit here on this rock, by the river, doing nothing.

There is so much work to be done for my people.

We have little food, we have few jobs, our fields are in shambles, and still land mines everywhere.

I am here to hear the quiet, the water, and singing trees. This is the sound of peace in the presence of my Allah Almighty.

After 30 years as a mujahedeen, I have grown old from fighting. I resent the sound of destruction. I am tired of war.

Our fourth day out of Kabul we reached the village of Eshkashem, at the mouth of the Wakhan Corridor. Here we met another strongman, Wohid Khan, a tall, taciturn, handsome Tajik in his early forties. As commander of the Afghan–Tajik border security forces, he oversees 200 Afghan troops in their patrol of a 330-mile stretch of the Afghan–Tajik border, including the entire northern boundary of the Wakhan. Khan granted us permission to traverse the corridor, from one end to the other, but he couldn't guarantee our safety once we crossed into Tajikistan. The most he could do was provide us with a handwritten note that vouched for our honorable intentions.

The entrance to the Wakhan was stunning. On either side of a flat, brown valley, enormous white mountains—the Hindu Kush to the south, the Tajikistan Pamirs to the north—rose like a mirror image. The huge teeth of these peaks, with a tongue of dirt down the middle, reminded me of a wolf's mouth. The valley disappeared into the distance, a throat of land that reached toward the steppes of western China.

The rough road that the Russian invaders had cut, following the camel path of the Silk Road, was all but gone, covered by rockslides or swept away by floods and avalanches. Our four-wheel-drive Toyota van crept alongside slopes where we were sure we'd roll, crossed fulvous streams so high we were almost carried away. When we sank axle-deep in mud and got stuck, it took hours of digging with ice axes to extract the van.

Many of the peaks on both sides of the valley are unclimbed. Doug kept shouting for the driver to stop so we could crawl over our duffel bags, spill out the side door, and take pictures.

Back in the early seventies, stories of expeditions to the Wakhan's 20,000-foot summits generated enormous excitement. The Brits, Germans, Austrians, Spaniards, Italians, Japanese—they'd all come here to climb. In 1971, Italian alpinists led by Carlo Alberto Pinelli explored the central Wakhan's Big Pamir range and climbed three of its highest mountains, Koh–i-Marco Polo (20,256 feet), Koh-i-Pamir (20,670 feet), and Koh-i-Hilal (20,607 feet). On the very western edge of the Wakhan, in the Hindu Kush, 24,580-foot Noshaq was once a popular peak.

But the 1979 Russian invasion put an end to Wakhan mountaineering for more than two decades. In 2003, Pinelli returned and managed to galvanize a successful expedition to Noshaq, but not a soul had summited in the heart of the Wakhan for a generation. Doug and I were itching for an ascent.

That first night in the Wakhan we slept in a *khun*, a traditional Wakhi home with a layered, square-patterned wood ceiling and red Afghan rugs spread over an elevated platform. The Wakhi, a tough-knuckled, wiry tribe, have ancient Iranian roots and have lived in the Wakhan for at least a thousand years. They speak Wakhi, an old Persian dialect, and adhere to the Ismaeli sect of Islam. Subsistence farmers, they use yaks to till the sandy soil and plant potatoes, wheat, barley, and lentils. The growing season is extremely short, the winters hideously harsh. One out of three Wakhi infants dies before the age of one, and women still commonly die in childbirth.

The extended family that took us in that night—grandparents, parents, kids, aunts, uncles—were old friends of Sarfraz, but it wouldn't have mattered; throughout the trip, wherever we stopped, we were warmly welcomed with food and a bed. An Afghan's wealth and generosity are measured by the kindness he shows strangers. Sarfraz's friends fed us ibex and brown rice, which we ate with our hands from a common plate. Several months earlier, the village school had been destroyed by an avalanche. Sarfraz spent the evening working on a plan to build a new CAI school.

The next day we continued up-valley, often walking ahead of the grinding, bottom-scraping van—our stubborn, modern-day camel. We were passing into the Wakhan's Big Pamirs, but the valley was so deep and the mountains to either side so high, we couldn't see any peaks beyond those along the front range. We were searching for what appeared on the map to be a cleft in the left-hand wall. We needn't have worried. It was obvious the moment we saw it—a V-shaped fissure with a 300-foot waterfall crashing onto boulders.

We stopped in a yak meadow near the falls, at 10,000 feet. Sarfraz was taking the van back to Faizabad to pick up Greg and bring him out to meet us. This was basecamp. We dragged out our backpacks and duffel bags, and then Sarfraz was gone. We had one week to climb the mountain.

• • •

As often happens in very remote, sparsely populated places, a man showed up out of nowhere: a Wakhi named Sher Ali, rough as a rock, with his own alpenstock. He helped clear away the yak pies and set up our tents, then stood off at a distance, staring.

"You guys know how to cook?" Teru asked, chewing on a chunk of jerky.

Doug and I looked at each other and laughed.

"Right," said Teru. Thenceforth, Teru the photographer was also Teru the basecamp cook. He was good—dicing onions, experimenting with spices—and each meal was better than anything we two dirtbags could have cooked up with a full kitchen.

That day Doug and I reconned above the waterfall, following a steep-walled drainage up to the snow line. Beyond was a spiky wilderness of white. We couldn't see Koh-i-Bardar—*Mountain of the Entrance* in Wakhi, the peak we hoped to climb—but we knew it was back there somewhere. Doug and I decided to attempt our sight-unseen peak in a single, unsupported push while Teru waited at camp with Sher Ali.

We busted out early the following morning with so much energy we could barely keep up with our legs. Doug and I had the same pace and made swift progress. By noon we were crossing brilliant snowfields, passing beneath Teton-like granite spires. By 12:15 we were marooned.

In the space of fifteen minutes, the temperature had warmed just enough for the four-inch crust to soften to the point that it wouldn't support our body weight. It was like breaking through ice. Suddenly we were both wallowing chest-deep, fracturing off chunks of crust as we tried to crawl back onto the surface.

"Time to camp," said Doug.

"Here? Now?"

"You wanna swim to the mountain?"

We tromped out a platform and spent the rest of the afternoon eating, napping, and sunbathing. Up at 4:00 the next morning, we reached our 16,000-foot assault camp on the Purwakshan Glacier by 10:00. We dropped our packs and did a fast recon up to the base of Koh-i-Bardar to find our line: a steep couloir to a knife-edge ridge to the summit. We were back by midday and had our tent up before we once again became castaways in an ocean of snow. We couldn't take one step off our tent platform without drowning.

"We'll have to climb it entirely at night," said Doug, while we were baking inside the oven of our tiny two-man tent.

Already Doug was one of the best partners I'd ever had. He was fast, funny, could sleep anywhere, farted like a horse, never whined, and, most important, simply loved the mountains. He was the epitome of parsimony—carrying the right, light gear and absolutely nothing extra, except Peet's French roast coffee, of course.

We watched snow squalls come and go that afternoon, trying to scare us, took sleeping pills at 6:00 p.m., got up at 11:00, and were crunching up the glacier before midnight. Headlamps burning, we blazed over the glacier in crampons, found the right couloir, front-pointed straight up, catwalked along the knife-edge, both fell into crevasses on the summit glacier, and swapped leads postholing right to the 19,941-foot summit of Koh-i-Bardar.

It was 6:45, forty-eight hours since we'd left basecamp. Standing atop the summit block, we saw the whole world spread below us—jagged, pale pink, chaste. There hadn't been another first ascent in the Wakhan since 1977.

• • •

Sarfraz, now with Greg in tow, met us back at basecamp and we drove farther into the corridor. Greg had another school meeting to attend in Sarhadd, a Wakhi village fifteen miles down the road.

At the welcoming ceremony all the children lined up, looking like brilliant, unidentifiable flowers in their rags and robes of reds and maroons. The little girls wore strings of lapis lazuli, and the little boys blue Chinese Wellingtons. Once again Greg gave a speech to the assembled elders, but for this crowd, it was different: more emphasis on the economic benefits of education, less on Allah. How one of these children right here, once they learned their three R's, could go to a trade school in Kabul and return home to fix the village tractor.

That night, when we were all in our sleeping bags—Teru already asleep, Doug busy noting the day's weather in his journal with hand-drawn symbols, Sarfraz somewhere outside negotiating our horses for the morning—Greg and I, insomniacs both, sat with our backs against the stone wall and talked about his vision for Afghanistan.

"The US fired eighty-eight Tomahawk cruise missiles into Afghanistan in 2001," he said. "I could build forty schools for the cost of one of them. The Taliban are still here. They're just waiting for us to leave. You can kill a warrior, but unless you educate his children, they will become prime recruits."

Greg pulled his scarf up around his face, looking just like an Afghan in the candlelight. He would not be coming with us deeper into the valley. About 550 Wakhi families live in the western Wakhan, and he and Sarfraz had identified twenty-one villages that needed schools. "Educating girls, in particular, is critical," he continued. "If you can educate a girl to the fifth-grade level, three things happen: Infant mortality goes down, birthrates go down, and the quality of life for the whole village, from health to happiness, goes up. Something else also happens. Before a young man goes on jihad, holy war, he must first ask for his mother's permission. Educated mothers say no."

• • •

Sarhadd, roughly halfway up the Wakhan Corridor, is at the end of the road. From here all travel would be on foot or by horseback. We had eighty miles in front of us to reach Tajikistan.

On a cold, windy morning, Sarfraz, Doug, Teru, and I left Sarhadd with four packhorses and four Wakhi wranglers. For two days we hiked along the bottoms of immense canyons, in the shadows, jumping boulders, fording side streams, imagining Marco Polo doing the same thing. We climbed two small passes to escape the canyons and reach the upper Wakhan settlement of Langar and Khan Bibi's grim stone hut.

From Langar we walked to Bazai Gonbad, a Kirghiz burial ground consisting of a dozen domed, chalk-white mausoleums. Beyond Bazai Gonbad, the Wakhan widens dramatically. The valley is too high for farming—12,000 feet—hence the eastern Wakhan is inhabited primarily by Kirghiz nomads. In general the Kirghiz are wealthier and healthier than the Wakhi, although since the borders were closed in 1949, there has been a symbiotic relationship between the two peoples. The Wakhi need animals and the Kirghiz need grain, so they barter.

The Kirghiz are cowboys, and Sarfraz, a great rider himself, managed to get us saddle horses. Teru, the New Yorker, was the most natural cowboy among the Americans, followed by Doug, who is originally from New Jersey. I grew up in Wyoming working on ranches and can't ride a horse to save my life.

The upper Wakhan is one of the last refuges for at least three endangered species—the snow leopard, the Himalayan wolf, and the Marco Polo sheep. All are still hunted by the Kirghiz. (We saw wolfskin coats for sale on Chicken Street in Kabul and were told the pelts came from northeastern Afghanistan.) In a heavy-snow winter, the Kirghiz hunt snow leopards and wolves that prey on their sheep and sometimes even on children; they hunt the sheep for food. But change is coming: Biologist George Schaller, vice president of science and exploration at the New York–based Wildlife Conservation Society, has been inventorying Marco Polo sheep in the area since the 1970s—most recently visiting in 2004 and 2005—and he's campaigning to make the entire region a protected international park.

One evening we stopped in a Kirghiz camp called *Uchkali—Place of the Ibex*—where there were nine families living in nine yurts and an untold number of goats and sheep and yaks. Kirghiz lives are interwoven with the lives of their animals, and they subsist almost entirely on red meat, milk, and yogurt. Although they speak a Turkic dialect, their ancient ancestors may have been Mongols. After welcoming cups of tea, the old chief, a man named Yeerali, set before us a battered cardboard box. Inside the box was a gas-powered generator.

Yeerali had bought the generator the previous autumn, along with several gallons of gas and a box of electrical supplies, and brought them here by horse in hopes of having lights during the long, snow-buried winter. Of course the generator broke soon afterward and the camp spent another winter in darkness.

We were Americans, were we not? Visitors from the land of machines. Certainly we would fix the generator.

After having been given so much by the people of the Wakhan, it was our chance to give something back. Besides, we were on the spot. Doug and I took up the challenge.

First we carefully examined the little beast, talking back and forth in a professional tone, making a good show of our diagnosis. Then we got out our multitools and went to town. We fiddled with the gas mixture and the throttle spring and the adjustment screws and the choke lever and the spark-plug gap.

The machine was no more complicated than a lawn mower, but the gaze of the entire camp was on us. After we'd done all we could possibly think of and then some, I yanked on the pull cord.

Nothing. The Kirghiz's disappointment was palpable.

We fiddled some more, I pulled the cord: a cough. Their eyes lit up. More adjustments, I pulled the cord, and the little engine that could roared to life.

Doug and I were instant heroes. Yeerali ordered two men to kill the biggest sheep of the herd, which they did forthwith, cutting its throat and skinning it right there in front of us. While the various parts of the sheep were being cooked, Doug and Sarfraz and I dug into the box of electrical supplies and proceeded to electrify the camp, stringing wire and lights to the nearest yurts as if they were Christmas trees.

When the platter of food arrived, we sat down beneath the abundant light of a single dangling bulb.

Now, there's something special about Wakhan sheep, a Central Asian breed called Turki qoey: They have two distinct camel humps of fat on their behinds. Like whale blubber to the Inuit, sheep-ass fat is a delicacy to the Kirghiz.

Two large lumps of steaming ass sat in the middle of the platter, surrounded by the boiled head and testicles.

Doug and I glanced at each other and, without hesitation, sprung open our belay knives, cut off large slices of greasy ass fat, and plopped them into our mouths.

"Not bad," said Doug. Then he cracked open the sheep's head and took a bite of the hot, soft cheek, and I ate one of the big, slippery testicles.

• • •

We traveled by horseback for two more days across the upper Wakhan, stopping in Kirghiz nomad camps along the way. We spent our last night in the Wakhan in Urtobill, a community of four extended families. Together they'd pooled their resources and bought Chinese solar panels, a car battery, a TV, and a video player. That evening we sat with them inside a Kirghiz *utok*, or community house, and watched their only video: a grainy 1975 documentary called *The Kirghiz of Afghanistan*.

The next day, we galloped up to the Tajikistan border, which was marked by a tangled, partly downed barbed-wire fence. Nobody was there. Just more open brown country.

It was the end of the road for Sarfraz. We dismounted and took pictures. Sarfraz had become a friend, and we were going to miss him—just how much, we had no idea. We hugged and shook hands, and then Doug and Teru and I walked into Tajikistan.

We followed a washed-out tank track due east along the barbed-wire fence, passing two tall, abandoned guard towers. After ten miles we still hadn't seen a soul. Up on the hill to our left were another guard tower, some tanks buried in tank pits, and some buildings, but the place appeared deserted, so we kept going.

A quarter-mile past the outpost, we heard a pop and a zing. "That's a shot," said Doug. He was brilliant.

We heard another round and spun on our heels to see an officer with an AK-47 running down the hill toward us. We put our hands in the air. In seconds the officer was upon us, screaming in Russian and waving his rifle in our faces. "Dokumenty! Dokumenty!"

He was the spitting image of a young Robert De Niro in *The Godfather: Part II*, and seemingly just as volatile and unpredictable. I could see his finger trembling on the trigger.

We slowly handed him our passports, along with the note from Wohid Khan.

"Wohid Khan, Wohid Khan," we said in high, choirboy voices. The name seemed to register.

He marched us to the base. All but one of the buildings were abandoned. We were taken inside, past a small kitchen into an even smaller office, and the door was closed behind us. A metal desk, a shelf with Russian military books, a couch. We sat on the couch while Vito Corleone laid his AK-47 on the table and allowed us to see that he was also packing a sidearm. He looked like the kind of guy who was waiting for us to do something stupid so he could blow us away right there.

Eventually he got up, opened the door, and motioned for us to step out. We were taken to a little kitchen and served tea and cookies. In the next room we could hear Vito calling his superiors. Two hours later another officer arrived.

"Welcome in Tajikistan," he said happily, then shook our hands. He looked like a bearded Antonio Banderas.

We thought he actually spoke English, but he didn't, so the interviews took a long time. Vito and Tony had some kind of comic-book interrogation manual that they used to extract information from us.

Were we al Qaeda? Were we Taliban? Were we CIA? Were we drug smugglers?

We answered no to all of the above.

What were we, then?

Tourists.

Tourists. Tourists who walked all the way across the Wakhan?

Yes.

We showed them our route on the map.

That is not possible, they said. No one has ever crossed this border.

We know. That's why we're here.

Vito and Tony were dismayed. They decided to go through the contents of our backpacks, one item at time. Toothbrush, dirty underwear, unwashed bowl. They made a complete inventory, but it was obviously a letdown. No guns, no drugs, no secret documents. Had we been real spies or at least drug smugglers, Vito and Tony would have been promoted and could have gotten out of this shithole outpost. On the other hand, since we really were three stupid American tourists, they could chill out.

So what did we want for dinner, asked Vito. How about Marco Polo sheep.

That night our interrogators gave us their bunks while they slept on the hard floor of the office.

I was so thrilled I couldn't fall asleep.

"We did it, guys," I whispered. "We crossed the Wakhan!"

"And now we're under arrest," said Teru.

"I would call it temporarily detained," said Doug.

• • •

In the morning we were supposed to be transferred to another military base for further questioning, but this outpost had no vehicle. Eventually a 1950s Soviet Muscovitch, a pint-size car, showed up. It was owned by two elders of the local village.

Doug, Teru, I, and Vito, Tony, and the two old men and two submachine guns, which Vito asked us to hold, all crammed into the car. We drove about a mile before it broke down. Vito and Tony stayed with the two old men and the car but told us to keep marching across the plain to the next military base so as not to miss our next interrogation.

Once out of their sight, I suggested we just light out for the mountains and cross into China. We were at the very end of the Wakhan valley.

"You're crazy, man," said Teru, outraged, "we're under arrest!"

I thought Doug would be into it, but he was lukewarm. "Let's just play this out and see what happens."

Late that afternoon we walked into the Kizilrabat military base. Our captors rolled in by car an hour later. We had another huge meal of Marco Polo sheep, and then Vito took us out to a hot springs for a much-needed bath. Vito was cool now, although when Teru asked him when we would be free to go on our merry way, Vito grimaced and said four or five weeks.

This deeply unnerved Teru. Doug and I didn't believe a word. If we didn't show up in China tomorrow, our backup plan would kick in: Greg would call the embassy.

That night we were transferred north by jeep to an undisclosed military base. A big meal was waiting for us when we arrived. Stew with chunks of meat, Russian bread with slabs of butter, cookies and candies and tea. We were given beds with clean sheets in a barrack with posters of pin-up girls lining the walls.

In the morning we were served a large breakfast but told to stay inside, out of sight of the soldiers. Teru moped back into bed, Doug read, I worked on my notes. But I'm constitutionally unsuited to sitting around. Out the window I could see a volleyball net.

When I stepped out of the barrack a soldier immediately sent an attack dog at me. I grinned and picked up a length of rebar. The dog turned around.

"Netch," I said in Russian, making the shape of a ball with my hands and pointing to the volleyball net. "I want a volleyball."

The soldier tried to hustle me back into the barrack but I stood my ground. A volleyball came bouncing out. Within minutes at least fifteen boy-soldiers had emptied out of the barracks for a rousing game of volleyball. It was straight out of *Hogan's Heroes*. Doug heard all the commotion and came out to play.

We bump–set–spiked our way through three games. It was a blast. We had the normally bored-to-death soldiers laughing out loud. After volleyball we moved on to a rope-climbing contest, then a chinup contest, then back into our barracks for lunch. Having gotten a little oxygen into the system, Doug and I were in high spirits, but Teru was morose.

"I bet we're outta here tomorrow," Doug said cheerfully.

"How do you know?" said Teru.

"I don't. I just think things will work themselves out."

"We could be stuck here for weeks, *months!*" Teru's voice was shrill.

Teru then told us that he had sent an SOS text message to Greg on his sat phone. He'd even sent the latitude and longitude coordinates of this military base.

That was spy behavior. It could get us in deep trouble. For the first time on the entire trip, Doug's face darkened. "We're a team. Teru, that was a team decision, not your personal decision."

Doug and I went back out into the yard to take a stroll and talk.

"Since we're not in China today," said Doug. "Greg already knows the score. He'll pull out all the stops."

The next morning we were transferred further north, to Murgob, then east to the military base in Chorug, where we underwent more entertaining questioning.

What elementary school did you go to?

How old is your mother?

Why did you fly from Denver?

What al Qaeda cell helped you get across the Wakhan?

That night we were put up in the interrogator's own home. I gave him a twenty and he went out and bought us vodka and salami. We had a long discussion about the merits of capitalism versus socialism. He insisted we sleep in his bed, but we slept on the floor.

The following day, more interviews, with each of us interrogated in a separate room. I gave my interviewer another twenty to buy vodka and we shared a few glasses, so my interview went splendidly. I learned that he was divorced and missed his son who lived in Dushanbe. Doug's interview also went well. He and I thought things were moving along quite smoothly. Then, through the wall, we overhead Teru angrily demanding to speak with the American embassy.

This made our captors suspicious, of course. They decided to do another thorough search of our clothes, our bodies, our packs, everything. I managed to stand beside Teru and whisper to him to ditch the sat phone in the toilet. Doug and I figured that if they found it, there couldn't be better proof that we were spies after all, and we'd be in for an extended stay. Teru obstinately refused.

Just as they started opening our bags, two armored-plated U.S. Embassy Land Cruisers roared into the compound. Cavalry to the rescue.

After five days of detainment, faster than you could say "we're outta here," Vice-Consul Evan McCarthy, Major Mark Handy, and two embassy cops expeditiously secured our release.

The moment the doors closed on the bulletproof embassy Land Cruisers, we were back home. Just like that, our trip was over. Outside it was

Tajikistan, inside it was America. We drove to a fancy hotel while listening to Van Morrison, eating Pringles, and drinking Coke.

• • •

Afghanistan is a country of horrific contradictions. Unfathomable kindness stands shoulder to shoulder with unspeakable cruelty. Extraordinary beauty sleeps next to wretched ugliness. The harshness of Afghanistan's history and its landscape have created a fiercely fragmented country. Much of this will never change.

But one thing could.

The Taliban—who sponsor al Qaeda—are once again attempting to take over the country and reinstate their misguided, draconian interpretation of Islam. They can only succeed if they can buy weapons. To buy weapons, they need money. This money comes from opium.

In 2005, Afghanistan produced 6,100 tons of opium, ninety-three percent of the world's total supply. The revenue from the illegal trade is estimated at more than $3 billion, almost equal to what Afghanistan receives in all foreign aid. In 2005, the United States allocated about $774 million to the effort to eradicate poppy farming in Afghanistan. Unfortunately, this too, is misguided.

After crossing the Wakhan, I eventually met back up with Greg in Bozeman, where we talked about the future of Afghanistan.

"Opium?" he said. "Honestly, it can never be eliminated from Afghanistan. Most villages are desperately poor. They're utterly dependent on the income from poppy farming. Eradicating the poppy crops will only cause more poverty and more hopelessness—and drive thousands of young men into the arms of the Taliban—which will only cause more killing and more wars."

There is an alternative: The Senlis Council, an international drug-policy think tank, recently proposed legalizing the farming of poppies in Afghanistan.

India is already licensed by the International Narcotics Control Board, an independent watchdog group that monitors the trade of illicit and medicinal drugs, to grow opium and produce generic pain medication for developing nations. Afghanistan could do the same. The cost of creating such a program has been estimated at only $600 million. Ideally, the farmers would get cash, the drug lords and the Taliban would be cut out, the developing world would get more pain-relief medicine, and the major demand for the global traffic in heroin would be drastically reduced.

It's a compelling strategy—accepting the reality on the ground rather than fighting it—and it's exactly how Greg Mortenson operates—which is why CAI has been so successful.

The war on drugs? The war on terrorism? They're both sickening oxymorons.

Violence begets violence. War begets war.

Conviction

OF LIFE OR LIMB

On Saturday, April 26, 2003, Aron Ralston started a solo descent into the deep, narrow slot of Bluejohn Canyon in southeastern Utah. Passing over and then under boulders that clogged the three-foot-wide penumbral passage, Ralston was negotiating a ten-foot drop between two ledges when an 800-pound boulder shifted above him. He managed to snap his left hand out of its path, but his right hand was instantly smashed between the boulder and the sandstone wall.

"The adrenaline was pumping very, very hard," Ralston, twenty-seven, later recounted from St. Mary's Hospital in Grand Junction, Colorado. "It took some good, calm thinking to get myself to stop throwing myself against the boulder."

Ralston was trapped, alone in a remote canyon. Rescue was unlikely: He'd neglected to inform anyone of where he was going.

Six foot two, long, lean, and fit, Ralston is an accomplished outdoor athlete. He first became interested in climbing in 1996, after reading about the Everest disaster in which eight mountaineers lost their lives in a single storm. "I wondered what I would do if I were in a situation like that," he told me.

Ralston grew up in Colorado and graduated with honors from Carnegie Mellon University in 1997 with a double major in mechanical engineering and French, then worked at Intel for five years, hopscotching to posts in Phoenix; Tacoma, Washington; and then Albuquerque, New Mexico, where he volunteered on a local search-and-rescue team. In the spring of 2002, he moved to Aspen, took a retail job at Ute Mountaineering, and began training to become a climbing guide.

According to his Web site, www.aralston.com, Ralston has topped out on thirty-four of the fifty states' highest points, soloed forty-five of Colorado's fifty-nine fourteeners in winter, and summited 20,320-foot Mount McKinley.

This kind of adventuring involves risk. In March 2003, Ralston and two companions were backcountry skiing on Resolution Peak, in central

Colorado, when they got caught in an avalanche. "I just remember rolling down with it. Powder was swirling all around and I was trying to breathe, but I would breathe a mixture of snow and air, swallowing it like seawater. It was horrible. It should have killed us."

It didn't. Buried up to his neck, Ralston was rescued by his friend, and together they dug out the third skier. It was less than a month later when he embarked on his solo day hike in the Utah desert.

After the boulder crushed his hand, Ralston said, "I very quickly figured out some of my options. I began laying plans for what I was going to do." He also inventoried his provisions: two burritos, one liter of water, and some candy bar crumbs.

One possibility was that "someone would happen along the trail" and rescue him. No one did, so he spent his first night in the slot canyon working on plan B: futilely chipping away at the rock with his multitool.

The next day, Sunday, using his climbing gear and his search-and-rescue skills, he moved to plan C: rigging ropes in an attempt to hoist the boulder off his hand. This also failed.

On Monday, he rerigged the ropes and again tried moving the rock. "At no point was I ever able, with any of the rope mechanics, to get the boulder to budge even microscopically," Ralston said.

He kept chipping away at the boulder, but over the next few days he would often simply stop and rest. "There were times when I thought that was the most efficient use of my time," he explained.

He thought a lot about dying and was afraid at first, but he eventually "came to peace with death."

On day four of his ordeal, Tuesday, April 29, Ralston ran out of water. Realizing he would die of dehydration within days, he prepared to reckon with his last resort: severing his hand with the blunt blade of his multitool.

"Essentially I got my surgical table ready and applied the knife to my arm, and started sawing back and forth. But I didn't even break the skin. I couldn't even cut the hair off of my arm, the knife was so dull."

On Wednesday, he managed to puncture the skin but realized he wouldn't be able to cut through the bone.

By Thursday, May 1, growing weak and having passed through stages of depression, hope, and prayer, Ralston decided he would have to break his arm near the wrist to extricate himself. "I was able to first snap the radius," he calmly recalled, "and then, within a few minutes, snap the ulna at the wrist, and from there I had the knife out and applied the tourniquet and went to task. It was a process that took about an hour."

Ralston sawed through the soft tissue between the broken bones and amputated his hand.

"All the desires, joys, and euphorias of a future life came rushing into me," Ralston stated. "Maybe this is how I handled the pain. I was so happy to be taking action."

Ralston rigged his rope, set his anchors, rappelled sixty feet to the floor of Bluejohn Canyon, and hiked five miles downstream into Horseshoe Canyon, supporting the bloody stump of his right arm in a makeshift sling. He ran into three hikers from Holland, who gave him Oreos and water and helped him carry his pack. At 3:00 p.m., he was finally rescued by a helicopter, which had begun searching for him when friends in Aspen, worried because he hadn't shown up for work, called the Utah authorities.

Flown first to Allen Memorial Hospital in Moab, Utah, Ralston was later transferred to St. Mary's Hospital in Grand Junction, where he underwent the first of several surgical procedures to prepare his right arm for a prosthesis.

Three days later, a team of thirteen rangers trekked into the canyon to retrieve Ralston's hand. Using a hydraulic jack and a grip hoist, it took them an hour to lift the boulder. Ralston had carved the words *Good luck now* into the rock just before he severed his hand.

• • •

In the days and weeks after the accident, more than 500 articles worldwide and hundreds of TV and radio news segments recounted the gruesome details of Ralston's self-rescue. His story held us spellbound. It trumped the repulsive sensationalism of *Fear Factor*, the voyeurism of *Survivor*, and the improbable terrors of *The Worst-Case Scenario Survival Handbook*. It was actually life or death. No safety net. No film crews. No prizes but the biggest: life.

A friend and I were discussing the incident when he confided, "You know, I guess I have doubts. I don't know if I could do that." This from a man who recently had climbed six peaks in Peru in six weeks. He wasn't the only one; I had dozens of conversations like this. Aron Ralston, through simple courage and cool self-appraisal, had cut through all the feckless fakery of "reality" TV and prompted us to ask ourselves the inescapable question: Could I do that?

Al Siebert, PhD, ex-paratrooper, founder of the Resiliency Center, an outreach program in Portland, Oregon, and author of the 1996 book *The Survivor Personality*, has studied hundreds of stories of survival and found that, in many cases, the answer may lie in a handful of specific behavioral traits.

"Survivors rapidly read reality," says Siebert. "When something horrible happens, they immediately accept the situation for what it is and consciously decide that they will do everything in their power to get through it." That is, they have the ability to rationally accept dreadful circumstances without becoming angry or passive, two common responses to stress.

"Getting angry is just a waste of precious energy," says Siebert, "and playing the victim dramatically increases your likelihood of dying."

After adjusting to the new circumstances, survivors start looking very hard, but also very imaginatively, for solutions. "I call it integrated problem-solving behavior," says Siebert. "By that I mean it's a mixture of left-brain thinking—logical, linear, Mr. Spock—and right-brain thinking—intuitive, creative, lots of leaps of faith."

One of Siebert's most intriguing discoveries is that survivors tend to exhibit "biphasic personality traits," which means they have oppositional, counterbalancing behavior. "It is to be proud and humble, positive and negative, selfish and unselfish, cooperative and rebellious, spiritual and irreverent," Siebert writes in *The Survivor Personality*. In other words, Hollywood has it all wrong: Survivors are not brutish, one-dimensional *Rambo* types or combustible *Scarface* maniacs; rather, they are complex, compassionate, and, most important, open-minded.

Peter Suedfeld, PhD, professor emeritus of psychology at the University of British Columbia, who has researched survival psychology for more than forty years, puts it this way: "Beyond the fundamental will to survive, the foremost character trait of a survivor is intellectual flexibility.

"People under high stress are more likely to become rigid, which only decreases their chances of survival," he continues. Even in a jam, "survivors are extremely adaptable people. They know how to improvise. If one solution doesn't work, they try another. They don't fixate on one answer. They keep an open mind, searching for options, developing strategies."

There are two other important survivor characteristics: optimism and unflappability. Optimists recognize that their predicament is temporary, isolate the problem, understand that even if they haven't found a solution yet, it doesn't mean there isn't one, and recognize that they do have a modicum of control over their fate.

To be unflappable is to be able to "tolerate bizarre experiences without freaking out." It's the old cliché: Don't panic. There are only three ways to cope in a tough situation—leave the environment, change the environment, or change your attitude. According to Suedfeld, "survivors are capable of recognizing which one, or which combination, will best increase their chances."

In short, considering the psychological profile of survivors, if you tend to react to dicey situations with impatience, intolerance, panic, pessimism, passivity, pigheadedness, anger, or any combination thereof, you may not make it out alive.

• • •

Fortunately it's not just a matter of innate character or instinct.

"People absolutely can be trained to survive," says Frank Heyl, a retired air force officer and director of the Combat Aviation Survival School in Helena, Montana.

"Everybody is born with the will to survive," says Heyl, "but it's like a muscle or a skill. You've got to nurture it, train it, build it up."

You can get the basics from any survival manual or wilderness safety course: Never venture into the backcountry alone without leaving word of your intended route and return date. Always, even on a dayhike, stock your pack with the fabled "ten essentials": knife, water, food, matches, map, compass, headlamp, cord, proper clothing, and sun protection. Heyl puts two additional items at the top of the list: "Your head is number one. It's the best survival tool there is. Number two: a basic medical kit and the understanding of how to use it."

Then you've got to take this knowledge into the field.

"It's all about hands-on experience," says Heyl. "Go into your local woods at night, in the wind, when it's raining, and see if you can build a fire. Go out in the winter and practice building a snow shelter. The more you practice survival skills, the better a survivor you become." Ralston's search-and-rescue skills and his previous experience with close calls in the backcountry—his own and others'—are what gave him this mental preparedness.

Even for a military veteran like Heyl, surviving isn't about being macho. "Men like to do things by the numbers. They like routine, but this kind of rigidity works against them in a survival situation. Women tend to be more flexible in their thinking, more adaptable, and this can make them better at survival," says Heyl. "It doesn't take Herculean strength to survive."

• • •

Aron Ralston clearly used his head, but would a medical kit or an informed friend have saved his right hand? Probably not. His experience lies at the outer limits of the backcountry-accident bell curve. "You are exponentially more likely to be hit by lightning in the backcountry than to be forced to amputate your arm," says Eric A. Weiss, MD, emergency physician and associate director of trauma at the Stanford University Medical Center and author of *A Comprehensive Guide to Wilderness and Travel Medicine*. "Lightning is the number-one natural-hazard cause of death, and a sprained ankle is the most common backcountry injury."

Statistics from NOLS, the National Outdoor Leadership School, bear this out. From 1998 to 2000, NOLS had 465,753 program days and only 526 injuries, forty-eight percent of which were either sprains or strains caused by slipping on the trail. Wounds, bruisings, and bee stings accounted for another twenty-one percent, fractures and dislocations a mere seven percent, and head injuries two percent. Frostbite, dental pain, burns, and infections made up the rest.

Even so, it's the fluky, once-in-a-lifetime accidents that keep us up at night, and it's the survivors' ingenuity—not their errors—that leaves the most lasting impression.

In 1997, Doug Goodale, a thirty-three-year-old Maine lobsterman, cut off his right arm above the elbow after getting it caught in a winch. In 1993, while fishing near St. Mary's Glacier in Colorado, Bill Jeracki, an emergency room technician, was pinned to the ground when a boulder crushed his left leg. Snow was forecast and he'd left his jacket in the truck; Jeracki, forty-seven, didn't believe he would survive the night. Fashioning a tourniquet out of his flannel shirt, he cut off his leg at the knee with his pocketknife, "like you fillet a fish," using metal clips from his fishing kit to clamp the bleeding arteries. Then he dragged himself to his truck and drove into town.

That same year, bulldozer operator Donald Wyman was clearing trees in a forest in western Pennsylvania when a massive oak crushed his left leg. Using a rawhide bootlace as his tourniquet (which he tightened with a chainsaw wrench) and a three-inch pocketknife as a scalpel, Wyman amputated his broken leg below the knee.

· · ·

Haven't we all done what Ralston did—just shot out into the wilds alone without telling anyone? Desperate for quiet, famished for rock, thirsty for streams, craving the smell of pines. And, yes, of course, the chances of our quick trip into the wilderness turning into a life-or-death struggle are remote, but what if? That's the clincher. What if that boulder, which has been in that same position for a thousand years, inexplicably shifts a fraction of an inch, just at the very moment that your hand is beneath it? What would you do? Would you die?

It's not being dead that scares us. What frightens us is being a witness to our own death. Watching it come, knowing we are trapped, alone, with no one to call for help. And what we fear most is finding ourselves in a situation where we actually have a choice, but lack the courage to fight, the resolve to tell death to go screw itself—whatever the cost.

Aron Ralston had a rough choice: to die or to mutilate himself. When a serac unexpectedly falls and instantly kills a climber, we are not fascinated, only touched by grief. There was no choice, no existential struggle, no opportunity for the human will to pull ancient power from the depths of its core and transform fear into focus.

This, the steadfast, implacable will to survive, is what Aron Ralston has. And what we all want.

ROW, ROW, ROW YOUR BOAT

The aching vastness of the ocean. A million mindless waves crawling up each other's backs like blue crabs. Through a monocular I glass the line where the paper-smooth blue of the sky attaches to the streaming blue of the sea.

She isn't even a speck out there. She's still beyond the curve of the earth, beyond imagination.

Farther down the beach a tall fishing vessel is dry-docked on blocks of wood. Up the rope ladder I go, onto the slanted roof of the forecabin, up the mast to the crow's nest.

There she is.

Still so far out to sea her absurdly small boat is almost unidentifiable. But she is undeniably extant, the palms of her oars flashing in the sunlight, like hands waving. She appears to be rowing strongly, steadily; landfall is still hours away. And yet what are mere hours after all this? She is rowing herself out from unspeakable desolation, like a figure walking out of a desert mirage.

Back at the pier in the Barbados resort of Port St. Charles, watercraft have been mustered for the mostly English press corps: the condescending BBC crew, stiff-necked British tabloid reporters, sunburned-but-sallow Fleet Street photographers, plus a few excitable Barbadian broadcasters. Our flotilla casts off and cruises out past the breakwater toward the tiny rowboat.

After 111 days at sea, ocean rower Debra Veal, twenty-six, should be scorched, stringy, blistered, trembling with exhaustion. Nothing could be further from the truth. An incredulous photographer shouts, "My God, Ms. Veal, you look as if you've just come off an ocean cruise!"

She smiles, teeth white as shells. "I have," she says.

Veal has her sun-blonde hair pulled back in a bouncy ponytail. She is exquisitely tanned (she often rowed naked), with the shapely, corded legs of an Olympic sprinter and the swooping curves of a Playmate. She's a Devonshire girl who's been an athlete all her life—tennis, kayaking, mountaineering. Veal is also a businesswoman who owns a London gallery called The Well-Hung Art Company.

A cheer rises from the crowd at the dock as she glides in. She raises an oar in the air and shakes it. Her husband, Andrew Veal, a tall, handsome gent, steps into the rowboat, giving her a kiss and a long hug. They'd set out together in the little vessel but, afflicted by a previously unknown phobia of the sea, he jumped ship after two weeks, and she'd carried on alone for ninety-seven days.

And now Debra Veal is the last-place finisher in what is indubitably the most grueling athletic event in the world: the quadrennial Atlantic Rowing Challenge, a 2,900-mile race across the sea from Spain's Canary Islands to Barbados in the southern Caribbean.

> DAY 15: At the launch Sir Chay Blyth addressed all the competitors. "As you are rowing across the Atlantic looking down at your little brown toes, ask yourself, 'Am I the happiest I could possibly be?'" Well, I've had a good look at my exceptionally brown toes and my answer at this point is a resounding yes.
> —from Debra Veal's e-mail diary

In 1896, two Norwegians, George Harboe and Gabriel Samuelson, rowed from Manhattan to Le Havre, France, in sixty days. Since humans had mastered the use of the sail several thousand years earlier, it is unclear how they came up with this throwback adventure—the first recorded crossing of an ocean by rowboat.

Seventy years later, in 1966, an Englishman and a Scot, John Ridgway and Chay Blyth, rowed an open twenty-foot dory from Cape Cod to Ireland's Aran Islands in ninety-one days. Like the Norwegians—indeed, like almost all sailors of the previous 500 years—Ridgway and Blyth carried all their own provisions and navigated by sextant.

In 1971, John Fairfax and Sylvia Cook of Great Britain rowed 8,041 miles across the Pacific Ocean from San Francisco to Australia in 361 days. That same year, Chay Blyth became the first person to sail singlehanded and nonstop around the world against prevailing winds and currents—a pitiless, 292-day voyage. Thereafter, taking on one challenge after another, he racked up victories in the toughest sailing races on the planet, including the Whitbread Round the World Yacht Race.

An intrepid sailor at sea, Blyth was and remains a bombastic self-promoter on land. In 1989, capitalizing on his fame, he created an event-marketing company called the Challenge Business. In 1992, Blyth's company put on the first against-prevailing-winds-and-currents-'round-the-world sailing race, the British Steel Challenge. In 1997, this impresario of endurance founded the Atlantic Rowing Challenge.

"When you talk about extreme sports, people come up with skate-boarding," says Sir Chay, who was knighted for his services to sailing. "Ha! Zooming up in the air and doing flips and flops. That's not an extreme sport. That's a technical sport."

We're poolside in Port St. Charles. Blyth flew to Barbados for Debra Veal's brilliantly hyped finish and is now redfaced and on his fifth rum punch.

"An extreme sport is one in which you put your life on the line," he continues. "If you survive, it was great sport. If you don't, then of course you made a mistake.

"The interesting thing about rowing the Atlantic is that people have only two opinions of it. Either they think it's fantastic and would love to do it, or they think it's bloody brainless and stupid and what's the point."

> DAY 24: It is horrible out here when you get this low and there is no one to pick you up and tell you it will be OK. You know you cannot afford to feel this sorry for yourself and that the highs outweigh the lows. But the lows cut deep and are difficult to bounce back from.
> —from Debra Veal's e-mail diary

In the inaugural Atlantic Rowing Challenge, thirty teams competed and twenty-four finished. The first-place team, New Zealanders Rob Hamill and Phil Stubbs, crossed the Atlantic in an unbelievably swift forty-one days, two hours, and fifty-five minutes. They traded two-hour rowing shifts twenty-four hours a day. The last to wallow in, after 101 days at sea, was an indomitable mother-and-son team from London; Jan

Meek was fifty-three at the time, and her son, Daniel Byles, twenty-three. Four years later, in the second Atlantic challenge race, thirty-six teams crossed the starting line on October 7, 2001, and thirty-three finished; a Kiwi team again took first.

The entry fee for the Atlantic Challenge is $19,500. The rules state that two people per boat must row nonstop from Los Gigantes Harbour on Tenerife, in Spain's Canary Islands, to Port St. Charles. (Debra Veal was technically disqualified the day her husband was plucked from their boat.) Two official safety yachts monitor the rowers. If you decide to pull the plug, you are rescued, and your boat, in proper Viking fashion, is burned at sea. Assistance of any kind results in disqualification.

Each team must use the same basic boat, purchased from the race organizers as a 500-piece, laser-cut plywood kit for $3,535. Assembled, the vessel measures twenty-three feet four inches, bow to stern, with a six-foot five-inch beam. It's an open rowboat with a miniature, coffinlike cabin in the stern.

"The so-called cabin is too low to sit up inside," says Tom Mailhot, forty-two, a thick-chested American rower who has come to Barbados to film Debra's arrival for a documentary he's making about the race. Mailhot and his partner, John Zeigler, finished the race in early December, in eleventh place. "Fifty-eight days, three hours, fifty-four minutes," Mailhot recites, smoothing out his blond pirate's mustache. "And that was the easy part."

Mailhot and Zeigler spent a year in man-hours and $35,000 in additional materials to put their boat together. Then they had to rig it: carbon-fiber oars, water-desalinating pump, solar panels to charge the batteries to run the satellite phone and the VHS radio and the stereo and the GPS. Sliding seats, steering system, sea anchor, oarlocks and outriggers, survival equipment, Emergency Position Indicating Radio Beacon, gas stove, food for many weeks.

"You need $150,000, minimum, just to get to the starting line," Mailhot says. "Then the fun begins."

All ocean rowers suffer. Asses and armpits chafed so raw they're bleeding, blistered palms, dehydration, seasickness, sleep deprivation, depression, mind-cracking boredom.

Would Mailhot do it again?

"Once across the Atlantic is enough."

DAY 26: It is unbelievably beautiful today. I am driving along a glassy surface that hardly has a ripple. Blue sky and white cotton wool clouds are reflected on the surface and everything is silent. I have never known peace and tranquility like it.
—from Debra Veal's e-mail diary

Tori Murden, thirty-nine, was the first woman to row solo and unsupported across the Atlantic. She did it in 1999. "When I began my quest, more people had walked on the moon than had rowed the Atlantic solo," she said when I called her at home in Louisville, Kentucky.

In 1989, Murden and partner Shirley Metz became the first women to ski to the geographic South Pole. Murden, who has a bachelor's degree from Smith College, a master's from Harvard Divinity School, and a law degree from the University of Louisville, had rowed in college and continued rowing afterward to stay in shape for mountaineering. She'd climbed all over the world by 1997, when she and Louise Graff became the only all-women team to enter the first Atlantic Rowing Challenge.

Food poisoning landed her in the Tenerife hospital for three days. After she and Graff once again pushed out into the Atlantic, they discovered that the electrical system for their water pump was shot. No water, no prayer. That ended her first attempt.

"I still wanted to finish what I'd started," Murden told me. "I wanted to extend the range of what we consider physically and mentally possible."

In June 1998, with an Italian watch company as a sponsor, Murden set out alone from Nags Head, North Carolina, to row to France. "I wouldn't have gone solo or unsupported if it weren't for the sponsor," she said. "Let's face it: If you can't afford to pay for the trip yourself, you need a sponsor, and a sponsor is only interested in something that's never been done."

On her eighth day at sea her boat capsized in a storm. Slammed onto the ceiling of her cabin, she recalled, "I was too busy pleading for my life to worry about the fact that my communications equipment was soaking in saltwater." The next morning, after the storm passed, Murden did not turn back. She would have no communication with the outside world for the next seventy-eight days.

"By early September," Murden continued, "I'd rowed more than 3,400 miles but covered fewer than 2,700. I was less than 1,000 miles from France when Hurricane Danielle swept across the North Atlantic."

With no radio, Murden had no idea what was coming. The sky blackened, then hell came. Her rowboat was tumbled end over end in seventyfoot waves: "Head over heels, heels over head. Wood, flesh, bone, it was all crashing." She stuck it out for four days before deciding she might not live through her ordeal. "I finally pushed the [emergency rescue beacon] button."

Murden, obsessively relentless, set out again a year later, once more solo and unsupported. She left Tenerife on September 13, 1999, and rowed into Port de Plaisance, Guadeloupe, eighty-one days later.

"The pivotal distinction between ocean rowing and mountaineering is the sameness of rowing," Murden said. "You wake up on the ocean and you can't tell where you are or where you've been. It's all the same. There is no way to gauge the passing of distance. You never get any perspective on your progress."

> DAY 65: The loneliness I have felt in the past ten days has been almost unbearable. Try as I might, I don't seem to be able to fill this empty hole which has developed within me. I haven't had any physical contact with another human being since Andrew left the boat. A number of people have asked what I would like for Christmas. A hug would certainly be high on the list.
> —from Debra Veal's e-mail diary

Rob Hamill, the cowinner of the 1997 Atlantic Rowing Challenge, wrote a book about the experience. It's called *The Naked Rower*, and there is no better explanation of the Sisyphean ordeal of ocean rowing, from the almost insurmountable task of raising sponsorship money to finding the right partner.

Hamill had rowed scull for New Zealand's Olympic team and recognized that the Atlantic race would require a "masochistic tolerance to pain." (This is the kind of thing rowers revel in.) Unlike many competitors who simply hoped to survive the crossing, Hamill entered the race to win.

"I wanted to test myself," Hamill, thirty-eight, told me from his home in New Zealand. "I had a vision that there would come a moment when I had to save my own life or save someone else's life. A shark attack or a boat capsizing. I wondered how I would cope in those circumstances. We all like to think that we'd react in the right way, but probably only five, maybe ten percent of us actually would."

Since the Blyth–Ridgway crossing in 1966, thirty-five years of high-tech innovation have transformed rowing the Atlantic from a life-or-death adventure into a relatively safe endeavor. And yet the ocean still kills. Although no one has died in the two challenge races, at least seven people have perished trying to row across the Atlantic. The most recent fatality was Nenad Belic, a sixty-two-year-old Chicago cardiologist who rowed out from Cape Cod in May 2001; 151 days later, in a storm 230 miles off the coast of Ireland, Belic's emergency beacon was activated. After a massive search by the English and Irish coast guards, Belic's beacon and boat were recovered, but his body was never found.

Hamill and Stubbs trained like rowers—that is, fanatically. They hired a shipwright to engineer their stock boat for maximum speed, and zealously trimmed each piece of gear and packed food down to the ounce. It paid off with the win and a world record that still stands.

Hamill returned in 2001 to defend his title but, in classic Kiwi style, managed to break a bone in his fist stopping a man who was beating a woman on a street in Los Gigantes. "He hit her with a Mike Tyson hook to the jaw," he said. "I did what any decent bloke would do."

Hamill was replaced by Matt Goodman, who with partner Steve Westlake missed setting a new record by only twenty-three hours and thirty-nine minutes. The pair again brought the title home to New Zealand.

> DAY 83: As I approach the three-month milestone I am recognizing that this journey is slowly wearing me down. Week after week of twelve hours a day of hard labour in solitary confinement is taking its toll. My body is screaming for some normality—a rest from rowing, a still bed, a toilet with a seat, regular showers and some fresh food.
> —from Debra Veal's e-mail diary

Debra Veal is relaxing beside the pool in Port St. Charles in a black one-piece swimsuit. The Fleet Street boys are drooling. It is only twenty-four hours since she came ashore in Barbados, and she has already finished her fifteenth photo shoot with the tabloids. Sir Chay has been boasting that her picture is on the front page of nearly every British newspaper. The press is fascinated and mystified by this petite woman who is both a gorgeous girl-next-door and a tenacious, courageous rower.

That night, Veal, her husband, and her friends and family manage to elude the reporters and sneak off to a Barbadian dance bar. After midnight, sweating from all the dancing, she pulls me aside.

We talk about her new celebrity—she welcomes it, but some of the attitudes behind the public fascination chafe. "Underneath, England is still stuck in a Victorian age where the wifey should be at home with her feet pressed against the sink," she whispers.

She tells me how proud she is of Andrew, her husband, for publically admitting his fear. About how she could never have finished the voyage without messages of support from Hayley, her twin sister. "Hayley saved my life over and over." About her secret cache of dreams she'd slip into to stave off the soul-crushing boredom. "One of my favorites? I'd think of all the extreme things I'd love to do."

In part because she didn't quit when her husband left her alone in the Atlantic, and certainly because she is beautiful and mediagenic, this young woman who came in dead last in the Atlantic Rowing Challenge is suddenly (briefly) more famous than the pioneers of the sport who came before her—extraordinary rowers, some of whom set world records. And yet, despite her glamour and bubbly nonchalance, Debra Veal belongs in that distinguished company. She belongs because her hands were crimped into claws for weeks; because she was bashed against the gunwale by a rogue wave, and was almost thrown from her boat—a virtual death sentence—when an errant oar nearly cracked the hull, and still she kept rowing.

She belongs because she fought the real struggle ocean rowers must face—the struggle in the mind. To be out in the unfathomably vast, borderless desert of the ocean, minute after minute, day after day, week after week, facing down the blue horizon vanishing in every direction, and the glancing visitations of insanity coming and going at the edge of your consciousness like a circling shark.

EL VEDAUWOO

"So this is the legend," Todd says with a grin. He sets another stick on our tiny campfire, slouches onto the tangle of climbing ropes, and begins rubbing the dried blood from his knuckles.

Back in the swirling dust devils of history, Fred Beckey, the über-dirtbag of climbers, lit out for Mexico. He dragged his partners from their beds and gunned across the moonlit desert in a low-slung station wagon. Beckey, an eat-from-the-can, skirt-chasing vagabond, had climbed more mountains than any man in America, and he was widening his search for *montañas*, or perhaps señoritas.

It is unclear how long Fred and his friends were down there, banging along mule-cart tracks between the cacti, living on tortillas and tequila, dancing with the dark-eyed, scarlet-dressed *mujeres*. Mexico is a labyrinthine dreamscape streaked with sunlight.

One day the gringos purportedly stumbled upon a gleaming mountain of white granite that rose up out of the burning desert. Beckey couldn't have been more dazzled if he'd found a forgotten bordello. According to legend, the stone was as clean and catholic as Yosemite, but with the rugosity of the rock at Joshua Tree. Beckey and his lump-fisted compadres are said to have climbed a chimney system on the southwest face before finding their way back across the border, elated, exhausted, and sworn to secrecy.

"The El Dorado of Mexican rock," I finally reply.

Todd and I are curled up close to the fire like two mangy dogs, utterly exhausted. Camped out on the summit of a rock tower in the mercurial *corazón* of Mexico, we have no sleeping bags, no water, no food. Our eyes are so bloodshot they've hemorrhaged.

"Already sounds apocryphal," rasps Todd.

• • •

I had tried hunting down the peripatetic Beckey, now in his late seventies but still living the road-tripping climbing bum's life. He supposedly lives in Seattle, but good luck finding him there. All I ever got was a letter from a friend of his named Lisa, who wrote to say she was leery of the legend: "I would say it was one of FB's stories. He takes great delight in starting rumors."

Then one morning my friend Todd Skinner phoned.

"Saddle up."

"Where we going?"

"Mexico."

He'd tracked down an ex-smoke jumper named Mark Motes, who claimed to have been on Beckey's fabled south-of-the-border sojourn in 1980.

"Motes says *el pico* is somewhere west of Durango near a pueblo called Peñon Blanco. It's all really vague. I'll bring the ropes and a rack."

"I'll get maps."

Like Beckey, Todd's life credo presupposes you can *vamos* at the drop of a sombrero—if not, what the hell kind of life do you have?

One week later we're switchbacking up into the Sierra Madre Occidental in a rented jeep. The road is called *El Espinazo del Diablo*—the Devil's Backbone—and it runs along an arête, with arid, incised canyons thousands of feet deep dropping off to either side. Ominously, all the rock is volcanic, most of it either rotten or overgrown with thornbushes.

For the entire day we have little idea where we are and no idea where we're going. Then, at twilight, we pass a startling sign that gives us our exact location: *TROPICO DE CANCER, LATITUD NORTE 23° 27', LONGITUD OESTE 105° 50'.*

Just after dark we grind down a twenty percent cobblestone grade into a village named Los Bancos.

Todd spots a roof with *Corona* painted in yellow. He hops out and is soon opening the wooden gate and hailing me in. I park, get out, and pass through a blanket into a kitchen. I shake hands with several leathery men and squat to shake hands with a half-dozen snot-nosed children. A thin woman carrying a child is setting out tamales on a blackened woodstove. A lightbulb hangs from a cord in the blue-stucco ceiling. Todd spreads the maps out on a table beside the stove and the men eagerly huddle over them, tracing their worn fingers along tracks and trails.

"*Donde esta el blanco peñon?*" Todd asks, forming a mountain with his hands.

"*Sí, sí,*" says the oldest man, placing a thick, yellowed thumbnail on a distinct spot: *Cerro el Peñon.* The closed contours clearly indicate a mountain. Near the peak is a village called Palo Blanco.

"Hah!" Todd is delighted. "I knew it! Maybe the village was called Palo Blanco and the peak itself Peñon."

But something doesn't fit. We have already passed this peak and surveyed its walls and all of them were unquestionably volcanic, not granite.

We discuss the many possibilities for these inconsistencies while the caballeros look on. Todd reluctantly points out that discrete, clear facts and amorphous old myths rarely jibe. Over time, small tales become tall tales. Words become fungible. *Blanco, palo, peñon.* Granitic, volcanic.

We go back to the maps. Our key words begin to leap out everywhere. *Los Blancos. Cerro Pelon. Cerro Blanco. Llano Blanco. Cerro el Pino.*

"Ever go snipe hunting, Todd?"

"*Peñon Blanco,*" Todd says again to the men, enunciating for all he's worth.

The old man pipes up. "*Peñon Blanco?* No, no, señor *escalador.* No, *ese no es el lugar.*" He begins scouring the maps, his dark, battered fingers moving from river to mesa to ridge crest.

"Ah, *aqui.*"

This time his cracked thumbnail has stopped in the far corner of a map we only brought by chance.

"That's over 150 miles in the opposite direction from the area we were told to search," Todd says incredulously.

"Exactly," I reply.

· · ·

We lie scrunched against the fading fire, staring up at silver bands of Mexican stars, too cold to sleep, too whipped to keep talking. It's past midnight. I hear Todd's breathing slow. I'm still awake, trying to puzzle him together.

Todd Skinner, forty-three, raised in Pinedale, Wyoming. Summited Gannett Peak, the highest in the state at 13,804 feet, when he was eleven. Elk hunting and horse packing guide for almost two decades, farrier when the horses needed shoeing. Connoisseur of antique saddles and renowned collector of vintage Old West guns. Directed and produced eight climbing films, Vietnam to Pakistan; husband of Amy; father of Hannah, three, and one-year-old twins, Jake and Sarah. Owner of Wild Iris, a Lander, Wyoming, outdoor shop.

And—oh, yeah—the most controversial rock climber in America.

Todd went to the University of Wyoming on an alpine-skiing scholarship in 1977 and left five years later with a degree in finance and a reputation as the most contentious climber since the late Warren Harding.

It all started at Vedauwoo, a granite outcrop near Laramie famous for its flesh-ripping off-width cracks, where both Todd and I apprenticed. Vedauwoo disciples like me adhered to a strict set of commandments passed down from the early days of mountaineering.

Never fall. If you do, lower off immediately; you shouldn't have been on the climb in the first place. Don't lead what you can't lead. All climbs are done ground up, no previewing. All bolts are put in on lead. Hanging on gear is a sin worse than coveting thy partner's girlfriend. All climbs must be done in stoic, heroic style—no hangs, no tension, whimpering of any kind is justification for paying out slack.

Then Todd Skinner showed up in the summer of '78. With heretical disregard for the old guard and the arrogant zeal of the apostate, he and partner Paul Piana began putting up routes so difficult it was impossible to do them without practicing. Bolts were placed on rappel and the climbs "worked" via "hangdogging." You fell all the time, relying on the bolts to catch you until you mastered the move. Attempting climbs that were over your head was the point.

As his reputation grew, Todd was excoriated, his ethics decried, his style lampooned. He was the bête noire for every mountaineering traditionalist from Boulder to Banff. And yet younger climbers were soon following Todd's lead, embracing hangdogging and safe, well-spaced bolts. Mortal boldness diminished, but ratings and skill levels leapt by two full grades. Rock gymnastics had come to stay.

Today, nearly twenty-five years later, many of Todd's early offenses are standard operating procedure in several climbing disciplines. All sport climbs are rap-bolted, to say nothing of the artificial world of gym climbing. World-class sport climbers may practice the same move, just like a gymnast or a figure skater, for years before perfecting it.

Todd Skinner was way ahead of his time.

• • •

The day before the climb:

I'm driving while Todd hangs out of the jeep, scanning the desert with binoculars.

"Well, I'll be gawddang!" he yells. "Pull over."

Off in the distance, poking miraculously above the red haze, is a white pyramid. We find a dirt road beelining for it and go.

An hour later we're scrutinizing the maps at a fork in the road when two vaqueros appear. They trail their cattle past us, stop, lean on their saddle horns, point when we ask a question, then ride off.

Passing through a one-street adobe village just before sunset, we are stymied by a wide arroyo. A villager strolls up to our jeep. We point to our glowing peak, pink in the evening light.

"*Ese es bonito Cerro Blanco*," he says regally. He tells us a better place to cross the arroyo, then passes a clear Pepsi bottle into the cab. We each take a swig. It is smooth, smoky, homemade tequila. The man winks and takes a slug himself.

"*Buena suerte*, amigos."

"That's as close as you can come to communion," Todd says.

By noon the next day we're there. We've forded half a dozen bone-dry streambeds and three streams, passed through numerous barbed-wire gates, parked in a cottonwood ravine, hiked for an hour up through a rock-walled col hirsute with giant yuccas, and now stand at the base, ogling Beckey's chimerical white mountain.

Most myths are best enjoyed around a campfire and not actually pursued. But some people can't help themselves. Todd has spent half his life being a myth destroyer—and, consequently, the other half being a mythmaker.

I examine the cone of white granite through binoculars, gradually moving up the south face. It is perhaps 1,000 feet high. Although there are several fissures—I can identify the Beckey chimney—only one crack cleaves the face bottom to top.

"Todd," I say fervidly, "the central line will go."

We have been traveling together for days, searching, and have not had one conversation about technical climbing. We've talked about Tom Daschle, Trent Lott, monks, artists, CEOs, small planes, kids, leadership, generals, solar energy, Stegner, Nietsche, tax law, the Arctic National Wildlife Refuge, saddles, and rifles.

"Good," says Todd. "I'm going to check out that boulder."

He is an incorrigible boulderer, so I assume he's off to test the rock. But when he returns, in his hand is a pottery shard, a broken spearhead, and a stone scraper.

"You know, Mark," Todd says, "It's the search itself I love, not what I'm searching for."

We spend the rest of the afternoon reconning the area and Todd discovers cave paintings underneath three different boulders.

Back in the jeep at dark, we creep down into the nearest village in search of water, food, and maybe even a bed. The one dusty street is deserted except for one man. He is sitting in a pickup with the door open listening to a Marty Robbins tape. We stop and try to explain in our useless Spanish what we are doing here and what we are looking for. The man wears glasses, has an open, smooth face, and listens intently.

"Would you like to spend the night in our church?" he responds in perfect English.

His name is Gabino Rico. He is the village preacher. He went to Pepperdine University. Four of his eight children live in the United States.

He shows us into a bedroom at the back of the mud-brick and concrete church. There is a bunk bed and clean blankets. He brings us a bucket of hot water and a bar of soap.

"After you have cleaned up, please come have dinner with us."

The sanctuary of the small church is also the meeting room and refectory. Two couples, part of the congregation, have prepared a meal. Fresh hot, homemade corn tortillas, frijoles, rice, salsa cilantro, meat stew, bananas, Nescafe.

Gabino, his congregation, and his village will take care of us—feed us, house us, educate us—for the rest of our stay in Mexico.

• • •

We've used up all our wood, and the fire is dying out. We're both awake now, talking in the darkness.

Todd spent eighteen winters in Hueco Tanks, Texas, training. Three summers in a tepee beside Devils Tower putting up outrageous routes, two more in a tepee at Mount Rushmore.

"I realized that you had to live with the rock," Todd says. "That was the only way to fully comprehend and then test the boundaries. After a while I began to see the limits of possibility in different places and started searching. I didn't have an apartment for seven years. I was looking for rock with a future."

Todd traveled to France, Switzerland, Spain, Egypt, the Soviet Union, Poland, Czechoslovakia, Thailand, Brazil, Vietnam, South Africa.

"I've searched the world over, and still come back to Wyoming," continues Todd. "History means jack. The places with the most history have the least future. Most rock-climbing areas are dead ends, due to the nature of the rock. Places to visit, but not places where you can live with the rock. To do that, the quantity and the quality of the rock must combine to allow limitless improvements in difficulty."

Todd and his partners have put up first ascents, none rated less than 5.12+, on the hardest continuous rock climbs ever attempted. He spent sixty nights on the east face of Trango Tower in Pakistan in 1995, completed a fourteen-pitch masterpiece up the strongest line on the Hand of Fatima in Mali in 1998, free-climbed the Geneva Dihedral on Ulamertorsuaq in Greenland in 1999, and made it up the east face of Poi in the Ndoto Mountains of northern Kenya in 2000. But they are not alpine climbs. They are well protected. You are not going to die. Todd believes in safety and, unlike almost all mountaineers the world over, does not equate adventure with risk.

"Adventure is pushing yourself into unknown realms," Todd says, "not dying just because the protection sucked."

•   •   •

Twenty-four hours earlier:

We are up at four. By daybreak we've battled 500 vertical feet of thornbushes to gain the base of the wall. I get the first lead. Classic 5.9 toe-heel off-width crack, eight inches wide—too big for my hands, too small for my body—with the occasional yucca to climb through to keep things interesting. On the next pitch, Todd leads up through 5.10, legs straddled and stemming, with no gear—hand jams, a fingertip lieback, then a dirt overhang that requires an ungainly belly flop onto an ill-placed cactus.

Pitch three starts in a chimney and shoots out to a giant roof hung with clumps of green moss the size of pineapples. I stem in full splits, tearing away the moss.

"Is there pro?" Todd yells anxiously.

"The rock is rotten!" I hear the fear and weakness in my voice.

Digging desperately with my fingers, I manage to hollow out a space for a camming unit in the wretched rock. There's an absurdly flaring crack that goes out the left-hand side of the roof. In a full-body stem, both feet on one wall, both hands on the other, I attempt to calmly assess the feasibility of the crack. But soon I start shaking so badly that at the last possible moment I cram a fist jam deep into an exfoliating hole—and fall.

To my surprise, the fist jam holds. Dangling by one arm, I slam in another cam and then promptly fall on it. Unbelievably, the piece holds, although only two of its four lobes have wedged in the deteriorating rock. It could pop at any second. I'm swinging in space.

I'm too scared to lower off this horrifying piece, so I climb. It is the ugliest off-width in Mexico. I use flared fist jams, chicken wings, arm bars, a shoulder wedge, stacked fists, a head jam, every single crack-climbing trick I ever learned in Vedauwoo. There is nothing for my feet. The upper half of my body is plugged up in a hole, and my legs merely flail in midair. I manage to insert one side of my body in the crack. But there's no protection. None! I'm so far past the point of no return I could vomit. I talk to myself. Calm myself. Consciously stop my legs from shaking. Inch upward.

For the next hundred feet of climbing I stab the dirt in the back of the crack and the wind blows it back into my eyes and mouth. Crazed with terror, I somehow wiggle in just two small, bad, no-hope-at-all-of-holding-a-fall pieces before hitting the end of the 175-foot rope.

The crack is too wide to protect. There is no belay, only clods of dirt. I have no choice: I futilely tie into them with a sling. My eyes are so packed with dirt I can no longer keep them open. I scream instructions for Todd, and he screams back at me, but neither of us can make out what the other is saying. I yell myself hoarse trying to make sure he knows he can't fall, no matter what. The dirt-clod belay would not hold us.

We are trapped midway up our mythical wall. The sun is falling from the sky, the wind screeching. We can't communicate. We have no alternative but to go on instinct and experience.

With my eyes crusted shut, I feel the rope. At the slightest change in tension, I delicately pull up. Time is of no importance. As long as Todd doesn't fall and drag us both to our deaths, I could belay for hours, days. I go into a half-conscious state, concentrating on sending good vibes through my fingers down the rope to Todd.

The next time I open my eyes, Todd has climbed through the roof and heaves into view on the face below me. He motions for me to yard up the haul line, which I do. To my everlasting relief, knotted to the end is a cam that Todd removed from the crack below. I jam it deep into the crack where it's solid enough to anchor a fall. Suddenly I have a real belay.

When Todd climbs up to me he's as shaken as I am.

"Holy Christ, hombre! That's harder than any 5.12 I've ever done! I would never have led it."

"You did, Todd. We both did."

There are two more difficult pitches to the top. It's dark when we pull over the lip. In a summit cave we gather wood and make a fire and settle in for a long, garrulous bivouac.

• • •

The ashes are cold and we're stiff as wood when the sun finally rises. It will take us half a day to find our way off the mountain. For the first time, we're actually talking about climbing, the pretext for our adventure in Mexico.

We agree that the middle pitch was absurdly dangerous, deserving of an X, or death fall, rating. We thus dub it the *Dos Equis* pitch.

And a name for the climb itself? El Vedauwoo.

• • •

Postscript: Todd died from a fall climbing in Yosemite on October 23, 2006.

NO EXIT

The search plane drops sickeningly, banks hard, tilting the fuselage windows downward, and sweeps across the south face of Mount Foraker. Denali National Park and Preserve rangers Joe Reichert and Tucker Chenoweth peer through the Plexiglas, searching for any sign of life. Somewhere down there, climbers Sue Nott and Karen McNeill are missing, lost in a vertical maze of ice and snow and rock.

At 17,400 feet, Foraker is the second-highest peak in the Alaska Range. The highest, 20,320-foot Mount McKinley, lies twelve miles to the northeast. Foraker's south face is fearsome—shattered stone walls, avalanche chutes, crevasses everywhere. Bisecting the south face is a severe arête called the Infinite Spur, a 9,000-foot line that extends from the glacier straight up to the summit. It is one of the hardest mountaineering routes in North America, having seen only seven ascents in almost thirty years, all by world-class two-man teams. Until now, no women have ever attempted the Infinite Spur.

Nott, thirty-six, and McNeill, thirty-seven, are two of North America's most accomplished mountaineers. They started the Infinite Spur on May 14, with approximately twelve days' worth of food and fuel. Today is June 8—they have been on the mountain for twenty-six days. Even rationing themselves, they'd have now been without food and fuel for more than a week.

They're also missing gear. Six days ago, on June 2, Nott's backpack was found atop old avalanche debris near the base of the route. Her foam pad was still tied to the pack. A two-way radio—considered standard safety equipment on Foraker—was inside. Nott's sleeping bag, a stuff sack, a glove, and a fleece jacket were discovered nearby, but there was no sign of the women.

Staring at the south face from the search plane, I'm struck by the topographic treachery of the Infinite Spur. A series of menacing hanging glaciers—death zones on any peak—press in on both sides of the arête. In the event of an accident, heavy snow, or Arctic wind, there are only two ways off the spur: Retreat directly back down the precipitous ridge or go up and over the summit and down one of Foraker's less technical routes.

The Navajo twin-engine circles tightly and we make another pass at 16,500 feet. We're looking for anything remotely human: a rope frozen to the ice, a half-buried tent, an ice axe, a hand waving from a snow cave.

Nothing. We make another pass and then another and another.

Speaking through his headset, Reichert asks the pilot, Ed Dearwent, to take the plane as high as he can in the hope of getting a clear view of the summit. But there's nothing to see. Less than an hour ago, rangers at 14,200 feet on McKinley radioed in to the search-and-rescue headquarters in Talkeetna, about fifty miles to the south, that Foraker was clear. We jumped into the plane and flew straight to the mountain, but by the time we arrived, smooth, lens-shaped lenticular clouds obscured the summit.

Dearwent begins to circle Foraker in hopes of getting a better perspective of the summit, but the weather is already so bad on the north side of the mountain that we're forced to turn around.

One more pass by the Infinite Spur. One more desperate look. One more chance for everything to miraculously work out. We see nothing. Another storm is devouring Foraker. We arc south, back to Talkeetna.

• • •

Nott and McNeill spent the past fifteen years working through a rigorous mountaineering apprenticeship. Sponsored by gear maker Mountain Hardwear, they climbed extraordinarily tough, technical routes that only other alpinists would know. McNeill, a Kiwi who'd relocated to Canmore, Alberta, made the first ascent of Dos Cuernos, on the Patagonian Ice Cap, in 2004, put up three new hard lines in Greenland, and climbed extensively in Canada and Alaska. She chose to do most of her expeditions with other women. Nott grew up in Vail, Colorado, and was a serious backcountry skier before a friend introduced her to ice climbing in 1990. She completed the first ascent of Glass Onion, a difficult ice-and-rock route in southeast Alaska, made four attempts on Patagonia's Fitz Roy, and climbed extensively in the French Alps.

"Climbing gives me so much joy, so much happiness," Nott told me when I interviewed her in the fall of 2003; she had been selected by *Outside* magazine as one of the top female athletes in the world. At the time, she was living in Chamonix, France. That year, climbing with her boy-friend, John Varco, Nott had become the first American woman to complete a winter ascent of the north face of the Eiger. "The climb was great," she told me enthusiastically. "It was cold and classic and everything you could possibly hope for."

When I spoke with Varco that fall, he gave her the ultimate alpinist's accolade: "Sue's motivation never wavers. She wants to get to the top. When it gets grim, there are a thousand reasons to go down, and it's hard to find just one reason to go up. Sue always finds that one."

McNeill was equally committed to the climbing life. After moving to North America in 1994, she spent four years as an instructor at Chicks with Picks, an all-women ice-climbing school in Ridgway, Colorado. According to cofounder Kim Reynolds, a close friend of both women, McNeill had three rules: "First, you could never say you're sorry while climbing," recalls Reynolds. "Second, as Karen lowered you off a climb, she would stop and hold you one foot off the ground until you said, 'I am a goddess.' Third, after you got off the climb, you always had to state one thing you did well."

For the past three years, McNeill worked as a teacher at the Morley Indian Reserve, near Canmore. "She encouraged the kids to get rid of the clutter and pressure of society, tune in to themselves, and pursue their own dreams," says Margo Talbot, forty-two, a Vancouver-based guide for Antarctic Logistics and Expeditions and a good friend. "She didn't have many female role models, so she lived her own dreams and grew into the role model she wished she'd had."

In 1999, Nott and McNeill teamed up for the first time, climbing in Peru. It was a natural fit: two women who were instinctively drawn to the mountains and found through climbing the confidence and courage to break out of hackneyed female stereotypes. In 2000, they climbed the west ridge of 21,466-foot Shivling, in India's Garhwal Himalayas, in a grueling five-day push. In 2004, they paired up to climb McKinley's highly coveted Cassin Ridge. They set out with five days of food and seven days of fuel. On the tenth day, when they didn't show up at camp at 14,200 feet on the West Buttress, the standard descent route, the Park Service launched a search-and-rescue mission. A high-altitude Lama helicopter found them snug, if hungry, in their tent on the summit, having become the first female team to complete the route.

Mount Foraker was their most ambitious climb to date. One of the most difficult and dangerous mountains in the Alaska Range, Foraker is described in one guidebook as the "ultimate test-piece and one of the world's finest alpine challenges." Since 1979, only twenty-four percent of climbers who've attempted Foraker have summited, and nineteen have died. Of the twenty-six climbers on the peak this spring before McNeill and Nott began the Infinite Spur, not a single one summited.

The Infinite Spur has been even more unforgiving. When renowned mountaineers Michael Kennedy and George Lowe put up the first ascent of the route, in 1977, it took them eight days and more than eighty pitches of roped climbing. Both men survived bad falls. The route was not repeated until 1989, then not again until 2000. The average time for teams climbing the route was five to eight days until 2001, when super-alpinists Steve House and Rolando Garibotti did a forty-five-hour speed ascent. All attempts on the Infinite Spur between 2002 and 2005 failed.

No one I spoke with described the two women as reckless or fearless or puffed up with their own egos. They were driven and competitive but realistic. They went into a climb with a plan and knew when to call it off. They'd turned around on 19,127-foot Taulliraju in Peru because they were dehydrated. High winds, deep snow, and ice-plastered rocks had forced them to abort their attempt on Shivling's east ridge; they retreated and, a week later, summited via the west ridge.

Both of them understood that for alpinists, death is just a mistake away. "Mountains make me dig deep, pull into myself, and overcome," Nott told me in 2003. "Alpine climbing is extremely hard mentally. You can't have meltdowns, because you can't, to survive. You get used to being careful and making deals with the devil: Just get me past this serac, just get me through this bergschrund, just get me through this storm . . ."

•   •   •

On May 14, two climbers, Will Mayo and Max Turgeon, retreating from a new line to the right of the Infinite Spur, met up with Nott and McNeill at the start of the route. The women were carrying huge packs and told Mayo and Turgeon that they hoped to be back at basecamp in ten days.

A week later, on May 21, Mark Westman—a member of the last team to summit the Infinite Spur, in 2001—flew over the south face on a routine flight back to Talkeetna and spotted tracks at the base of the arête. He saw no one on the route, but there was little cause for concern. The pair had planned to move slowly and steadily, and by their own most optimistic estimates they would have had several more days of climbing before they finished the route.

Later that same day, an Arctic cold front from the northwest collided with a high-pressure system in the Bering Sea, producing eight days of unimaginably high winds. From May 25 to 28, winds at the 14,200-foot camp on McKinley were clocked at fifty to seventy miles per hour, with gusts as high as one hundred miles per hour reported at higher elevations. During this tempest, Foraker and McKinley were lost inside lenticulars.

Winds dropped enough on the twenty-ninth for Will Mayo to get a "pretty good look" at the upper half of the Infinite Spur from the window of a bush plane. He saw no tracks and no humans. Alarmed, Paul Roderick, owner of Talkeetna Air Taxi and the bush pilot who had taken Nott and McNeill into basecamp, flew over the route the next day. He found no trace of the two women.

"I was worried," Roderick told me a week later from his hangar. "That windstorm was unbelievable. Just brutal. It was the first time weather had actually grounded me in years. I couldn't imagine what it must have been like high up on Foraker."

In Talkeetna, he called Daryl Miller, Denali's South District Ranger. A Vietnam vet who did two tours of duty as a combat marine, Miller, sixty-two, joined Denali's search-and-rescue squad in 1991 and has since participated in hundreds of rescues and dozens of recoveries. In 1996 he was presented with the International Alpine Solidarity Award for saving so many lives.

"I spent the thirty-first evaluating the information we had," Miller told me solemnly when we met in his Talkeetna office on June 6. "The weather events, the ability and personality of Sue and Karen, the route. And the next day we launched the search and rescue."

It was deemed too dangerous to search the Infinite Spur on foot, so Miller dispatched a Lama helicopter to fly a reconnaissance mission. The pilot spotted tracks at around 14,000 feet, but no other sign of the climbers. The next day, Lama pilot Jim Hood, along with climber Mark Westman and ranger Meg Perdue, flew multiple sorties over the route and discovered Nott's pack, pad, and sleeping bag. Due to the risk of avalanche, they used a hydraulic "grabber" suspended below the Lama to retrieve the gear.

Lashed to the outside of the battered pack was the sleeping pad; it was sun-faded, indicating that it had been in that position for a number of days. The radio inside still worked but had not been used. Judging by the position of the pack's shoulder straps and hipbelt, Miller ruled out the possibility that Nott had been wearing the pack when it was lost. A more likely scenario, he hypothesized at the morning briefing on June 3, was that it had been accidentally dropped or blown off from somewhere above 11,000 feet—and that Nott and McNeill had continued climbing without it.

That day, the Lama flew the lower sections of the route. A fixed-wing aircraft scoured the Sultana and Southeast ridges, the standard descent routes off Foraker's summit, but saw no tracks. Two searchers were stationed with a spotting scope at an 8,000-foot camp a mile east of the Infinite Spur. Nothing.

• • •

Back at the Talkeetna ranger station, the atmosphere was strained. As search efforts continued, there was a palpable but unspoken sense of doom. John Varco, along with a dozen of Nott's closest friends, had arrived in Talkeetna a week earlier to help with the rescue effort. Sue's mother, Eve, and her two sisters, Karen and Sarah, had flown in as well. Karen's mother and father, Elaine and Neil, and her sister Wendy were en route to Alaska from New Zealand.

From the start of the operation, Daryl Miller had been in daily contact—either in person or by phone—with the families and close friends of Nott and McNeill. He kept them apprised of every flight, every new discovery, every evolution in the thinking and execution of the operation—often speaking with the parents two or three times a day.

"Constant communication is imperative," Miller told me. "They need to know exactly what's happening. My mission was to keep all those who loved these two women in the loop at all times." Which meant that as each day passed and Nott and McNeill didn't turn up, everyone was coming closer to accepting the heartbreaking reality.

On June 4, the Lama flew four separate sorties up and down the route. Pilot Jim Hood spotted tracks at 15,600 and 15,800 feet. Flyovers on day five revealed tracks at 16,400 and 16,600, and the focus of the search shifted to the summit.

Our flight on June 8 with Reichert and Chenoweth yielded no further clues—and then another storm moved in, blasting Foraker for five consecutive days and grounding all aerial search efforts.

Three days later, in consultation with the search-and-rescue team, Miller conducted a survivability analysis—a detailed investigation into the likelihood of the two women still being alive. They began with the essential facts: Nott and McNeill started the route on May 14 with almost two weeks' worth of food and fuel. They'd have now been without food and water (you need fuel to melt snow for water) for two weeks. There had been a solid week of mortally high winds. Their route had been aerially scoured—more than twenty-seven hours of flying—with no luck.

That evening, after informing the families of the decision, Denali National Park and Preserve officially announced that the search-and-rescue operation for Sue Nott and Karen McNeill was transitioning into a "limited search"—a body-recovery effort, not a live rescue.

It was over.

• • •

So what happened? How could two extremely experienced alpinists vanish on Mount Foraker?

Reconstructing a mountaineering accident is much like reexamining the evidence in a criminal investigation: You try to piece together all the clues to create potential scenarios.

"Three things are certain," says Miller. "Sue and Karen started the route on the fourteenth of May, lost the pack several days later, and continued climbing, reaching at least 16,600 feet."

Was it a mistake to keep climbing without the radio (their best shot at summoning help should they need it), sleeping bag, and pad? Probably not. According to Miller, McNeill and Nott had initially considered attempting Foraker with just one sleeping bag, to save weight, a common practice among serious alpinists. Depending on where the pack was actually blown off, it might well have been safer and easier to finish the route, rather than retreat and rappel down dozens of pitches. At that stage, somewhere between May 15 and 20, the weather was still good and the two women were climbing in the sun and on pace.

Studying photographs of the tracks above 15,000 feet, it's clear they climbed this section of the route before the windstorm—the footprints are raised pedestals of compacted snow, indicating that they were made when the snow was still deep, before it was blown off the ridge. Which means that despite the loss of a pack, pad, and sleeping bag, McNeill and Nott probably finished the Infinite Spur on schedule in eight to ten days and were on their way up the lower-angle, mile-long snow slope to the summit when the wind started to maul Mount Foraker.

What happened then is pure speculation, but there are only two realistic scenarios: They were blown off or they tried to burrow into the snow and froze to death in −50°F windchill.

"When you're that high on a difficult and committing line like the Infinite Spur," concludes Miller, "you cannot descend back down the route you just completed. Your only escape is up, and you just hope that when you reach the top to exit, the weather window will allow you safe passage. Sue and Karen were hit by winds so strong it would have been impossible to go up. They had no exit."

On June 18, a thousand people—climbers, friends, family—packed Vail's Ford Amphitheater for a service celebrating the life of Sue Nott; two days later a memorial was held in Canmore for Karen McNeill.

"Sue and Karen were in the right place at the wrong time," John Varco told me afterwards, in a voice barely more than a whisper. "There was nothing they could do about it. It would have been like trying to climb in a tornado. Anyone up there—you, me, the best alpinist in the world—would have met the same fate.

"But don't call it a tragedy. Yes, it's tragic for those of us left behind, but Sue and Karen were living big. Huge! They were celebrating life. We should do the same."

TIME TRAVELER

An icy wave crashes down into the open boat. The four cramped, wool-clad seamen are bailing desperately, yet faithfully as monks. Trapped in a gale, sailing west between Iceland and Greenland, they have not slept in thirty-six hours. Stunned by prolonged hypothermia and weak with exhaustion, spirit alone is keeping them alive. That and the unlikely hardiness of their craft, the thirty-six-foot *Brendan*, a twin-masted Irish curragh featuring the latest sixth-century design and materials. Built to flex like a sea serpent, the hull was hand-stitched from forty-nine ox hides, each a quarter-inch thick, waterproofed with wool grease, and stretched over a rib cage of Irish white ash. Two miles of leather thongs bind the frame together.

Another wave curls high over the leather boat and explodes down upon the heavily-bearded sailors, knocking them off their feet. They are knee-deep in gelid water, food and clothing, skinned seagulls and whale blubber, sheepskins and oilskins—the ancient flotsam of death at sea—sloshing about them. Thick tarps, stretched gunwale to gunwale, deck three-quarters of the *Brendan*, but where the helmsman must stand there is a gaping hole. If it is not covered, the boat will founder, and the ocean will summarily swallow the sailors and their dream.

The captain suddenly remembers the spare ox hides stowed aboard to patch a potential tear from icebergs. In the midst of the gale, the hides—stiff as war shields—are dragged out, perforated with a knife, and lashed together. The makeshift shell is mounted over the gap. The helmsman must now stand in a small porthole, ribs brutalized by the edges of the leather shell, fingers frozen as wood, but: the boat stops sinking. The helmsman can only bear the intense cold for fifteen minutes, then he is replaced by a crewmate. The bailing and rotation continue sleeplessly for another twenty-four hours.

In time, the tempest, unsuccessful at killing the sailors, thunders away, and fog settles upon the cold sea. Like a ghost ship, the curragh floats onward, into the maze of icebergs off the east coast of Greenland.

• • •

According to legend, Saint Brendan sailed from Ireland to Newfound-land 1,400 years ago, but the expedition described above took place in the late twentieth century, led by a heretical explorer named Tim Severin.

"There's no question that the Brendan voyage was my most danger-ous journey," says Severin, speaking so softly my tape recorder barely picks up his voice. "The margins were very slim. It set the threshold for fear. Once you've been really, really scared and then you come through and everything's fine at the end, it's very difficult to get as frightened again."

Severin and I are having lunch at the Casino House, in the quiet hills of County Cork, Ireland, Severin's home for more than thirty years. A slight, sixty-three-year-old man with liquidy blue-green eyes, a lean, handsome face, and a thin neck wrapped in a paisley cravat, Severin looks more like a distinguished British intellectual than one of the finest mod-ern adventurers. In truth, he is both: recipient of the prestigious Found-er's Medal of the Royal Geographical Society as well as the Livingstone Medal of the Royal Scottish Geographical Society, author of fifteen books, and winner of the Thomas Cook Travel Book Award, the Book of the Sea Award, and the literary medal of the Académie de Marine, Severin is the only man to have built and sailed five different seagoing vessels of ancient design.

In an age when stunts of extraordinary physical skill are regularly performed with little apparent purpose beyond fifteen minutes of fame—kayaking one-hundred-foot waterfalls, snowboarding Everest—and the risks transparently outweigh lasting value, Tim Severin is an adventurer cut from a different cloth.

"No one's tried another Brendan voyage, and my advice is, don't," Severin says, laughing. "It's like a doctor who injects himself with some sort of unknown drug. The hypothesis has been tested. Further risk is unwarranted."

Severin's 1976–77 Brendan expedition became his benchmark for exhaustive research and methodical preparation. Studying the eighth-century Latin text *Navigatio Sancti Brendani Abbatis*, which describes a precise if phantasmagoric voyage to the New World by Saint Brendan, an Irish monk and missionary, Severin began to believe that such a journey may have actually taken place.

But the only way to prove it was to do it, so he did. He spent two years building a replica of the early Irish skin boat, then, using the *Navigatio* as a travel guide, sailed the craft 4,500 miles from Ireland to Newfoundland via the Hebrides, the Faroe Islands, and Iceland. Though he nearly died trying, Severin proved that seafaring Irish monks could have discovered North America in the sixth century, well ahead of the Vikings and almost a millennium before Columbus.

In 1978, Severin's account of the journey, *The Brendan Voyage*, became a global bestseller, was translated into twenty-seven languages, and established Severin as Thor Heyerdahl's rightful successor.

• • •

Even before touching land in the *Brendan*, Severin was dreaming of his next project: retracing the route of perhaps the greatest literary seafarer of all time, Sinbad the Sailor. In 1980–81, Severin built a medieval ship and sailed the 6,000-mile trade route described in *The Arabian Nights*, from Oman, on the Arabian Peninsula, to Canton, China.

In 1984, he designed a twenty-oar galley to exact Bronze Age specifications and, with a seventeen-person crew of neo-Argonauts, rowed it from Greece to the Soviet republic of Georgia, proving that the Greek myth of Jason and his quest for the Golden Fleece was based on geographical fact. The next year, Severin used the same boat to tackle the über-myth of Western literature, retracing Ulysses' odyssey from Troy to Ithaca. Following that, he completed two overland expeditions by horse, one tracking the 2,500-mile route of the First Crusade across Europe, the other exploring the Mongolia of Genghis Khan; two more sea passages, the China Voyage and the Spice Islands Voyage; followed by two expeditions searching for the historical roots of *Moby-Dick* and *Robinson Crusoe*.

Severin wrote a book about every expedition he completed. All told, he devoted two to four years to each project, using the book contracts to fund his unorthodox life of adventure and creating a bankable franchise of historic reenactment. To connoisseurs of British sailing literature, Severin the author is legendary. However, unlike much contemporary travel writing, his work is free of emotional outpourings. He is eloquent at description, fastidious about mythic details, but maddeningly reticent about his inner feelings. (He was married for ten years, then divorced, and has a grown daughter named Ida—but you won't find any of this in his books.) Much like the nineteenth-century English explorers, Severin keeps his own counsel and sticks to facts. No confessional effusion, no dark psychological secrets, no wanking.

Reading his work, you realize that Severin is an anachronism: Rigorously disciplined, he is willing to go back in history and re-create the conditions and crafts of ancient travelers, and then physically experience their difficult journeys himself, risking his life to better understand the complex intertwining of history, myth, and geography.

Severin, in short, is a time traveler.

• • •

Born in Assam, India, in 1940, Severin credits his upbringing for igniting his exploratory instincts. His father was an English tea planter born in South Africa; his mother, half British, half Danish, was born in India. At the age of six, Severin was shipped off, like so many children of expats, to boarding school in England.

"Look, this was ordinary," says Severin. "It made us extremely independent and self-sufficient at a very early age. We could cope perfectly well, thank you very much. No need to be led by the hand.

"I took my holidays in England with my grandmother, who had spent her entire life in India. Everything in the household, all the photographs on the walls, all the reference books, all the literature, came from India. I grew up with this whole mythology around me."

Severin was educated at Oxford, where he received a graduate degree in medieval Asian exploration. In researching his thesis, he and two companions retraced the route of Marco Polo, from Venice to Afghanistan, by motorcycle, a journey that resulted in his first book, *Tracking Marco Polo* (1964). It also foreshadowed his lifelong obsession with epic voyages, and the lengths to which he would go to achieve historical accuracy.

Of all his journeys, the Sinbad Voyage may be the most astounding. Building Sinbad's ship, a ninety-foot motorless vessel with 2,900 square feet of sail, required 140 tons of hardwood Severin hand-selected in the forests of India, 50,000 coconut husks that were spun into 400 miles of coconut rope to bind the hull planks and ribs together, and twenty Laccadive shipwrights working nonstop for 165 days. Impressed by Severin's commitment to the seafaring heritage of Arabs, the project was ultimately financed by Qaboos bin Said, the sultan of Oman.

In November 1980, Severin launched the *Sohar*—named after the ancient Arabian port and purported home of Sinbad—sailing from Muscat, Oman, bound for China. During the seven-and-a-half-month voyage, Severin and his sailors endured many of the struggles early Arab seamen—the prototypes for Sinbad's character—must have faced. They shared quarters with all kinds of creatures: fruit flies that burrowed into their nostrils, a plague of cockroaches that skittered over their faces, mice in the food lockers, rats in the bilge.

Then there were the mind-warping doldrums. On the 900-mile crossing of the Indian Ocean, from Sri Lanka to Sumatra, the ship began sailing backward in a headwind. Soon the *Sohar* was stranded at sea.

"We were facing the long, slow, gnawing doubts of boredom, frustration, and the ultimate possibility of thirst," wrote Severin in *The Sindbad Voyage.* "We had truly moved back into the days of sail on ocean passages. Our time scale was longer, slower, and ultimately dependent on nature."

For the next thirty-five days, the *Sohar* zigzagged aimlessly in the middle of the sea. As food and water began to dwindle, the twenty-seven-man crew became resourceful. They fished constantly, but instead of eating their catch, they used it as bait to hook sharks for food. Once they managed to bring in seventeen sharks in just ten minutes. During storms, they rigged canvas tarps under the mainsail, funneled the rainwater into buckets, and refilled the ship's cistern.

"Patience is very easy to display," Severin explains when I ask him about his cool stoicism, a rare quality in this age of instant gratification. "If you believe what you're doing is something truly worthwhile, you stay with it. Frustration arises when you think what you're doing is empty and useless. If the project is worth doing in the first place, it's worth being patient about."

And what makes a project worthy? For Severin there are two inflexible criteria:

"First, it must be original—something that no one has ever done before. Second, it must stand a reasonable chance of advancing knowledge."

Just days after escaping the doldrums, an abrupt, violent shift in wind slammed the mainsail against the mast and broke the foot-thick, eighty-one-foot main spar in two. "*Sohar* had been crippled as effectively as a butcher snapping the leg bone of a chicken by twisting it against the socket," Severin wrote. They were 450 miles from Sumatra. Improvisation in times of calamity is one of the defining characteristics of great adventurers, and Severin immediately put a plan into action. Within seven hours, the crew had salvaged the long section of the broken main spar, smoothed off the fractured end, rigged it with a spare mizzen sail, and *Sohar* was once again "moving briskly through the water."

Intriguingly, although Severin has managed to display equanimity in the face of countless dangers over four decades of exploration, none of his books address the issue of courage.

"I don't see my journeys as tests of courage," he explains, "but more as tests of knowledge. When I select a project, I examine the evidence. I search for the kernel of truth within the legend. Could a ship of that kind have made such a journey? I gather information, do my homework, dig. If, after a year of research, the project still seems worthy, I build a boat as true to the original craft as possible, then we go out and do it. You get into heavy weather and there are some fraught moments, but I've done the calculations and think the risks are acceptable. There's no courage involved."

• • •

Although he has had more than 200 teammates over the course of fifteen expeditions, Severin has never lost a single man—perhaps the truest testament to his leadership.

"Severin has a deep sense of responsibility for his crew members," Joe Beynon told me from his home in Switzerland. The coordinator for health and detention at the International Committee of the Red Cross in Geneva, Beynon, thirty-nine, crewed on and photographed Severin's 1993 China Voyage, a test of whether the Chinese could have crossed the Pacific 2,000 years ago in a bamboo raft. Three years later, he rejoined Severin for the 1996 Spice Islands expedition, which retraced the route of Alfred Russel Wallace, a nineteenth-century naturalist who recognized the possibility of natural selection before Darwin.

"Tim's very up-front about the risks and wants to bring people back safe and well," Beynon continued. "He's not in the breed of the British mountain climbers: "people die, nature of the game." It's never a question of people dying. He sails original ships, minimizes the risk, and you all go home safely. Tim's very meticulous at planning, very workmanlike, and leaves nothing to chance."

Thinking of all the trips I've been on where conflict has blown the team—and sometimes the expedition—completely apart, I ask Severin how many people have dropped out of his projects.

"Two, maybe three; all the others were really first-rate," he says cheerfully. "People seem to rise to the occasion—they do more than cope; they learn, they make a great contribution. I'm a big believer that almost anyone can handle a remote journey."

So what is the most valuable characteristic of a good teammate? Bravery, stamina, technical skill?

Severin grins. "I would say being laid-back, easygoing."

"With Tim, there's no rush, no desperation," said Murdo McDonald, thirty-five, a geography teacher from the Outer Hebrides who accompanied Severin on his most recent project, a search for the sources of the fictional character Robinson Crusoe. "Tim takes time to understand a culture. He doesn't have a predefined idea of where the end will be or what he'll find. He goes slowly, conscientiously, and lets things unfold.

"It's all about the myths and legends for Tim. If nobody in the world knew about his projects, he would still do them—and he'd still be happy."

Most telling of all, both Beynon and McDonald added that if Severin were to call today, they'd both drop everything to go with him.

• • •

Nansen, Amundsen, Shackleton. I put Severin in this elite company of great adventurers who have left a meaningful legacy. Not for his skill at re-creating ancient vessels, or for his ability as a captain at sea, not even for so thoroughly succeeding in his vast ocean voyages, but rather for his incisive, field-informed interpretations of some of the greatest literature of humankind.

Upon reaching Sumatra on the Sinbad Voyage, Severin was able to connect the original tales of cannibalistic tribes that fed their victims drugged food to modern tribes that still use the island's marijuana in their cooking.

In retracing Wallace's journey through the Spice Islands of Indonesia, Severin resurrected one of the most unheralded evolutionary theorists of all time, filling in the biographical blanks that no professor scouring libraries ever could.

And in his most recent book, *In Search of Robinson Crusoe* (2002), Severin discovers that an obscure runaway white slave named Henry Pitman, who was once marooned on an island in the Caribbean, provided Daniel

Defoe with his prototype for Robinson Crusoe, rather than the infamous Scotsman Alexander Selkirk.

When I list these examples for Severin, he is visibly pleased but says nothing. For several minutes his eyes stare right through me, as if he were out upon the ocean. Then he grins and his whole face lights up.

"From the first book I wrote, my editors have said, 'Put more of yourself into it.' And my response has always been: No. It's not about me. The book is about the project, the ideas."

So what is Severin's next adventure? He refuses to say.

"I much prefer to do it first, then talk about it."

ZEN MASTER

Yvon is leading. It's what he does best. He's guiding his feet along a lip of rock, maneuvering himself under an overhang. Positioned directly below the obstacle, he slides his hands up into a fissure and leans back. He holds himself horizontal, 700 feet of empty Wyoming sky beneath him, studies the problem, and begins to climb.

He doesn't narrate the possibilities, nor does he appear to make any cerebral calculations; he just moves. His body—his hands and his feet coming in direct contact with the rock—will solve the problem.

He's focused. There's no wasted movement. His right hand shoots out and grabs an edge, quickly followed by his left hand, and then he steps up both feet. For a moment he is hanging upside down, crouched like a monkey about to leap for a branch. But he doesn't leap. He pushes out with his legs and pulls in with his arms, and his body smoothly shifts to one side.

It would seem an awkward position for a man, pushing and pulling simultaneously, but somehow it creates a kind of dynamic tension, an internal, counterbalancing opposition. Yvon Chouinard is struggling precariously but also magnificently, paradoxically balanced. He's using a classic climbing technique called the lieback: a difficult albeit direct solution to overcoming a crux. Another solid handhold, another foothold, and he rises gracefully onto the overhanging face. No hesitation, no desperation. Two more moves and he flows up and out of sight.

Then I hear him roar with delight.

• • •

"Don't bring those damn cams," Yvon had grumbled over the phone. "Don't need them. A few stoppers and hexes, that's enough. And don't bring those heavy ten-millimeter ropes. Ridiculous!"

He was just back from salmon fishing in Iceland. (Or was it trout fishing in Newfoundland? Or perhaps bonefishing in the South Pacific?) We were planning a climbing trip into Wyoming's Wind River Range. For thirty years Yvon had had his eye on an unclimbed line on the south face of 12,972-foot Mount Arrowhead. "And we don't need a tent," he bellowed. "I've spent a hundred nights in the Winds without a tent."

When I mentioned helmets, he scoffed at that, too, and said he'd only used one once or twice in his life. How about a headlamp? "I prefer to stumble around in the dark."

On the other hand, the fact that I wasn't intending to bring a fly rod represented a serious problem. "It's practically a crime to walk through the Winds and not fly-fish," Yvon said gravely. And when I suggested that a few cans of sardines and a tub of peanut butter would suffice for the week, he said tersely, "I'll do the cooking."

As a shakedown for an impending Andean expedition, I wanted to try using llamas. I volunteered to be the llama wrangler. Yvon had invited along two brothers from Hawaii, George and Kent Kam, so I figured the llamas could carry all our climbing gear and food, and said so. Yvon's predictable response: "Don't need them."

• • •

We met at the Elkhart Park trailhead, on the west side of the Wind River Range, at noon on a forest-fire-dry day in August. I had the gear and the llamas, Josey Wales and Guy Sado; Yvon had the food and the Hawaiians, George and Kent.

It would be hard to find two more good-natured brothers than the Kams. They're Yvon's buddies from another of his life passions: surfing. George, forty, is as ebullient and outgoing as a maître d'. He'd retired at the age of thirty-two after making a small fortune as a marketing manager for apparel companies in the surfing industry.

"It's just fashion, really," George said, smiling. "But everything's fashion. For every real-life surfer, or climber, or fly fisherman, there are a thousand wannabes."

Kent, forty-two, is quieter, but equally open. He had designed and built surfboards, then worked as a commercial pilot, and now is a firefighter in Honolulu, where he lives with his three-year-old daughter and his flight-attendant wife.

We weren't on the trail for more than an hour, Guy Sado trotting along like a trouper and Josey Wales already showing ominous signs of being an outlaw, when out of the blue Yvon said, "Who needs a $450 raincoat?"

He was apparently reacting to the conspicuously outfitted backpackers we'd been passing on the trail, many of whom looked to be carrying the entire inventory of a small outdoor shop.

"What's wrong with getting wet!" Yvon cried.

When I reminded Yvon that Patagonia Inc.—the $223 million clothing company that he founded and owns, lock, stock, and barrel—sells precisely such items, he groused, "I know. I know. But they don't need them."

Hypothermia is what's wrong with getting wet, of course. And Yvon knows it—few men have spent more time in the mountains. Climbing together in Yosemite for a week last year, we'd talked for hours about shell design, and he'd gone on at length and in exquisite detail about the engineering of seams alone. Still, Yvon is prone to radical pronouncements. He's like an old philosophy professor of mine who started every class by posing a new existential problem: "Who can prove to me that the world wasn't created ten seconds ago, complete with memories, fossils, and computer files?"

"Yvon likes to say and do things for the shock value," says Doug Tompkins, a fellow climbing pioneer and businessman who has been Yvon's close friend for more than forty years. "It shakes people up. Gets them thinking."

While George, Kent, and I each carried a pack with shoulder straps and a hipbelt, Yvon carried his with a tumpline strapped across his forehead. He learned this trick twenty years ago during a forty-five-day expedition across the Himalayas. He claimed the United Nations had done a study on tumplines and found that, once your neck and back muscles were sufficiently developed, they were more efficient than shoulder straps and hipbelts. "I had chronic back pain until I started using a tumpline," Yvon declared. He'd sent me one and I'd tried it, but found I was walking miles staring at my feet instead of the landscape—just like the women I'd seen humping conical baskets of rice all across Asia.

On our first night in the Winds we camped in a brittle alpine meadow beside seemingly fishless Seneca Lake. I put up our tent—Yvon had relented on this issue—while he gave dryland fly-casting lessons until dusk. Kent was a natural. George, in his enthusiasm, sometimes forgot the ten-and-two dictum. (Norman Maclean: "It is an art performed on a four-count rhythm between ten and two o'clock.") I was no better with a rod than I had been as a kid.

After dark, sitting around the camp stove, Yvon said he knew a guy in Bozeman, Montana, who lived for years in a stainless-steel, tubular camper that you entered from underneath. He was a master welder and was working on fuel-efficient stove designs at Yvon's behest

"You know, your average kitchen stove is a total piece of crap," he said. "They're over eighty percent inefficient. Imagine if the pot set down inside an insulated casing. The heat lost to the air would be minimal, the fuel efficiency dramatically increased."

It was a good example of the way Yvon's mind works: constantly questioning, rethinking, reformulating, innovating. As George told me, "It's Yvon's instinctual quest for the best. He's always looking for ways to improve everything. How to make it better, simpler, lighter, more environmentally friendly. I don't know anyone like him. In everything he does, he strives for perfection."

"You should hear him talk about board design," says John McMahon, a California stockbroker who's another of Yvon's surfing buddies. "He wants to create the perfect surfboard."

It galls Yvon that most surfboards break so easily; he's offended by anything that's disposable but doesn't have to be. Quality and simplicity have always been guiding principles for Yvon and his wife, Malinda. Their son, Fletcher, twenty-six, spends his days working on the problem, building and shaping surfboards in a shop less than a stone's throw from the shed in Ventura, California, where his dad once shaped pitons. Their daughter is a designer as well; says Yvon, "She has a very clear sense of what is practical and functional."

Where Yvon can sometimes be caught up in his own ideas, Malinda is the pragmatist. She interprets their vision, she sends the e-mails, she makes things happen. She is the nexus.

"Yvon has always been willing to push forward without a template," says novelist Tom McGuane, a passionate fly fisherman and a longtime friend. "He is not bound by psychological cinctures like so many of us, but it is Malinda who has given him this freedom. Malinda allowed Yvon not to lose contact with his instinctive ability to take great leaps forward. She is always there. Malinda is a visionary just like Yvon, but she's the tactician, the one behind the scenes. Without Malinda, many of Yvon's ideas would never have seen the light of day. What Yvon and Malinda have, really, is a very productive, very creative partnership."

• • •

On our second day in the Winds, Yvon told us that "the most important thing I ever taught my kids was how to eat roadkill."

He explained: "We hit a sage grouse on the road one day when they were young, so we stopped and picked it up. I taught them how to skin it, then I taught them how to cook it, and we ate it. Then I taught them how to tie flies with the feathers. Then we went fishing with the flies and I taught them how to catch fish."

This was Yvon the survivalist talking now, another distinct character among his dozen or so personalities. Designer, climber, writer, kayaker, environmental activist, lover of rivers and fish, philosopher, surfer, businessman, ascetic, aesthete—at the age of sixty-two, he morphs from one role to the next effortlessly.

Here is Yvon the pessimist: "I knew Man was doomed when I realized that his strongest inclination was toward ever-increasing homogeneity—which goes completely against Nature. Nature moves toward ever-increasing diversity. Diversity is Nature's strength. Nature loves diversity."

And you don't get diversity without adversity, according to the Chouinard theory of the universe. We'd talked about this extensively in Yosemite.

"Adversity is what causes organisms to change and adapt," he'd said. "Adversity is the catalyst for evolution. Take away adversity and evolution stops. And what do you have then? Devolution: America."

Late that afternoon, we camped at the northern end of Upper Jean Lake, the south face of Mount Arrowhead looming above us. Yvon cooked the first of five straight dinners of his bowel-busting, carrots-and-onions tsampa. When Kent happened to mention the profusion of pine needles and dirt in the entrée, Yvon replied, "They're good for you!"

And then the lesson: "You know, I absolutely forbade my children to wash their hands before they ate. Weakens their immune system. You have to learn how to handle germs. I drink from every stream I fish for the same reason."

I asked him if he'd ever had giardia.

"Oh, God," he cackled. "So bad the farts would clear out a bus. But that's not the point. The point is, I'm trying to adapt myself to the environment. Not the other way around."

Later that evening I reconned our approach to the base of Arrowhead while Yvon gave George and Kent more fly-casting lessons. Studying the south face with my monocular, then swinging the lens down onto Yvon beside the lake, it occurred to me that he was far more focused on showing his Hawaiian pals how to cast than on climbing a new route.

"Yvon's a big-time sharer of knowledge," says John McMahon. "At this point in his life, I think he's more interested in teaching than doing."

• • •

The next morning we rose at 5:30. I thought it a late start for climbing a new route, but Yvon seemed unconcerned. It took the four of us two hours to hike to the base of the south face. George and Kent intended to scramble to the summit via the west ridge, while Yvon and I had identified the gorgeous, curving line that creased the thousand-foot face. It cut straight to the summit.

When Yvon discovered that, despite his admonitions, I'd brought a number of cams, he cut the biggest ones off the rack. He also cut a third of the slings and carabiners. He climbs with no helmet, no chalk, no tape, no headlamp, no sunglasses, no sunscreen—his way of adapting to the mountain.

"I've cut everything superfluous from my life," he declared.

Even though I knew it was yet another bit of Chouinard hyperbole, I still chewed on this sentence for the first several pitches of the climb. Yvon is a man who owns three homes: an oceanfront house in Ventura, an oceanfront home made from recycled materials on California's Central Coast, and a home in Wyoming with a jaw-dropping view of the Tetons. Yvon is a man who flew to South America five times last year just to fish. But he doesn't use chalk.

The climbing was pure fun, compelling but not difficult. We didn't say much. We simply climbed—smooth, in sync, swapping leads.

I was watching Yvon lieback through the overhang on the sixth pitch, his movements poised and precise, when I remembered something else McMahon had told me: "You should see him surf. He just glides. He has no hesitation throwing himself out onto huge waves."

One time, I don't even remember what Yvon and I were talking about—writing, free diving, business—when he suddenly said, "Forget about the end result. It means nothing. The end result is we die. What matters is the process. The process is everything."

It was hackneyed Buddhist rap, but here's the thing: Yvon, despite—or perhaps because of—his many contradictions, lives it. For Yvon it wasn't the fact that we were climbing a new route in the Winds; it was all about how we were doing it. To him the ascent became more elegant each time something unnecessary was eliminated. Gear, chalk, words, signals. He believes, with all his being, in the Antoine de Saint-Exupéry line that regularly appears in Patagonia Inc. literature: "In anything at all, perfection is finally attained not when there is no longer anything left to add, but when there is no longer anything to take away."

·   ·   ·

We completed our directissima of Arrowhead's south face in three hours, and then spent the afternoon back at camp in a pleasing, postexertion fog, erratically debating this and that. At one point I told Yvon that I thought Patagonia clothing was too expensive.

"Not compared to Calvin Klein," he responded.

He went on to defend his company by saying that, because of the renowned durability of Patagonia apparel, everybody from dirtbags to billionaires buys it.

"Dirtbags don't buy anything," I exclaimed. "They schwag it. I know—I used to be one."

"I still am one!" Yvon countered.

Now hold on—Yvon does wear the same old clothes for days on end. And he did sleep with his clothes on the whole week we were in the Winds. And no matter the protean conundrums of his mind, he's snoring in less than two minutes. And most of his climbing gear belongs in a museum. And he's completely satisfied eating sardines with a piton. And he doesn't need a shower. And he flies economy just like the rest of us. And he sleeps on friends' couches instead of paying for hotel rooms. And he drives vintage beater Toyotas. But . . .

"C'mon, Yvon, you're a multimultimillionaire."

"I give it all away. I don't even have a savings account."

True, I already knew that Patagonia Inc. had given millions upon millions to environmental causes.

"But that's not even the point," he continued. "Being a dirtbag is a matter of philosophy, not personal wealth. I'm an existential dirtbag."

"You're not a dirtbag anymore, Yvon, you're a businessman. A very successful businessman. Dirtbags don't own companies. Somewhere along the way you must have wanted to be a businessman."

"Never!" There was real vehemence in his voice. "All I ever wanted to be was a craftsman."

"He's in denial," George told me later. "He's an entrepreneur. He's a capitalist. He just can't bear being lumped in with all those businessmen he doesn't respect.

"But he also is a dirtbag. It's a statement as much as anything else. You know those Patagonia ads—'Committed to the core'? Well, Yvon is the core."

● ● ●

The next day we continued trekking north. I was hoping we might make one more ascent, but I think Yvon had already gone back to trout-fishing dreams.

We stopped for lunch at Summit Lake. It was the geographic fulcrum, the halfway point between our start at Elkhart Park and our finish at Green River Lakes. George and Kent and I lolled in the tundralike hummocks while Yvon cast a line.

It was high noon, that unluckiest of fly-fishing hours, but a cutthroat took his fly and promptly snapped his 5x tippet. He replaced it with a 4x and immediately caught a one-pounder, then a pound-and-a-halfer. As he was popping the fish off the hook with a one-handed flick of the wrist, a big sloshing sound rolled across the water. Yvon looked back over his shoulder just in time to see the splash. In a seamless series of motions, he let go of the hook; began snapping the line in great big sky S's, streaking out more and more line; spun 180 degrees while the hook was floating in the air; cast, throwing all the line off the reel; dropped the fly bull's-eye inside the concentric circles; and caught a two-and-a-half-pounder before the one-and-a-half-pounder had time to swim away.

He issued his familiar, exuberant roar, and then allowed himself a brief commentary: "Now that's . . . that's fly-fishing."

● ● ●

Two hours later it was raining, and our llama Josey Wales had sat down on the trail for the hundredth time. We'd climbed our climb and caught our fish and now the trip was about to fall apart, even though we were still a three-day walk from the trailhead. George volunteered to cajole and kick Josey along the trail while the three of us double-loaded Guy and hustled down to Three Forks Park.

The downpour kindly commenced only after we got our tents up. By the time we'd eaten Yvon's homemade tsampa, we were bone-cold and drenched. George and Kent hit the sack, but Yvon and I couldn't help ourselves. We hung around our miserable little campfire, choking on smoke, watching a heavy mist come off the high park grass and drift into the trees. We took swigs of Glenlivet and let ideas bounce and tumble around us.

Yvon told me about the time his son, Fletcher, speared a wild pig and cooked it using one of Yvon's recipes. He told me about his dream of inspiring the biggest companies in the world to give one percent of their gross sales to environmental causes, just like Patagonia Inc. does. He called it a revolution, and his eyes showed white in the dark.

"Imagine! Just imagine if Conoco and IBM and Microsoft and GM all gave one percent. It would be billions of dollars. It could save the planet!"

("People criticize Yvon," says Tompkins, "but 99.9 percent of these people can't match what he's doing for the environment. Yes, he owns a big company and he could do more—I could do more, you could do more, we all need more courage to do more. But for everything Yvon takes out of this world, he gives back more than anybody I know. And that's the bottom line.")

Yvon, the maker of his own myth, was growing tired, but he had to tell me about this free diver he knows who has adapted himself so well to the underwater environment, has become so tuned in, that fish will guide him to lobsters, that dolphins have saved him from shark attacks.

Yvon, a Henry David Thoreau and a Ralph Lauren and a Muhammad Ali all forged into one, was tired, but he wanted me to understand that sustainability is the only hope for the planet. "Sustainability, sustainability . . . " He repeated it like a mantra.

Yvon, the master of market semiotics, was so tired, but he said he has been trying to write a book for nearly a decade. "Writing is too hard," he complained. It's a book about business. What else. "You know what the business of most businesses in America is? To sell the business. The business is to sell the business. Cash out. Go golfing. Well, not me, god-damn it."

We were standing hunch-shouldered in the dark, rain draining off the bills of our baseball caps, mist flowing into the black woods like a river, the campfire long since drowned. Yvon had to sleep now, but first he had to tell me something.

"I am guilty," he said quietly. This in reference to his profligacy, for his burning fossil fuel to stand in icy water on some remote river and try to think like a fish instead of a human.

He was going to his sleeping bag now, but before he did he wanted to tell me his favorite joke. He'd told it to me before. "There once was this Zen master sitting on a small stone bench, studying his small Japanese rock garden . . . "

There are only five rocks in the master's garden. Each was chosen for its individual perfection, as well as for its unique relationship to the other stones. One day a visitor comes to the garden. The visitor steps slowly around the tiny space, contemplating the rake-grooved gravel and the stones. Eventually the visitor turns to the Zen master and exclaims, "It is perfect." The Zen master shakes his head solemnly and says, "No, it will be perfect when there are only three stones."

Yvon chuckled and said good night. I offered him my headlamp, but he waved it away and stumbled into the dark.

THE BIG PRINCE

En route to Casablanca, flying north across the Sahara, the plane is lost. It is an inky, moonless night in the early 1930s. The two leather-helmeted men, Antoine de Saint-Exupéry, the French pilot and poet destined to become the bard of the nascent art of aviation, and a man named Néri, his navigator, lean out of their plane and stare down at the desert, just a few hundred feet below. Through a cosmic sleight of hand, it has vanished. They peer through their goggles into a black abyss, as though suspended above some starless expanse of space.

Intermittent radio bearings from ports along the desolate Atlantic coast—Dakar, Villa Cisneros Agadir—have been unaccountably wrong and pulled the aircraft far off course. The navigator has no idea where they are. The elementary control panel is of little help, although it does indicate that there is less than an hour of fuel left. Sensing that the plane is out over the ocean, rather than the desert, the pilot arcs the craft to the right.

To go down in the ocean is certain, if not entirely disagreeable, death. Drowning, Saint-Exupéry will later tell a reporter, would be his choice of endings: "You don't feel yourself dying. You simply feel as if you're falling asleep and beginning to dream." But at this point in his life, at age twenty-nine and ardently in love with the adventure of flying the mail back and forth over the savage Sahara, Saint-Exupéry is not ready for death. Better to ditch in the desert, as he has been forced to do many times before. Shipwrecked in a sea of sand, there is some chance of rescue before you die of thirst—after desperately drinking and then puking up the plane's radiator fluid—or are captured by nomadic Bedouins who will torture you, or behead you, or ransom you, perhaps all three.

Soon they are sailing through a miasma of clouds and fog. Néri is passing notes to Saint-Exupéry. "No bearings. No bearings." The pilot is left to navigate on passion and instinct—traits fortuitously acute in this airman. (One colleague will later say, "When the flight is normal, Saint-Exupéry is dangerous; given complications, he's brilliant.") These were the daring early years of aviation; one mail pilot died almost every month. Humans had been crossing deserts by camel for millennia, sailing seas for a thousand years, climbing mountains for a hundred—the sky was the last great terra incognita for adventurers.

The wood-and-metal airplane, a French-made Latécoère 26 that Saint-Exupery dislikes, is plummeting through a void. Up could be half-way down or three-quarters sideways. The compass needle jerks errati-cally, the fuselage shudders, the wings creak. Néri has begun to pray. Saint-Exupéry steadily steers the aircraft and dreams of the calming familiarities of earth. Laughter. A bowl of hot milk and coffee in a Moroccan café.

He has had multiple near misses, most of them in the primitive Breg-uet 14, a slow, ungainly biplane he flew for a decade. It had no real nose, but rather a flat forehead plugged with a large wooden propeller. The Breguet 14's singular redeeming attribute was a noble resoluteness founded upon mechanical simplicity. With a control panel hardly more sophisticated than that of a Ford Model T, it would still fly with a broken tail, flopping wing, or coughing engine. Saint-Exupéry, an intuitive mechanic, crash-landed the Breguet many times, repaired its Renault 300-horsepower engine with a hammer and screwdriver, then lifted right back into the sky. He would elegize the obsolescence of the simple Breg-uet 14 years later. For him, there was no charm in modern airplanes. They were soulless rockets, and flying one was a "bureaucratic affair . . . a life without surprises."

The pilot and his favorite airship shared an uncanny resemblance. On the ground, in old black-and-white photos, both the Breguet 14 and Saint-Exupéry appear bulky and awkward. Saint-Exupéry was a head taller than most men, clumsy and uncomfortable in his bearlike form. (In his 1942 book *Flight to Arras,* a nonfiction account of the fall of France in WWII, Saint-Exupéry described his body as a "flunky" that he was required to dress, bathe, and feed. "It is in your act that you exist, not in your body.") Unkempt, two thick fingers pinching a hand-rolled ciga-rette, a quizzical expression on his face, Saint-Exupéry, despite the regal name, was patently unheroic in appearance, an outsize man who might have been mistaken for a provincial baker.

But put the hulking Frenchman in the cockpit of a plane and send him into the sky, and a transformation occurred. The wings became extensions of Saint-Exupéry's arms, the cables became his tendons, the enormous, fallible engine his own thundering heart. Man and machine became one—a graceful, athletic, airborne organism. "The machine does not isolate man from the great problems of nature," Saint-Exupéry wrote, "but plunges him more deeply into them."

Suddenly, in the black night sky, a pinprick of light is spotted off the nose of the plane. It must be the beacon of an airport! Néri bursts into song from sheer relief. Saint-Exupéry swings the craft toward the tiny light.

Then it vanishes.

Another diamond of light springs from the murk. Néri believes it can only be the Villa Cisneros airport in Spanish Sahara. He radios a request that the airport flash the light three times. The incandescent speck they are pursuing doesn't so much as blink.

Saint-Exupéry has been chasing stars.

"And with that we knew ourselves to be lost in interplanetary space among a thousand inaccessible planets," he writes in his 1939 memoir *Wind, Sand and Stars*, "we who sought only one veritable planet, our own, that planet on which alone we should find our familiar countryside, the houses of our friends, our treasures."

Believing their fuel now depleted, they prepare to drop to earth, to crash into the oblivion of the Sahara. But, in the final moments, a radio call from their base in Toulouse, France, reaches them, providing bearings and a reprieve: "Your reserve tank bigger than standard. You have two hours' fuel left. Proceed to Cisneros."

Once again Saint-Exupéry escapes disaster through some ineffable alliance of luck and faith, ability and hubris. It's the story of his life, and the reason why his death, a decade later, would haunt his readers and admirers for years.

● ● ●

Flying across the Ligurian Sea back to Corsica, the plane was lost. It was a beautiful day in late July 1944 and the world was at war for the second time in as many generations. Saint-Exupéry, now the famous author of seven books, was returning from an unarmed, solo reconnaissance mission to the Rhône Valley.

Patriotic to the marrow, Saint-Exupéry had, through sheer force of personality, managed to inveigle himself a dangerous flying assignment

for the Allies, despite the fact that he was forty-four years old and showing the strains of a tumultuous life. Over the past fifteen years he had
survived innumerable airplane crashes, but two in particular had left lasting scars: a smashup in Africa in 1935, followed by a five-day, 125-mile
trek across the Libyan Desert during which he nearly died of thirst; and
an accident in Guatemala that caused serious head wounds and a half-
dozen broken bones. Add to these wrecks the tender disaster of a marriage to a childish, voraciously partying wife. Worse, the boundless wild
world he had known as a mail pilot in West Africa—where survival was
dependent on ingenuity, improvisation, and pluck—was gone forever.

Now, bent on helping liberate France at all costs, Saint-Exupéry was
flying a highly sophisticated aircraft he detested and only marginally
understood. The American-made Lockheed Lightning P-38's control
panel had 148 knobs and dials and was one of the fastest planes of its time.
On almost every previous sortie in the P-38, he had experienced potentially fatal problems—engine failure or malfunction, a wing fire, near
asphyxiation from a faulty oxygen mask. He had flown low over enemy
territory and inexplicably survived. He had been pursued by enemy fighters and barely escaped. Like fuel leaking from a bullet hole in the wing
tank, the good luck Saint-Exupéry had once had as a young pilot was
dribbling away.

He took off at 8:30 a.m. from Bastia, on the northeastern coast of
Corsica, and was due back in four hours. He didn't return. By 2:30 he
would have been out of fuel. At 3:30 he was reported missing and pre-
sumed dead.

For more than half a century, friends, family, reporters, and writers
opined on how Saint-Exupéry might have died. Perhaps he experienced
engine trouble and crashed in the Alps. Perhaps he was shot down over
the Mediterranean. Perhaps he failed to properly use the oxygen equipment and blacked out. Even suicide was suggested, an act inconsistent
with the pattern and pride of his life: Saint-Exupéry was quite willing to
die for his country, but only at the hands of the enemy or the elements.

It is hard to imagine a more poignant and fitting way for Saint-
Exupéry to have left this planet than by vanishing into oblivion, for this
is precisely what happens to the boy in his best-known work, *The Little
Prince*, a slim autobiographical parable published in 1943 and since translated into eighty languages.

"You understand . . . it is too far. I cannot carry this body with me," the title character, a phantasmal spirit of adventure, says. "It is too heavy. But it will be like an old abandoned shell. There is nothing sad about old shells."

And with that, there is a "flash of yellow close to his ankle," and the Little Prince evaporates.

In 2004, sixty years after Saint-Exupéry's enigmatic disappearance, the wreckage of a P-38 was discovered a mile and a half off the southern coast of France near Marseille. Winched up from the mud of the Mediterranean, it was positively identified as Saint-Exupéry's aircraft. The discovery placed boundaries on the mystery but did not solve it: No trace of his remains was found.

Still, the precise circumstances of Saint-Exupéry's death are insignificant. Stacy Schiff, author of the 1994 *Saint-Exupéry: A Biography,* believes it could have been pilot error.

"But does it really matter?" asked Schiff when I spoke to her recently, and then she answered her own question: "No. All reconnaissance pilots ran huge risks. His death was a matter of probability. What is so thrilling was Saint-Exupéry's life, a ragged, glorious series of close calls."

• • •

Born in 1900 into a declining aristocratic French family, Saint-Exupéry was raised with his three sisters and one brother in a Louis XVI château near Lyon by a household of intelligent, tolerant women, including several aunts and a grandmother. His father died of a stroke before he was four years old, and he became deeply attached to his mother. A dreamy, artistic child, Saint-Exupéry was writing poetry and plays by age seven, the plays often extravagantly performed before his indulgent family. He routinely wrote his poetry very late at night, and would wake one of his siblings or cousins to listen to his latest composition.

Saint-Exupery received his *"bapteme de l'air"* at the age of twelve after hanging around the tiny Ambérieu airport, in southeastern France, for several weeks pestering the mechanics and pilots. His mother forbade him to fly, but insubordination was already one of his more well-developed traits. He got himself taken up for two short circles: thus began his life-long love affair.

To quench his "irresistible thirst" for flying, he took private flying lessons in the summer of 1921 and spent the better part of his two-year military service flying the Breguet 14, sometimes making six flights a day. In 1926 Aéropostale, the private French mail service, hired Saint-Exupéry. He began his apprenticeship as an airplane mechanic, was soon test-flying each new Breguet 14 the company bought, and within a year was transporting the mail from France to Spain over the Pyrenees.

Beginning in 1927, Saint-Exupéry spent four years flying the mail over northwestern Africa, Patagonia, and the Andes. It was an emotional calling as much as a career, something that he would not experience again until World War II.

Saint-Exupéry spent most of the thirties and early forties doing more writing than flying. He covered the Spanish Civil War; wrote for magazines like *Paris Soir* and *Harper's Bazaar*; and published books, including *Night Flight,* a 1932 novel about flying the night mail over South America, *Wind, Sand and Stars,* and *The Little Prince.*

After his plane was found, I was spurred to revisit *The Little Prince* with my two daughters. We read it together over two evenings, taking chapters in turn. Teal, my nine-year-old, particularly enjoyed the miniature prince's encounters with the inhabitants of other minuscule planets—the king, the conceited man, the lamplighter—in which the obvious allegories are outweighed by the simple, outlandish magic of the tale. Addi, a twelve-year-old realist, found the whole thing a bit absurd for her tastes.

On the surface, *The Little Prince* is a pleasingly quirky fairy tale that reveals the obsessions of adulthood and deserves its worldwide popularity. Read with the knowledge of the author's private anguish, it is a symbolic tale of loneliness and loss. Either way, it would be an injustice for Saint-Exupéry to be remembered solely for this one small gem.

• • •

If you want to know who Antoine de Saint-Exupéry was, and why he should be read and remembered, you must dive into *Wind, Sand and Stars* and *Flight to Arras,* two of the finest adventure books of the twentieth century. *Wind, Sand and Stars* won the Grand Prix du Roman de l'Académie Française in 1939 and the National Book Award in 1940, whereas *Flight to Arras* was banned in his homeland for being unpatriotic. My copies of both books—thumb-worn and underlined—are large stones in my literary foundation.

Wind, Sand and Stars is a lyrical memoir of Saint-Exupéry's formative years of flying—his annealing by winging the French mail over the blazing Sahara, the pride of responsibility, the satisfaction of perfecting his craft, the love found among comrades of cause. These same themes resound in *Flight to Arras,* a much darker, conspicuously spiritual book that chronicles the fall of France to the Nazis through the experiences of a French fighter pilot. Together, the two books are an homage to a life of personal integrity and action.

"The notion of looking on at life has always been hateful to me," Saint-Exupéry writes in *Flight to Arras.* "What am I if I am not a participant? In order to be, I must participate." Like Whitman, Conrad, and Hemingway, Saint-Exupéry believed that complete immersion in one's chosen métier was fundamental, that "one needs to live in order to write. One needs to have something to say." And then he must say it with clarity, passion, and precision.

"In anything at all, perfection is finally attained not when there is no longer anything to add, but when there is no longer anything to take away." I've had this quote from *Wind, Sand and Stars* tacked to my office wall for twenty years.

Saint-Exupéry wrote at night and flew at night and wrote while he was flying at night. "Night, the beloved," he rhapsodizes in *Flight to Arras.* "Night, when words fade and things come alive. When the destructive analysis of day is done, and all that is truly important becomes whole and sound again. When man reassembles his fragmentary self and grows with the calm of a tree."

What raises Saint-Exupéry's work above mere adventure writing into the realm of literature is his willingness to go beyond the vagaries of one life and openly examine the universal questions of humankind. By today's standards, his language is unfashionably lofty and affirmative, neither reveling in minutiae nor discreetly concealing his opinion. Saint-Exupéry was not a postmodern writer. He was a thinker and a doer, a philosopher and an adventurer—as unafraid of making bold proclamations as he was of flying faulty planes over treacherous routes.

In *Wind, Sand and Stars*, Saint-Exupéry meditates on the meaning of his fledgling mail plane, recognizing it as evidence of a larger human impulse: "The central struggle of men has ever been to understand one another, to join together for the common weal. And it is this very thing that the machine helps them to do. It begins by annihilating time and space."

Near the end of *Flight to Arras*, grappling with the blight of fascism and the militarism required to fight it, Saint-Exupéry asserts, "It is easy to establish a society upon the foundation of rigid rules. It is easy to shape the kind of man who submits blindly and without protest to a master. . . . The real task is to succeed in setting man free by making him master of himself."

Saint-Exupéry would not have been remembered as a pilot; he was just one of many valiant aviation pioneers. But it was the act of flying that set him free, and it was through the process of writing that he mastered himself. Sailing above the earth for so many years gave him an aerial perspective on the human condition, and yet his writing was always more about compassion than courage, more about brotherhood than boldness.

Near the end of *Wind, Sand and Stars,* Saint-Exupéry writes, "It is another of the miraculous things about mankind that there is no pain nor passion that does not radiate to the ends of the earth. Let a man in a garret but burn with enough intensity and he will set fire to the world."

And he did.

Lessons

FAME AND GLORY

A kangaroo squats in the red dirt road. Head drooping, front paws limp, it can barely hop out of the way. The sun, an evil globe scorching the earth, is literally cooking the meat inside the kangaroo's tattered fur. I pull over, pour several quarts of my emergency water into a makeshift bowl, and set it beside the road along with some food; but I know it's too late.

The drought is that bad. Kangaroo carcasses dot the desert like the skeletons of dead explorers, their hides stretched taut over rat-gnawed bones, sand drifting into their pecked-out eyes.

I stop for the night in Tibooburra (population 130), a ghostly, dirt-blown town 600 miles north of Melbourne, in the northwestern corner of New South Wales. The Tibooburra Hotel is a dilapidated two-story sandstone building with a peeling wooden porch. Tiny rooms above the pub, bathroom down the hall. I am the only guest.

In the pub, a prosthetic leg and a dusty saddle hang from the ceiling, cowboy hats are nailed in rows along the walls, and the smell of cigarette smoke and abandonment fills the air. I order a mug of beer that immediately goes warm.

A crooked little man in a crushed cowboy hat bounds through the screen door, takes a stool at the bar, pours a mug of beer down his creased, stubbled throat, and orders another.

"I'm the water hauler," he volunteers.

Turns out Tibooburra, an Aboriginal name meaning "heaps of rocks," went dry two years ago, and locals have had to truck in drinking water from an aquifer-fed reservoir.

"A third of an inch of rain in two years," adds the Pooh-bellied bartender.

"We got a 3,000-gallon tanker," says the water hauler, raising his mug to me. "Goin' tomorrow 3:00 a.m. for the fill-up, mate, if you care to come along."

"I'm heading to Innamincka," I say, "to see the Dig Tree."

The Dig Tree is a gnarled coolibah that stands in the burnt heart of the outback beside the warm, green water of Cooper's Creek. It is the most famous tree in Australia because of the cryptic instructions carved into its trunk and the part it played in this country's most notorious expedition.

In 1860, Robert Burke and William Wills set out to become the first white men to cross Australia, a historic south–north traverse from Melbourne to the Gulf of Carpentaria. Their eight-month journey took them through the Tibooburra region in October of that year en route to a basecamp on Cooper's Creek and then into vast, desperate stretches of the interior. Burke and Wills were like the Lewis and Clark of Australia, famed icons of early outback exploration—although, by the time it was all over, they'd become legends for very different reasons.

"Burke and Wills—now they were some bloody tough bastards!" says the bartender, suddenly animated. "I hope they're still teaching the schoolchildren about our heritage."

To get a taste of what they experienced, I've come to the desert in the dead of summer—January—after one of the driest years in Australian history.

"Tracin' their path, are ye?" says the water hauler. "Bugger, they was brave."

• • •

The Australia that Burke and Wills ventured into was an immense, uncharted continent. Roughly the size of the United States, it had been the home of Aborigines for 60,000 years when, in 1788, a British penal colony was established near present-day Sydney. By 1860 there were 1 million European immigrants living on the coastline; two-thirds of the continent, including the entire western half, remained unexplored by whites.

Discovering what lay inland had far-reaching implications for communication and commerce. It took two months for news to travel by ship from England to its Australian colonies, and yet a telegraph line already extended from Europe to India to Southeast Asia. What if a line could be strung from Melbourne, the major port on the southern coast, straight through to the northern coast and linked by cable with Asia? News would take a mere two hours, a reply a day or two. Certainly, untold acres of prime grazing land would be discovered in the process, maybe gold as well.

Members of the Royal Society of Victoria, a Melbourne gentlemen's club composed of scientists, businessmen, and armchair explorers, took it upon themselves to solve the mystery of Australia's frontier. In January 1860, they announced plans to fund the Victorian Exploring Expedition and placed an ad for a leader in the Melbourne papers. After much internal politicking, the Royal Society chose Robert O'Hara Burke, thirty-nine, an Irish emigrant and small-town police superintendent, as the expedition's unlikely chief.

"The idea of Burke leading any expedition anywhere at all was ludicrous," writes former BBC correspondent Sarah Murgatroyd in *The Dig Tree*, her 2002 history of the epic journey. "He was neither a surveyor nor a scientist and had no exploration experience."

Australian historian Alan Moorehead cites references to Burke in his 1963 book *Cooper's Creek* as a "wild eccentric dare-devil" who was in "no sense a bushman" and whom "some thought not quite sane" because of his habit of lying for hours in a bathtub in his backyard wearing only a pith helmet.

"Burke was popular, charming, and intelligent, but excitable, impulsive, and headstrong," writes Murgatroyd. By all accounts, Burke appears to have been guided not by an explorer's fundamental trait—curiosity—but by two esteemed Victorian values: fame and glory.

Good thing, then, that the expedition's twenty-six-year-old surveyor, William John Wills, was a diligent student of natural history and the sciences. According to his father, he was "ever pining for the bush . . . his love fixed on animals, plants, and the starry firmament."

A novelist couldn't have fashioned two more disparate characters.

On August 20, 1860, the Victorian Exploring Expedition left Melbourne, bound for the Gulf of Carpentaria, 1,500 miles of Sahara-like desert to the north. It was a circus from the start: nineteen men, twenty-six heavily laden camels imported from India, twenty-three horses, a train of six bizarrely overloaded wagons, and a semisubmersible dray. All told, they were hauling twenty tons of accoutrements, including twelve sets of dandruff brushes, four enema kits, an oak table with two oak stools, and a large bathtub.

Burke declared that he would cross Australia "or perish in the attempt."

• • •

The consensus at the Tibooburra pub is that I should stick to the main dirt track to reach Innamincka, a day's drive through scrub plains and foot-deep bull dust. It's one of the few regions on earth where it's possible to die if your car breaks down. You hide out in the sweltering shade of your vehicle, drink emergency stores of water, and wait for another car to pass by. If no one happens along in forty-eight hours, you're cooked. In 1963, a family of five perished this way.

Instead, I navigate an obscure sandy path to a watering hole called Olive Downs, where I count twenty-seven kangaroo carcasses locked in the fractured mud. I bump along "jump-ups," hillocks of rock and sand, and, following a trail that's no wider than my truck, cross the breadth of Sturt National Park. Named for Charles Sturt, one of only a handful of explorers who preceded Burke and Wills, the desolate country seems little changed since the summer of 1844, when Sturt and several teammates rode horses north from Adelaide into the desert. Some 800 miles inland, they found a network of channels and permanent warm-water billabongs, which they christened Cooper's Creek after a South Australian judge.

That same year, a Prussian named Ludwig Leichhardt walked an astounding 3,000 miles from Brisbane to Port Essington along the north-eastern coast. But he disappeared on his next expedition, and surveyor Augustus Gregory was dispatched to find him.

Between 1855 and 1858, Gregory made several bold desert journeys, including an enormous boomerang-shaped trek that ran from Brisbane on Australia's east coast clear out to Cooper's Creek, then hooked south to Adelaide, leaving only a 700-mile section between Cooper's Creek and the Gulf of Carpentaria unexplored. Gregory and his men went on horseback, lived off the land, and set a precedent for traveling extraordinarily light. But they never found Leichhardt.

Likewise, his fellow explorer John Stuart accomplished five successful journeys in the early 1860s, eventually crossing Australia east to west. Stuart also traveled light, with his horse, Polly, and a few saddlebags. In more than 12,000 miles of desert, he never lost a man.

In contrast, the Burke and Wills expedition began falling apart even before making it out of Melbourne. The axles of several sagging wagons snapped and three team members were sacked.

Four weeks later and 250 miles north, Burke realized he was dangerously overburdened. He dismissed seven more men and jettisoned gear willy-nilly—everything from a useless camel stretcher to a store of lime juice, an essential preventive of scurvy. Still, a week later the draft horses were so exhausted they were set free, the wagons left to rot in the bush. Even the camels began collapsing in the heat.

Burke's temperamental character wrought havoc. He fired and hired personnel at random. Two months into the journey, he dismissed his deputy leader George Landells—who later wrote that Burke's conduct as a leader was horribly wanting in "judgment, candour, and decision"—and named young William Wills his second in command.

Burke did not keep a diary; instead he relied on Wills to do so. Wills took copious notes on the flora and fauna, navigated and plotted the team's course through the desert, and now indefatigably tackled the day-to-day headaches of expedition management.

After traveling 465 miles in fifty-six days—a distance a horseman like Gregory or Stuart could have covered in ten days—Burke reorganized again, leaving five men, tons of gear, and most of the horses beside the Darling River. The Victorian Exploring Expedition was disintegrating.

Temperatures rose to 140°F in the sun, yet Burke ignored the advice of Aborigines and often passed up shaded watering holes where "bush tucker"—game and desert vegetables—was plentiful. Each day was a sixteen-hour forced march. The expedition reached Cooper's Creek, the oasis of the Australian outback, on November 11, 1860.

• • •

Innamincka (population fourteen) is a forlorn cluster of ramshackle buildings beside Cooper's Creek—a gas station in the sand, a pub hidden in the middle of millions of acres of nowhere, a dusty airstrip used to transport oil and gas crews and the occasional mail pouch. It's the kind of grit-chafed, end-of-the-earth outpost that's so existential, a director might choose it for a movie set.

In fact, I book into the Burke Lodge Cabins, a set of three trailers left over from the 1985 film *Burke and Wills*. As the only guest, I'm given the director's trailer, which contains four midget beds, a screeching, wall-mounted AC box, and a shower where a snake keeps poking his head through the drain.

"Out here, it's either drought or deluge," explains Joan Osborne. She's a landscape painter; her husband, John, is a retired aluminum-plant foreman. Together they're Innamincka's longest-lasting residents and unofficial mayors.

"Some years, the flies are so bad, your food is black if you try to eat outside," says Joan. "For a few years, we had a rabbit infestation, which meant there were lovely wedgetailed eagles everywhere. Things don't change here so much by season as by years. We had a stretch where it rained so much, Cooper's Creek was constantly flooding."

"This year, it's snakes," John tells me, his face as tan as sand. He's wearing traditional outback attire—sweat-soaked T-shirt, ratty shorts, slip-on boots. "Eight-foot king brown bit a mate. Came through the ductwork and dropped onto his bed. Bite nearly killed him."

So why do they live here?

Joan sighs, disappointed that I haven't already figured this out for myself.

"It's so beautiful." Her eyes almost water. "There is nothing like the desert. Nothing in the whole world."

• • •

Because Cooper's Creek has permanent water in the billabongs and ample shade under the coolibahs, it was a center of commerce for the Aborigines for a thousand generations. They would travel hundreds of miles to trade shields, wooden bowls, axe heads—or simply to socialize.

When Burke and Wills arrived at Cooper's Creek, they were welcomed by the Yandruwandha Aborigines with offerings of fish and invitations to ceremonies. Burke rebuffed them by blasting bullets into the air.

Summer and its mortal heat had descended. Although the Yandru-wandha had warned Burke not to venture farther into the desert during the hottest months, he was insistent. He ordered four men to stay behind at the basecamp at Cooper's Creek to guard a stock of provisions against a plague of rats. They were instructed to wait three months for Burke's return—until March 15, 1861—before forsaking the post.

On December 16, Burke, Wills, and two other men—ex-soldier John King and ex-sailor Charley Gray—strode defiantly into the unknown. They took six camels, one horse, and barely three months' worth of food. The terrain varied from dismal rows of dunes to baked claypan, rock-tiled wasteland to savage, waterless mountains. On some days, Burke and his men managed a meager five miles; other days they slogged thirty-five or more across the punishing landscape.

Through inhuman persistence, Burke and Wills reached the Gulf of Carpentaria on February 9, 1861. But they never saw the ocean. They marched until they were knee-deep in a mangrove swamp, then simply turned around. The Victoria Exploring Expedition had triumphed—although what began as "the finest expedition ever assembled in Australia," according to the journalists of the time, was now down to four emaciated men in rags. And it was 900 miles back to their supply base at Cooper's Creek.

• • •

"Ya see, mate, they weren't Aussie bushmen, now were they?" Bomber Johnson chides, wiping his forehead with a neckerchief in the 110°F shade.

Red-faced, yellow-haired, bushy brows falling into his eyes, sixty-nine-year-old Bomber is the self-appointed historian and personal guide to the Dig Tree, a forty-four-mile drive north from Innamincka along a twisting sand track.

"They were arrogant. They didn't try to learn from the Aborigines," says Bomber. He's a jackaroo (Aussie for cowboy) pilot who has spent thirty-five years mustering cattle in his Cessna 172.

Bomber tells me tale after tale of Aborigines: the trackers who could follow outlaws across bare rock by finding the grains of sand that fell from beneath their toenails, the jackaroos who could survive on goanna lizard flesh for weeks. "They knew how to live in this nice big slice of hell," he says appreciatively.

Bomber directs me to an unassuming coolibah distinguished only by an encircling boardwalk. Carved into the twisting trunk are the letter B, for Burke, and the roman numerals LXV, for the expedition's sixty-fifth camp. Over the last century, Bomber explains, folds of bark have covered up the most famous inscription:

> dig
>
> under
>
> 3 ft nw
>
> april 26, 1861

On February 13, 1861, Burke, Wills, Gray, and King began dragging themselves southward from the gulf. With supplies almost gone, Burke cut rations in half. Although Wills was a good shot and King would later report that they were surrounded by "kangaroos, emus, and any quantity of ducks and pelicans," Wills was too debilitated to hunt.

Burke, by this point, had likely gone mad. Once, when a camel dropped and couldn't continue, he inexplicably abandoned the beast instead of eating it.

On March 15, 1861, the day they were due back at basecamp, Burke and his men were still 680 miles to the north. Burke cut rations again. They were drinking three quarts of water a day when their bodies needed ten and burning twice the number of calories they were consuming.

Gray began lagging behind, his legs in excruciating pain. He became delirious and then unable to speak. He died at sunrise on April 17, 1861, less than one hundred miles from Cooper's Creek.

Four days later, Burke, Wills, and King stumbled into Cooper's Creek and, upon seeing the inscription in the coolibah tree, collapsed. King felt the still-warm ashes of the campfire. The four men at basecamp had waited an extra five weeks at their post but had left that very morning.

After eight months of unspeakable hardship, Burke, Wills, and King had missed salvation by eight hours—and now were too exhausted to catch up.

Buried beneath the Dig Tree in an old camel trunk were stores of flour, sugar, tea, and dried meat left behind by Burke's men, but it wasn't enough. Robert Burke and William Wills died of starvation and exhaustion beside Cooper's Creek. In September 1861, King was found living with Aborigines near Innamincka. Of the men left behind along the way, five perished, most of them from scurvy.

• • •

They are still teaching the Shakespearean tale of Burke and Wills to Australian children, whereas Sturt, Gregory, and Stuart—efficient and capable, paradigms of exploration—were consequently forgotten. Tragedy and irony always play better than common sense. We humans adore martyrs, as long as we don't have to be one.

The five rescue missions dispatched to find Burke, Wills, and the stragglers from their party further opened the interior. On August 22, 1872, the first telegram was sent from London to Adelaide, passing through an underwater cable from Java to present-day Darwin and then across the blazing expanse of outback.

A few miles northwest of Innamincka, on the banks of languorous Cooper's Creek, there is a concrete cairn marking Burke's grave. As I stand before it in the dizzying heat, swatting flies and staring at the simple plaque, it occurs to me that, in the end, Robert O'Hara Burke got exactly what he wanted.

FLIGHT

I'm rising up into a lavender dawn, the desert dropping beneath me as if in a dream. A thousand feet above the red earth of southwestern Utah, I throttle back, level off, and glide through the expanse of sky. Yo, Icarus, check it out! I feel like a twelve-year-old who has just lifted off in a flying machine he built in his backyard. Which—given the fact that I'm piloting what is essentially a three-wheeled go-cart powered by an oversize lawn-mower engine and hung by cords from a parachute—isn't too far from the truth.

There is no riveted metal fuselage enclosing me, no scratched cockpit Plexiglas to peer through. I'm seated outside in the open sky, a thrumming propeller at my back and a cool breeze skimming across my face.

This ultralight, a fifty-horsepower Powrachute Rascal, has only three flight controls: the throttle, which determines your rate of ascent or descent, and two foot-operated steering bars. A pair of on/off switches power the engine and a lever mounted to the front wheel steers the vehicle, but only when it's on the ground.

I gaze down between my legs through fathoms of nothingness. Wriggling gravel roads, straight-shooting fences, dendritic arroyos, clusters of cottonwoods, the sprawl of Saint George. On the ground, with nothing but the restrictive horizontal perspective—the curse of all flightless, earthbound creatures—it's a labyrinth. But from up here, Zeus's view, everything becomes cartographically clear. Saint George, population 55,000, is transformed into a toy town with checkerboard blocks and tiny sidewalks. Highway 9 and Interstate 15 are logical lines connecting Saint George with the nearby communities of Washington and Hurricane. The Virgin and Santa Clara rivers snake easily between flat-topped mesas, following the paths of least resistance. A miniature world exists down there, appearing so orderly and purposeful that it inspires a wondrous sense of serenity.

Until: "Mark!" The voice on the helmet radio screeches in my ears. "This is Frederick. Looks like you're enjoying yourself up there. Ready to try landing?"

I check my watch. I've been flying for over an hour, buzzing around in giant, meditative circles.

"Uhh, right. Why not."

"Okay, Mark. Finish off the downwind leg, drop to one hundred AGL on the base, turn into the upwind leg, and let's see if you can bring her in."

No sweat. I cruise over the landing zone (LZ) and give Frederick Scheffel, my instructor, a heroic thumbs-up, stomp the left steering bar, arc tightly, ease back on the throttle, float down to one hundred feet above ground level (AGL), and line up the landing field.

But something's wrong. I seem to be sliding sideways in the air, drifting to the left. The aircraft is unwilling to fly straight. For a moment I can't figure it out. Then my eyes snap toward the orange windsock on a pole in the field. On my final pass over the LZ, I have been explicitly told to observe the orientation of the windsock. Now I realize that the wind has shifted ninety degrees since I took off. I'm descending perpendicular to a gusty crosswind—a stupid, potentially dangerous mistake.

Suddenly I'm quite close to the ground. The wind is blowing me toward a barbed-wire fence. Scheffel's cautionary horror stories ricochet through my head: the "brainless fool" who tried to land on a moving train, tangled with some utility wires, and died when he smacked head-first into the moving cars; the "idiot" who crashed into a barbed-wire fence and had to be sewn back together with forty stitches. Starting to panic, I instinctively grab the front-wheel lever and try to steer away from the fence rushing toward me, but my terrestrial reflexes won't help me now, and turning the front wheel won't turn the damn aircraft. I frantically jam the lever as far as it will go, but, of course, the ultralight will not respond.

I realize I'm going to smash into the flesh-shredding barbed wire and become the next idiot.

"Mark! What the hell . . . ? Throttle. Throttle!"

My flooded brain is unable to translate this strange language, but somehow my right hand gets the message and shoves the throttle to the hilt. At the last second, when I can almost feel the barbed wire snagging on the seat of my pants, I zoom back up into the soft, welcoming sky.

• • •

Even before there were written words, humans dreamed of flying, envying the freedom of flitting songbirds and marveling at the raptors soaring overhead. The desire to fly is so ubiquitous in ancient myth and folklore that it seems hardwired into our consciousness.

Four thousand years ago, the Chinese emperor Shun was said to have taken off by flapping two large reed hats. Egypt's sun god, Ra, is often depicted wearing falcon wings. Greek mythology recounts the fatal flight of Icarus, whose wax wings melted when he flew too close to the sun. The Tang dynasty poet Li Po claimed to have been borne aloft in a chariot pulled by a phoenix and a dragon. Milarepa, an eleventh-century Tibetan Buddhist monk, was said to have attained the gift of flight and ridden a small drum to the top of holy Mount Kailas.

It was only a matter of time before mortals attempted takeoff. In the early eleventh century, a monk named Eilmer leaped from a tower in Malmesbury, England. With winglike contraptions strapped to his arms, he managed to glide several hundred yards before tumbling from the sky and breaking both legs.

Four centuries later, over a period of forty years, Leonardo da Vinci produced more than 400 sketches and 35,000 words in his obsessive attempts to figure out the mechanics of flying. In the late eighteenth century, a British scientist named George Cayley formulated the basic principles of flight: lift, drag, weight, and thrust. In 1853, Cayley convinced his coachman to climb aboard a glider and soar above the English countryside; he became the first human being to fly and survive unscathed. Fifty years later, two American bicycle manufacturers, Wilbur and Orville Wright, ushered in the era of powered aviation with Orville's twelve-second flight at Kitty Hawk, North Carolina, on December 17, 1903.

The rest is history. Biplanes, the Red Baron, mail planes, Lindbergh, World War II bombers, jet planes, commercial airliners, the Concorde, the space shuttle. Decade by decade, planes grew bigger and faster until routine flight became about as adventurous as a bus ride across Kansas.

But even as aeronautical innovation accelerated, a small core of purists were determined to recapture the visceral sensation of birdlike flight. In the early seventies, aviation throwbacks would haul their rudimentary hang gliders up some remote hillock and leap off. Crashes were common; tinkering with new designs, habitual.

In 1975, a thirty-two-year-old glider pilot named John Moody attached a ten-horsepower, two-stroke Chrysler motor to his glider, the

Icarus II. A year later, he flew it at the Experimental Aircraft Association Fly-In Convention, in Oshkosh, Wisconsin, introducing the world to ultralight flying. By early 1980, Dick Eipper, founder of San Diego–based glider manufacturer Quicksilver, began selling the first commercially successful fixed-wing ultralight kit, for $2,995. Three years later, the powered parachute (PPC), a twin-engine version powered by two counter-rotating propellers, made its debut at the Sun 'n Fun air show in Lakeland, Florida. It was the rebirth of adventure flying: retro, counter-culture, seat-of-the-pants.

"We were renegades back then, and I guess we still are," says Scott Wilcox, veteran pilot and editor-in-chief of *Ultralight Flying!*, a twenty-nine-year-old publication based in Chattanooga, Tennessee, not far from Lookout Mountain, one of the original hang-glider hills. "Ultralight flying isn't about transportation; it's about the magic of pure, simple flight."

Today there are more than 15,000 ultralight pilots and more than one hundred ultralight manufacturers in the United States. Defined by the Federal Aviation Administration as an aircraft that weighs less than 254 pounds and carries no more than five gallons of gas, modern ultralights fall into six different categories: fixed-winged aircraft that resemble stripped-down versions of conventional small airplanes; trikes, which have a hang-glider-type wing with a carriage for engine and pilot; motorized hang gliders; powered paragliders, in which the engine and caged propeller are mounted on a backpack and connected by cords to a parachute; gyrocopters; and the go-cart-like PPCs. Although regulated by the FAA, ultralighting does not require a pilot's license. For the price of a used car, you can buy your own flying machine and soar away.

• • •

But first you need to learn to fly. That's why I'd signed up for a four-day course at SkyTrails Ranch, a PPC training center in Saint George. Founded in 1999 by Scheffel and fellow pilot Paul Gooch, SkyTrails takes advantage of the high desert's stable weather and consistent flying conditions.

At first glance, the powered parachute appears a hermaphroditic aircraft—half loud, thrusting engine, half soft, pliant airfoil. But the combination creates a surprisingly forgiving flying machine. The cart—which carries the engine, prop, and pilot—hangs like a pendulum below the thirty-six-foot-wide canopy. In the air, the craft always self-corrects. For example, press a steering bar as far as it will go and you'll begin to spiral downward, the cart swinging outward with considerable centrifugal force. Simply let off on the bar, however, and the cart will stabilize beneath the rectangular chute.

The parachute, a series of sewn-together hollow tubes that inflate when airborne, has the unique ability to rebuild itself in less than fifty vertical feet of drop. Translation: If for some reason your wing collapses in a freak wind, the chute will balloon back into shape within seconds. The PPC, in other words, is its own emergency landing device. Top speed for the PPC is thirty-two miles per hour, and its maximum range (due to the five-gallon fuel limitation) is about fifty miles.

Straightforward as they are to fly, PPCs are still aircraft, and not idiot-proof; learning aeronautical basics is essential. Three other students and I spent the first day at SkyTrails in ground school, working through the 260-page *Powered Parachute Guide and Training Manual*: Bernoulli's principle, thrust versus drag, lift versus weight, wing loading, propeller/engine torque compensation, wake turbulence, density altitude—flight theory that seemed complicated on the ground but began to make sense once I was airborne. On day two, after practicing taxiing, turning, and kiting (accelerating until the chute pops up above your cart) on a dirt field southeast of town, we notched our inaugural flight, an instructor-assisted soar in a two-seater PPC.

Later that day, I took my first solo flight. Following my near miss with the barbed-wire fence, after my heart rate dropped below 200, I managed to land into the wind, safely and properly. As I rolled to a stop and cut the engine, Scheffel ambled toward me.

"Just practicing my below-radar maneuvers," I said, pulling off my sweat-drenched helmet.

Scheffel grimaced and stared at me through his aviator sunglasses. A stubby, suntanned, sandy-haired fifty-two-year-old, he is normally chipper as a sparrow.

"The powered parachute is the safest ultralight there is, Mark. Only twenty-six people in the past two decades have figured out how to kill themselves flying one." A smile was sneaking up on him. "I've taught hundreds of people to fly, and no student of mine has ever even broken a fingernail. I don't expect this to change. Now, what'd you do wrong?"

I humbly enumerated my mistakes. Showing off and not checking the windsock. Consequently trying to land across the wind. In a panic, mixing up ground steering (wheel-turning lever) with aeronautical steering (foot bars). Forgetting to throttle up when it was apparent the landing should be aborted.

"You got it," Scheffel said. "Put your helmet back on. I want you to kite your chute and do a preflight. You're going right back up."

I refueled the PPC, gave it a thorough inspection, and flicked the engine switch on. As soon as the motor warmed up, I shoved the throttle forward and began rolling fast down the dirt. Within a few seconds, the chute leaped up above me, and I was airborne.

An hour later, when I came safely back to earth, I'd been grinning so hard my teeth were speckled with bugs.

•   •   •

Because of their unique ability to fly low and slow, ultralights offer pilots an unparalleled proximity to the avian world. In 1982, ultralight pioneer Tracy Knauss filmed the endangered Peruvian condor for ABC Sports' *The American Sportsman* series, setting a precedent for ultralight-assisted wildlife research. In 1988, an organization called Operation Migration began using ultralights to teach flight routes to Canada geese; for the past seven years, it's been raising and training flocks of endangered whooping crane hatchlings to follow safe migratory paths.

Certainly the most poignant and widely acclaimed example of the use of ultralights is the 2003 documentary film *Winged Migration*, by French director Jacques Perrin. Using ultralights, Perrin and his crew of eighteen pilots and dozens of cinematographers flew in formation with greylag geese, red-crowned cranes, white storks, and two dozen other species on their astounding thousand-mile global journeys. Taking advantage of birds' ability to imprint on their human "parents," Perrin's team of ornithologists spent a year breeding, raising, and training the chicks to tolerate close-quarters filming and three years shooting the documentary. The result is the most intimate portrait of avian flight captured on film. It makes you want to fly. It made me want to fly.

On day three at SkyTrails Ranch, I'm drifting through the sky at 1,000 feet AGL. This morning I practiced flybys: cruising over the LZ and attempting to hold the ultralight level at various elevations. First one hundred feet, then fifty feet, then forty, then twenty. In the early afternoon I practiced touch-taxi-and-go landings, in which you graze the earth, kite your chute, then rocket right back into the sky. I reduced the propeller's RPMs on each landing, finally alighting with the engine at a low idle.

Now for the final test: an "emergency" landing with the engine turned off.

"Mark, this is Frederick. Are you ready?" I'm not, but I say I am.

"All right, anytime you want."

I reach out my arm, place my fingers on the engine-off switch, and hesitate.

The powered parachute's engine is needed only for propulsion. Without the engine, the PPC will float back to earth at half the rate of an ordinary parachutist, practically landing itself. I know this intellectually, but that doesn't mean squat. It seems like unshakable common sense to believe that when an aircraft's engines go, everybody dies. For a split second, ugly scenes try to squeeze into my brain: planes nosediving, twirling, screeching, explosions on impact.

I hit the switch. The engine sputters, the propeller slows to a click. Silence.

My heart jumps when I find that I am not falling out of the sky. I have tipped slightly downward and am gradually, gracefully descending. The experience is so viscerally thrilling, so primeval and satisfying, a laugh of relief and joy escapes from my chest. I float back to earth as calm as a feather.

• • •

On the last day of class, I fly a cross-country loop. Out over a sea of red sand dunes, I skim just above one butte after another, eventually arcing left and following the silvery Virgin River back to the landing field.

It's supposed to be the end of the course, but I can't get enough. I want to go up just one more time.

It is early evening when I lift off; long purple shadows streak the scarlet desert. I head off in a direction I've never gone before and fly higher than I've ever flown—1,000, 2,000, 3,000 feet. From this height I can see the gentle curve of the earth. From this height the magnificence of landscape overwhelms the minuscule marks of humankind. Up here, there is only open sky and unspoiled earth. It's a perspective so holistic that every human should have the opportunity to experience it.

At 3,500 feet AGL I shut off the engine. The empty silence surrounds me. I am alone in space. Only the faint flutter of the nylon wing above me can be heard. I've spent much of my ascent looking down; now I look up and out and am shocked to find I'm not alone. From out of a clear blue sky, a bird: Flying beside me is a juvenile bald eagle. For unknown reasons, perhaps just youthful curiosity, the eagle is escorting me through the warm welkin.

We are parallel, so close to each other I can see the animal's feathers tremble. The eagle twists its head, looks me in the eye, and turns its regal beak back into the wind.

LEAP YEAR

At last we alighted on the south coast of Spain. A family of four from America, traipsing through the Málaga airport with overstuffed daypacks and four bulging duffels, four bulging bicycle boxes, and two sturdy computer cartons. Disheveled and greasy with the residua of transit, so exhausted that our two daughters' heads were bobbing, in any other country (especially our own) our huddled little mass would have been easy prey for customs officials with a taste for harassing tired refugees. Fortunately, this was España. The officers had trim Franco outfits but a languid indifference, and we barreled our laden carts straight out into a sweltering Iberian afternoon, no one even bothering to check our passports.

We had hoped to catch a bus, train, or taxi up the Mediterranean coast to our destination, the pueblo of Salobreña, but none would accommodate our small mountain of possessions. Instead, we rented an absurdly large moving van, loaded our bags, squeezed into the cab, and set off just after dark along a winding contour line of asphalt. My wife and girls fell instantly into dreams while I navigated a causeway suspended between an indigo sky and the sable sea, two voluptuous bodies winking at each other like old lovers.

Creeping into Salobreña, I parked by moonlight and woke my family. The air was moist and perfumed with jasmine. It was not possible to drive to our new home. The road up to the house started out only five feet wide and narrowed down to the width of my shoulders—"*la calle más estrecha de Salobreña*," the narrowest street in town. So we half-sleepwalked up the cobblestone lane to our oblong courtyard, gladly leaving our ponderous luggage in the van. Traveling light we were not, but then we weren't traveling—we were moving.

At noon the next day, eyelids heavy from jet lag and cascades of sunshine, we set about exploring. Our new casa was old whitewashed stucco, and its big windows faced south, like all the other houses built into the hillside. We shared walls with our neighbors, who shared walls with theirs, and so on—a contiguous community called El Barrio de la Fuente, situated just below the ruins of a tenth-century Moorish castle. It had stone-tile floors and ceramic-tile walls, a porch lined with potted plants, and two terraces: a lower one, which looked out over a clanking welding shop and the town park, and another on the rooftop, affording a 270-degree panorama. To the west spread the hazy, azure Mediterranean, with Africa out there somewhere; straight ahead, to the south, the ancient alluvial sugarcane fields and the new condos inexorably consuming them; and to the east, the dusty brown foothills of the Alpujarras set against the cool whaleback of the Sierra Nevada.

It didn't feel like home, but that was the point.

• • •

Three months later, as I look out from the wide-open window of my office-cum-living room, the mercurial seascape is flat navy blue, as unmoving as an abstract painting. It is late morning, and my daughters, Addi, eleven, and Teal, nine, have caught the bus to their Spanish school, their backpacks stuffed with heavy textbooks. Sue, my wife, is taking a long run on the beach and then circling back to buy fresh shrimp for supper. Magdalena, our octogenarian neighbor, who is tinier than Teal, has taken her wee, blind, crippled, octogenarian dog—a beast whose bark sounds exactly like a baby crying (I've daydreamed of surreptitiously easing it into the afterlife)—for a walk, in her arms. Next door, infirm Antonia has flung a pail of mop water into the courtyard, and her grandson is feeding the exotic, egg-size canaries in the lightless rock cave beneath her house. Belinda, behind us, is bellowing from her terrace at little Manuelito, in the park two blocks away, to come home and pee before he pees his pants. *El panadero* has made his house-to-house deliveries with the large sack of baguettes; the propane-gas man has lugged an orange canister up to our front grate; *el cartero*, who buzzes around town on a yellow moped outfitted with yellow saddlebags, has delivered our day's mail from the States. And my father has sent an e-mail telling me not to worry—he fixed the toilet in our house, which churlishly broke right after we left Wyoming.

So I guess we've settled in.

Sue and I talked about moving abroad for years, scheming and dreaming and putting aside money. It was part of my family history—when I was thirteen, my family moved to northern Holland for a year; my father, a mathematician, was on sabbatical. Although we spoke not a word of

Dutch, all six of us kids were plunged directly into local schools. We floundered valiantly out of sheer desperation, quickly learned how to float with just a few words, began to kick a bit, then dog-paddled, and eventually swam (not gracefully, but passably). Submerged in a new culture, that one year abroad altered us all. The world would forevermore be beckoning—vast beyond imagination, resplendent and revolting, perplexingly complex, contradictory, ceaselessly intriguing. Sue and I wanted our girls to have their own eye-widening opportunity.

Being a writer, I'm fortunate enough to have a transplantable job, so that wasn't an obstacle. And yet life got in the way and the years clicked by until one day we looked up, noticed that Addi and Teal were already half grown, and realized that it was now or never. It was a simple decision, really: In six months we would leave on a yearlong sojourn. Thereafter, each piece more or less fit into an unfinished puzzle that we solved as we went along.

The high plains of Wyoming are rightfully famous for their brutal weather, and we all agreed that we wanted a change of climate. Sue is fluent in Spanish, hence a Spanish-speaking country seemed sensible. Beyond that, each of us had personal criteria. Sue wanted the girls to learn classic Castilian—the most widely used form of Spanish—versus Catalan, Galician, or Basque. I wanted to be no more than one hour from the mountains and, for my work, no more than two from an international airport. Addi and Teal, realizing we were presumptuously making decisions for them and convinced that they had thus far led deprived childhoods living 1,200 miles from the nearest ocean, insisted that we be no more than an hour from the beach.

In this way, we chose Spain.

Unspoken but understood was that we wanted a community small enough to perambulate but that also had DSL. A community that was still Spanish—not an expat colony of Brits, Swedes, or Germans—but wasn't hidebound in medieval prejudices. A community that had paella and pizza. A tall order.

"Andalusia. That's where we'll go!" Sue announced one night at dinner.

In April, Sue and I flew over on a reconnaissance mission, rented a car, and found Salobreña on the first day. A town of 10,500 inhabitants, it could be traversed on foot in eight minutes. The beach was a five-minute walk away; 800-foot limestone climbing crags a ten-minute drive; the Sierra Nevada, Spain's highest mountain range, only an hour north. Before we left, we signed a lease on a furnished house, paid our first month's rent, and spoke with the principal of an elementary school for the girls.

In early August, after renting out our house in Laramie (fully furnished, plates to computers), rearranging our banking to live off ATM cards, and loaning our two cars to kin, we pulled up stakes and fired ourselves, as if out of a cannon, over the big pond. In less than twenty-four hours, we had traded the dry, landlocked spread of Wyoming—where there are more deer and antelope than people, and nine months of winter—for the sticky, flesh-covered Costa Tropical, where some form of summer reigns year-round.

By day two, the bikes were reassembled and Addi and Teal were out exploring. In one week, we had obtained a *certificado de empadronamiento*, our census certificate. In two weeks, we had willingly converted from expensive microbrews to cheap micro-*riojas*. In three weeks we had purchased a used Volkswagen Golf, the standard Euro family car, with 130,000 kilometers on the odometer. After a month, we had a high-speed Internet connection, supplementing our addiction to the BBC.

A little patience, *poco dinero*, a lot of running around, and before I could properly pronounce *destornillador* (screwdriver), we were rookie members of the European community.

• • •

Living abroad, like isolationism and xenophobia, is a venerable American tradition. Benjamin Franklin lived in England for almost eighteen years and in Paris for more than seven. Mark Twain settled in Europe for a decade. Hemingway and Fitzgerald, Matthiessen and Plimpton, and many other Yanks temporarily sank roots into foreign soil.

According to a 1999 US Bureau of Consular Affairs report, there are almost 4 million American civilians living abroad: a thousand in Tanzania; 38,000 in Taiwan; 450 in Mongolia; a hundred or so in Turkmenistan; about 95,000 in Spain. Among the millions are diplomats, Peace Corps volunteers, teachers, nurses, exchange students, and multinational corporations' employees. All have chosen to forsake close friends and relatives, fine neighborhoods, and favorite routines to live overseas for a time.

Many go for the same reasons we travel: to experience the unfamiliar. To eat goat cheese from the green cave of Magaha, *queso de cabra* that is so acridly tart it makes your mouth water. To follow doglegging lanes in a mountain village until you're convinced you're lost, only to suddenly realize that you're right back where you started (the recursive metaphor of travel, again). To witness customs that we could hardly imagine: two oxen, say, garlanded with delicate violet blossoms, pulling a cart carrying a small statue of Santa Maria del Rosario, the patron saint of Salobreña.

Yet moving abroad is more profound than traveling. It goes beyond curiosity to commitment. If to travel is to be a stone skipping lightly over the water, to move abroad is to stop and allow yourself to sink into an alien world, gulping to breathe a different language. Moving abroad is full immersion in a strange country, being forced to make a new life there, using little more than whatever wit, wisdom, openheartedness, and evenhandedness you carry inside you.

Perhaps the principal difference is this: To travel is to expect much of the places you visit; to move to one of these places is to expect much of yourself. No longer just passing by, to function at all you must step through the façade of pageantry and figure out how things actually work in your adopted nation.

Some of this is banal. When is garbage collected? (Midnight.) Where is the wine-bottle-recycling container? (By the bus stop.) What is the word for the female end of a telephone jack? (I still have no idea.) Which *ferretería* (hardware store) has *clavos pequeños* (little nails)?

And some of this is sublime. Discovering the back way to the girls' school, a paved path beneath limestone caves, past a baaing-goat pen, through tall sugarcane, around the last sugarcane factory in all of Europe, through the burnt-maple air to *Colegio San Juan de Ávila*. Sleeping on the rooftop on warm summer nights. Drinking a new red wine with a late dinner on the terrace and finding that *Sangre de Toro* has the more poetic name, but that nondescript *Tarragona de Baturrica* has a more robust flavor. Learning words that are so much more mellifluous than their English counterparts—*melocotónes meloso, ciruelas redondo, chorizo* (sweet peaches, round plums, sausage). It is through such words and such modest, quotidian undertakings that one begins, *poco a poco*, to learn a new language— the central challenge of living abroad.

At this moment, my daughters are at school. Addi is perhaps studying geography, learning the Spanish names for countries she never knew existed, or maybe she is working on division, which Spaniards write backward and which schoolchildren are taught to do entirely in their heads. Teal has a test today spelling out the ordinal numbers, *primero hasta tregísimo* (first through thirtieth), and later she'll be practicing the Spanish terms for the anatomy of the eye. All three of us will get another kitchen-table language lesson from Sue tonight. At the last tutorial, Sue informed me that it was time I stop speaking Spanish like a Latin Tarzan and get cracking on my conjugations.

It is not possible to know a country well without knowing its language. Language is the magic key that opens the imposing gates to another kingdom. Once inside, everything looks different, not the least of which is your mother country on the other side of the fence. What you actually see and feel and believe—that is, who you are—depends a great deal on where you're standing on the globe. Once again, geography is destiny.

· · ·

I've just returned from my noon bike ride. The loop begins with a cruise through the groves of cherimoya trees—which grow a sweetish fruit that you spoon out of its scalloped green skin—along the broad Guadalfeo River bottom. A gushing canal runs along the narrow strip of asphalt. Beyond the fruit trees, the road climbs into long-ago-terraced mountains, passing through several small villages where old men in berets sit in the shade of somnolent stone churches.

As the road curls deeper into the mountains, it becomes ridiculously steep, which makes for a fabulous workout. (No wonder Lance Armstrong trained in Spain.) It is a road steeper than anything ever allowed in the United States, but rules, wonderfully, are anathema to the Spanish. Speed-limit signs are as rare as traffic police, and people drive as fast as their little tin boxes will move. Drivers graciously give cyclists a wide berth but, oddly, appear to aim for pedestrians. When a vehicle finally comes to a halt, it does so wherever the driver pleases, like a toddler falling asleep in the middle of the living-room floor. Double parking is de rigueur, triple parking fair play. Of course, the narrow cobblestone streets were originally designed to accommodate little more than a mule and cart. Triple parking usually blocks the entire thoroughfare, giving all involved something to honk and yell and wave their hands about, which they seem to enjoy far more than actually getting to where they're trying to go.

But this is to be expected—Americans always whine about how foreigners drive, from Madrid to Madras. Now that I'm the foreigner, I've quite happily learned how to park with half the car up on the sidewalk and take joy in using my horn. It's the consciousness of a culture that really matters, not so much its formal regulations. Fathoming this takes time and requires forbearance, a virtue that matures immensely when you choose to live abroad. Suddenly you are an uninformed minority—a healthy experience for an American. We are, after all, a nation of immigrants, yet within only one or two generations we so easily forget how difficult it can be to adapt to unfamiliar territory.

America's immense economic and military strength make us believe we are a majority on this globe. Nothing could be more ludicrous. There are more Europeans than Americans, more Africans, more Indians, more Chinese, more South Americans. And yet, living only in the United States, you could easily imagine that being number one in all things is a divine birthright. This has the potential to breed an ugly closemindedness. Not surprisingly, then, one inevitable outcome of a move overseas is a renewed respect for the teeming diversity of humankind, a recognition that there are at least a dozen ways to skin a cat—and they're all right.

Of course, living abroad—even speaking the language and settling there for years—doesn't make you a true insider. You will always be a foreigner, but if you're lucky you may come away with a perspective on your new home that the locals don't have and find you've become a fledgling connoisseur of red wine and olive oil.

As I rolled back down into Salobreña, it was just after 2:00 p.m. From every household, the soul-nourishing aromas of home cooking wafted out the open windows and along the streets. Nose uplifted, I gloried like a bloodhound in the different smells: *cerdo* (pork) sautéing in garlic, *papas fritas* (fried potatoes), *sopa de albóndigas* (meatball soup).

We didn't move to Spain to recover some rustic, romantic, agrarian life. That's been gone for some time. Rather, we moved to live surrounded by whatever traditions are here now. As when, at the stroke of 2:00, citizens one and all pull down the heavy metal grates of their work life, physically and metaphorically, and go home to their families for *la cena grande*—the big meal. Somehow, amid all the shove and shuffle of the modern commercial world, the Spanish have had the good sense to still organize work around life, instead of the other way around. Imagine stopping right in the middle of your fervid workday and taking a three-hour break. One hour to enjoy your meal with your family, one hour to converse extravagantly, using all body parts, and one hour for a deep, restful siesta. Can you think of anything more decadent or more civilized?

Pulling up beneath the kitchen window of my house, I could hear the girls, already out of school for the day, laughing, and I could smell Sue's shrimp paella cooking on the stove.

Vivir la vida.

MEDITATION ON MEDITATION

Sit still. Focus on the breath.

Breathe in, breathe out. Breathe in. . . . I can't help but notice that the petite blonde beside me is exhaling so loudly—with rhythmic nasal hoots—that she must have fully transcended her thoughts. Am I the only loser in the room who's not in a trance?

I'm at meditation camp. I know—I can't believe it either. If there are two things in this world I'm fundamentally incapable of, they are sitting still and not thinking. I was walking at seven months old, running at eight months. When I was nine years old, my Sunday-school teacher apprised me that I was "headed for hell" for asking impertinent questions. In college, I majored in philosophy—Nietzsche, Kierkegaard, and Heidegger were my gurus. Later, between expeditions, I spent years training myself to write, which is just thinking on paper.

There I go again.

Focus, please. Breathe in, breathe out. Breathe in. I lift my eyes ever so slightly and sneak a peek out the window. Freedom! All I want is to be outside, hiking, biking, mowing the lawn even—it doesn't matter. I just have to move.

I think, therefore I am; I do, therefore I live—my two mantras for as long as I can remember. So why subject myself to a three-day sufferfest of sitting?

I blame it partly on Grasshopper. The TV series *Kung Fu* caught me at an impressionable age, and its star, a martial-arts apprentice named Grasshopper, was my idea of cool. ("Grasshopper, when you can walk on the rice paper without tearing it, then your steps will not be heard . . .") He was always getting himself into some kind of exciting mess, meditating on it, then kicking ass.

Science is responsible for the rest. It's no big secret that meditation is known to reduce stress, but recent research suggests that it may also improve athletic performance. Erik Ekker Solberg, a sports-medicine specialist and cardiologist in Oslo, Norway, has been researching the psychobiological effects of meditation for more than a decade. Among his discoveries: For competitive marksmen, regular meditation enhances the accuracy of shooting; and in a study of thirty-one male runners, those who practiced meditation twice a day for thirty minutes showed significantly reduced levels of lactic-acid buildup after exercise. Lactic acid is the burning sludge that forms in your muscles when you exert yourself. You can meditate that out of your system? Sign me up!

• • •

As it happens, a world-renowned institution of meditation, the Shambhala Mountain Center (SMC), is located just down the road from my Wyoming home, across the state line in Colorado. Founded in 1971 by Chögyam Trungpa Rinpoche, a Buddhist lama exiled from Tibet after the 1949 Chinese invasion, the SMC is an idyllic 600-acre Buddhist campus. Located at 8,000 feet in the Rockies, amid meadows and ponderosa forests, with a meditation hall, dorms, and a magnificent Buddhist shrine, the SMC is a place where Western idealism and Eastern spiritualism happily coexist. The center hosts 10,000 overnight visitors a year, most of whom are participating in personal quests, from three-day yoga seminars to month-long meditation intensives.

I signed up for an introductory weekend retreat in shamatha, or sitting, meditation. The SMC program description promised a regimented schedule—multihour sittings each day, relieved only by meals, a bit of walking meditation, and discussion. Yoga, the only optional activity, started each morning at 6:45 a.m.; lights-out was at 10:30 p.m. I booked a bed in the bunk room and bought the recommended reading, *Turning the Mind into an Ally*, by Sakyong Mipham Rinpoche (son of Chögyam Trungpa Rinpoche and spiritual leader of the SMC). I read it twice, underlined obsessively, and started training. Yes, training.

I admit it: I was scared. I don't think twice about climbing an unknown mountain in Uganda, tramping through waist-deep slime in the jungles of Burma, or riding horseback across Afghanistan, but the idea of driving less than an hour from my home to sit quietly in a room for three days freaked me out. I worried about keeping absolutely still, surrounded by a bunch of serious people, thinking serious thoughts when I shouldn't be thinking any thoughts at all.

So, as often as I could get up the nerve, I'd unroll a deep green Tibetan rug on the hardwood floor of our living room and sit. (The rug is symbolic to me; I bought it in Lhasa in 1986 from Tashi Tsering, author of *The Struggle for Modern Tibet*.) I'd sit still on the wool rug amid its twelve lotus flowers and attempt to focus on my breathing, and fail. One thought after another kept popping up, like those damn gophers in the carnival game—this story's due in two weeks, I'm thirsty, why aren't I outside climbing?—and I'd try to clobber every one with a fat mental bat.

I knew I was in trouble.

· · ·

Sure enough, on the first evening at camp, sitting with thirty-seven other students on blue cushions arranged across heated wood floors, I found myself thinking as hard as I could about not thinking. Our instructor, Greg Smith, a slight fifty-three-year-old with a gray beard who's been teaching meditation for nearly twenty-five years, had told us in a deep metronomic voice to "put your eyes in the middle distance and just focus on your breath. That's meditation. That's actually all there is to it." Closing your eyes all the way was strongly discouraged; you might fall asleep.

When I'd surreptitiously look around, it appeared everybody else already knew how to do this. The real estate agent to my left, the wildlife biologist to my right, the insurance consolidator behind me, the pharmaceutical salesman in front of me—they all looked tuned in. It was true: I was the worst meditator on the planet.

Back to the breath.

I concentrated with all I had and managed to hold on to the sensation of breathing for exactly three full breaths. Then I had to shrug my shoulders because of a sharp ache in my back, and then I had to shift my legs, and I thought about how sitting cross-legged isn't all that comfortable, and then I remembered how the Chinese can squat for hours, and I thought about all the monks I've met in Tibet and how, through years of practice and discipline, they can sit in the lotus position on cold stones for hours, which made me start thinking about what a weenie I was, which made me absolutely certain that I couldn't sit still for one more minute. . . .

When the gong finally sounded, I tried to stand up slowly and casually, as if I were waking from some perfect dream—when what I really wanted to do was to leap to my feet, howl obscenities, dash outside, and roll in the snow like a dog.

During the question-and-answer session that followed, I was secretly relieved to hear that others were struggling, too. When I told the group that my willful desire not to have thoughts was in itself a thought that was getting in the way of my not thinking, people chuckled in acknowledgment—or maybe pity. Smith eyed me with concern and said emphatically, "Let that go. Accept that you are going to have thoughts, just don't let them drag you around."

That night, lying in my sleeping bag in the dorm, I reread (by headlamp) portions of *Turning the Mind into an Ally*. "A bewildered mind is like a wild horse," Mipham writes in a chapter called "Bewilderment and Suffering." The wild horse needs to be tamed, but through gentle coaxing, not brute force. In a chapter called "How to Gather a Scattered Mind," he explains, "Holding the mind too tightly can be harmful. When our control is too tight, the mind will bolt at the earliest opportunity."

Mipham was affirming what I already knew: I was trying too hard.

I switched off my headlamp, dressed, and slipped out of the dorm. I was breaking curfew, but I needed some exercise. The sky was black above the aspens, the snow like an ocean. Walking alone through the forest, I thought back to when I had learned to ride a horse.

I worked on a ranch as a boy and was a terrible horseman. I was often reprimanded for holding the reins too tight, which would make my horse whinny and struggle and jerk its head. "Not too tight, not too loose," a cowboy once told me from the saddle, spitting brown tobacco juice and wiping his face with the back of his hand. Back at the dorm, when I picked up Mipham's book again, I noticed that "Not Too Tight, Not Too Loose" is the title of chapter ten.

• • •

So where have I been? Meditation made the cover of *Time* years ago, a sure sign that a trend has reached critical mass and the whole world's doing it. There are seemingly more meditation options than there are lattes at Starbucks: transcendental meditation, transformational meditation, tantric meditation, mantra meditation, vipassana meditation, shamatha meditation, and a hundred others. And the whole world's gone Zen: Zen golf, Zen gardening, Zen and the art of ferrets, Zen and the art of the mosh pit, Zen and the art of pumpkin bombing. Even Grasshopper—actor David Carradine—has been resurrected as a twisted Zen master in Quentin Tarantino's *Kill Bill* films.

Meditation is a practice older than Hinduism and Buddhism. Although the dogmas of both religious philosophies have become intertwined with meditation, the most basic reason for meditating is to calm the mind and live in the present. Shamatha, also called "peaceful abiding," is a physical and mental discipline. You sit cross-legged, back straight, head erect, eyes lowered, and train your mind to follow the breath. In and out, in and out—steady, calm, fluid. The point is to unshackle yourself from external distractions, the incessant discursiveness of thoughts, and any emotional roller-coasting. The goal is to be with yourself, in the moment, which will help you—voilà—unlock the secret to true happiness.

Or so they say. That first night at meditation camp, I dreamed I was trapped in a tight glass box in the sitting position.

The next morning, I shuffled through the snow from my dorm to the Sacred Studies Hall. Friends had raved about yoga for years—"It would be so good for you"—but I'd held out.

Only a third of the class showed up. For an hour and fifteen minutes, while focusing on our breathing, we went through a series of poses that both stretched and tensed my body: sun salutations, cobra, upward-facing dog, downward, triangle, corpse—the names sounded exotic to a neophyte like me. But I was sweating and my body was doing something and my mind was focused. Which is to say, my friends had been right.

After breakfast, it was back to the meditation cushion for a marathon four-hour session. This time I loosened up the reins, and the natural divagations of my mind seemed to distract me a little less. I discovered I could focus on the breathing, but still for only a few seconds at a time. In my best moments, my mind shifted from concentrating on my breath to hearing my heart inside my chest. I could feel the blood surging down through my arms and out to my fingertips, moving down my legs and into my feet.

We took a break for walking meditation—strolling so slowly that it's quite possible to lose your balance and fall over—and then did another Q&A with Smith. He asked us to describe the sensations we were having.

Some of us said we could only hold on to a single breath; others said they could go for five or ten. When I mentioned that I could feel the blood streaming through my body, Smith seemed surprised. "That could be indicative of a deep state of meditation," he said.

I wish.

• • •

For the afternoon, we were instructed to abide by noble silence. Meaning: no talking for the next six hours. I suspect we all wanted to get to know everybody else, but that wasn't the point of this retreat. Like it or not, we were here to get to know ourselves.

After a silent lunch, we walked in single file—slowly, solemnly, and silently, with our hands clasped in front of our stomachs like friars—through the snow up to the stupa. I kept thinking about hitting the woman in front of me with a snowball.

A stupa is a religious monument meant to remind humans of their potential for enlightenment. The Great Stupa of Dharmakaya, at the Shambhala Mountain Center, took thirteen years to build and enshrines the teachings of Chögyam Trungpa Rinpoche. Having seen hundreds in Asia, I can report that this stupa, right here in the middle of modern America, is one of the most stunningly beautiful ones on the planet. Resembling a tall, narrow, gold-topped crown, it's exactly 108 feet tall and (excuse my floridity) radiates tranquility.

We all sat and meditated inside it, although I spent most of my time staring up at the mandala on the ceiling, a gorgeously complex, worlds-within-worlds Buddhist version of the Sistine Chapel, painted by our instructor, Greg Smith, and a team of volunteers.

That afternoon, back at the Sacred Studies Hall, we meditated for two more hours. Like a kid after recess, I found I could relax better and focus more easily. I let my mind settle onto my breath and then, naturally, to the comforting thump of my heart. I could feel the blood circulating through my body like wind through the mountains. My breathing almost seemed to stop. Between my ordinary salmagundi of thoughts about sex and mayhem, I discovered that, now and again, I could actually be still and be in the moment. And whenever I got there, I was surprised to find that I recognized the feeling. I'd been there before.

We ate dinner in silence, which I enjoyed—back at home with my family, I can barely get a word in edgewise. Noble silence was then lifted for *rota*, or chores. I volunteered for kitchen duty, which I've always considered a good chance to goof off. Then someone broke out a bottle of wine (yes, it's allowed), which struck me as promising—maybe we'd get to know each other—until people started wandering off to bed. Just in time for lights-out.

Later, after everybody in my dorm room was asleep, I slipped out again. It was snowing, and I decided to hike up to the stupa. I didn't move fast or slow; I just walked at a natural pace. There are few experiences more grounding or more peaceful than walking through snowfall in the dark. When I reached the stupa, it was luminescent, bathed in faint light from four floodlights, one in each corner of the grounds.

I began to circumnavigate the monument clockwise. I walked and listened to the snow crunch underfoot. Ever since yoga practice, I'd been coming to something in my mind. I just didn't know what it was.

The floodlights created four wedges of light separated by four large spaces of darkness. A line of prayer flags curved upward from each of the floodlights to the top of the stupa. On each circle, I stopped beneath a different line of red flags, put my head back, and stood there inside a magical curtain of falling snow. Tiny flakes wet my face like rain. At an undetermined moment, I would step out of the panel of twinkling light back into the empty blackness.

The snowfall was so faint it could hardly be felt or seen between the floodlight beams. I was listening to my footfalls in the snow, making my seventh circumambulation of the stupa, not thinking a thing, when I was struck by something: There had been many times in my life when I was calm, limpid, and fully present—they just didn't happen when I was sitting. They happened when I was climbing.

When I'm leading on rock or ice, I'm usually so focused that it's impossible for a thought to slip in. There is no chatter, no emotion, no analysis. It must be the feeling experienced by a single-handed sailor when he centers all his energy on surviving a storm, or by a kayaker when he's fluidly running dangerous whitewater. Smith had said that in deep states of meditation you don't simply feel the breath; you become the breath.

Perhaps it's the innate fear of falling, but when I'm leading well, I'm not merely moving; I feel like the movement itself. I could have it all wrong, but I'd bet the sensation a monk experiences after meditating is much the same as the rush of euphoria and peacefulness that comes over me after leading a pitch.

I practically danced back to the dorm that night. Along the way, I remembered once asking my fourteen-year-old daughter, Addi, who is a competitive swimmer and has loved water since she was a baby, what she thought about lap after lap.

"Nothing. Water washes away all my worries. I'm just moving through the liquid."

No matter what hormone-fueled teenage mood she's in when she goes to swim practice, she inevitably comes home flushed and cheerful.

I remembered what my wife told me after running the Boston Marathon. Minutes after she'd crossed the finish line, I asked, "What are you thinking about mile after mile?"

"I'm not," she said.

The next day, back in the Sacred Studies Hall, I once again failed miserably at sitting meditation, but it didn't bother me too much. After all, I'm just beginning. Then again, maybe I've been meditating my whole life.

THE PATH OF APPRENTICESHIP

I glide through the forest. As I sink into each turn, the powder rolls up my thighs. My skis carve crescents through the open firs, neither fast nor slow but with ease, like a looping stroke of calligraphy.

This is my third ski tour in Yellowstone. Today I skied from basecamp up to Heart Lake and back, traversing a couple of small passes, navigating by compass through two snow squalls, and fording a river. Now it is dusk, and so cold that my beard has frozen into a thicket of ice bristles.

I slide into a broad meadow and cut silently over the drifts. My wax, a blue kicker over buffed green, is splendid. I'm practically levitating. Kicking, floating on one ski balanced like an ice skater, then kicking with the other leg. It's a rhythm so natural and elegant that once you've mastered it, the movement—instead of the speed or the distance covered or the day's destination—becomes an end in itself. Kick, glide . . . kick, glide . . . kick, glide . . .

Through this motion, this mantra of muscle, I slip into a state of grace. Everything fits. The darkling sky mirrored in the violet snow. The snow feeding the trees and the hidden creek. The creek cutting the mountains. The mountains and me. We all dovetail together.

The tent comes into view, an orange speck set inside sentries of thin-limbed aspen. I stop. I'm drawn to the tent, but also reluctant. I don't want this long day, so smooth and solid, to end.

My mind goes on ahead. Not far from the tent, steam is rising into the frigid air. Ah, the thermal pools, the deep warmth of summer in the dead of winter. Dan Moe and Keith Spenser, my companions, will already be there. Long johns hung on upended skis, heads back against a mossy log, white bodies sunk up to their sunburned necks in the gorgeous hot water.

Soon I'll join them. In an hour it will be night and −20°F and dark as only distant mountains can be. Soaking, we'll lean back and stare up at the crystalline stars. Dan will name the constellations: Gemini with Castor and Pollux, Canis Major, Ursa Major, Boötes the Herdsman. An hour later, like a resurrection, the moon will rise and the snow will sparkle and we'll still be luxuriating in the delicious pools. After all but dissolving, we'll climb up the five-foot rim of snow, dash naked to the tent, and dive into our sleeping bags.

I see myself safely cocooned in down, my toes curled around a hot-water bottle, writing in my journal and plotting the day's travel on the topo. When the coyotes begin to sing, the call and response bounding over the luminous snow like the nimble animals themselves, I'll switch off the headlamp and listen, more at home than I am at home.

Standing on my skis and leaning on the poles, I turn and look back. I can just make out the faint line of my tracks scalloping down the last steep slope, then running straight to me, as if bringing a secret message. This simple line, disappearing backward, gives me a profound sense of satisfaction.

It occurs to me, as I push off and begin again to kick and glide, that I almost know what I'm doing. The next thing that comes to mind is Woody Jensen.

• • •

Like other callow young men, I took up karate in college. *Okinawa-te.* Woody Jensen was the instructor. He was fluid, lean as a marathon runner. Every muscle was defined, from his corded neck to his knotted calves. He was spareness itself, every kick, every step, every word precise.

We stretched for twenty minutes before each lesson. Woody could touch his palms to the floor. He could do Chinese splits. After stretching, we practiced kicks. Side kick, front kick, roundhouse. Again and again. Woody would walk among his pupils, wordlessly repositioning the angle of an ankle or the twist of a hip.

We spent less time punching. "The leg is seven times stronger and one-third longer than the arm," he told us. We were expected to rehearse the kicks until our legs moved with alacrity and accuracy.

I was always eager to try, if incapable of executing, the more difficult kicks. While other novitiates were humbly perfecting the simple front kick, I would be leaping into the air and spinning like a Bruce Lee wannabe.

Woody also emphasized the katas—formalized, sequential routines that, if diligently practiced, teach one the basic skills of karate: blocks, feints, kicks, punches, steps, turns. My favorite was the *Seiuchin* kata, but I can't say I worked at it consistently or intelligently. To get it right was a slow process. I was impatient.

One evening Woody was watching me go through the motions.

"You are a fast learner," he said. "It is unfortunate."

I was dumbfounded by this hard-shelled nut of truth. It became my own personal koan, one that would take me years to crack open.

Woody knew I was far more passionate about the outdoors than about karate. One spring day when it was snowing hard—huge flakes dashing themselves against the windowpane like desperate hummingbirds— Woody called me out of a kata and told me to leave class and go cross-country skiing that minute. On another occasion, when honeyed sunlight came pouring through the window and I felt trapped indoors like a bug in a jar, he excused me from class early and suggested I go rock climbing.

After I had been in karate for about six months, I was allowed to spar. I was fearful and reckless. One evening I sparred with Woody. I was fighting—kicking and punching and spinning—while he was dancing— swaying his hips, deftly bobbing his head, sweeping his arms. Nothing I did touched him. Exasperated, I attempted a spinning back kick—a committing move. Instead of ducking out of the way (I telegraphed badly), Woody slipped inside my flailing offense and stabbed his foot on the little toe of my pivoting foot. My toe broke instantly and I fell to the mat. Woody used athletic tape to bind the painful little piggy to its neighbors.

"It will heal in a few weeks," he said. "In the meantime, I'd like you to use that time to think about why you are studying karate."

I tried, but abandoned the soul searching to play outside. I went skiing despite the toe, and did a winter ascent of Medicine Bow Peak.

A week after I returned to lessons, Woody asked me to stick around after class. When everyone had left, he sat down in front of me.

"So, Mark, why are you studying karate?" he asked, peering up.

I told him I liked it.

"You like the image of karate, or karate?"

I started to protest.

Woody stood up. "One day perhaps you will teach me how to cross-country ski."

He held out his hand and we shook.

"Good-bye, Mark."

. . .

Two years later, still in college, I did my first ski tour of Yellowstone: an ambitious one-month circumnavigation. It was meant to be an epic.

Skip Mancini was my partner. We mailed food drops to the park's east, north, and west entrances and went superlight—so light we took summer-weight sleeping bags, and froze almost every night. But we were green-horns, and anxious to suffer. How far we skied every day was paramount, so we cruised right past the elk and buffalo. Absurdly, we passed up every chance to relax and soak in the park's hot pools. We were in a hurry to do something big.

On the last night of the trek, we cooked in our tent. We were tired of fixing dinner one hundred yards away, hunched against snowstorms, stomping our feet to keep warm. We hadn't seen any grizzlies anyway, only the occasional long-clawed prints. Skip mixed up a batch of biscuits and we ate one honey-and-butter-smothered delicacy after another. It was heaven.

Later that night, I woke up hearing snapping in the forest. I wanted to believe it was merely branches breaking from the weight of snow. Nope.

Something was circling our tent. Several big somethings were circling our tent. I woke Skip. We didn't have to say what we both knew: Our tent smelled like a biscuit. Our bags smelled like biscuits. We were like pigs-in-a-blanket.

I told Skip that I'd heard grizzlies were afraid of fire. We both lit our Bic lighters as if we were at a Grateful Dead concert.

"I don't think this is the kind of fire they meant," Skip whispered.

"I got a plan," I squeaked. "We'll light the tent on fire. Nylon burns like anything."

"They don't care if their meat is cooked or not."

"I'm serious."

"You're stupid."

"Okay," I said, "what if we light our sleeping bags on fire and swing them around our heads screaming at the top of our lungs—"

"Listen!" Skip said abruptly.

"I don't hear anything."

"Exactly."

I feel certain we set the world speed record for breaking camp. Shimmying out of our bags, we dropped the tent, crammed everything onto the sleds, tiptoed past the griz tracks encircling our camp, and frantically skied away.

• • •

After college, I was fortunate enough to be unemployable (a degree in philosophy helps) and moved into a twelve-foot-by-twelve-foot mountain cabin in Wyoming. It seemed the natural thing to do.

One of my treasured books as a boy was Charles Sheldon's *The Wilderness of Denali* (1930), which describes the three years he spent living alone on the slopes of Mount McKinley between 1906 and 1908. Sheldon was an indefatigable hunter and naturalist, a consummate observer of wildlife. His book records everything from the cannibalistic habits of shrews to the mating behavior of Dall sheep. Five species of mammals were later named in Sheldon's honor, and his crusading work led to the establishment of Mount McKinley National Park in 1917, which in 1980 was combined with Denali National Preserve to create Denali National Park and Preserve.

Sheldon's vigor and competence as an outdoorsman were legendary. He always traveled alone and much preferred winter. Temperatures in the −30°F range were his favorite, so he could snowshoe hard without overheating. He regularly covered thirty miles in a day lugging a rucksack heavy with specimens.

Living in a cabin through the winter, I tried snowshoeing, but found it slow and cumbersome. Snowshoeing is to skiing what rowing is to sailing. You have this vast ocean of snow to traverse. Why muscle every inch of it when, with practice, you can sail? I didn't know how Sheldon did it, and I wasn't going to.

I skied every day and thought I was improving, but I didn't have a teacher. I didn't think I needed one. I believed in the nobility of being self-taught. It wasn't until I took an on-snow test in Colorado, hoping to become a certified cross-country ski instructor, that I suddenly saw myself as I really was: a yokel with the strength and endurance of a mule, my technique inversely proportional to my ability to suffer.

Bill Hall was the examiner, a tall, tan master of the planks whose technique was so effortless, so flawless, that he flowed over the snow like the wind.

"You're kicking backward instead of down," Bill told me. "Imagine there's a nail going straight through your foot. Kick down. Try it."

I did.

"Good, good—but you're still dropping your back leg too soon. Shift your weight." He stepped forward, raised my leg, and pressed my chest down.

"It's all about balance. Try it again."

I did, and suddenly, miraculously, I was skiing correctly for the first time.

In the optimistic zeal of youth, it is our right to shun teachers and passionately reinvent the wheel. This, too, is part of the process. Without mentors, we make mistakes by the bushel, and often make ourselves miserable. Still, it can be a wholesome way to toughen our mettle and create our own tall tales. For a while we believe we are going where no human has gone before. When reality eventually wears through this illusion, we seek out teachers.

· · ·

Between the ages of eighteen and twenty-eight, I spent maybe 500 nights camping in the snow. It was total trial and error. I made countless screw-ups, some of which I was lucky to live through. Still, I learned how to build a passable snow cave, how to track elk on skis, how to forecast the weather from clouds. It was an apprenticeship, although it's only now that I recognize it as such.

On my second tour of Yellowstone in winter, four friends and I did a smaller loop. We had nothing to prove. The point was simply to be out there, not to epic. My skiing, honed by hundreds of hours of practice and the advice of teachers like Bill, was flowing and easy. And we took our time on a fifteen-day circle through the Bechler Canyon region, stopping at as many hot pools and geyser basins as we could. It was surreal to loll buck-naked, surrounded by snow ten feet deep. This was one of two good reasons for touring through Yellowstone versus anywhere else.

The other reason was the animals. We slid around herds of steam-snorting buffalo buried up to their necks. We discovered small herds of elk hiding in the timber. Around Shoshone Geyser Basin, where the ice had melted, flocks of geese and ducks bobbed on the black water and chattered away. Along the Snake River we spotted sandhill cranes, moose in the willows, a fox trotting gaily along the bank, killdeer, chickadees, ravens, bald eagles, a red-tailed hawk. We went slow enough to see them all.

We brought lots of food and thick sleeping bags, wanted for nothing, lived like kings in the wilderness, and never once asked ourselves why we were there. It was self-evident.

. . .

Apprenticeship—taking the time to thoroughly learn the fundamentals—is a sedimentary, accretionary process. For such an old-fashioned concept, it took me an embarrassingly long time to get it. As Americans, we're almost trained to be impatient. Fast this, fast that, we can too easily rush our lives away.

Here's a rule I try to remember: Rushing is almost always wrong. Rushing robs you of the charm of the moment. To rush is to have your mind always out ahead of your body, which is so unnatural that stupid mistakes are inevitable. The opposite of hurrying is not slow, but swift. To be swift you must be efficient. Efficiency in the outdoors is a form of mindfulness. It's about focus and having the knowledge and ability to make the right moves—and that requires experience, which, alas, takes time.

Cross-country skiing is a craft. Kayaking is a craft. Mountain climbing is a craft. Pick your sport or adventurous avocation: To become competent takes us all years of practice. So why do we climb the bump in our backyard and immediately want to take on Everest? Climbing Everest without actually having incrementally developed the requisite skills is like putting a quarter in a player piano and pretending you are a pianist. Who're you kidding?

So here's another rule I'm trying to accept: Shortcuts are pointless. If you're engaged in an activity because you truly enjoy it—the motion of your body, the refinement of your skills—what's the sense of skipping ahead? It's like skipping the middle of a novel or the middle of a song. The power of any experience is a function of its depth, a depth that can be fathomed only through dedication and discipline.

To apprentice is to accept the unfolding beauty of progression. To become at ease with where you are in the spectrum of expertise. I have a good friend who has killed the simple, visceral joy of cycling and climbing because he never believes he's good enough. He sets his sights so high that his performance is always a disappointment to him. Being covetous of what you are not is corrosive. Enjoy the slow blossoming of your own expertise. This is the craft of developing a craft.

Last rule: The process is the point. It's a cliché, I know. It's also what Woody was trying to teach me so many years ago.

Mastery is an illusion, grace a momentary gift, apprenticeship endless.

•   •   •

Case in point: that third Yellowstone trip.

The morning after my excursion to Heart Lake, I went for another long jaunt. (This in itself was an insight gained from the previous Yellowstone journeys: Instead of touring in a circle, thus being forced to drag the whole heavy camp along every day, we had skied in for two days, then set up a basecamp from which we could do fast, light, all-day tours.) I planned to retrace yesterday's tracks for several miles, then veer south.

Approaching the slope I had so leisurely carved down the evening before, I was stopped dead. My tracks were buried. They still came swooping over the crest, but then vanished at a long, deep shelf in the snow. The entire slope had avalanched. The crown wall was two feet deep, the debris pile at the base enormous. If the collapse had caught me, I would have disappeared without a trace. When I'd crested the slope, it had briefly occurred to me that I should probably dig a snow pit before skiing down.

But I'd been telling myself I knew what I was doing.

Last Rites

THE END

The water is so cold that icebergs are floating in the middle. It's June in Wyoming, at 11,000 feet, and Lookout Lake is only half melted out. The snow is still five feet deep along the shore, and chunks have calved into the water.

Mike Moe and I have hiked in to climb the Diamond, a 600-foot quartzite face in the Medicine Bow Mountains. People rarely climb here—it's too high, too harsh, too dangerous. There are often snow squalls, rockfall, route-finding debacles. Mike and I have been climbing the Diamond for twenty years; it's where we train for epics. This summer we're going on separate expeditions to Canada: Mike to attempt a ski traverse of Baffin Island; me to try a new route on Mount Waddington. This is our last chance to climb together.

Scrambling through the jagged terrain down to Lookout Lake, I feel nimble and at ease. We've done this so many times before, it's as though I'm sliding back through time.

At the water's edge, Mike leaps out onto a flat rock and begins to strip. He stuffs his socks into his boots, wraps his shirt in his trousers, and plugs it all inside his backpack. Then he stands there naked, stroking his short red beard, contemplating the still, black water.

The surface of the lake is a mirror, perfectly reflecting Medicine Bow Peak and its series of stone faces. Here, at the bottom of the mountain, we are still in night's shadow, but dawn is beginning to gild the summit. Long, pink clouds, like giant rainbow trout, suddenly appear in the water. Except the trout are swimming upside down above a mountain that is pointing inward instead of upward. It is a surreal reflection—as if we're looking at the other side of life.

"Last one to the other side . . . " Mike says, and dives into the lake.

At that moment, a scene from another time fills my mind.

Diving in from the vine bridge, Mike was immediately swept out of sight. The huge brown river just took him. It had been pouring buckets in Guinea for months and the Niger was swollen fat as a snake that's swallowed a goat, and we couldn't

tell how many trees had been pulled into the water that might trap us in our kay-
aks, so Mike said he'd swim the river to find out—use his body as a proxy for us
and our boats. "It's the only way to test it," he'd insisted. It was the fall of 1991
and his wife was pregnant and my wife was pregnant and we were in Africa hoping
to pull off one last big expedition before life changed for good.

He's done this before, but it still stuns me. The water is so cold it
would instantly paralyze anyone but Mike. Will alone keeps him warm.

I grab his pack and begin hopping boulder to boulder through the
snowfield. This is our ritual. I'll hike around the lake, he'll swim across
it. We'll meet on the far side, just north of the Diamond.

It's getting light now and the air is a cool violet. I can see Mike chop-
ping through icy water, his feet fluttering. Unlike me, he is utterly
unafraid of water. It is his natural element. In high school he was a state-
champion swimmer.

I meet him on the far shore. When he comes out of the water, he's so
frozen his skin is a waxy, translucent blue and his movements jerky. His
jaw is clenched and he can't speak, but he's grinning. He fumbles putting
his clothes back on; I have to tie his boot laces for him because his fingers
are wooden. Heaving on our packs, we continue up through the talus,
across a hard tongue of snow.

• • •

Mike is a wit, peculiarly quick-minded. He has an ever-changing reper-
toire of voices, a dozen nicknames for me. We rarely get the chance to go
into the mountains together anymore, so when we do, we gleefully revert
to our younger, bolder selves.

At the base of the Diamond, Mike stacks the rope and, finally able to
talk, says, "Suppose you think you're leading."

We both want to lead—it has been this way since the beginning—but,
eager beaver that I am, I already have my rock shoes on. I point to
them.

"I see, Rhubarb the Black's got 'iz scuppers on already," says Mike in
his pirate's brogue. "Then the sharp end be yours."

Mike and I gravitated to each other as teenagers. We both lived on the
edge of Laramie, the boundless prairie our backyard. We were predeter-
mined to be wild and became perfectly matched partners in misadventure: Mike and Mark. Climbing came naturally to us, and we scaled
everything in sight. University buildings, boulders, smokestacks, moun-

tain walls—our adolescent enthusiasm and daring far exceeding our abil-ity. Soon enough even wide-open Wyoming started feeling small. We lied about our ages, got jobs on the railroad, lived in a tent behind the Virginian Hotel in Medicine Bow, banked the cash, then left high school to spend half a year hitchhiking through Europe, Africa, and Russia, climbing and chasing girls. We got arrested in Tunisia, Luxembourg, and Leningrad. We got robbed. We slept in the dirt.

Through college at the University of Wyoming, Mike and I double-dated, debated Nietzsche, and stood back to back defending atheism, dis-membering our Christian attackers with rapier tongues. We ice climbed and skied the backcountry and went on expeditions. Close calls were commonplace, and we thought nothing of them. We pushed each other but willingly stood in for the other whenever one of us was weak or scared or lost. We were outdoors brothers-in-arms. We would die for each other without flinching—and almost did a dozen times.

"You're on," Mike announces, and I start up a dihedral between the wall and a delicate pillar. The pillar—ten feet wide, ten feet thick, and 200 feet tall—leans precariously against the Diamond. We have used this route to gain the upper face multiple times, but it always feels dicey. We console ourselves with the fact that the pillar has stood here for thousands of years.

Today the crack is running with water and dangerously slippery. Half-way up I mention this fact.

"Is that whining I hear?" cries Mike in his Monty Python voice. "Courtesy slack coming your way."

We were sixteen and just learning how to climb and we made a pact that whin-ing was prohibited. No matter how freaked you were, you had to keep your mouth shut. To enforce this rule Mike came up with a penalty called "courtesy slack": The belayer fed out extra rope—so you'd take a longer fall—whenever even a whimper was heard. Over the years, this bred a black, Brit-like humor in Mike. The more desperate the situation, the more he made fun of it: "It's absolutely grand—no handholds whatsoever" or "If the ice were only a wee bit thinner and more rotten I could actually enjoy myself." We were ripe with hubris. As far as we could tell we were indestructible.

At the top of the pillar I move onto the wall, set up a belay, and Mike begins climbing. I notice that he moves more slowly than he used to, but then he doesn't climb so much anymore. He has other passions now.

After college, we both did big expeditions—I went to Shishapangma and Everest; Mike walked the Continental Divide with his younger brother, Dan, then two years later mountain-biked it—but our priorities were diverging. The year I went to Everest, 1986, Mike took an internship in Washington, DC, working for the hunger-relief organization Bread for the World. In 1987, we both went to Africa. With my girlfriend, Sue Ibarra, I climbed Mount Kilimanjaro and Mount Kenya and traveled far and wide writing adventure stories. Mike went to Swaziland to work for CARE, teaching poor Swazis how to get small-business loans. He helped start a daycare center. His girlfriend, Diana Kocornik, was teaching in Swaziland for the Mennonite Central Committee. Mike started going to church.

We all moved back to Wyoming in 1990, bought houses, and started families. When I got married, Mike was my best man. At his wedding, I was a groomsman—his brother, Dan, was his best man. My daughter Addi and his son Justin were both born in January 1992; my daughter Teal and his twins, Carlie and Kevin, were born one month apart two years later. I kept writing stories; Mike took a job as the director of Wyoming Parent, a nonprofit family-advocacy organization.

Halfway up the leaning pillar, he yells, "Wish it were wetter in here!"

• • •

Mike pulls himself up onto the top of the pillar and steps over to the belay.

"Mike, what if the pillar suddenly collapsed?" I ask.

"Won't," he says. "It's been here forever."

"But what if it did?"

"Buck, you'd catch me."

Mike is the most optimistic person I know. He is sanguine, imperturbable.

"What if you lost your ice axe?" Mike asked one day in 1979. "Could you still climb the couloir?" We were training for McKinley by climbing the snowy chutes on either side of the Diamond. So we tried it without our axes, scraping little holds in the snow with our woolen mittens. What if you lost your ice axe and crampons? I asked. Could you still get up the couloir? We kicked tiny steps with our heavy leather boots and gouged mitten holes and climbed it. But what if you were descending? We practiced glissading with nothing to stop the death slide but a sharp rock in our hands.

Thus began our private game of what-if. What-if was meant to make us more resourceful, more capable of surviving desperate situations. And it did—for a time.

We swap leads and Mike moves out onto a sheet of gray rock split by a pencil-thin crack.

"But, Mike, what if I couldn't and you were killed? Was it worth it?" I'm baiting him and he knows it.

"Yup. Right up until the moment I die . . . then it's completely not worth it."

"That's not an answer and you know it."

The crack has closed off and Mike is holding on by his fingertips. He uses this predicament not to respond.

Our game of what-if was good fun for more than a decade, but it changed after we had kids. Before, we always assumed we'd come home. That was the principle behind what-if. What if this or that happened—how would you get yourself out of the fix? But after kids, we both began to wonder what if . . . we didn't? What if we were killed? By a grizzly, by a river, by a collapsing pillar of stone. It's a natural thing to ask once you start thinking about someone besides yourself. We may be leaving on expeditions to Canada soon, but we are dads now, not Huck and Tom. Justin and Addi are three years old; Teal and Carlie and Kevin will turn one this summer. Our game of what-if has evolved into the fundamental conundrum of our lives: Is it morally possible to be a serious adventurer and a father?

For my part, I hide behind the hackneyed and sophistic excuse that it's who I am. That if I were to quit adventuring, I wouldn't be Mark Jenkins—which I know is bullshit. People change all the time and don't lose their identity. They often become someone better. I just don't have the willpower.

Mike does. He's been trying to reform himself for years. He's weaning himself off adventure like a heavy drinker weans himself off scotch. Slowly, with frequent relapses. He has promised Diana—and himself—he will do only one big trip every two years, but I sense this expedition to Baffin will be his last. Inside, I know Mike believes serious adventure, expeditioning, is incompatible with being a father—you are imperiling not simply your own life but the lives of your children, which is immoral. So he will have to give it up.

To calm his existential qualms, Mike has taken to putting more and more effort into planning the logistics of an expedition. This upcoming trip to Canada is a case in point. He's spent weeks testing gear, studying maps, developing contingencies. He told me he thinks he can bring the risk down to something acceptable. I told him he's in denial. Risk is integral to adventure. A freak accident, an unanticipatable rockslide, an avalanche. No risk, no adventure. He knows this, but he's torn between being the man he is and the man he believes he should be.

• • •

I feel a tug on the rope and look up. Mike is far above his last piece of protection, and the crack has vanished. There are no handholds and nothing to stand on. Most climbers would back down.

"Watch me!" Mike yells, and dives for a thin ledge.

A letter arrived for me from Swaziland. It was 1989 and I was in Novosibirsk, crossing Siberia by bicycle. Mike wrote, "Dear Dostoyevsky the Big Legs—expect you have saddle sores the size of rubles and lungs like a hippo but the KGB has no doubt caught you by now so I'll soon be mounting a daring rescue . . ." He went on for several paragraphs in his clumsy handwriting and terrible spelling, and between the lines I knew he was worried about me and that he was really saying he would do anything for me, march to the ends of the earth if I needed him. I missed him so much I reread the letter over and over, asking myself why I never told him how much he meant to me, why I never just told him I loved him.

Mike barely catches the lip of rock.

He belays me up and I lead the final pitch. We're 800 feet above Lookout Lake, but the climbing is relaxing and fun. Mike got the sketchy pitch, the bastard. I realize now that that's why he didn't argue for the first lead.

I reach the summit, lean against a warm slab of rock, bring Mike up, and we sit there side by side, staring out across Wyoming.

"Mike, remember Lhasa?"

He grins, but I can tell it's really a grimace.

We went to Tibet in 1993 to climb an unknown peak, and after two days in Lhasa Mike got pulmonary edema, just like he did when we were on McKinley, except there was no way to go down and his lungs filled up with fluid, and we went to the hospital, but they could only give him a Chinese army balloon of oxygen that he sucked on while we waited for the plane. His lungs were gurgling so badly he couldn't lie down, so he had to sit up all night, but even then he was still drowning from the inside. His face was bloated and gray, and if the plane didn't come in the morning he would die, but he was the funniest he'd ever been. He kept making me laugh, and I was so scared I was sick to my stomach, and when I heard the sound of the plane I began to weep.

Atop the Diamond, feet dangling in space, we are on the roof of our world. We eat the lunches our wives have packed for us and silently observe the landscape that made us: snow and ice and rock and sky. We sit there together for a long time, feeling as close as we ever have.

After a while we coil the rope and pack up the gear and begin discussing our upcoming expeditions. I'm going to Waddington with my friend John Harlin. It took a lot of persuading. His father died climbing the Eiger, and John has spent much of his adult life struggling with what that means. In his early twenties, John had a partner who died while they were descending from British Columbia's Mount Robson. After that, he promised his wife, Adele, and his mother that he would give up alpinism. Going to Waddington with me means he's breaking his promise.

Mike will attempt to ski across the Barnes Ice Cap on Baffin Island with his brother, Dan, and two other good friends of ours, Brad Humphrey and Sharon Kava. I have tried to convince Sharon not to go—I worry that she doesn't have the experience for an Arctic trip—but Mike's enthusiasm is magnetic. It is something we disagree on. Mike believes that self-confidence and sangfroid—both of which he has an abundance of—are more valuable than technical ability. I don't.

I ask him what he fears most.

"Same as ever, bro."

Years ago, Mike confided that his deepest fear was that something would happen to Dan while they are on a trip together. Dan, quiet and happy, the kid who fainted during sex-ed films in junior high, a man who has never said a bad word about anyone, has always looked up to Mike. Mike is the natural-born leader, Dan the disciple.

"I couldn't bear it," Mike whispers.

· · ·

To descend, we walk along the edge of the Diamond, passing right by where the plaque will be, but of course it's not there yet.

We mounted the plaque in the summer of 1996. Tim Banks and Keith Spenser and I—Mike's closest friends—climbed the Diamond at midnight in honor of Mike's motto, "Any real adventure begins and ends in the dark." I led and Keith carried the engraved metal plaque, heavy as a headstone, in his pack, while Tim hiked around the back side to the summit. Halfway up, at about 3:00 a.m., Keith and I were shocked by little orange explosions all around us. Keith thought someone was using a nightscope to shoot at us and this seemed insane but the cracking was everywhere and then we smelled it and realized they were firecrackers. Tim was throwing bottle rockets down at us, hooting with laughter. We finished bolting the plaque to the summit block right as the sun came up.

On the hike down from the Diamond, Mike is talking about changing the world, as usual. He's been reading the research. Most kids with problems come from single-parent families. As director of Wyoming Parent, he plans to change this. He's got some ideas, but he needs state funding. He knows he can get it. He believes in legislation. He believes in laws that encourage citizens and companies to act in the best interest of the community. He believes in the basic goodness of people.

I'm listening, but I don't have Mike's faith. I used to, but I've spent too much time in screwed-up countries. I've spent too much time in places where evil things happen purely because of evil people.

In 1998 I awoke in a black, hot, locked room in northern Burma and realized I'd been dreaming about Mike every night for weeks. I desperately needed his companionship and judgment because things were getting perilous and if he'd been with me we would have balanced each other and I wouldn't have gone off the rails, or better yet I wouldn't have even come to Burma.

We've dropped down the back of the Diamond and swung around to Lake Marie and we're sloshing back through the snow to the car.

"What do you say we take Justin and Addi up here this winter?" Mike says. "Build a snow cave, teach them how to wipe with snow, howl with the wind."

I tell Mike I'm in, of course.

• • •

It was late August 1995, and Diana and the kids were over at our house for a backyard barbecue and we were all eagerly speculating about when Mike and Dan and Sharon and Brad would be home because it would be anytime now. Later that evening Diana called and her voice was so strange I didn't recognize it. She asked us to come over to her house, and when I walked in the door Perry and Greta, Mike and Dan's parents, were sitting stone still on the couch, and I knew immediately and my legs failed me and I dropped to my knees.

The telephone rang. It was the Royal Canadian Mounted Police out of Clyde River, Northwest Territories. Diana asked me to speak to them. I couldn't speak, so I just listened.

The team had successfully crossed Baffin Island, the expedition was over, and they were on their way home. They were coming back across Baffin Bay in a small aluminum motorboat with an Inuit guide named Jushua. They saw a pod of bowhead whales among the icebergs, and then the whales disappeared beneath the black water; then one breached right under their boat and flipped it over. They were two miles from shore and couldn't right the craft because of the plywood steering shed. Jushua was wearing a marine survival suit, but the team had only life jackets.

On the way home from the Diamond, Mike drives. I shove in an old cassette tape I find on the passenger seat. Turns out to be *Abbey Road.* We know every song by heart. "Come Together," "Here Comes the Sun," "Golden Slumbers," "The End." We sing along like we have on so many road trips. I take bass and Mike sings tenor, slipping into falsetto just to make me laugh. We think we sound terrific. We sing at the top of our lungs. "And in the end, the love you take is equal to the love you make."

Jushua was found alive, washed ashore after eighteen hours in the sea. He said they held hands across the hull of the boat for as long as they could, but the water was so cold. Mike was encouraging them all and cracking jokes and reassuring them that the mighty Mounties would be sending out a search flight any minute and to just hold on, just hold on. After a while Mike was the only one who could still talk.

First Sharon slipped away, face down in the water, then Brad. Dan and Mike held on to each other, hands clasped over the hull, for six hours. Then Dan began to slip away and Mike tried to grab him, tried to hold on to his brother, but he couldn't. Mike clung to the upturned boat for two more hours, talking to himself, going mad, before floating away into the Arctic. He was thirty-seven.

When the tape ends Mike and I stop singing and are quiet for a spell. Just driving across the high plains, antelope in the distance, wind combing the tall brown grass.

It was October that same year and snowing and we were below the Diamond and I was trembling holding Justin's tiny hand as he threw the ashes. Perry would never accept the death of his sons and died of heartbreak three years later. I'd see Greta alone in the park and we'd just hold hands and cry.

Years later, none of us were the same or ever could be, and the shock and despair now blessedly came only in the middle of the night. And on one of those nights in the dead of winter the giant pillar leaning against the Diamond collapsed and shattered into a thousand pieces, but the plaque we'd mounted on the summit in memory of Mike and Dan and Brad and Sharon is still there.

Eleven years after they froze to death in the Arctic Ocean, I called Diana to tell her I was writing this story. She said Justin and Carlie and Kevin would have been such different people, and we both broke down on the phone.

Then she said: "But, Mark, there are so many ways to lose your life besides dying."

As we glide into Laramie we're talking about our kids. Mike and I have big plans. As soon as they're a little older we'll take them climbing at Devils Tower, like we did together when we were young. We'll take them cross-country skiing in Yellowstone so they can sit in the hot pools like we did. We'll teach them to climb Fear and Loathing, a face route that is all about balance, about deftly moving on invisible edges, never thinking about falling, and believing with all your heart that you can stand on air.